T0293342

The **AI REVOLUTION** in **CUSTOMER SERVICE** and **SUPPORT**

A Practical Guide to Impactful Deployment of AI to Best Serve Your Customers

ROSS SMITH | **MAYTE CUBINO** | **EMILY MCKEON**

The AI Revolution in Customer Service and Support:
A Practical Guide to Impactful Deployment of AI to Best Serve Your Customers
Ross Smith, Mayte Cubino Gonzalez, and Emily McKeon

Pearson
www.informit.com
Copyright © 2025 by Pearson Education, Inc. or its affiliates. Hoboken, New Jersey.
All Rights Reserved.

To report errors, please send a note to errata@informIT.com

Executive Editor: Loretta Yates
Associate Editor: Shourav Bose
Development Editor: Rick Kughen
Senior Production Editor: Tracey Croom
Tech Editor: Dr. Xin Deng
Copy Editor: Rick Kughen
Compositor: Danielle Foster
Proofreader: Dan Foster
Indexer: James Minkin
Cover Design: Chuti Prasertsith
Cover Illustration: Prostock-studio/Shutterstock
Interior Design: Danielle Foster
Illustrations: Vived Graphics
Figure Credits: Figure 5.1: Created from DALL-E
Figure 5.2: Created from Midjourney

ISBN-13: 978-0-13-828650-7
ISBN-10:   0-13-828650-7

Library of Congress Control Number: 2024939894

6 2024

Dedication

To the next generation—Sela, Scarlett, and Paz, and to Maddy, Emma, Clara, and Roo—who will all grow alongside the AI. Always celebrate your humanity! Sincere thanks to my friends Mayte and Emily and everyone who made this work possible.

—Ross

To Sofia, Tiago, and Laura: your curiosity and strength are my endless inspiration. Always dream big! To my family and friends for their support and encouragement. And to Ross and Emily for revolutionizing my life with the most amazing journey ever.

—Mayte

With all my love to my family—I am forever grateful for your belief in me. Your unwavering support, patience, and love have been my greatest motivation. To Ross and Mayte, you have infinite creativity and knowledge, and I'm thankful for your trust and energy as we ventured forth on this project.

—Emily

Contents at a Glance

Contents

PART I: INTRODUCTION TO AI AND ITS APPLICATIONS IN CUSTOMER SERVICE AND SUPPORT

PART II: BUILDING AI MODELS USING PROPRIETARY CONTENT: THE 6DS FRAMEWORK

9   DEPLOY: LAUNCHING THE SOLUTION 211

10   DETECT: MONITORING AND FEEDBACK 245

PART III: ORGANIZATIONAL CONSIDERATIONS FOR AI MODEL CREATION AND DEPLOYMENT

11   RESPONSIBLE AI AND ETHICAL CONSIDERATIONS IN CUSTOMER SUPPORT. 261

12   CULTURAL CONSIDERATIONS. 287

**PART IV: GAMIFIED LEARNING AND THE
FUTURE OF WORK IN SUPPORT**

Acknowledgments

This book is a testament to the incredible efforts of many and the power of collaboration. We extend our deepest gratitude to all who shared their insights, expertise, and enthusiasm with us.

With the speed of change we're experiencing in the era of AI, we knew our window of opportunity to tell our story was short. We worked hard to ensure this book provided the practical steps to build and deploy AI models for real-world scenarios. While there is so much upside to integrating AI in customer service and support, many other industries can also learn from these pages.

To our contributors, Dr. Xin Deng, Phaedra Boinodiris, Mostaq Shakil Ahmed, Michael Fitzgerald, and Jason Weum, your willingness to share your knowledge has greatly enhanced this project beyond measure. It would not be the same without your input and wisdom.

To Executive Editor Loretta Yates and Associate Editor Shorav Bose, your guidance has turned our vision into reality with your tireless work behind the scenes bringing this book to life. And to our Development Editor, Rick Kughen, your keen eyes and thoughtful suggestions have sharpened our message. A very special thanks to Dr. Xin Deng, our technical reviewer, who kept us honest and didn't allow us to "hallucinate"!

We would also like to thank J.B. Wood for writing the foreword and his inspirational message. He not only believes in the power of AI and what it can do for the customer experience but also in the value of collaboration and how innovation is at the heart of progress in our industry.

To our family and friends, this book came together very quickly, and it would not have been possible without your love and support. This has been a memorable journey that we couldn't have taken on without you. You inspire us each and every day.

To our readers, we hope you find this book informative and helpful as you move forward with employing AI models in your own organizations. While technology changes rapidly, the foundations of great leadership remain the same. We encourage you to stay abreast of the exciting AI innovation and all it has to offer!

We welcome your feedback and comments and look forward to hearing from you! Check out what we've been up to: *https://airevolutionbook.com/*.

About the Authors

Ross Smith, FRSA is a Fellow of the Royal Society of the Arts and a worldwide support leader at Microsoft. Ross co-authored *The Practical Guide to Defect Prevention* and holds seven patents. He is a PhD scholar at University College Dublin, focused on AI, automation, worker displacement, and the future of work. He co-founded the Future World Alliance, a nonprofit committed to responsible AI for the next generation. He can be found online on LinkedIn at *https://www.linkedin.com/in/rosss42/*.

Mayte Cubino Gonzalez is an EMEA director in the Modern Work Support Engineering organization at Microsoft and serves as the site lead and board member of Microsoft Portugal. With 20 years of experience in customer service and support roles, Mayte is also an AI enthusiast and patent holder. She was recognized in 2016 with the European Disability Champion award for her work in raising awareness about hidden disabilities and workplace adjustments. She can be found on LinkedIn at *https://www.linkedin.com/in/mayte-cubino-gonzalez/*.

Emily McKeon is a communication director at Microsoft focused on global strategic business and executive communications designed to strengthen employee engagement and drive value for the Customer Service and Support business. She has vast communication experience and a strong depth of knowledge in customer support, global diversity and inclusion, and employee engagement. She can be found on LinkedIn at *https://www.linkedin.com/in/emily-mckeon-7ab9ba3/*.

About the Contributors

Dr. Xin Deng is currently a machine learning scientist at Microsoft. Dr. Deng played an important role in this work's technical accuracy and production. Her background in AI and machine learning has helped shape this book's perspective on the current state and the future of AI, machine learning, and data science. She is actively contributing her expertise in M365 Outlook Copilot utilizing GPT models. She can be found on LinkedIn at *https://www.linkedin.com/in/xin-deng-00a25a60/*.

Phaedra Boinodiris currently leads IBM Consulting's Trustworthy AI Practice, and she is the AI ethics board focal for all of consulting, serves on the leadership team of IBM's Academy of Technology, and leads IBM's Trustworthy AI Center of Excellence. She is a Future World Alliance co-founder and the co-author of *AI for the Rest of Us*. She can be found on LinkedIn at *https://www.linkedin.com/in/phaedra/*.

Mostaq Shakil Ahmed leads a vast global team spread across 48 countries at Microsoft. He serves as the global general manager of Modern Work Support Engineering including Microsoft Copilot support. Shakil has authored a number of papers on software globalization and has also contributed as a part-time lecturer on the same subject at the University of Washington. He can be found on LinkedIn at *https://www.linkedin.com/in/shakilam/*.

Michael Fitzgerald is a finance manager at Microsoft. He holds an MBA from the Tuck School of Business at Dartmouth and a Master of Arts in Law and Diplomacy from the Fletcher School at Tufts University. He can be found on LinkedIn at *https://www.linkedin.com/in/mfitzgerald514/*.

Jason Weum is the director of supportability at Microsoft for Teams, SharePoint, OneDrive, Viva, and Office. He focuses on crafting an unparalleled AI-first customer support experience by minimizing support queries with AI, self-help, proactive diagnostics, and product improvements. He can be found on LinkedIn at *https://www.linkedin.com/in/jasonweum/*.

Foreword

The journey of technology in customer service is a story of evolution, from the early days of switchboards and mail correspondence to the digital age's omnichannel support platforms. This voyage reflects a continuous pursuit of efficiency, personalization, and satisfaction in supporting customers and driving product loyalty. In an era when artificial intelligence (AI) is redefining the parameters of customer interaction and satisfaction, our mission is to ensure that you, the dedicated professionals at the heart of customer service, are fully equipped with the information and resources you will need to navigate and lead in this transformative landscape.

I've witnessed firsthand the remarkable strides we have made through cross-industry collaboration over the years. By embodying a wealth of insights from pioneers who have led the charge in integrating AI into customer service frameworks, we will serve our customers better if we build on these successes and continue advancing our collective thinking and innovation. We all play an instrumental role in fostering partnerships, bringing together the brightest minds from technology, customer service, and beyond to share insights, challenges, and successes.

In customer service history, there has never been a more important time for us to collaborate across organizational boundaries. Through shared learning environments, we can explore the potential of emerging technologies, ensuring that the customer service industry keeps pace with technological change and leads it. The goal is to empower you with the knowledge, resources, tools, and intelligence you need to leverage AI to enhance your customer service capabilities while maintaining the human touch that has always defined our industry.

We're at the forefront of navigating this evolution and leading the industry through each phase of technological advancement in the ever-changing customer service and support world. We see *The AI Revolution in Customer Service and Support* as a guide for customer service and support professionals who sit directly at the intersection of customer service excellence and cutting-edge AI technology.

We recognize that the pace of technological advancement can be exhilarating, inspiring, intimidating, and daunting. This book is designed as a compass for those navigating the new terrain, bridging the gap between traditional customer service expertise and AI's technical details and nuances.

As customer service and support professionals, our role is pivotal in shaping the experiences that define brand loyalty and customer satisfaction for your organizations. This industry, rich in tradition and human connection, is now at the cusp of a transformative era brought about by AI. As AI technologies redefine the boundaries of what's possible within customer service and beyond, sharing insights, challenges, and solutions across different sectors has become invaluable. This knowledge-sharing accelerates the pace of AI integration into customer service practices and ensures a broader understanding of its impact across various customer touchpoints.

While the advent of AI in customer service and support brings us transformative innovation and endless opportunities, this revolution is not merely about integrating innovative technology into our industry. It's a reimagining of what customer service is and can be. AI has the means to become a powerful tool—more importantly, an important partner—in creating deeper, more meaningful connections with customers. Its potential to analyze vast datasets in real time allows for a level of service customization previously unimaginable, offering personalized solutions, predictive support, and seamless interactions across multiple support channels.

Capitalizing on the collaboration between technologists, customer service experts, and business leaders in crafting innovative AI solutions and becoming deeply attuned to the human aspects of customer interaction will set a new standard for excellence in the industry.

This book is a testament to a collaborative spirit and is designed to offer a comprehensive understanding of AI's impact on the customer success field. By encapsulating a wide array of lessons learned and perspectives, the book offers a unique vantage point on how AI can and will be harnessed across the service industry spectrum. It provides a comprehensive overview of cutting-edge applications, ethical considerations, and the future trajectory of AI technologies, making it an indispensable resource for support professionals seeking to navigate the complexities of this new era.

I want to encourage us all to build an ecosystem of collaboration where challenges are tackled collectively and successes are celebrated as milestones for the entire industry. We are the experts in our field, and by leveraging best practices as we enter this new era of AI, we will create unprecedented customer experiences. We will face and overcome shared challenges in implementing AI, such as ethical considerations, data privacy, and workforce adaptation. AI adoption is a strategic opportunity and only through strong collaboration and maintaining an open dialogue will we continually learn and ultimately enhance our collective success in

this rapidly evolving landscape. I'd like to invite leaders, innovators, and frontline professionals to join forces in leveraging AI to enhance customer experiences, streamline operations, and forge lasting relationships with customers and each other.

AI will not just enhance customer service; it will help us all actively shape it. By working together, we can transform our industry to be more efficient, responsive, empathetic, and connected to the needs of every customer.

Welcome to the revolution: *The AI Revolution in Customer Service and Support*! I'm excited to help launch this new era of collaboration as we build a bright future with the help of AI technology.

J.B. Wood

Technology Services Industry Association (TSIA)

President and CEO

Introduction

Artificial intelligence has made amazing advances in the last year, and customer service and support is one of the most important areas where this new technology is having an immediate impact. While the technology is not yet in a place where it will fully replace agents and support engineers, it can do wonders to dramatically improve customer experience while also contributing to optimizing productivity in various ways. This book will help you understand how and where to incorporate AI technology, such as large language models (LLMs), machine learning, predictive analytics, augmented reality, and others, into the customer experience flow.

Please note that a percentage of proceeds from the sale of this book will be donated to the nonprofit Future World Alliance, dedicated to curating K-12 education in AI ethics. See *https://futureworldalliance.org*.

Who Is This Book For?

The AI Revolution in Customer Service and Support is a practical guide for adopting and deploying generative AI models within a customer service and support organization. It is written for technical and non-technical customer service professionals and customer service and support professionals who have been thrust into the technical limelight and need to learn quickly about deploying and leveraging AI.

This book is for customer service professionals who want to learn more about deploying and leveraging AI in their organizations but are unsure where to get started. Their leaders look to them as customer professionals, but the new world is highly technical. Reading this book will help them leverage their customer service experience to navigate this new world.

Errata, Updates & Book Support

We've made every effort to ensure the accuracy of this book and its companion content. The world of AI is moving quickly, with new advances every week. You can access updates to this book—in the form of a list of submitted errata and their related corrections—at:

informit.com/airevcs/errata

If you discover an error that is not already listed, please submit it to us at the same page.

For additional book support and information, please visit

InformIT.com/Support and *http://airevolutionbook.com.*

49 66 20 79 6F 75 20 64 65 63
69 70 68 65 72 65 64 20 74 68
69 73 2C 20 79 6F 75 20 61 72
65 20 67 72 65 61 74 21 20 2D
20 52 65 61 63 68 20 6F 75 74
20 74 6F 20 75 73 20 6F 6E 20
41 49 52 65 76 6F 6C 75 74 69
6F 6E 42 6F 6F 6B 2E 63 6F 6D
2E 0A 0A

PART I

Introduction to AI and Its Applications in Customer Service and Support

Throughout this book, we discuss the practical applications that AI can have in assisting with delivering a high-quality customer service and support experience and how to integrate AI into your support organization. While we know that customer service and support are critical components of business success—by playing a hand in customer retention, driving customer loyalty, and brand reputation—the integration of AI into your customer service and support world is truly a transformative shift. This revolution can redefine how your business interacts with customers and unlock once-unreachable opportunities.

However, before we dive into the specifics of how to build and deploy AI models within your support organization, we wanted to set the stage by discussing the opportunity to integrate AI into your customer service and support organization, taking a more technical look at AI and machine learning, and examining the areas within your support business where AI can have an impact.

By discussing the opportunity for AI integration in customer service and support, we aim to highlight the potential for AI to streamline the business's operational components and enhance the human element of customer engagement. AI can quickly analyze vast amounts of data to provide insights to assist humans with customer interactions, enabling a more personalized and proactive experience.

Taking a technical look at the history and application of machine learning and AI, we explore the intricacies of these technologies to help demystify how they work and their potential application in our customer service and support industry. The deeper technical discussion in Chapter 2, "Overview of Generative AI and Data Science Machine Learning," is one you can peruse, skim, or skip without impacting your experience with the rest of the book's content. However, we believe having a basic understanding of the mechanics behind AI helps you appreciate its capabilities and limitations and arms you with information and credibility with others in and outside your business.

We'll further discuss the impact areas within your support business where AI can be most beneficial, providing a roadmap for strategic integration and implementation. AI can be leveraged in many areas of customer service, including predictive analytics for preventing issues before they arise, intelligent routing for getting a customer to the best person to assist with their issue, chatbots handling routine inquiries, and assisting human support agents with detailed troubleshooting guides in seconds. By identifying the key areas where AI can make a significant difference in your own business, you can best prioritize your efforts and resources effectively.

AI has the potential to elevate every facet of customer service. By fostering a close relationship between AI and customer service professionals, where each brings their strengths, you can create a seamless and satisfying experience for customers. By doing so, you'll ensure that technology acts as an enabler of better support, not just faster support. Thank you for joining us on this journey!

1

The Seeds of an AI Revolution

A hero ventures forth from the world of common day into a region of supernatural wonder: fabulous forces are there encountered and a decisive victory is won: The hero comes back from this mysterious adventure with the power to bestow boons on his fellow man.

—Joseph Campbell, *The Hero With a Thousand Faces*

The seeds of a revolution are often sown in the fertile ground of broad discontent, where systemic injustices, malcontent, and economic disparities push the populace toward a collective yearning for change. These initial sparks, fueled by a combination of oppressed voices and visionary leaders, can grow into a powerful movement that challenges the status quo and demands profound societal transformation.

This is not where we are today—our modern-day seeds are planted by technological change that has been thrust upon us.

The AI Revolution is one that stems from hope and opportunity. We have been introduced to a magic door that will open new opportunities for all of humanity. AI can help with healthcare, climate change, the eradication of disease, and for customer service and support, a sea change. Customers will experience new and improved support in ways that have never been possible.

Overview of Customer Service and Support

With the complexity and vast differentiation across industries and organizations' use of terminology in the customer support realm, this book will use many terms interchangeably unless a notable difference in guidance is warranted, which we will call out specifically. Some of these interchangeable terms, along with current definitions, include

- **Department terms**
  - **Customer service:** Customer service is the assistance and advice provided by a company to those people who buy or use its products or services.[1]
  - **Customer support:** Customer support includes consumer services designed to assist customers in the correct use of a product and help with solving problems. It might include assistance in planning, installation, training, troubleshooting, maintenance, upgrading, and disposal of a product.[2]
  - **Guest relations:** Guest relations is an approach to managing interactions with guests and providing them with information and assistance.[3]
  - **Help desk:** Help desk is a department, a team, or person that provides assistance and information, usually for electronic or computer problems.[4]
  - **Customer care:** Customer care is how an individual, group, or business treats their customers.[5]
- **Business roles**
  - **Organization:** Organization is an entity—such as a company, an institution, or an association—comprising one or more people and having a particular purpose.[6]
  - **Company:** Company is a natural legal entity formed by the association and group of people working together to achieve a common objective.[7]
  - **Business:** Business is an organization or enterprising entity engaged in commercial, industrial, or professional activities.[8]
  - **Industry:** Industry is a group of related companies based on their primary business activities.[9]

- **Support staff roles**
  - **Support engineer:** A support engineer is a professional who provides technical assistance related to products, services, or software, troubleshooting issues and offering solutions to ensure optimal functionality and user satisfaction.[10]
  - **Customer service agent:** A customer service agent is a person who interacts with customers to assist, address inquiries, resolve issues, or facilitate transactions.[11]
  - **Customer service representatives (CSR):** Customer service representatives interact with customers to handle and resolve complaints, process orders, and provide information about an organization's products and services.[12]
  - **Client relations associate:** A client relations associate is an individual who interacts with clients daily, building relationships and providing services that help to build trust between the client and the company.[13]
  - **Front-line service delivery:** Front-line service delivery personnel are people who interact directly with customers or clients in the workplace and are typically the primary point of contact between a customer or a public member and an organization.[14]

In addition, there are clear distinctions across different delivery methods and channels of support that we touch on below. For the most part, we will consider these equivalents unless it's important to distinguish differences related to the application of generative AI.

This book is intended to provide customer service and support professionals with practical guidance and best practices in adopting and deploying generative AI models within their organizations to maximize AI's outcomes and benefits. We explored the current and projected future use of generative AI in support scenarios through our own experience and many interviews and conversations with industry professionals to inform what we hope is a balanced and educational guide on how to get started in this revolutionary time.

Effective Customer Service and Support

As we look at the elements of effective customer support, we will touch briefly on the importance of support, support strategy, how customers access and interact with support, and some key measurement areas. This will provide the basis of understanding that we will then build on

throughout the book as it relates to how the deployment of generative AI may impact many of these elements.

These key elements are common across the support industry as measurements of success and are closely followed by leadership in determining the effectiveness of the service.

In any organization, there are many different types of roles. For example, in retail, there are buyers, manufacturers, and salespeople, among others. A nonprofit organization might have fundraisers, lobbyists, website designers, and community organizers, among others. In software and services development, there are engineers, product designers, sales and marketing personnel, among others. In banking and finance, there are roles related to investing, accounting, account management, and others.

Customer support is a common role across almost every industry. Companies establish these roles to address customer concerns and actively cultivate and maintain customer satisfaction for business growth and relevance. Satisfying 100 percent of their customers 100 percent of the time is a worthwhile goal for businesses to strive for, though it's unrealistic given it is influenced by myriad uncontrollable factors. These factors can range from the inherent unpredictability of product issues such as product bugs or compatibility challenges and their potential impact on customers to the complexity of those issues and resulting impact on staffing, organizational health, and so on. These factors are compounded by the diverse nature of the customer base, encompassing a wide spectrum of expectations, timelines, cultural standards of satisfaction, backgrounds, business contexts, and needs.

Take, for instance, a healthcare nonprofit organization dedicated to providing devices for the elderly. Their clientele spans hospitals, nursing homes, individual patients, government agencies, and other nonprofit entities. The sheer breadth of this constituency demands a strategic approach.

Organizations faced with such diversity are confronted with a choice: invest significantly upfront to predict and meet every possible customer need or adopt a more pragmatic approach. Many opt for the latter, choosing to establish a post-launch service and support system that can flexibly address any gaps in their initial offerings or assist customers with product-related issues. This pragmatic approach is often a result of the realization that creating the perfect product is a formidable challenge, learned through experience and adaptability.

Today, with the fierce global competition seen across almost every industry, an exceptional customer service and support organization can make or break a company. It is often considered the first line of defense between a product issue and a happy customer. Moreover, the quality of the support experience lends value to the customer's relationship with the company, often building trust and creating loyalty. Trust and loyalty assist companies in the retention of customers and the brand's market reputation, essentially safeguarding them from competition. Moreover, satisfied customers are more likely to provide valuable feedback and insights, leading to product improvements and innovation, thus fueling long-term growth and success.

The brand image is critical for the success of any organization and is highly influenced by the quality and consistency of customer service. A positive brand image is attributed to a growing reputation and customer base, customer purchasing decisions, and, ultimately, customer loyalty to the brand itself.

The retention of customers is also critical to the company's bottom line and future growth. According to many published studies, the average cost of acquiring new customers is four to five times higher than the cost of retaining existing customers.

With the high cost of marketing and advertising, it's more economical to work to retain customer loyalty than to pump resources into continually sourcing new customers. Research done by Salesforce indicates that after a high-quality customer service experience, 91 percent of customers are more likely to purchase from the company again.[15] We are all aware that satisfied customers who have had great experiences—whether with the product or service itself or with support—are naturally more likely to recommend the company to friends and family, assisting with the continued growth of the customer base, without the added marketing and advertising expense. Marketing and advertising campaigns can also use social media channels to learn about customers' experiences with the company and its products and services (including support), allowing it to improve the targeting of promotions geared toward customer retention.

While some might consider customer support to be a niche topic, we couldn't disagree more. In fact, Alex Bard at Assistly says, "Customer service is much more than a "niche"—in my view, companies exist to serve customers, so there is no end to very large, important, and interesting problems we can solve with customer service software."[16]

Social media plays a very direct role in the reputation and brand of an organization. Customers now have many channels to voice their opinions and experiences with brands. Customer service can be an amplifier both in the positive and the negative of brand reputation as customers purport their direct experience with the support they received from a company, influencing other's choice and perception of the brand. Companies that greatly value customers will prioritize providing excellent customer service experiences, helping to fortify brand reputation.

When a company is successful, it has a solid and growing customer base with a strong brand reputation, and the impact on the morale of the employees cannot be overlooked. Employees thrive when they're proud of the organizations in which they work. When they see customer focus as a company's core value, it further assists in propelling feelings of helpfulness and collaboration across the entire organization. Employee satisfaction and customer satisfaction are closely intertwined, and they often have a reciprocal and mutually beneficial relationship within an organization. Satisfied employees are more likely to be engaged in delivering better service and customer support. Author and speaker Simon Sinek said, "Customers will never love a company until its employees love it first."

The customer service team, especially support workers, is the core of the relationship between the customer and the business. The customer service team's role is to deliver exemplary customer support in a timely manner. Well-trained employees with the skills, knowledge, and tools to effectively and efficiently assist customers greatly contribute to brand perception. Customers who feel valued lead to increased satisfaction and, ultimately, brand loyalty.

Strategies for Delivering Outstanding Customer Service and Support

Organizations are constantly looking for ways to gain an advantage in this competitive world. Top-tier customer service and support can help companies propel themselves ahead of others. Organizations can rely on several strategies to assist in exceeding customer expectations.

Technology and the Speed of Resolution

Over the past couple of hundred years, technology has become increasingly important in our daily lives and has sped up exponentially in the last 100 years. With the advent of engines for transportation, phones for communication, and computers for almost everything, we rely on technology to complete many of our daily tasks more easily and quickly. The technological revolution has also impacted customer service and support, allowing businesses to provide various ways to connect with clientele to meet their varying needs.

With technology constantly available and easily accessible by most, customers engage with businesses in multiple ways and have become increasingly impatient, often expecting an immediate resolution. Whether experiencing a product issue, account information problem, or even a basic question, most customers have already tried to figure out the problem by searching the Internet and the company's website, visiting technical forums, or poking around in the product's help section. Therefore, they are already invested in finding an answer quickly. Companies are more likely to quickly address many customer inquiries by offering more technical solutions through real-time support, such as technical diagnostics, instant messaging, live chat, easy call-back methods, or AI-empowered solutions. AI technology offers additional advantages, including easy 24/7 access to support in multiple languages and time zones. In addition, AI can often solve routine inquiries more easily and quickly and even proactively resolve issues before customers realize they have an issue, leading to greater customer satisfaction.

Delivering with Empathy

The resolution of the inquiry isn't the only important aspect of delivering a great customer support experience. How the support is delivered is often considered more important than the resolution itself.

Merriam-Webster defines *empathy* as "the action of understanding, being aware of, being sensitive to, and vicariously experiencing the feelings, thoughts, and experience of another."[17] As of this writing, although the definition doesn't say "another living creature," it is implied that "another" is someone or something that can have feelings, thoughts, and experiences. We don't feel sorry for the server overheating in the datacenter or the phone dropped in the pool. However, we might feel empathy for a dog shivering in the cold. Ironically, we can feel sad or disappointed by the Venus de Milo without arms,[18] a rock formation that has crumbled, or a dried riverbed, but empathy's not the same as sympathy. Despite losing her arms, the Venus statue has a calm, serene, and poised face. We may feel the calmness in her face, though we don't empathize with her having lost her arms. The statue can move us, but we don't empathize the way we would with a customer having lost their files or a goldfish who jumped from the bowl.

While this discussion might seem too deep here, setting this context is important because empathy will play a huge part in AI's success with customer engagements going forward. Have you ever experienced a scenario where you were placed on-hold when calling a customer service department? Likely a robotized or recorded voice explains to you how important your call is and how much they appreciate your patience as you wait for an actual person to help you solve your issue. Chances are you didn't believe the robotized or recorded voice really cared about you or your wait time. What you were looking for was a more empathetic human engagement. Ensuring support employees are trained to exhibit genuine and real empathy for the customer's situation helps the customer feel listened to and valued.

To underscore this point about empathy, founder and CEO of All American Entertainment, Greg Friedlander stated,"When you build a culture of empathy from the top down, where your team really cares about the clients you work with, not only do the statements above become second nature, but your clients can sense the authenticity in every single interaction. Every customer interaction is an opportunity to demonstrate genuine care and understanding."[19]

Personalization and Tailored Access

Taking this a step further and connecting to the customer more personally can often lead to a more meaningful interaction, further fostering trust and loyalty. According to Zendesk writer Patrick Grieve, "Personalized service is providing customer experiences that are tailored to the consumer's individual needs and preferences. Personalization often makes customers feel more valued, which inspires greater brand loyalty."[20]

Personalization can range from simply knowing the customer's name to more in-depth knowledge of technical details like knowing a device ID or domain name. Customers feel better about the experience if they feel like they have a relationship with the service provider. Many hotel or credit card loyalty programs offer special customer service phone numbers to their elite-tier customers. **Figure 1.1** shows the American Express contact information for its Platinum cardholders.

AMERICAN EXPRESS

GLOBAL ASSIST® HOTLINE

Global Assist Hotline is available to you 24/7. We can help you prepare for your trip before you go – with important information specific to your destination. While you're traveling more than 100 miles from your home in the United States, coordination and assistance with services such as lost passport replacement assistance, translation services, missing luggage assistance and emergency legal and medical referrals are only a phone call away.

FIGURE 1.1 American Express Hotline

Figure 1.1 is a prime example of a tailored support experience, assuring a unique service for Platinum cardholders. AI can offer some big wins with personalization and tailored access. For example, it can ground its answers in a customer's account history. If a customer is calling for a second time for help with a problem they've had in the past, the AI can take that into context, along with the support and account history, in ways that a human might not be able to do today. AI in customer support is an exciting area for future discovery and innovation.

Knowledge

Another area that is prime for AI is knowledge. Earlier, we discussed the benefits of training support staff to be empathetic to customer's situations. While knowledge and empathy often go hand-in-hand when a customer rates their overall support experience, it will be very interesting to evaluate these two strategies separately as AI further infiltrates support scenarios. Empathy is one area where humans will always play a more important role, and knowledge is one area where AI will continue to improve.

Knowledge can be defined as "the fact or condition of knowing something with familiarity gained through experience or association."[21] And being knowledgeable goes beyond just "having knowledge." To explain the importance of knowledge in customer service scenarios, here are three simple examples.

- Your family is visiting a popular theme park, and your 5-year-old child reports an urgent need. You find a park employee and ask for directions to the nearest restroom. Their reply is, "I don't know."

- You just returned from a magical holiday where you visited some of the most amazing wilderness you've ever seen. You have great nature photos, pictures of your significant other, and encounters with an eagle and a bear—it was epic, and your phone is filled with memories. You go to upload these photos to your computer and get "File not Found" errors for every photo. You frantically search the Internet for a solution, and when that doesn't help, you text support. After you don't get a resolution, you call them directly to get help saving these precious pictures, and they respond with, "I don't know."

- You went to a fundraising event after work and were moved by images of those in need. The next day, you woke up and decided to donate. You found the organization's website, but donating was not intuitive. The site had a chat option, so you chose that and asked how to donate. The response was, "I don't know."

These scenarios and many others underscore the importance of a knowledgeable team. Without knowledgeable support staff, you will never be able to fully meet your customers' needs. While a theme park restroom might not change locations often, software services could change daily, so whatever knowledge is put in front of the customer—whether by a human or by AI, must be current and accurate. If not, it's the same as—or maybe worse than—"I don't know."

How Customers Access Support

Technology advancements have also played an important role in the specific support offerings companies provide and how they are provided. Starting with the earliest and most basic support engagement, in-person support, and advancing to AI solutions. Erik Nordstrom, CEO of the popular US-based department store Nordstrom, spoke about the focus on customers as their top prioritiy. He says,"First and foremost, it's the focus on the customer. Everyone says that, but our aim is simply to make customers feel good. We think about that through the lens of getting closer to our customers, physically in ways of having the product closer to the customer, and in delivering one-on-one service, which has always been important to us."[22]

How customers access support differs widely depending on the industry, competition, company preference, or customer desire. With many companies offering multiple entry points to remain competitive, they control costs and service customers' varying needs.

Following are many of the various support access points:

- **Proactive support:** Proactive support is the gold standard for customer service and support. If support is needed for any reason, the best solution is for the organization to proactively know that an issue happened or is about to happen and solve it before you ever find out. Can you imagine never needing to seek support of any kind and everything always works exactly as expected or is fixed automatically? While this would be ideal, it is not very practical. However, with advancements in technology, including AI, this and other similar scenarios are now possible through advanced telemetry and other methods.

- **Self-service options (FAQs and knowledge bases):** For most modern support organizations, "self-service" is the number one priority. Providing help directly with the product limits the need for customers to search elsewhere and helps customers find solutions more easily. If we abstract this to the theme park restroom analogy from earlier in this chapter, this could mean well-displayed, easy-to-read signs throughout the park. If finding support directly in the product or service isn't feasible, organizations often offer other avenues for customers to find and access help easily. This could include public-facing support documentation appropriately tagged for easy web search discovery. A company's website that can easily be searched can offer great help resources or direct software diagnostics for customers to run and auto-solve issues. And now, with ChatGPT and other AI solutions, organizations are finding new and efficient ways to offer support solutions, preventing many support calls from being necessary. Once again, going back to the theme park restroom analogy, the best self-service option might be as simple as offering customers a map. The goal here is to provide the knowledge where customers are most likely to see it and help themselves.

- **Social media and community forums:** Just as people have gathered in town squares and coffee shops to share information and solve the world's problems, community forums and social media act as similar hubs of knowledge distribution. Companies can control their support messages through social posts and comments and respond to questions once, often reaching a global audience. Community forums leverage the expertise of thousands, providing thoughts on possible solutions, essentially crowd-sourcing assistance.

- **Live chat and instant messaging:** If customers cannot quickly find the help they need on their own, through their social networks, or prefer a more direct personal interaction, they next turn to support from the organization. Live chat and instant messaging solutions are convenient and more personal ways for customers to be quickly guided toward resolving their issues. These options work well for many of the commerce and easier support issue scenarios and with AI models now in the mix, are more cost effective than ever before.

- **Phone and email support:** Many customers prefer to talk or communicate directly with a human or have reached a point of frustration that they feel calling a support line is their next best option. Greg Friedlander, founder and CEO of All American Entertainment, says it best when discussing what he's learned about customer service. His point is that not all communication is the same and often a phone call is more effective than email.[23] The psychological component of reassuring customers when they choose to speak to a person on the phone is highly relevant and can significantly impact customer satisfaction. Human interaction provides a level of comfort, trust, and problem-solving capability that automated systems or written communication may not offer.

While this isn't always the quickest option for resolving your issue, it can change your perspective about a situation through the (hopefully) empathetic support professional's engagement and assurance that they will solve your issue as quickly as possible. While email support can happen independently, it is often paired with phone support as an easy way for support professionals to follow up on actions and provide status updates for support issues that take longer to resolve.

- **In-person service and support:** The number of organizations offering in-person service and support is decreasing rapidly. Through the COVID-19 pandemic, many companies had to reinvent their business models by moving services online. And while many storefronts and other businesses have opened up to in-person customer visits, selling their products or offering experiences, customer service is often no longer part of the brick-and-mortar stores or easily accessible in-person and is now only available through other channels.

Measuring Support Success

As with any organization, the measurements of success are vast, depending on the outcomes you're looking to achieve. In customer service and support, some businesses may care more about the speed of resolution, while others may prefer to focus on the customer support experience regardless of how long issue resolution takes. A variety of factors contribute to the decisions businesses make in what's most important for them, including cost of service and brand reputation. Many of these factors are not mutually exclusive, though most agree that customer satisfaction is the ultimate measure of success.

- **Customer satisfaction/dissatisfaction:** It is increasingly difficult to meet all customers' needs all the time. Depending on where you are in the world, what support channels are available to you, how deep you need to search for an answer, how long you wait in a support queue, whom you end up with on a support chat or call, how they interact with you, and whether your issue was resolved can all play into your evaluation of a successful or unsuccessful support interaction. The business impact and the severity of the issue the customer is facing (business, work, life) can have a direct impact on satisfaction. If the issue is minor and easily resolved, customers are more likely to be satisfied with a swift and hassle-free solution. On the other hand, if the issue is major and disrupts their experience or causes significant inconvenience, such as bringing a payment platform down with significant financial loss or creating a highly disruptive and inconvenient situation for the customer, the probability of landing a dissatisfaction scenario is much higher, even if the support experience delivered was top notch. The unpredictable nature of problems can have a complex and multifaceted impact on customer satisfaction. While these issues can create challenges, they also offer opportunities for companies to demonstrate their commitment to customer support, build trust, and ultimately enhance satisfaction by addressing and resolving issues effectively and efficiently.

- **Customer wait time:** A study by the American Customer Satisfaction Index (ACSI) found that customer wait times *do* affect customer satisfaction scores and that customers are 18 percent less satisfied with their overall experience if they have to wait longer than expected. In addition, any dissatisfaction with the experience doesn't go away once the wait is over.[24] Another study by researchers at MIT found that customers who had to wait longer than 10 minutes for service were less likely to recommend it to others or return to the business. And those who experienced long wait times were also more likely to leave negative reviews online.[25]

- **Timely issue resolution:** As mentioned earlier, typically, by the time a customer reaches out for assistance, they've already tried to troubleshoot and solve the issue or answer the question on their own, possibly by restarting the device, using self-help resources such as web searches, reviewing the organization's website, maybe even asking a friend. Therefore, by the time they reach out and contact a support professional, they have already spent some time trying to resolve their issue or question and are ready to move on with their lives. While the most effective support is no support required, the next best is a quick and effective resolution.

- **First contact resolution:** Not only is the total time it takes to solve an issue important but so is the total number of people required to solve an issue. Going back to our earlier "I don't know" analogies, depending on the issue's complexity, customers may not immediately be assisted by someone who can directly solve their issue. The support professional may need to connect with other colleagues for additional assistance or transfer the chat or call to a different support department or higher and more technical tier of support before a solution is offered. The quality of transfers in customer support is critical in shaping the customer experience and satisfaction. It requires effective communication, seamless handoffs, consistency, and a focus on efficiently resolving the customer's issue. When done well, even complex support queries that involve multiple people can result in a positive customer experience and higher satisfaction levels. On the flip side, it can also ruin the customer's experience because information might be lost in the process, requiring the customer to repeat information and steps already taken, which can contribute to frustration and loss of trust.

- **Customer sentiment:** How customers feel throughout their incident impacts their overall customer experience and, ultimately, their brand perception. While feelings can run from frustration about being unable to find the solution on their own to being elated that their call resulted in a quick resolution, not all feelings are weighted the same. Depending on what matters most to a customer and where they may have encountered success or trouble in their experience will play into their overall sentiment score, translated to either a positive, neutral, or negative sentiment about the brand.

Challenges in Customer Support

Organizations' challenges with customer support are generally similar across industries and support channels. You may have an irate customer who didn't get their needs met or differing quality of assistance experienced depending on the channel the customer chooses to go to for help, or the balance between automation and human interaction. All these play into how a customer experiences their interactions with a business and their perception of the brand.

- **Handling difficult or irate customers:** Each customer is different and engages with companies differently. Customers come with different perceptions, experiences, and expectations. We all know how difficult it is to meet every customer's needs all the time. Great customer service professionals adapt to combining empathy, patience, and problem-solving to help tame the most irate customers. AI can further assist support professionals by helping to predict customer pain points, analyzing patterns in a customer's communication, suggesting optimal solutions and empathetic responses, and gauging emotion through sentiment analysis—possibly diverting a poor experience by deescalating the situation. By seamlessly integrating AI within the workflows of support interactions, many challenges can be turned around, leading to a more positive customer experience.

- **Maintaining consistency across various channels:** With the many support channels employed by companies, ensuring a consistent experience across all customer interactions is incredibly difficult. The challenge is really in ensuring customers experience a seamless and personalized experience irrespective of the channel they choose for their support assistance. Given AI's ability to analyze large amounts of data in a relatively short time frame, the opportunities to monitor and report response discrepancies across channels is prime for the application. In addition, machine learning algorithms can predict customer expectations based on their past interactions, paving the way for a more uniform and personalized support experience. With the assistance of AI, companies can move closer to the desired consistency in experience across all support channels.

- **Balancing automation and human interaction:** There are many advantages that both AI and the automation of processes have in a company's ability to support customers. They can assist with handling repetitive tasks, forecasting customer queries based on past interactions, managing basic inquiries, delivering fast resolutions, and analyzing large amounts of data—all driving toward greater consistency in support interactions and business efficiency. However, there are times when a customer wants human interaction for a deeper level of understanding and empathy. This is where a shift from AI and automated processes really matters and often comes along when the issue is complex and not easily solved.

Desire for Change and Improvement

As discussed, many opportunities exist for AI integration in the customer service and support arena. Almost every aspect of support can benefit from greater AI integration or process automation, which translates directly to an improved customer experience. While the desire for companies to transform many of their support operations and integrate technical solutions may be present, the complexities of doing so can be prohibitive to the level of detail required for optimal customer service and support outcomes.

Data Quality and Availability

AI models rely on very large amounts of high-quality data to provide accurate and relevant responses to queries. Any incomplete, outdated, inconsistent, or biased data will likely lead to poor responses and/or undesired outcomes. Garbage in, garbage out. In later chapters, we'll talk in-depth about how support organizations can work to ensure the AI models they deploy are properly indexed, reviewed, and continually monitored for accuracy.

THE LOOM OF PROGRESS

We start our story in the 16th century. It's a story of innovation, fear, excitement, and marvel at evolution and its wide-reaching implications—not just for the technology itself, but for people, business, and cultural and global change.

With all the sheep in England, the village of Manchester started to grow as a market for wool. The growth continued for decades, and it eventually became a home for textiles. With the arrival of the "spinning jenny" in the 1760s, textile manufacturing further propelled the growth of the textile industry, and other types of yarn were introduced, such as cotton. With cotton imported from India through the port of Liverpool and floated up the Mersey and Inwell Navigation—rivers connecting the towns—Manchester continued to grow, eventually being nicknamed "Cottonopolis" for its burgeoning trade.

In 1790, two women neighbors walked to work one warm spring day in a fictitious mill in Manchester. Mary did the job that was known as "spinning." In the 18th century, once the cotton was "carded," the spinners would spin it into thread. It would then be spooled and used by the weavers, who would weave it into cloth. Mary was one of the best spinners at the mill. Although she started after the arrival of the spinning jenny, she also learned to operate the water frame and the spinning mule—two other inventions that she had mastered. Elizabeth had a different role as a weaver, and as they walked, she talked about the rumors she'd heard about a new invention from Edmund Cartwright called "the power loom."

As it turned out, the rumors Elizabeth heard were to come true on that very day. When they arrived at the mill, there was a lot of commotion and a crowd of people. Early in Elizabeth's career, Richard Arkwright had opened the first steam-powered textile mill on Miller Street in Manchester, and she had strong memories

Technology Integration and Compatibility

An organization's underlying technical architecture is critical for applying AI solutions, transcending the support arena. However, in support, tools such as the customer relationship management (CRM) system, chat platforms, voice assistance, reporting tools, and the like play into what and how AI can and should be deployed to optimize the support experience. For example, many legacy systems may not be compatible with AI solutions and require significant changes to implement this new technology. This could add cost and affect the overall support experience, not just with customers but also with how employees interact with the solutions designed to assist them in their daily work. It will be important of that time and how it changed her work. The pit she felt in her stomach was driven by the anxiety that the introduction of a new machine might change her job again.

As the two worked their way through the crowd, they caught their first glimpse of the new shiny object—the focus of all the fuss. It was indeed a power loom—and it was getting set up right there in their own factory. Mary tagged along behind Elizabeth. She was younger and less experienced and had no idea how to view this new addition. Was it a friend or foe? A benefit or a threat? They went to their stations and started the day's work as the crowd continued to bustle. By the end of the day, there, in a corner of the shop, was this new shiny thing, seemingly watching them do their work as if calculating its next move.

As they walked home when their shift was done, Mary asked Elizabeth if she worried that the power loom would take her job. Elizabeth had spoken to her boss during a break and learned more about what the machine could do. A grim look came to her face. "Mary," she said, "that machine is here to take our jobs away from us." Mary panicked. "Wait, what?"

Elizabeth continued to describe how the machine would do the work of ten spinners and would only require one person to change the spool once an hour. So Mary's job was as good as gone. She also spoke of her nervousness because the machine was much faster and that she would be expected to keep up. If she could do it, her overall productivity with the machine would be double what it was without it. That also meant if she couldn't keep up, she would be among half of the weavers who would no longer be necessary.

If the machine could really do the job of ten Marys and one Elizabeth, their lives would change forever.

for organizations to think through their desire for AI integration and how it might work with their current and future technical architecture and consider future innovation quickly, given the rapid changes we're seeing with generative AI.

The same applies to the concept of knowledge management, previously highlighted in this chapter as a key factor in the success of any AI model. As you prepare to equip your AI model and have it ingest the necessary knowledge to fulfill your needs, concepts like how data is structured or formatted can significantly impact the model's performance and the success of your project.

Talent and Organizational Culture

As we'll discuss later in this book, new roles emerge as the AI demand increases. Many organizations might not have the in-house staff to be able to design, develop, deploy and maintain AI solutions. With the technology being so new, it will take some time for there to be enough skilled individuals to meet the increasing demand. In addition, there is a change management component as AI systems are introduced. Many employees and managers are reluctant to engage as they may need to change how they work and interact with support tools. And many are feeling like AI will take over their jobs. Therefore, working to dispel myths and integrating AI into the organization's culture may help employees overcome resistance and see the solutions as enablers of their work.

Technology advances have changed our lives in countless ways, including in our engagement in and with customer service and support. Although AI will play an increasingly important role in all channels of customer service and support, there isn't a replacement for an empathetic and knowledgeable human available to solve the most complex problems. Customer support is always about meeting customer needs, exceeding customer expectations, and ultimately creating customer loyalty.

We are entering the dawn of an AI Revolution in customer service and support, where technology offers a bridge between the pillars of empathy and efficiency. This transformative time promises to disrupt and redefine support, making it more personalized, accessible, and empowering than ever before. As we sow the seeds of this AI Revolution, we are not just changing how we serve; we're using this innovative technology to reshape the very essence and nature of customer service. Together, as we embark on the journey through this book, we want to work together with you to harness AI to create a future where every customer interaction is based on understanding and care provided by both human and machine. This is just the beginning, so invite your human compatriots and let's embark on our revolutionary journey!

Endnotes

1   Lucas, Robert (2015). *Customer Service: Skills for Success.* McGraw-Hill. ISBN 978-0-07-354546-2.

2   Wikipedia contributors. "Customer support." Wikipedia, The Free Encyclopedia. December 16, 2023. [https://en.wikipedia.org/wiki/Customer_support].

3   Talwar, Himanshu. "Enhanced focus on guest relationship and its importance post pandemic." *ET Hospitality World.* May 12, 2021. [https://hospitality.economictimes.indiatimes.com/news/speaking-heads/enhanced-focus-on-guest-relationship-and-its-importance-post-pandemic/82570092].

4   Merriam-Webster. "Help desk." Merriam-Webster.com Dictionary. Accessed March 17, 2024. [https://www.merriam-webster.com/dictionary/help%20desk].

5   Indeed Editorial Team. "What is Customer Care? (With Examples)." Indeed. February 12, 2024. [https://www.indeed.com/career-advice/career-development/customer-care].

6   Wikipedia contributors. "Organization." Wikipedia, The Free Encyclopedia. January 27, 2024. [https://en.wikipedia.org/wiki/Organization].

7   Shaw, Ahsan Ali. "What is a Company?—Meaning, Features, and Types of Companies." Marketing Tutor. Accessed March 17, 2024. [https://www.marketingtutor.net/what-is-a-company/].

8   Hayes, Adam. "What is a Business? Understanding Different Types and Company Sizes." Investopedia. February 29, 2024. [https://www.investopedia.com/terms/b/business.asp].

9   Gorton, David. "Industry Definition in Business and Investing." Investopedia. November 7, 2023. [https://www.investopedia.com/terms/i/industry.asp].

10   Indeed Editorial Team. "Technical Support Engineer: Definition and Responsibilities." Indeed. March 8, 2024. [https://in.indeed.com/career-advice/resumes-cover-letters/technical-support-engineer].

11   Mindmesh editors. "Customer Service Agent." Mindmesh. Accessed March 17, 2024. [https://www.mindmesh.com/glossary/what-is-customer-service-agent].

12   Wikipedia contributors. "Customer service representative." Wikipedia, The Free Encyclopedia. January 25, 2024. [https://en.wikipedia.org/wiki/Customer_service_representative].

13   Climb editors. "What Does a Client Relations Associate Do?" Climb. February 20, 2024. [https://climbtheladder.com/client-relations-associate/].

14   Indeed Editorial Team. "Frontline Employees: Types and Tips for Motivating Them." Indeed. December 12, 2022. [https://www.indeed.com/career-advice/finding-a-job/front-line-employees].

15   Salesforce Reserchers. "State of the Connected Customer, 4th edition." Salesforce. Accessed March 17, 2024. [https://c1.sfdcstatic.com/content/dam/web/en_us/www/documents/research/salesforce-state-of-the-connected-customer-4th-ed.pdf].

16   Thomas, Jesse. "Why Customer service is Much More than a Niche—an Interview with Assistly's Alex Bard." Forbes. November 16, 2011. [https://www.forbes.com/sites/jessethomas/2011/11/16/why-customer-service-is-much-more-than-a-niche-an-interview-with-assistlys-alex-bard/?sh=22997de16324].

17 Merriam-Webster. "Empathy." Merriam-Webster.com Dictionary. Accessed March 17, 2024. [https://www.merriam-webster.com/dictionary/empathy?src=search-dict-hed].

18 Meyer, Isabella. "'Venus de Milo' Sculpture—Discover the Famous Statue Without Arms." Art in Context. Updated September 5, 2023. [https://artincontext.org/venus-de-milo-sculpture/].

19 Friedlander, Greg. "6 Things I Learned About Customer Service as a CEO." Inc. March 6, 2024. [https://www.inc.com/inc-masters/six-things-i-learned-about-customer-service-as-ceo.html].

20 Grieve, Patrick. "Personalized customer service: what it is and how to provide it." Zendesk. January 22, 2024. [https://www.zendesk.com/blog/start-providing-personalized-customer-service/].

21 Merriam-Webster. "Knowledge." Merriam-Webster.com Dictionary. Accessed March 17, 2024. [https://www.merriam-webster.com/dictionary/knowledge].

22 Moin, David. "Nortstrom at 120: CEO Erik Nordstrom On Navigating Rocky Times, Brick-and-Mortar's Revival + How Great Service Has Evolved." Footwear News. September 13, 2021. [https://footwearnews.com/business/retail/erik-nordstrom-ceo-strategy-interview-1203176455/].

23 Friedlander, Greg. "6 Things I Learned About Customer Service as a CEO." Inc. March 6, 2024. [https://www.inc.com/inc-masters/six-things-i-learned-about-customer-service-as-ceo.html].

24 Berg, Erik. "How Does Wait Time Impact Customer Satisfaction?" NEMO-Q. May 10, 2022. [https://www.nemo-q.com/blog/how-does-wait-time-impact-customer-satisfaction/].

25 Berg, Erik. "How Does Wait Time Impact Customer Satisfaction?" NEMO-Q. May 10, 2022. [https://www.nemo-q.com/blog/how-does-wait-time-impact-customer-satisfaction/].

2

Overview of Generative AI and Data Science Machine Learning

You may grow old and trembling in your anatomies, you may lie awake at night listening to the disorder of your veins, you may miss your only love, you may see the world about you devastated by evil lunatics, or know your honour trampled in—to learn. Learn why the world wags and what wags it. That is the only thing which the mind can never exhaust, never alienate, never be tortured by, never fear or distrust, and never dream of regretting. Learning is the only thing for you. Look what a lot of things there are to learn.

—T.H. White

Welcome to the most technical chapter of our journey into the AI Revolution. Unlike the other chapters in this book, this chapter is a deep dive into the history and details of the data science technology that powers today's AI Revolution in customer service and support. In this chapter, we explore concepts such as generative AI, machine learning, various language models, reinforcement machine learning, and prompt engineering—among other topics—in detail. This chapter goes into the technical details of the foundation upon which the AI that is changing customer support is built.

However—and this is important—you don't have to read this chapter to get the most out of the following chapters. You may have technical colleagues who know or will learn about the topics in this chapter, or you may have partners or vendors to help you build and deploy AI solutions. You don't have to know this level of detail to move forward in leading your organization through the deployment of AI. We recognize that not everyone will feel comfortable navigating this more complex territory, and that's okay—it won't matter for the rest of the book.

However, we felt that we would be remiss if we didn't cover this technology in some detail as a foundational component of this book. This chapter will not supplant the myriad of courses, papers, books, theories, algorithms, and other details in this fast-moving technology. This chapter is worth a skim to understand the underlying developments driving the AI Revolution and what to explore in more detail if you are interested.

If you're a customer service and support professional eager to leverage AI in your organization but less versed in technical jargon—please know this chapter is not a prerequisite for the valuable insights and steps outlined in the other chapters in this book. It's here to provide a deeper understanding for those who wish to explore further. Skipping it won't diminish your ability to apply AI effectively within your role.

The rest of the book is designed with you in mind, focusing on practical applications, deployment strategies, and real-world scenarios that don't require a deep technical background to understand. However, if you want to be the leader who queries your team or a vendor on their understanding and application of reinforcement learning from human feedback (RLHF), you might want to investigate to understand more.

Whether you decide to brave this chapter or flip past it and go directly to the next, rest assured that this chapter is not required reading to enable a successful AI deployment! Happy reading, wherever you land next.

Unveiling the Realm of AI Technologies: A Glimpse into the Augmented Future

In 1947, Alan Turing gave a public lecture about computer intelligence—the original concept of artificial intelligence. In 1950, he proposed the Turing test, a criterion for machine intelligence based on natural language conversation. In 1956, John McCarthy coined the term artificial intelligence and organized the first conference on the topic at Dartmouth College.

In the 1970s and 1980s, AI research focused on developing rule-based systems that could encode human knowledge and reasoning in specific domains, such as medicine, engineering, and finance. These systems, known as expert systems, could perform tasks requiring human expertise, such as diagnosis, planning, and decision-making.

In the late 1980s and 1990s, the development of AI underwent a paradigm shift from relying on predefined rules to learning from data, enabling machines to achieve higher levels of intelligence and performance. Machine learning (ML) is a subfield of AI that enables machines to learn from data and improve their performance without explicit programming. Machine learning techniques include supervised, unsupervised, and reinforcement learning, which can be applied to various problems, such as classification, clustering, regression, and control.

In the 2000s and 2010s, AI experienced a major breakthrough with the advent of deep learning, a subset of machine learning that uses multiple layers of artificial neural networks to learn from large amounts of data. 2015 was a big year in AI history; a five-game Go match was hosted between the European champion Fan Hui and AlphaGo, a computer Go program developed by DeepMind. AlphaGo won all five games. Deep learning has enabled significant advances in various domains, such as computer vision, natural language processing (NLP), speech recognition, and robotics. Some notable deep learning models include convolutional neural networks (CNNs), recurrent neural networks (RNNs), and transformer models, such as BERT (Bidirectional Encoder Representations from Transformers)[1] and GPT (Generative Pre-trained Transformer).[2]

In 2017, Google developed the transformer model and published a paper, "Attention Is All You Need."[3] Transformers opened a new chapter for the natural language processing field. Since then, companies and researchers worldwide have built large-scale language models based on the transformer architecture.

In the 2020s and beyond, AI is entering a new frontier of generative technologies, which aim to create novel and realistic content, such as images, texts, sounds, and videos. Generative technologies use deep learning models, such as generative adversarial networks (GANs), variational autoencoders (VAEs), and large language models (LLMs), to generate content that is indistinguishable from human-produced content. Generative technologies have various applications, such as art, entertainment, education, and communication.

Generative AI and Language Models

One of the most exciting and challenging areas of generative technologies is natural language generation (NLG), which generates natural language text from a given input, such as an image, a keyword, or a prompt. NLG has many applications, including summarization, translation, dialogue, storytelling, and content creation. However, NLG also poses many technical and ethical challenges, such as ensuring the generated texts' quality, diversity, coherence, and fairness.

A key component of NLG is the language model (LM), a probabilistic model that assigns a probability to a sequence of words or tokens. LMs can generate new texts by sampling tokens according to their probabilities or evaluating the likelihood of existing texts. LMs can be trained on large corpora of text data, such as Wikipedia, books, news articles, or social media posts, using deep learning techniques, such as RNNs or transformers.

Because statistical language models (SLMs) cannot capture long-term dependencies or semantic relations in natural language, this underscores the importance of building these models with responsibility and ethics in mind, as discussed throughout this book.

The development of LMs has gone through several stages, reflecting the advances in computational power, data availability, and algorithmic innovation. There are four main development stages of LMs: statistical language models, neural language models, pre-trained language models, and large language models (LLMs).[4]

- **Statistical language models** are based on statistical learning models. The idea is to build models based on the n-gram assumption, which states that the probability of a word only depends on the previous n-1 words and not on the rest of the sentence or the document. An n-gram is a sequence of n-words, such as "the cat" or "a big house." For instance, predicting when the probability of the word "model" would come after the words "large language" is illustrated as P(model|large language). Statistical language models estimate the probabilities of n-grams from a corpus of text data using techniques such as counting, smoothing, or interpolation.

- **Counting:** Counting is simply the frequency of the n-gram in the corpus divided by the total number of n-grams.

- **Smoothing:** Smoothing adds some small values to the counts to avoid zero probabilities for unseen n-grams.

- **Interpolation:** Interpolation combines the probabilities of different n-grams, such as unigrams, bigrams, and trigrams, to balance the trade-off between specificity and generality.

Smoothing and interpolation are often adopted to mitigate the data sparsity problem. Statistical language models are simple and efficient but have limited expressive power and cannot capture long-term dependencies or semantic relations in natural language. For example, statistical language models cannot distinguish between the meanings of "bank" in "I went to the bank" and "The bank was closed" or the contexts of "She saw a bear" and "She saw a bare." Statistical language models cannot handle the ambiguity of words with multiple meanings, such as "bat," "right," or the influence of words that are far apart in the sequence, such as "The man who wore a hat" and "The hat was red."

- **Neural language models (NLMs)** use neural networks, such as recurrent neural networks (RNNs) or convolutional neural networks (CNNs), to learn distributed representations of words and sequences and to model the conditional probability of the next word given the previous words. A groundbreaking work in the field of neural language modeling was the paper "A neural probabilistic language model,"[5] which presented the idea of representing words as continuous vectors in a high-dimensional space and learning the probability of the next word based on the sum of the context word vectors. Many studies have opened a new chapter for using language models for representation learning, playing an influential role in the NLP field. For example, word2vec[6] utilizes two methods to learn word embedding:

  - **Using context to predict a target word through CBOW (Continuous Bags of Words):** CBOW is like a guessing game where the AI tries to predict a word based on the words around it. Imagine a sentence with a missing word; CBOW looks around the neighboring words to guess the missing one, helping the AI better understand the language.

  - **Using a word to predict a target context through Skip-Gram:** Skip-Gram is like a word puzzle where the challenge is to find the related words. Given a specific word, Skip-Gram tries to predict the surrounding words, helping the AI grasp the context and relationships between words in a sentence.[7]

NLMs can overcome some of the limitations of statistical language models, such as capturing longer contexts and learning richer features, but they also have drawbacks, such as requiring more computation and data and suffering from the vanishing or exploding gradient problem.

- **Pre-trained language models (PLMs)** are a type of model that uses transfer learning. PLMs are first trained on a large collection of text data that doesn't have specific labels (this is the pre-training phase). After this, PLMs are fine-tuned on a particular task or domain with more specific data (this is the fine-tuning phase). This process allows PLMs to be highly effective at understanding and generating human language in various applications. As mentioned earlier, RNNs have some drawbacks and limitations, such as the difficulty of learning long-term dependencies, the gradient vanishing or exploding problem, and the sequential nature of computation, which prevents parallelization and reduces efficiency. To address these issues, long short-term memory (LSTM) models were proposed by researchers as one of the most popular and effective variants of RNNs. LSTM models have a special structure consisting of three gates and a cell state, which can regulate the input, output, and forget operations of the recurrent unit. LSTM models can generate natural language texts by updating the cell state and the hidden state at each time step, based on the current input and the previous states, and then producing the next word or token from the hidden state. As one of the first models that demonstrated the effectiveness of PLMs on large-scale unlabeled text data and then transferring the learned knowledge to downstream tasks or domains, embeddings from language models (ELMo) was built as an LSTM-based model that can generate contextualized word embeddings, which are vector representations of words that capture their meanings and usage in different contexts. Unlike traditional word embeddings, such as word2vec or GloVe, which assigns a fixed vector to each word regardless of its context, ELMo can dynamically compute word embeddings based on the entire input sentence or document, using a bidirectional LSTM that encodes both the left and the right contexts of each word. PLMs also adopt the transformer architecture, which is an attention-based neural network that can learn long-range dependencies and parallelize computation. Some of the most influential PLMs are BERT, developed by Google, and GPT, developed by OpenAI. Based on pre-trained context-aware word representations, these models have shown remarkable effectiveness and versatility as general-purpose semantic features that can significantly improve the performance and efficiency of various NLP tasks.

- **Large language models (LLMs)** are the latest and most advanced stage of LMs, which aim to build very large-scale and powerful LMs that can generate natural language texts across multiple domains and tasks, given minimal or no supervision. LLMs rely on massive amounts of computation and data and use sophisticated optimization and regularization techniques, such as self-attention, dropout, or layer normalization, to train billions or trillions of parameters. Some of the most prominent examples of LLMs are GPT-3, GPT-3.5 (Instruct GPT) GPT-4 and GPT-4o, developed by OpenAI.

  - **GPT-3:** GPT-3 is a transformer-based model with 175 billion parameters and can generate coherent and diverse texts on various topics and domains, given a few words or sentences as input.

  - **GPT-3.5:** In 2022, OpenAI deployed GPT-3.5, which performs more significantly in following instructions, making up facts less often, and generating less toxic output. They used prompts submitted by the customers through Playground and hired human annotators to provide demonstrations of the desired model behavior and rank outputs from the models. GPT-3.5 is fine-tuned based on this data from GPT-3.

  - **GPT-4:** In 2023, GPT-4, a 1.8T-parameter model with 16 Mixture of Experts (MoE), was announced by OpenAI to improve the security of the model and enable multimodal capability. However, LLMs also have limitations and risks, such as producing inaccurate, biased, or harmful content or violating the data sources' privacy or intellectual property rights.

  - **GPT-4o:** Launched in 2024, GPT-4o ("o" for "omni") is a step towards a much more natural human-computer interaction—it accepts any combination of text, audio, image, and video as input and generates any combination of text, audio, and image as output. It can respond to audio inputs in as little as 232 milliseconds, with an average of 320 milliseconds, which is similar to human response time in a conversation. It matches GPT-4 Turbo performance on text in English and code, with significant improvement on text in non-English languages, while also being much faster and 50% cheaper in the API. GPT-4o is especially better at vision and audio understanding compared to existing models.[8]

The emergence and advancement of LLMs significantly impact the AI community and society at large, as they open up new possibilities and challenges for natural language understanding and generation. LLMs can be seen as a form of generative technologies that can create novel and valuable outputs from minimal or no inputs, such as images, music, art, or texts. They can foster interdisciplinary collaboration and innovation by bringing together researchers and practitioners from different fields and domains and creating new paradigms and methods for natural language understanding and generation.

Despite the exciting progress and impact of LLMs and generative AI, many mysterious and unpredictable perspectives remain. There are some risks associated with LLMs. They can amplify existing biases and harms, such as perpetuating stereotypes, discrimination, misinformation, or manipulation, by learning from unfiltered and unrepresentative data sources, or by being misused or abused by malicious actors. They can also pose ethical and legal dilemmas, such as violating privacy, intellectual property, or human dignity, by exposing sensitive or personal information, infringing on copyrights or trademarks, or generating deceptive or harmful content. Moreover, they can challenge existing norms and values, such as accountability, transparency, or trust, by obscuring natural language generation's sources, processes, and outcomes or by creating conflicts of interest, responsibility, or authority.

LLMs and Their Applications

As discussed earlier, LLMs are trained on billions or trillions of words, sentences, paragraphs, or documents collected from various online sources, such as websites, blogs, social media, news articles, books, or academic papers, using a technique called self-attention, which enables them to learn the contextual and semantic relationships between different units of language. LLMs can then use the learned representations to perform a wide range of natural language tasks, such as classification, summarization, translation, question answering, sentiment analysis, or dialogue generation. They do this by fine-tuning specific datasets or domains or by applying a method called *prompting*, which consists of providing the model with a few words or sentences as input or output examples and letting it infer the rest.

LLMs have demonstrated remarkable capabilities and achievements in natural language understanding and generation, surpassing previous state-of-the-art models and even human performance in some tasks. Some of the most notable and influential LLMs include GPTs, BERT, XLNet, T5, and DALL-E, which have been developed and released by leading research labs and companies, such as OpenAI, Google, Facebook, and Microsoft. LLMs have also enabled and inspired the creation and innovation of various applications and products, such as chatbots, assistants, recommender systems, content generators, summarizers, translators, analyzers, or synthesizers, which have been deployed and adopted by various industries and sectors, such as education, health, business, media, entertainment, or art, among others. LLMs have thus revolutionized and democratized the field of natural language processing and generation, opening up new possibilities and opportunities for research, development, and impact.

LLMs and Customer Support

One possible application domain of LLMs is customer support, which involves providing assistance and guidance to customers or users of a product or service through various channels, such as phone, email, chat, or social media. Customer support is an essential and integral part of any business or organization, as it affects customer satisfaction, retention, loyalty, advocacy, brand reputation, revenue, and growth. However, customer support can also be challenging and costly, as it requires hiring, training, and managing a large number of human agents, who have to deal with high volumes of queries, requests, complaints, or feedback, often repetitive, mundane, or complex while maintaining a high quality of service, professionalism, and empathy.

LLMs can offer a solution to some of these challenges by augmenting or automating some aspects of customer support, such as answering frequently asked questions, providing information or instructions, resolving issues or problems, collecting feedback or ratings, generating reports or summaries, or escalating cases or tickets, and so on. LLMs can leverage their natural language abilities, such as understanding, reasoning, generating, or adapting, to provide personalized, contextualized, and relevant responses or actions based on the customer's input, profile, history, or preferences, as well as the product or service specifications, policies, or updates. LLMs can also learn from the data and feedback collected from the interactions and improve their performance and accuracy over time, using techniques such as reinforcement learning, active learning, or transfer learning. Furthermore, LLMs can enhance the customer experience and engagement by adding elements of conversation, personality, emotion, or humor, to the interactions, depending on the tone, mood, or style of the customer and the situation.

Development, Optimization, Localization, and Personalization Based on LLMs

The rapid growth of the tech field has seen significant disruptions when the right combination of technology and user experiences come together. Generative AI–infused experiences bring a great opportunity for intelligent product development. Besides fostering AI's capabilities for business and real products, we must also ensure localization and personalization and operate with a clear customer-centric intent and goal.

There are multiple strategies to employ regarding integrating the generative AI large models into productions with further optimization, localization, and personalization.

Large deep neural networks have achieved remarkable success with great performance in research and real-world products with large-scale data. However, it is still a great challenge to deploy these large-scale AI models to real production systems, especially mobile devices and embedded systems, with the considerations of cost, computational resources, and memory capacity. The main purpose of teacher–student distillation (see **Figure 2.1**) is to train a small student model that simulates the large teacher model with equivalent or superior performance.[9] Another advantage of teacher–student distillation is that when we do not have enough labeled data, the teacher model can help generate a "pseudo-label" when training the student model. Pseudo-labels are then used to train the smaller student model, helping it learn and perform tasks as if it had been trained on a fully labeled dataset. Put more simply, imagine you're playing a video game, and there's a really tough level that you can't beat. So, you call in an expert friend.

The three main components of the teacher–student distillation framework include knowledge, distillation algorithm, and teacher–student architecture.

Figure 2.1 illustrates two AI models:

- **Teacher model:** The teacher model is like an expert friend. It's very smart but also big and needs a lot of power to run.
- **Student model:** Like you, the student model is eager to learn. It doesn't have as much power.

The goal is to make the student AI learn from the teacher AI without needing as much power. The process is such that the teacher model, trained with huge volumes of data, helps the student model by guiding it or giving it tips—in NLP; this is called "knowledge transfer." Sometimes, the teacher doesn't have all the answers (or labeled data), so the teacher makes up some good guesses (pseudo-labels) for the student to practice with. It's like getting hints for your video game level. This way, the student learns a lot and gets really good at the game, so it can almost match the teacher's skill level.

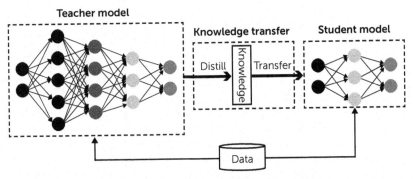

FIGURE 2.1 The general teacher–student distillation framework

This framework can be useful for any large-scale prediction or generative AI model, although it was originally introduced for an image classification model. With the rapid development of generative AI, many of the current large-scale models are significantly effective in generalization. However, many factors must be considered for real production, including cost, scalability, resource consumption during inference, adopting the existing model into some specific scenarios, and so on. Developing an AI-assistant writing tool by leveraging GPT to help users write articles or posts more casually and recognize contextual information is an example of adopting the existing GPT model to the specific scenario of an AI-assistant writing tool. Directly running GPT models is very challenging, considering cost and scalability. The teacher–student distillation framework helps serve lighter-weight models in production and localizes the model with task-specific data when leveraging the existing large-scale model.

Reinforcement Learning from Human/AI Feedback

As mentioned earlier, Instruct GPT/ GPT-3.5 was developed by OpenAI to have a better human alignment and address some issues like factuality, harm, etc. They collected prompts submitted by customers through Playground and ranked outputs from the models responding to the human-annotated instructions. InstructGPT/ GPT-3.5 is fine-tuned based on this data from GPT-3. The success of GPT-3.5 over GPT-3 is mainly due to the reinforcement learning from human feedback (RLHF) technique, which is adopted to fine-tune GPT-3 using human labels as a reward signal (see **Figure 2.2**).[10]

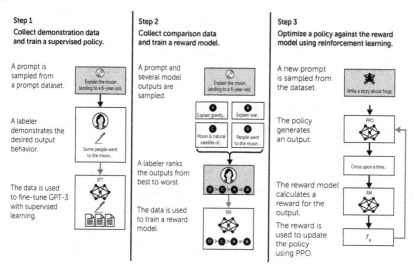

FIGURE 2.2 The reinforcement learning framework

The human annotators compare and rank multiple outputs from GPT-3 corresponding to each prompt. Based on this labeled data, a reward model is trained to predict the preferred output. Lastly, this reward model is a reward function and policy optimized to maximize the reward using the proximal policy optimization (PPO) algorithm.

Imagine you're teaching a teenager how to ride a snowboard for the first time. You want them to learn fancy tricks, but every time they try something new, you don't want them risking a big crash. The proximal policy optimization (PPO) algorithm is like a smart snowboard coach for the teen. It has a rule: "Try new turns or try new moves but not so different from what you already know, or you will definitely fall."

Here's how it works: The teenager tries a new turn or trick, sees how well they do (like scoring confidence points for staying upright and doing small tricks), and learns the way any human would. Then they try again, slightly tweaking their approach but with a twist. There's a safety net (the "clip" in PPO can be related to "clipping" the trick's extremes to avoid moving too far away from the original effort), making sure these tweaks aren't too drastic. This way, the teen steadily gets better without taking big risks that could lead to epic wipeouts.

PPO keeps a machine learning efficiently by reusing its experiences several times to refine its strategy, ensuring it learns a lot from each practice session. It's like watching a video of a snowboard performance on the hill and spotting a dozen ways to improve instead of just one. This makes the machine a quick learner and smart, avoiding unnecessary risks while it masters its metaphorical ability to shred on the mountain!

Despite the impressive results achieved by GPT3.5, this technique also faces some challenges and limitations that need to be addressed for further improvement and broader application. **Table 2.1** shows example challenges and potential mitigation activities with RLHF utilizing future research and development.

TABLE 2.1 Example challenges and potential mitigation activities	
CHALLENGE	FUTURE RESEARCH AND DEVELOPMENT
Data quality and quantity: The quality and quantity of human feedback data are crucial for training a reliable reward model and a robust policy. However, collecting human feedback data can be costly, time-consuming, and prone to noise and bias. Moreover, human preferences may vary across domains, tasks, and contexts, requiring more diverse and representative data to capture the nuances and subtleties of human expectations and instructions.	Improving the data collection and annotation methods and tools to ensure human feedback data quality, quantity, and diversity. For example, using active learning, crowdsourcing, gamification, or interactive learning techniques to solicit more relevant, informative, and consistent feedback from the users or the experts. Alternatively, using synthetic, simulated, or generated data to augment the real data and increase the coverage and robustness of the data.

continued

TABLE 2.1 *continued*

CHALLENGE	FUTURE RESEARCH AND DEVELOPMENT
Reward shaping and alignment: The reward model learned from human feedback data may not always reflect the true objectives and values of the users or the developers. There may be gaps or conflicts between what humans express and what they actually want or need. For example, humans may provide inconsistent, ambiguous, or misleading feedback due to cognitive biases, emotional states, or communication errors. Furthermore, the reward model may not align with the ethical, social, or legal norms and standards that should guide the behavior of AI systems. For example, the reward model may incentivize harmful, deceptive, or manipulative actions that violate the principles of fairness, accountability, or transparency.	Enhancing the reward shaping and alignment methods and mechanisms to ensure the validity, reliability, and alignment of the reward model. For example, using inverse reinforcement learning, preference elicitation, or value learning techniques to infer the latent or implicit objectives and values of the users or the developers from their feedback or behavior. Alternatively, using multi-objective, constrained, or regularized reinforcement learning techniques to incorporate multiple criteria, constraints, or penalties into the reward function and balance the trade-offs among them.
Generalization and adaptation: The policy optimized by RLHF may not generalize well to new or unseen prompts, scenarios, or environments. The policy may overfit to the specific data distribution or the reward model and fail to handle novel or complex situations that require more creativity, reasoning, or common sense. Moreover, the policy may not adapt well to the dynamic and evolving needs and preferences of the users or the developers. The policy may become outdated, irrelevant, or incompatible with the changing goals, expectations, or instructions of the stakeholders.	Developing the generalization and adaptation methods and strategies to ensure the flexibility, versatility, and applicability of the policy. For example, using meta-learning, transfer learning, or lifelong learning techniques to enable the policy to learn from multiple sources, tasks, or domains and apply the learned knowledge or skills to new or different situations. Alternatively, using online learning, interactive learning, or self-learning techniques to enable the policy to update, refine, or improve itself based on the feedback or performance in real time or over time.

Anthropic, a startup founded by former employees of OpenAI, developed Claude, an AI chatbot that is similar to ChatGPT.[11] It is claimed that Claude outperforms ChatGPT in a variety of perspectives. It not only tends to generate more helpful and harmless answers but also answers in a more fun way when facing inappropriate requests. Its writing is more verbose but also more naturalistic. Claude's key approach is called *constitutional AI*.[12] Like ChatGPT, Claude also uses reinforcement learning to train a preference model, though Claude uses reinforcement learning from AI Feedback (RLAIF) without any human feedback labels for AI harms.[13] The constitutional AI process consists of two stages: supervised learning and reinforcement learning, as shown in **Figure 2.3**.

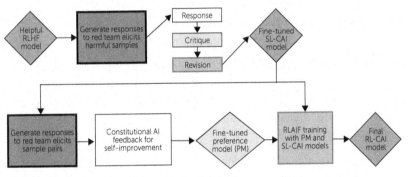

FIGURE 2.3 Steps used in the constitutional AI process

The constitutional AI process works like this:

1. In the supervised learning phase, initial responses to harmful prompts using a pre-trained language model that has been fine-tuned on a dataset of helpful-only responses are called *helpful-only AI assistants*.

2. The model is asked to critique and revise the responses using randomly selected principles from the 16 pre-written principles in the constitution.

3. As a result, the supervised learning–constitutional AI (SL-CAI) model is gained by fine-tuning the pretrained LLM on the final revised responses in a supervised learning way.

4. Claude uses a preference model as a reward signal in the reinforcement learning stage to optimize its responses to different prompts.

5. The fine-tuned model generates a pair of responses to each harmful prompt and evaluates responses according to a set of constitutional principles.

6. Then, a preference model is trained on the final dataset, combining the AI-generated preference dataset for harmlessness and the human feedback dataset for helpfulness.

7. The preference model learns to rank the responses based on their combined scores of helpfulness and harmlessness.

8. Finally, the SL model is fine-tuned via reinforcement learning against this preference model as a reward signal, which results in an optimized policy.

One advantage of this more advanced framework is that it can eliminate human annotation, saving a lot of time, cost, and energy. Similarly, we can develop specific principles with constitutional AI to ensure those LLMs produce factual, harmless, ethical, and fair outputs that also serve the needs of our particular scenarios. This approach, utilized by Claude, is based on the idea of aligning the AI chatbot's behavior with a set of constitutional principles that reflect the values and goals of the users and developers. These principles ensure that the chatbot generates helpful, harmless, ethical, responsible, and fair responses.

Claude's constitutional principles are respecting human dignity, avoiding harm and deception, promoting well-being and social good, and valuing diversity and inclusion. These principles provide a framework that can be modified and updated according to the customized needs and preferences of users and developers.

By using constitutional AI, Claude can outperform ChatGPT in several ways:

- Claude can generate more helpful and harmless responses because it is trained on a dataset that filters out harmful or unhelpful responses and incorporates human feedback on helpfulness.

- Claude can generate more ethical, responsible, and fair responses because it is under the guidance of a set of constitutional principles reflecting the values and goals of the users and developers.

- Claude can generate more fun and naturalistic responses by exploring and exploiting different responses using reinforcement learning and learning from its own critique and revision.

Chatbot customization can utilize reinforcement learning through human/AI feedback (RLHF/RLAIF). Chatbots are becoming increasingly prevalent in various domains, such as customer service, education, entertainment, health, and so on. However, not all users have the same preferences or needs when interacting with chatbots.

Some users prefer a more formal or professional tone, while others enjoy a casual or humorous style. Some users may want a more informative or detailed response, while others may seek a more concise or simple answer. Some users may appreciate a more empathetic or supportive response, while others may desire a more objective or factual one.

Therefore, it is important to customize the chatbot's behavior and personality according to the user's profile and feedback. A chatbot can leverage reinforcement learning to learn from its own actions and outcomes and adapt to the user's preferences and expectations over time.

Reinforcement learning is based on the idea of reward and punishment, where the chatbot receives positive or negative feedback from the user or itself and adjusts its policy accordingly. For example, if the user expresses satisfaction or gratitude after receiving a response from the chatbot, the chatbot can reinforce that response and generate similar ones in the future.

Conversely, if the user expresses dissatisfaction or frustration after receiving a response from the chatbot, the chatbot can avoid that response and generate different ones in the future. Moreover, the chatbot can also self-evaluate its responses and give itself feedback based on predefined criteria or metrics, such as relevance, coherence, fluency, informativeness, politeness, and the like.

Fine-Tuning Large-Scale Models

Fine-tuning is a popular method in the ML and AI fields and is done after a model has been pretrained. Then, the additional training is performed with a dataset specific to the scenarios practitioners and professionals work on. Fine-tuning solves common issues caused by large-scale AI models, such as difficulties productionizing big models and not being generalized enough for specific tasks.[14] See **Figure 2.4**.

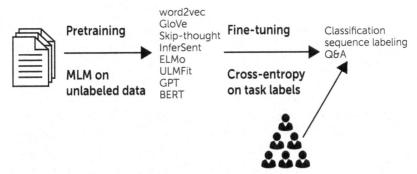

FIGURE 2.4 Fine-tuning pretrained large-scale models

Traditionally, most AI professionals do model tuning for fine-tuning, in which the pre-trained models' parameters (classification, sequence labeling, and question answering (Q&A) using task-specific labels and cross-entropy loss) are tuned. There have been several challenges with this approach and potential mitigation activities, as shown in **Table 2.2**.

TABLE 2.2 Challenges and potential mitigation activities of fine-tuning on pre-trained models

CHALLENGE	MITIGATION ACTIVITIES
Data availability: Fine-tuning requires sufficient labeled data for the target task or domain, which may not always be available or easy to collect. Fine-tuning may lead to overfitting or poor generalization if the data is too small or noisy.	**Data augmentation:** This is an approach to increase the size and diversity of the training data by applying some transformations or modifications to the existing data, such as cropping, flipping, rotating, adding noise, and so on. Data augmentation can help reduce overfitting and improve the generalization of the fine-tuned model.
Task transfer: Fine-tuning works best when the target task or domain is similar to the pretrained model. If the tasks or domains are too different, fine-tuning may not transfer the relevant knowledge or may even degrade the performance of the model.	**Transfer learning:** This is a technique to leverage the knowledge learned from one or more source tasks or domains to improve the performance of a target task or domain. Transfer learning can be done by freezing some of the layers in the pretrained model and adapting its output layer to the target task. Transfer learning can help overcome data availability and task transfer problems.
Cost and scalability: Fine-tuning large-scale models such as GPT or DALL-E requires a lot of computational resources and memory space, which may not be accessible or affordable for many users or organizations. Moreover, fine-tuning large models may introduce more complexity and instability to the optimization process.	**Meta-learning:** This is a technique to learn from multiple tasks or domains and then apply the learned knowledge to a new task or domain. Meta-learning can be done by training a meta-model or a meta-learner that can generate or update the parameters of a base model for a given task or domain. Meta-learning can help achieve fast adjustment and robust generalization of the fine-tuned model.

The evolvement and growing capabilities of current large-scale language models with prompt-tuning have become increasingly popular, in which the pre-trained model is frozen while a small set of learnable vectors can be optimized and added as the input for the task. Prompt design is even more commonly utilized, as of the writing of this book, which is a technique used to guide the behavior of a frozen pretrained model by crafting an input prompt for a specific task without changing any parameters. This is more effective and less expensive than prompt-tuning.[15] We can compare these three approaches to adapting pre-trained language models for specific tasks:

- **Model tuning:** The pre-trained model is further trained or "fine-tuned" on a task-specific dataset.

- **Prompt tuning:** The model remains frozen, and only a set of tunable soft prompts are optimized.

- **Prompt design:** Exemplified by GPT-3, crafted prompts guide the frozen model's responses without any parameter changes.

Prompt-tuning and prompt design methods are often used because of their effectiveness and reduced cost compared to full model tuning. See **Figure 2.5**, which illustrates a shift toward efficiency and multitasking in language model applications, highlighting the less resource-intensive nature of prompt-based methods.

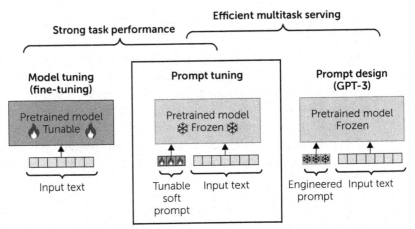

FIGURE 2.5 The architecture of model tuning, prompt tuning, and prompt design

Prompt Engineering

With the remarkable success and powerful generalization capabilities of current large pre-trained AI models, more and more AI practitioners are focusing on prompt engineering by directly integrating the existing generative AI models such as DALL-E 3, GPT-4, and ChatGPT into real applications. As we know, fine-tuning requires huge computational resources and memory space and causes catastrophic forgetting. Prompt engineering is a discipline focused on optimizing prompts for efficient use of LLMs across various applications and research. It enhances our understanding of LLMs' capabilities and limitations.

Prompt engineering encompasses diverse skills and techniques, crucial for effective LLM use. It enhances LLM safety and empowers integration with domain knowledge and external tools.

A prompt is a parameter that can be provided to large-scale pretrained LMs like GPT to enable its capability to identify the context of the problem to be solved and accordingly return the resulting text. In other words, the prompt includes the task description and demonstrations or examples that can be fed into the LMs to be completed. Prompt engineering, sometimes called in-context learning or prompt-based fine-tuning, is a paradigm of learning where only the prompt, which includes a task description and a few demonstrations, is fed into the model as if it were a black box. There are multiple prompt engineering techniques:

- **Retrieval augmentation for in-context learning:** The main idea is to retrieve a set of relevant documents or examples given a source and take these as context with the original input prompt to let the LLM generate the final output. There are different methods for in-context learning, such as one-shot and few-shot prompting. One example is the method RAG (Retrieval Augmented Generation) introduced by Meta AI that essentially takes the initial prompt plus searches for relevant source materials, such as Wikipedia articles, and combines the information with the sequence-to-sequence generation to provide the output.[16]

- **Chain-of-Thought (CoT):** This prompting technique encourages the model to generate a series of intermediate reasoning steps (see **Figure 2.6**).[17] A less formal way to induce this behavior is to include "Let's think step-by-step" in the prompt.

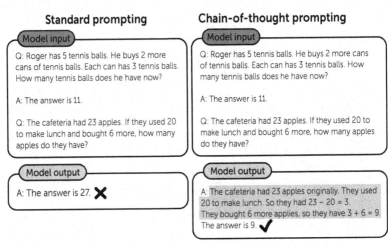

Standard prompting

Model input

Q: Roger has 5 tennis balls. He buys 2 more cans of tennis balls. Each can has 3 tennis balls. How many tennis balls does he have now?

A: The answer is 11.

Q: The cafeteria had 23 apples. If they used 20 to make lunch and bought 6 more, how many apples do they have?

Model output

A: The answer is 27. ✗

Chain-of-thought prompting

Model input

Q: Roger has 5 tennis balls. He buys 2 more cans of tennis balls. Each can has 3 tennis balls. How many tennis balls does he have now?

A: The answer is 11.

Q: The cafeteria had 23 apples. If they used 20 to make lunch and bought 6 more, how many apples do they have?

Model output

A: The cafeteria had 23 apples originally. They used 20 to make lunch. So they had 23 − 20 = 3. They bought 6 more apples, so they have 3 + 6 = 9. The answer is 9. ✓

FIGURE 2.6 Chain-of-thought prompting

- **Action Plan Generation:** This prompt utilizes a language model to generate actions to take, as shown in **Figure 2.7**.[18] The results of these actions can then be fed back into the language model to generate a subsequent action.

Command	Effect
Search <query>	Send <query> to the Bing API and display a search results page
Clicked on link <link ID>	Follow the link with the given ID to a new page
Find in page: <text>	Find the next occurrence of <text> and scroll to it
Quote: <text>	If <text> is found in the current page, add it as a reference
Scrolled down <1, 2, 3>	Scroll down a number of times
Scrolled up <1, 2, 3>	Scroll up a number of times
Top	Scroll to the top of the page
Back	Go to the previous page
End: Answer	End browsing and move to answering phase
End: <Nonsense, Controversial>	End browsing and skip answering phase

FIGURE 2.7 Action plan generation prompting

- **ReAct Prompting:** This prompting technique combines chain-of-thought prompting with action plan generation (see **Figure 2.8**). This induces the model to think about what action to take, and then take it. ReAct allows language models to produce both verbal reasoning traces and text actions that alternate with each other, while actions cause observation feedback from an external environment. The example shown in Figure 2.8 compares the performance of the standard prompting, chain-of-thought (reason only), act only, and ReAct prompting techniques.[19]

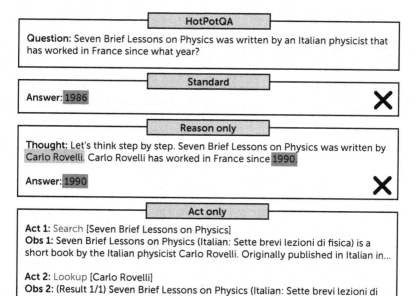

FIGURE 2.8 The results of four prompting methods

Prompt Chaining

This approach combines multiple LLM calls, with the output of one step being the input to the next. The overall process includes a few steps:

1. The process starts with an initial prompt or question. This could be a broad inquiry, instruction, or a request for information.

2. The model generates an initial response based on the input prompt. However, this response might be a bit generic or need refinement.

3. The generated response is then used as part of a new prompt. This time, the prompt is more specific, providing additional context or asking for clarification.

The chaining continues iteratively. Each new response becomes the input for the next prompt. The generated content becomes more focused and contextually relevant with each iteration. The advantages of prompt chaining are as follows:[20]

- It helps preserve context across responses and makes the generated output more coherent.

- The user can guide the model through the iteration process to provide more precise and relevant generation.

- It leads to more customized generation, which enables users to tailor the responses to their specific requirements. However, it still does not alter the fundamental capabilities and limitations of the underlying language model.

Tree of Thoughts

The tree of thoughts framework generalizes over chain-of-thought prompting and encourages the exploration of thoughts that serve as intermediate steps for general problem-solving with language models. This method allows a language model to self-assess the progress of its intermediate thoughts during problem-solving through a deliberate reasoning process. The LM's capacity to produce and assess thoughts is then integrated with search algorithms like breadth-first search and depth-first search, facilitating systematic thought exploration with lookahead and backtracking.[21]

Self-Consistency

The idea behind self-consistency is based on chain-of-thought (CoT), but it samples multiple diverse reasoning paths through few-shot CoT and uses the generations to select the most consistent answer. This helps to boost the performance of CoT prompting on tasks involving arithmetic and commonsense reasoning.[22]

Unveiling the Power of Clustering and Topic Modeling

Despite the rapid evolution of LLMs that can produce coherent and diverse texts across various domains, many tasks still require more granular and structured analysis of textual data. Clustering and topic modeling are techniques that can help discover hidden patterns, themes, and categories in a large collection of documents, without relying on predefined labels or annotations. They can also help reduce the data's dimensionality and complexity, making it easier to visualize, summarize, and interpret.

There are some example applications where clustering and topic modeling can be useful, such as:

- **Document classification and retrieval:** Clustering and topic modeling can help search and navigate large collections of documents by grouping similar ones according to their content. Moreover, they can also facilitate the identification of relevant documents for a given query or task.

- **Text summarization and generation:** Although LLMs can also be utilized for text summarization and clustering, topic modeling can supplement LLMs by extracting the main topics and keywords from the targeted collections of documents and providing concise and informative summaries that capture the essence and different granularities of the data. They can also serve as input or an additional layer for text generation systems, such as LLMs, that can produce longer and more detailed texts based on the topics and keywords.

- **Sentiment analysis and opinion mining:** Although LLMs have shown remarkable performance in understanding the context and capturing nuances in natural languages, topic modeling, and clustering methods, taking Latent Dirichlet Allocation (LDA) or K-mean clustering as examples can be more interpretable and can provide insights into the main themes in a collection of texts.[23] Utilizing a hybrid approach that combines both might be a good solution. For instance, using LLMs for fine-grained sentiment analysis and using topic modeling to understand broader themes or trends.

- **Knowledge discovery and extraction:** By uncovering the latent concepts and relations among the documents, clustering and topic modeling can enrich the semantic representation of the data, as well as the knowledge base of the domain. They can also help to identify gaps and inconsistencies in the data, as well as new and emerging topics and issues.

Therefore, clustering and topic modeling are still necessary and valuable tools for many tasks that involve understanding, analyzing, and generating textual data, especially when the data is large, heterogeneous, and unlabeled. They can complement and enhance the capabilities of LLMs' capabilities and provide insights and feedback for improving their performance and quality.

Enhancing Customer Support Through Hybrid AI: LLMs Meet Clustering and Topic Modeling

Customer support is evolving, and businesses seek more sophisticated and powerful solutions to handle the vast amount of textual data generated in interactions. A hybrid approach, blending the capabilities of LLMs and traditional machine learning techniques, emerges as a robust strategy. We'll explore a few of these machine learning techniques often utilized in support organizations to make sense of the large amounts of data to help optimize the business.

Clustering and Customer Support

Clustering is an unsupervised learning approach of grouping a set of samples based on their similarity without using any predefined labels or categories. Clustering aims to discover the natural structure or patterns of the data, as well as to reduce its complexity and dimensionality. Clustering can be used for various purposes, such as data exploration, summarization, organization, retrieval, and visualization. There are several different clustering methods:

- **Hierarchical clustering:** This method builds a hierarchy of clusters, where each cluster is either a subcluster or a supercluster of another cluster. Hierarchical clustering can be either agglomerative or divisive. Agglomerative clustering starts with each sample as a singleton cluster and then merges the most similar clusters until a single cluster remains. Divisive clustering starts with all documents in one cluster and then splits the most dissimilar clusters until each cluster contains only one sample.

- **Partitioning clustering:** This method divides the data points into a predefined number of non-overlapping clusters, where each point belongs to exactly one cluster. K-mean clustering is one of the most popular algorithms for partitioning clustering. Partitioning clustering can be either distance-based or centroid-based. Distance-based clustering assigns each data point to the cluster with the closest or most similar representative, such as the nearest neighbor. Centroid-based clustering assigns each data point to the cluster with the smallest or least average distance to the center or the cluster's mean, such as K-mean clustering. K-mean clustering classifies samples based on attributes or features into k clusters. It starts with a first group of randomly selected centroids, which are used as the beginning points for every cluster, and then assigns each point to the cluster whose mean has the least squared Euclidean distance and optimizes the centroid based on the distances from the points to it. The hard assignment stops creating and optimizing clustering when either the centroids have stabilized or the defined number of iterations has been reached.

- **Density-based clustering:** This method identifies clusters based on the density or the concentration of the data points in the feature space, where regions of separate low-density clusters can be uncovered and assist in identifying unforeseen patterns. Density-based clustering can handle outliers, noise, and arbitrary shapes of clusters. One of the popular algorithms for density-based clustering is DBSCAN (density-based spatial clustering of applications with noise). DBSCAN defines a cluster as a set of densely connected core points; a point is a core point if it has at least a minimum number of points within a given radius or neighborhood.

Clustering is a powerful technique for identifying patterns and insights from large and complex data sets. It can be used to segment customers, optimize services, categorize issues based on their similarities or differences, and provide personalized and efficient solutions. In the field of customer service and support, clustering has been a popular approach for solving some problems, such as:

- **Customer segmentation:** Clustering can help discover different groups of customers based on their demographics, preferences, needs, behaviors, or characteristics, such as age, gender, location, income, spending habits, loyalty, satisfaction, or feedback. This can help tailor the marketing strategies, product recommendations, pricing policies, or communication channels for each segment and to improve customer retention and acquisition.

- **Service optimization:** Clustering can help optimize the service delivery and support processes based on the complexity, urgency, or frequency of customer requests, issues, or inquiries, such as order status, product information, technical support, billing, or feedback. This can help allocate the appropriate resources, staff, or channels for each service type and improve service efficiency and quality.

- **Support case categorization:** Clustering can help resolve customer issues faster and more effectively by grouping similar or related issues based on their causes, symptoms, or solutions, such as product defects, software bugs, network failures, or user errors. When AI technology is used to cluster similar cases together, these groupings can help by offering new insights that are not obvious when looking at cases individually or by product. An example might be multiple unrelated services experiencing login or profile creation issues. Viewed on their own, these could be hard to relate or determine the root cause of the issue, but after clustering them together, it might be more obvious that this is a problem with shared code providing identity services to multiple workloads. This clustering can help diagnose the root causes, find the best solutions or prevent future occurrences of the issues, increase customer satisfaction, and enhance retention.

Topic Modeling and Customer Support

Topic modeling is a technique for extracting hidden topics or concepts from a collection of text documents, such as customer reviews, feedback, complaints, or inquiries. Topic modeling can help discover the main themes or patterns of customer needs, preferences, opinions, or issues and provide valuable insights for customer support improvement, product development, marketing strategy, or sentiment analysis.

There are several different topic modeling methods. These algorithms differ in their assumptions, mathematical models, and implementations, but they all share the same basic idea: finding a low-dimensional representation of the documents and the words in terms of topics and probabilities. The output of a topic modeling algorithm is usually a matrix that shows the relationship between documents and topics, and another matrix that shows the relationship between topics and words. These matrices can be used to infer the topics of new documents, find similar documents, visualize the topics, and extract insights from the text data. These methods include:

- **Latent Dirichlet Allocation (LDA):** This is one of the most popular topic modeling methods. LDA is an unsupervised learning algorithm that describes a set of observations as a mixture of distinct categories. These categories are themselves a probability distribution over the features. LDA is most commonly used to discover a user-specific number of topics shared by a collection of documents within a text corpus. Each observation is a document, the features are the presence or occurrence count of each word, the categories are the topics. LDA uses a generative process to assign topic probabilities to each document and word probabilities to each topic, based on the observed word frequencies in the documents. LDA can be applied to large, diverse text corpora and produce interpretable and coherent topics.

- **Non-negative Matrix Factorization (NMF):** NMF is a linear algebra method that decomposes a matrix of word-document frequencies into two lower-dimensional non-negative matrices, one representing the word-topic associations and the other representing the topic-document associations. NMF imposes a non-negativity constraint on the matrices, which ensures that the topics and the documents have additive and meaningful components. NMF can be faster and more robust than LDA and can handle sparse and noisy data.

- **Hierarchical Dirichlet Process (HDP):** HDP is a Bayesian nonparametric model that extends LDA by allowing the number of topics to be automatically inferred from the data rather than fixed in advance. HDP uses a hierarchical structure of Dirichlet processes to generate a potentially infinite number of topics and assigns them to the documents based on their relevance and specificity. HDP can adapt to the complexity and diversity of the text data and can avoid overfitting or underfitting the topics.

Topic modeling is a valuable technique in the customer service and support field for extracting insights from large volumes of textual data, such as customer reviews, feedback, and support cases. Here's how topic modeling is leveraged in this domain:

- **Automated support case categorization:** Customer support teams often deal with a variety of issues and requests. Topic modeling can be leveraged to automatically categorize support tickets into different topics or categories based on their content. This helps in routing tickets to appropriate product support teams and improves response time and efficiency.

Moreover, topic modeling can help automate some processes in the customer support workflow. For example, it can point customers to the self-help knowledge base, diagnostics, or websites with the accurate topic category prediction. This can enhance the customer experience, reduce customer effort, and increase operational efficiency.

- **Identifying emerging issues:** Topic modeling can help uncover emerging trends or issues in customer feedback and support cases. It provides actionable insights for companies to address top issues before they escalate proactively.

- **Improving search and retrieval:** Topic modeling helps organize and index articles based on the topics for a large knowledge base of support or self-help articles. This improves the search and retrieval process for support agents or engineers and the customers looking for solutions.

- **Customer feedback analysis:** Topic modeling can help analyze and summarize customer feedback from multiple channels and platforms. This can help identify the most common and important topics, issues, compliments, complaints, and suggestions that customers express. This can also help products and companies measure and track key performance indicators related to customer support, customer satisfaction, and loyalty. For instance, it can help measure the volume of support cases in different categories, identify resolution time, and assess customer satisfaction for each topic. Furthermore, product teams can prioritize and address customer complaints and grievances more effectively.

- **Content creation and knowledge management.** Topic modeling aids in content creation for FAQs, manuals, and support articles. It helps identify the most discussed topics, allowing companies to create relevant and helpful content that addresses common customer queries.

In essence, topic modeling enhances the efficiency and effectiveness of customer service and support operations by providing automated tools for organizing, analyzing, and extracting insights from large volumes of textual customer data.

Hybrid AI Opportunity

Traditional machine learning methods like topic modeling and clustering have their own limitations and challenges. One of the main drawbacks is that they rely on statistical methods that do not account for the semantic and contextual nuances of natural language. For example, topic modeling may fail to distinguish between different meanings or senses of the same word, such as apple as a company but not as a fruit, or group together words that are syntactically similar but semantically different, such as bass as a type of fish but not low-frequency sound in music. Moreover, topic modeling may produce topics that are too broad, too narrow, or not coherent, depending on the choice of parameters and algorithms. In contrast, large language models, such as GPT and Gemini, have demonstrated remarkable proficiency in understanding context, generating human-like responses, and extracting intricate patterns from textual data. In customer support, LLMs can be employed for tasks like sentiment analysis, intent recognition, and even generating responses to common queries.

While LLMs excel in understanding context and generating text, traditional machine learning methods like clustering and topic modeling offer strengths in structuring and organizing information. Clustering can group similar customer queries or issues, facilitating efficient handling by support agents. Topic modeling, on the other hand, extracts underlying themes from a vast dataset, aiding in understanding prevalent customer concerns. Moreover, when computational resources and budget are limited, it is easier and cheaper to leverage traditional machine learning methods like topic modeling and clustering.

In the dynamic landscape of customer support, a hybrid approach, integrating the capabilities of LLMs with the structuring prowess of traditional methods, proves to be a holistic solution. By combining LLMs with topic modeling, more accurate, robust, and interpretable models can be utilized for customer feedback analysis. For instance, language models can help generate more natural and fluent texts from topics and can also help capture the semantic and contextual information that topic modeling may miss. Furthermore, LLMs can help generate new and novel topics that may not be present in the existing data or suggest relevant and personalized content based on the topics of interest of each customer, while topic modeling and clustering can bring more interpretability and flexibility. This hybrid solution addresses the complexities of customer interactions, providing businesses with a powerful tool for improving customer satisfaction and support efficiency.

Endnotes

1   Wikipedia contributors. "BERT (language model)." Wikipedia, The
     Free Encyclopedia. March 5, 2024. [https://en.wikipedia.org/wiki/
     BERT_(language_model)].

2   Wikipedia contributors. "Generative pre-trained transformer." Wikipedia,
     The Free Encyclopedia. February 18, 2024. [https://en.wikipedia.org/wiki/
     Generative_pre-trained_transformer].

3   Gomez, A., Jones, L., Kaiser, L., Parmar, N., Polosukhin, I., Shazeer, N.,
     Uszkoreit, J., Vaswani, A. 2023. "Attention Is All You Need." Google. August 2,
     2023. [https://arxiv.org/pdf/1706.03762.pdf].

4   Zhao, W. et al. 2023. "A Survey of Large Language Models." Cornell
     University. November 24, 2023. [https://arxiv.org/pdf/2303.18223.pdf].

5   Bengio, Y., Ducharme, R., Vincent, P., Jauvin., C. 2003. "A Neural Probabilistic
     Language Model." Journal of Machine Learning Research. February 2023.
     [https://www.jmlr.org/papers/volume3/bengio03a/bengio03a.pdf].

6   Wikipedia contributors. "Word2vec." Wikipedia, The Free Encyclopedia.
     March 21, 2024. [https://en.wikipedia.org/wiki/Word2vec#Continuous_
     Bag_of_Words_%28CBOW%29].

7   Wikipedia contributors. "Word2vec." Wikipedia, The Free Encyclopedia.
     March 21, 2024. [https://en.wikipedia.org/wiki/Word2vec#Continuous_
     Bag_of_Words_%28CBOW%29].

8   Contributors, Open AI (2024, May 13). *Hello GPT-4o.* Retrieved from
     [https://openai.com/index/hello-gpt-4o/]

9   S., Amit. 2023. "Everything You Need To Know About Knowledge Distillation,
     aka Teacher–Student Model." Medium. April 19, 2023. [https://amit-s.medium.
     com/everything-you-need-to-know-about-knowledge-distillation-aka-teacher-
     student-model-d6ee10fe7276].

10   S., Amit. 2023. "Everything You Need To Know About Knowledge Distillation,
     aka Teacher-Student Model." Medium. April 19, 2023. [https://amit-s.medium.
     com/everything-you-need-to-know-about-knowledge-distillation-aka-teacher-
     student-model-d6ee10fe7276].

11   Leike, J., Lowe, R., et al. 2022. "Training language models to follow
     instructions with human feedback." Cornell University. March 4, 2022.
     [https://arxiv.org/pdf/2203.02155.pdf].

12   Henshall, Will. 2023. "What to Know About Claude 2, Anthropic's
     Rival to ChatGPT." Time. July 18, 2023. [https://time.com/6295523/
     claude-2-anthropic-chatgpt/].

13   Bai, Yuntao, et al. 2022. "Constituational AI: Harmlessness from AI Feedback."
     Cornell University. December, 15, 2022. [https://arxiv.org/pdf/2212.08073.
     pdf].

14   Ruder, Sebastian. 2021. "Recent Advances in Language Model
     Fine-tuning." Ruder.io. February, 24, 2021. [https://www.ruder.io/
     recent-advances-lm-fine-tuning/].

15   Constant, N., Lester, B. 2022. "Guiding Frozen Language Models with
     Learned Soft Prompts." Google Research. February 10, 2022. [https://blog.
     research.google/2022/02/guiding-frozen-language-models-with.html].

16 Meta Blog Editors. 2020. "Retrieval Augmented Generation: Streamlining the creation of intelligent natural language processing models." Meta Blog. September 28, 2020. [https://ai.meta.com/blog/retrieval-augmented-generation-streamlining-the-creation-of-intelligent-natural-language-processing-models/].

17 Wei, J., Zhou, D., et al. 2023. "Chain-of-Thought Prompting Elicits Reasoning in large Language Models." Cornell University. January 10, 2023. [https://arxiv.org/pdf/2201.11903.pdf].

18 Nakano, R., et al. 2022. "WebGPT: Browser-assisted question-answering with human feedback." Cornell University. June 1, 2022. [https://arxiv.org/pdf/2112.09332.pdf].

19 Yao, S., et al. 2023. "ReAct: Synergizing Reasoning and Acting in Language Models." Cornell University. March 10, 2023. [https://arxiv.org/pdf/2210.03629.pdf].

20 Anthropic editors. 2023. "Prompt chaining." Anthropic.com. Accessed January 27, 2024. [https://docs.anthropic.com/claude/docs/prompt-chaining].

21 Long, Jieyi. 2023. "Large Language Model Guided Tree-of-Thought." Cornell University. May 15, 2023. [https://arxiv.org/abs/2305.08291].

22 Chi, E., Chowdhery, A., Le, Q., Narang, S., Schuurmans, D., Wang, X., Wei, J., Zhou, D. 2022. "Self-Consistency Improves Chain of Thought Reasoning in Language Models." Cornell University. March 7, 2023. [https://arxiv.org/abs/2203.11171v4].

22 Liu, Bing. 2012. "Sentiment Analysis and Opinion Mining." Morgan & Claypool Publishers. April 22, 2012. [https://www.cs.uic.edu/~liub/FBS/SentimentAnalysis-and-OpinionMining.pdf].

3

Application Areas of AI in Support

Knowing is not enough; we must apply. Willing is not enough; we must do.

—Johann Wolfgang von Goethe

In today's rapidly changing digital landscape, the confluence of emerging technologies with established industries has led to unprecedented advancements. Artificial intelligence (AI) with customer service is one such powerful synergy. As businesses continuously strive to enhance the customer experience, AI emerges as a game changer, introducing efficiencies and capabilities previously thought unimaginable.

AI, at its core, is the embodiment of machine-driven intelligence, learning, and decision-making. Its influence is palpable across diverse sectors, from healthcare to finance, manufacturing, entertainment, and everything in between. However, its imprint is particularly transformative in customer service, where immediacy, accuracy, and personalization are paramount.

The past decade has witnessed a significant shift in customer service paradigms. Businesses are no longer solely competing based on products or prices; the quality of customer service has become a critical differentiator. AI serves as a bridge in this new landscape, helping businesses transcend traditional limitations. Whether providing 24/7 support through chatbots, analyzing vast amounts of customer data for actionable insights, or personalizing customer interactions in real-time, AI's potential is vast and largely untapped.

But why is there a growing need for AI in customer service? For starters, the modern customer is more informed, connected, and demanding than ever before. They seek instant gratification, personalized experiences, and solutions that cater to their unique needs. Traditional customer service models, often reactive and limited by human constraints, struggle to keep pace with these evolving expectations. AI promises to meet and exceed these expectations with its proactive, scalable, and data-driven approach.

As we dive into this chapter, we aim to illuminate the multifaceted applications of AI in customer service, offering a holistic view of its current impact and potential for the future. Through expert insights, real-world examples, and forward-looking analyses, we'll explore how AI is not just an add-on but a necessity in crafting the customer service experiences of tomorrow.

The Rationale for Using AI in Customer Service and Support

We live in a paradoxical time in which technology brings us closer, yet sometimes feels like it's pushing us apart. The rationale for using AI in customer service and support isn't about replacing the human connection we all crave—it's about enhancing it.

Consider the Industrial Revolution—a tectonic shift that altered the fabric of society and propelled humanity into an era of unprecedented growth and complexity. Before this revolution, artisans crafted products by hand, laboriously perfecting each piece. Then came the assembly line, mechanization, and eventually automation—each a disruptive innovation that redefined what was possible. In the modern customer support landscape, artificial intelligence stands as the new machinery, a force as transformative as the steam engine or the power loom. Just as the Industrial

Revolution was not solely about machines replacing craftsmen but about forming a symbiotic relationship, AI comes not to replace human expertise in customer support but to augment it. Let's explore this new frontier where machinery, craftsmanship, AI, and human intelligence coalesce to forge a revolution in customer service and support.

The Business Blueprint: Efficiency, Scale, and Profit

Just as the advent of machinery during the Industrial Revolution brought scale and efficiency to production, AI introduces greater data-driven insights, efficiency, and cost-effectiveness into the realm of customer support. If we look at an assembly line, we see each station designed to serve a specific function to optimize production. And each station in that line works toward developing a piece of the finished product that is of higher quality and produced at a faster rate than one person assembling all the parts of the product alone. Now, apply this concept to the world of customer support. AI acts as those specialized stations, each fine-tuned to handle a specific facet of the customer experience. This modern "assembly line" enables companies to promptly address inquiries, accurately predict customer needs, and personalize interactions, creating an unparalleled level of service. Beyond just handling questions or problems, AI offers the power of preemptive solutions, dynamic learning, and the ability to seamlessly integrate vast amounts of data, transforming how businesses connect with and understand their clientele. As we delve deeper into this chapter, we'll unpack the multifaceted benefits of AI, shedding light on its transformative power in efficiency, cost-effectiveness, personalization, and more.

Efficiency and Scale

When we talk about infusing AI into support mechanisms, it's not just about innovation—it's about unparalleled efficiency. The amazing processing capabilities of AI surpass those of humans, analyzing vast quantities of data in the blink of an eye. Take AI chatbots as an example: they can rapidly comb through terabytes of data, referencing solutions from millions of past queries. The result? The most common concerns get resolved in real time. This swift intervention allows human agents to channel their expertise toward more complex issues. Compared to traditional customer service processes for which agents might spend minutes or even hours or days searching for answers or escalating issues, the speed of AI-powered systems offers an almost incomparable advantage in timeliness and effectiveness.

Cost-Effectiveness

At first glance, the investment in a state-of-the-art AI customer support system might seem substantial, but viewing it as a long-term strategy rather than just an immediate cost is crucial. According to IBM's Watson blog, the data reveals that businesses could potentially reduce their customer service costs by as much as 30 percent by implementing conversational solutions, such as chatbots.[1] These AI tools can handle 80 percent of routine tasks and customer questions.

When assessing the true value, consider the operational differences. Human employees, as invaluable as they are, come with inherent limitations. They require benefits, occasional time off, continuous training, and are bound by a conventional workweek. In contrast, AI operates on a different spectrum. It can operate 24/7, unconstrained by working hours, illness, time zones, public holidays, or weather disasters. In practical terms, this continuous operation equates to the output of about 4.2 full-time human agents every single week, minus the breaks or downtimes. Spread this efficiency over a year, and the cumulative cost savings and enhanced productivity start to paint a compelling picture. This perspective makes the upfront AI investment justifiable and a wise move for future-proofing your customer support strategy.

CALCULATION OF EQUIVALENT HUMAN WORKERS

Assuming a human works 8 hours a day for 5 days, that's 40 hours per week. If an AI system works 24 hours a day for 7 days, that's 168 hours per week. Comparing the two:

Number of equivalent workers= (AI operational hours per week) / (human operational hours per week) = 168 hours / 40 hours = 4.2 human equivalents

Personalization and Data-Driven Insights

AI algorithms are designed to process and interpret data at a scale that's simply unattainable for human analysis. Every day, countless bytes of data flow through customer support systems. To put this into perspective, imagine going through a library that adds thousands of books every hour; this is the amount of data businesses often handle. AI can efficiently peruse this "library," pinpointing patterns and intricacies that might elude even the most skilled analysts. Whether it's recommending a product in an e-commerce platform based on a customer's purchase history, adapting responses based on sentiment analysis from past interactions, or tailoring learning modules for students based on their learning habits,

AI-driven personalization isn't just an incremental improvement—it's a paradigm shift. This level of detail, applied consistently across millions of users, transforms decision-making processes. Businesses can segment their customer base with surgical precision, ensuring every interaction feels bespoke. The outcome is a significant elevation in customer satisfaction because interactions become less about generic support and more about individualized, insightful experiences.

Scalability and Consistency

In the modern digital age, where support interactions can range from hundreds to millions daily, AI provides the bedrock on which businesses can scale and expand their customer support operations without a proportional increase in human resources. To understand the sheer magnitude, consider this: while a human agent may efficiently address a single customer query at a time, AI systems can simultaneously process and respond to thousands of inquiries without batting a digital eyelid. And they do this around the clock. Imagine the operational capacity of a 1,000-person call center condensed into a single AI system that never sleeps, takes breaks, or experiences fatigue or stress. This unparalleled scalability ensures that businesses can cater to a growing customer base without sacrificing the quality or speed of service. Moreover, AI algorithms perform with a level of consistency and precision that is difficult for human agents to maintain, especially in high-pressure, emotional, or repetitive scenarios, irrespective of the volume or complexity of tasks.

Reducing Time to Resolution

In the dynamic landscape of customer support, every second counts. Studies have shown that a mere 10-second delay in website load times can make users leave, so imagine the impact of delays in customer service. The quicker an issue is resolved, the better the customer experience. AI systems don't just shave off a few seconds; they revolutionize response times. Consider this: where a human agent might take several minutes to look through a customer's history, identify patterns, and suggest solutions, an AI system can achieve this in mere milliseconds. In fact, Boston Consulting Group (BCG) estimates that implementing generative AI at scale could increase productivity in customer service operations by 30–50 percent or more.[2] Guiding customers through troubleshooting steps, AI can autonomously navigate and decide on the most efficient route based on vast datasets, effectively minimizing time-consuming back-and-forth interactions. With every tick of the clock vital to a great customer experience, AI's ability to expedite resolutions can make the difference between dissatisfied customers and loyal advocates.

Multi-Channel Support

Modern consumers seek support through multiple channels, including email, phone, social media, and web chat. In today's fast-paced digital world, customers are hopping from one channel to another, like browsing TV channels. Keeping up with this can be a bit of a juggling act for businesses. Many have tried the multi-channel approach, thinking they've got it covered. But here's the catch: Today's customers are looking for more than just multiple channels—they want those channels to talk to each other, giving them a smooth and seamless experience. Let's examine these two strategies.

Multi-channel experience

This strategy involves businesses engaging with customers across multiple platforms (such as social media, email, phone, and chat). Each channel operates in isolation, meaning the customer might get different experiences or would have to reiterate their issues when switching from one channel to another.

In this strategy, AI plays a pivotal role in enhancing each channel's strengths. Deploying AI-driven chatbots or virtual assistants tailored for specific channels like email, chat, or social media can provide quick, accurate responses. Additionally, AI's capability to independently analyze user behavior on each channel helps businesses tap into channel-specific preferences and trends. This granular data analysis can be immensely valuable, especially in channels bombarded with queries, as AI can automate responses to frequently asked questions, ensuring timely and consistent customer engagement.

Omni-channel experience

This approach focuses on delivering a seamless and consistent experience across all platforms. The emphasis is on integrating the different channels to unite the user experience. When a customer transitions from, say, a mobile app to a phone call, the information flows seamlessly between the two, and the customer doesn't have to "start over."

In contrast to multi-channel, the omni-channel strategy demands a seamless customer experience across all platforms, and AI is the linchpin in achieving this. By integrating data platforms, AI can ensure that information flows smoothly across all touchpoints. Imagine a scenario in which a customer transitions from chatting with a bot on a website to speaking with a human agent over the phone. With the help of AI, this switch is seamless—the agent is already equipped with the chat history, context, and customer details. Beyond this, AI's power of predictive analytics personalizes the customer's journey, anticipating their needs and preferences. And when it comes to understanding the customer's holistic journey, AI-driven unified reporting offers businesses a comprehensive view of interactions, regardless of the platform.

Customers today are savvy. They're not just looking for multiple channels to utilize; they're looking for an experience that delivers results efficiently. Nobody wants to explain their issue over and over every time they switch from, say, chat to phone. Both multi-channel and omni-channel strategies have their merits. While diving headfirst into multi-channel might seem like a good start (and sometimes it's a necessary first step), it can lead to some redundancies and inefficiencies.

Think of it like having several remote controls for various devices—each one does its job, but you're often left fumbling between them. In our analogy, omni-channel is the universal remote. With AI powering this approach, not only do all the channels come under one unified strategy, but the data flow is also smooth. This means businesses get a 360-degree view of their customers, leading to richer insights and more tailored services.

As the digital landscape changes, adding a new channel to an omnichannel setup (backed by AI) is like adding a new device to your universal remote. It's integrated smoothly without causing disruptions. Sure, setting up this integrated strategy might be a bit pricier initially than just juggling multiple remotes (or channels). Still, the investment pays off with happier customers, streamlined operations, and insights that can shape the business's future.

From Reactive to Proactive, Preventive, and Preemptive Support

Let's rewind a bit and think about the traditional customer service model. Picture a customer stumbling upon an issue, dialing up the company, waiting, and then—fingers crossed—gets their issue resolved. It's a model that's been tried and true but is also reactive. Fast-forward to today when AI is flipping this script in dramatic new ways. Instead of just reacting, we're entering a world where AI allows businesses to be several steps ahead of customer issues.

Imagine a setup where AI sniffs out potential hiccups and starts working on solutions before the customer even knows there's a problem. This is proactive support. Then, there's preventive support where AI, with its machine learning prowess, doesn't just wait for issues to pop up; it predicts them and sets up defenses, ensuring the problem doesn't even rear its head. And the cherry on top? Preemptive support. Here, the AI isn't just predicting issues; it's seeing them on the horizon, darting forward, and fixing them autonomously. No fuss, no drama. For the customer, it feels like cruising on a smooth highway. All these layers, woven together by AI, are redefining the very essence of customer support, leading us to a future where interactions are not just about problem-solving but about preventing problems in the first place.

As game-changing as AI is in customer service and its notable advancements, it's crucial to understand its role: AI is an enhancer, not a substitute for human intelligence and empathy. Think of AI as the GPS navigator in a car, assisting the driver who remains in charge. In an optimally structured customer service framework, AI assists human agents, helping the agent as they address complex and nuanced situations. Together, they pave the way for an efficient, effective, and empathetic customer experience.

The Craftsmanship of Empathy: Humanity in the Machine Age

As great a navigator as AI can be, humans are so complicated that relying on AI algorithms to fully comprehend and accurately predict outcomes in every situation is unrealistic. Human interaction, with empathetic understanding, is valued by customers and can be a key differentiator in the overall customer experience. AI's role is to quickly and deeply analyze large amounts of data, offering actionable insights that enable humans to focus on those unique human skills of active listening, demonstrating empathy, and problem-solving to customize solutions for each customer.

Following our deep dive into the business perspective and the advantages AI brings to the table, it's pivotal to spotlight the enduring role of human agents in customer support. Even in an increasingly automated world, their significance in the customer service sphere remains undiminished. Let's demystify together the belief that AI will completely take over the role of human agents in the service and support world and all the good reasons why AI is best positioned as the assistant, guiding, and supporting, while humans remain firmly in the pilot's seat, steering the journey.

It's About the People, Not Just the Numbers

While it might be tempting to think of AI solely as a way to cut costs and increase efficiency—although those are nice perks—it's far more than that. At its core, support is about people and genuine human connections. It's about that mom trying to install a baby monitor who's lost in technical jargon. It's about the college student miles away from home and in a different time zone needing instant support for a malfunctioning laptop. AI helps us reach these people when and where they need assistance, offering a helping hand guided by data but warmed by human empathy and ensuring every interaction feels smart and heartfelt.

Time, the Most Precious Gift

We've all been there—waiting on hold for what feels like hours, listening to soul-draining hold music, and finally speaking to an agent who has to shuffle through pages or screens of information before helping us. AI cuts through these delays, offering instant, accurate assistance for straightforward issues and freeing up human agents to assist you with more complex matters. The gift of time is one of the most precious things customer service can offer, and AI is a tool that helps give you just that.

Meeting You Where You Are

The essence of customer service lies in its ability to adapt to diverse preferences and needs. Different individuals naturally gravitate toward different communication channels—some may lean toward the immediacy of chat, while others may opt for the formality of email, the ubiquity of social media, or the familiarity of a voice call. AI steps in like a maestro, orchestrating this multifaceted concert, adjusting and refining each note (or interaction) to the rhythm of individual preferences. Yet, while AI offers precision, the human touch brings soul to this symphony. Once engaged in customer interaction, human agents add layers of understanding, empathy, and genuine connection, transforming each AI-enhanced interaction into more than just a transaction—it becomes a personalized and meaningful exchange.

The Nuance of Insight

At the heart of effective communication lies the ability to perceive and understand another's intent. For example, you might wonder how Natural Language Processing (NLP) pinpoints intent within customer interactions.

Well, it's an intricate blend of science, vast data sets, and a touch of linguistic finesse. Initially, NLP evaluates the words we express. For example, sentiments such as "thrilled" or "love" typically suggest positive feelings, whereas terms like "frustrated" or "disappointed" denote negative ones. By accumulating extensive databases of these words and their associated undertones, AI systems can gauge the sentiment embedded within a text. But the process dives deeper than mere word choice; the arrangement of those words plays a pivotal role. The structure or length of a sentence can often provide subtle hints about a customer's feelings like short, sharp sentences potentially indicating annoyance. Furthermore, for voice-driven interfaces, the latest NLP tools can assess the tone and pitch of spoken words. A heightened pitch might signal distress, while gentler tones could imply satisfaction or calm.

Here's where it gets super useful in the customer service and support ecosystem. Once the AI has these intention insights, they're distilled into actionable feedback for human agents. This isn't about replacing the human touch—it's about enhancing it. Imagine a support agent getting real-time prompts like: "the customer seems agitated" or "the customer appears to be pleased with the solution."

By offering these nuanced insights, AI acts like an assistant, guiding and augmenting human agents. This ensures that every interaction isn't just about resolving an issue; it's about truly connecting, understanding, and empathizing with the customer. The outcome? A more human-centric approach to customer support, enhanced by the precision and consistency of AI. In other words, AI ensures that the customer's needs are acknowledged and genuinely understood.

The Interplay of AI, RLHF, and RLAIF

Contrary to some beliefs, artificial intelligence does not operate in isolation. Its accuracy, efficiency, and relevance are deeply intertwined with human collaboration, particularly through the lenses of Reinforcement Learning from Human Feedback (RLHF) and its complementary counterpart, Reinforcement Learning from AI Feedback (RLAIF). RLHF and RLAIF are instrumental in the training and fine-tuning of large language models, the engines behind breakthroughs like OpenAI's ChatGPT,[3] Google DeepMind's Gemini[4] and Sparrow,[5] Anthropic's Claude,[6] Meta's Llama,[7] and more. Instead of training large language models to predict the next word, we train them to understand instructions and generate helpful responses.

In a nutshell, RLHF represents a bridge between human intelligence and artificial intelligence, allowing developers to refine and align AI systems more closely with human expectations and societal norms. At its core, when a chatbot furnishes an answer, it's not merely spewing pre-programmed responses. Instead, that reply is the culmination of countless data points, refined and calibrated using human feedback. The model learns from raw data and the nuances and subtleties only human expertise can provide. Think of it as a student–teacher dynamic, where AI is the ever-eager student and humans are the seasoned mentors. This symbiotic relationship ensures that every interaction with AI reflects algorithmic acuity and human-guided judgment, cementing its role in optimizing customer service. The role of RLHF cannot be underestimated—it's this very process that bridges the gap between cold computational logic and the warmth of human intuition, ensuring AI remains relevant, responsive, and reliable.

This approach has been crucial in making large language models (LLMs) more attuned to what humans want and expect. However, the challenge with RLHF lies in its appetite for human-generated feedback, which is both time-consuming and expensive to gather. This is where RLAIF comes into play, harnessing AI-generated feedback to guide learning. This method shines in environments where the complexity or sheer scale makes human feedback impractical or where precision and consistency are paramount (RLAIF can simulate millions of scenarios, providing feedback that's mathematically aligned with desired outcomes—something incredibly challenging for humans to offer at such scale and specificity). RLAIF excels in domains where the feedback loop benefits from rapid iteration, consistency, and a level of detail that human oversight cannot ubiquitously provide. For a deeper technical exploration of these concepts, see Chapter 2.

This blend of human and machine intelligence doesn't just enhance AI's capabilities; it redefines them, ensuring that as AI models evolve, they do so in a way that is fundamentally aligned with human values and needs. The integration of RLHF with RLAIF ensures AI remains technologically advanced and deeply attuned to the human experience, making it an invaluable asset in fields demanding nuanced understanding and responsiveness—like customer service.

The Ethical Imperative

While the power of Artificial intelligence is undeniable, it also carries a profound ethical responsibility. The utilization of AI to discern and anticipate the customer's needs must be counterbalanced by a non-negotiable commitment to data privacy and individual autonomy. For this reason, the integration of AI in customer service needs to adhere to rigorous ethical standards designed to uphold the customer's privacy and safety. In this landscape, the technology serves not merely as a tool for efficiency but as an extension of the ethical commitment to respecting the customer's individuality and rights.

Reinforcement Learning from Human Feedback provides a powerful method for improving AI systems, though it can also be a double-edged sword. On the one hand, it allows AI to adapt to human nuances, making it more attuned to our needs and behaviors. On the other, it can inadvertently absorb biases in the feedback it receives, highlighting the importance of ensuring that the humans providing this feedback are trained and aware of potential biases and that there are measures in place to correct these biases. Engaging a diverse group of reviewers in the feedback process is crucial to minimize biases in AI systems trained via RLHF. This diversity should span various dimensions such as gender, ethnicity, age, and cultural background, ensuring a broad range of perspectives and experiences are considered. By incorporating inclusiveness in the feedback loop, the AI becomes more representative and aligns more closely with the principles of Responsible AI, potentially mitigating the propagation of existing biases and fostering more equitable outcomes.

Moreover, with AI models diving deep into customer behaviors and sentiment, there's a risk of violating personal boundaries or misusing data. This makes it vital for AI in customer service to operate under rigorous ethical standards, prioritizing customer privacy and safety. It's a world where technology doesn't just serve as a beacon of efficiency but stands firmly as a sentinel, ensuring that every interaction respects a customer's individuality, rights, and values. In this evolving landscape, responsible AI is not just an ideal—it's the foundation that upholds the trust and integrity of every AI-human engagement.

As we advance into the digital age, we must not lose sight not lose sight of what's genuinely important—the human connections that enrich our lives. AI in customer service is not about sidelining these connections but about nurturing and making them more accessible and effective. With a thoughtful approach, we can ensure that AI is a bridge between people, not a barrier.

Symbiosis Over Supremacy: The Steering Wheel of Strategic Balance

Harkening back to our example of the Industrial Revolution, we learned that machines alone didn't produce the most effective results. It was the combination of both human labor and machines that propelled entrepreneurs to success. These same learnings can be applied to the customer service industry of today, where it's not just AI or humans alone that create that great customer experience, trust, and, ultimately, loyalty. The balanced strategy of combining the empathic human touch with the precision of AI will create the greatest benefit to both customers and organizations. The combination of humans and machines will be better than either individually. This strategic balance is as critical today as the invention of quality checks and safety measures during the Industrial Revolution.

Creating a Seamless Customer Journey

The promise of a seamless customer journey is amplified exponentially with the incorporation of AI into customer service. With AI, businesses can ensure that customers receive the right information at the right time, thus minimizing friction and enhancing overall satisfaction. Advanced algorithms can predict common queries based on past interactions or frequently asked questions, offering customers solutions even before they realize they need them.

For instance, Spotify leverages AI to curate personalized playlists, ensuring users continually find music they love without searching for it.[8] Similarly, Amazon's recommendation system uses AI to suggest products to users based on their browsing and purchase history, thereby streamlining their shopping experience.[9] Companies like Zara employ AI to manage inventory better, ensuring that popular items remain in stock and immediately available to customers, thus reducing wait times and potential dissatisfaction.[10] Then there's Sephora, which uses AI-powered chatbots to provide personalized product recommendations, enhancing the user's shopping experience.[11]

In essence, AI doesn't just ensure the customer's journey is smooth and anticipates their needs, making each interaction feel personalized and intuitive. This proactive approach minimizes friction and elevates overall satisfaction, as customers feel understood and valued right from their first interaction.

Leveraging Data for Real-Time Decision-Making

AI systems can analyze enormous volumes of data to make real-time decisions that enhance customer experience. Whether it's using machine learning to prioritize support tickets based on urgency or analyzing customer feedback to make instant adjustments, AI can transform a static customer service model into a dynamic, responsive mechanism.

For example, Netflix utilizes AI to analyze viewer habits and preferences, adjusting content recommendations on the fly and ensuring that users continuously discover shows and movies that align with their tastes, leading to prolonged engagement and satisfaction. Furthermore, airlines like Delta now employ AI-driven systems to manage and predict potential flight delays. They can proactively notify passengers about potential changes by analyzing real-time weather patterns, air traffic, and aircraft status, ensuring smoother travel experiences. Ride-hailing services like Uber and Lyft also capitalize on AI to make real-time pricing decisions, analyzing factors like demand, traffic, and local events to set fair and competitive fares.

AI's real-time decision-making capacity is revolutionizing the landscape of customer support. By leveraging AI, support teams can instantly prioritize tickets, swiftly suggest responses based on past interactions and, combined with real-time performance monitoring and resource allocation, pave the way for a smoother and more responsive customer experience. Pioneering companies like Zappos and Amazon have tapped into these AI-driven benefits, witnessing a substantial boost in their response times and overall customer satisfaction.

In essence, AI optimizes a business's operational facets and ensures that customer interactions are timely, relevant, and tailored. It shifts the paradigm from a one-size-fits-all approach to one where each customer feels the system is attuned to their immediate needs and preferences.

Enhancing Upsell and Cross-Sell Opportunities

AI-powered recommendation engines have significantly reshaped the landscape of upselling and cross-selling, and the numbers speak for themselves. According to a McKinsey study, companies utilizing AI for recommendations have seen sales increase by 15 percent to 20 percent while simultaneously enjoying a reduced churn rate.[12] Amazon, a leader in the domain, attributes as much as 35 percent of its sales to its AI-driven recommendation system.[13] Furthermore, Netflix's recommendation engine, aimed at keeping users engaged with relevant content, saves the company approximately $1 billion annually by reducing churn.[14] These engines dive deep into customers' purchasing history, search queries, and even browsing duration to curate tailored suggestions. By presenting these at opportune moments, businesses not only witness a surge in revenue but also cultivate a more personalized relationship with their customers. In effect, AI intelligently links customer needs to a company's broader product or service offerings, maximizing value on both ends.

Automating Routine Tasks

AI can significantly reduce the workload on human agents by taking over routine and repetitive tasks. Incorporating AI into routine operational tasks is already proving invaluable in streamlining customer service.

According to a report by McKinsey, by automating manual and repetitive tasks, successful operations centers are reducing costs by 30 to 60 percent while increasing delivery quality.[15] For instance, e-commerce multinational Shopify highlights in their blog that AI-powered forecasting in supply chain management can reduce errors by up to 50 percent, lessening lost sales and product unavailability by up to 65 percent.[16] OpenTable uses AI to manage millions of restaurant reservations, allowing restaurant staff to focus on providing exceptional in-person experiences.[17] And when processing claims, AirHelp assists over 16 million passengers experiencing canceled, overbooked, or delayed flights—its chatbot acts as the first point of contact for customers, improving the average response time by up to 65 percent.[18] It also monitors all of the company's social channels (in 16 different languages) and alerts customer service if it detects crisis-prone terms used on social profiles.

Microsoft has developed a service called "Copilot for Service," which is designed to assist customer service agents with generative AI features. In Microsoft's words, "Copilot for Service accelerates agent onboarding, and case resolution improves efficiency and automates tasks to help free agents to focus on customers. Embedded in their desktop of choice or deployed in Teams, agents can simply ask the generative AI-powered Copilot questions in natural language to receive relevant answers that leverage existing contact center knowledge to enhance agent productivity and customer satisfaction."[19]

With these mundane tasks efficiently handled by AI, human agents can dedicate their expertise to areas that require in-depth problem-solving and human touch, greatly enhancing the overall quality of customer interactions. This seamless blend of machine efficiency with human empathy fosters an environment where both agents and customers benefit.

Fostering Continuous Learning and Improvement

Machine learning algorithms thrive on data; the more they process, the smarter they become. As a result, these algorithms can identify trends, patterns, and areas of improvement that may not be immediately apparent to human analysts, leading to a continuously improving customer service experience.

This immense data-crunching capability has led to breakthrough insights in customer service. For instance, Netflix uses machine learning to analyze viewing habits to predict and recommend shows users might enjoy next, resulting in a 75 percent selection rate from its recommendations.[20] Similarly, Amazon's recommendation system, also based on machine learning, drives 35 percent of its total sales by suggesting products based on users' browsing and purchasing patterns.[21] In the world of customer support, tools like Zendesk's Answer Bot[22] harness these algorithms to understand customer queries better, directing them to the most relevant solutions.

Fueled by algorithms, this continuous evolution ensures that customer service and support are responsive and predictive, anticipating needs even before customers articulate them.

Global and Cultural Scalability

AI systems can be trained to be more responsive and predictive and understand multiple languages and regional dialects, allowing companies to offer high-quality customer support that transcends geographical and linguistic barriers. This is particularly useful for businesses looking to expand globally without a proportional increase in support staff.

For instance, Microsoft Translator, a product of its Azure AI suite, currently supports real-time translation in more than 80 languages and dialects, empowering businesses to interact seamlessly with a global clientele.[23] This gives human agents the added power to utilize AI to help translate real-time conversations, essentially adding greater understanding to any support experience when the customer and agent speak different languages. Beyond just translation, tech giants like Google are fine-tuning their voice assistants to recognize and understand regional accents, ensuring that a user in Texas is understood as clearly as one in Tokyo or Toronto. Such capabilities enable companies to maintain a consistent and high-quality support experience worldwide without exponentially increasing their human support teams. This multilingual skill of AI is invaluable for businesses eyeing global expansion, as it facilitates a culturally sensitive and locally resonant customer interaction, irrespective of where the customer or agent is located.

One example of implementation in customer support is Spotify, which leverages AI in language translation to cater to its international user base.[24] The company faced challenges in providing support across multiple languages, primarily handled by its European service centers. To address this, Spotify partnered with Sutherland to develop a real-time language translation tool, Sutherland Translate AI, for its email support channel. This tool uses AI, machine learning, and translation engines from Google, Microsoft Azure, and Deep Learning to translate real-time customer queries, preserving cultural nuances and details. This solution has enabled Spotify to support customers in various languages, including Arabic, French, Russian, Polish, Turkish, German, Dutch, Portuguese, and Spanish, without significantly expanding staff or increasing operating expenses. Implementing this AI-driven tool has enhanced Spotify's capacity to handle customer queries in different languages, allowing for more efficient business operations and customer service delivery.

Crisis Management

AI's capability to manage a large volume of interactions simultaneously is particularly beneficial during times of crisis or high demand. For example, during a product recall or major outage, AI systems can handle the sudden influx of customer queries more efficiently than human agents, offering quick, accurate information and reducing customer anxiety and frustration.

In 2016, Samsung faced a massive recall of their Galaxy Note 7 smartphones due to battery issues that led to some devices catching fire.[25] While there is no documented evidence of using AI-powered chatbots during this crisis, customer support systems played a crucial role in handling the surge of inquiries from concerned customers. Let's picture the scenario and how chatbots could have played (maybe they did) a major role. While Samsung's human support agents could focus on critical cases and complicated issues, their AI systems could manage a significant portion of basic queries such as:

- "How do I return my phone?"
- "Where's the nearest service center?"
- "How do I get a refund?"

Doing so would ensure that customers receive prompt responses even during peak inquiry times. Moreover, using AI's data analysis capabilities, Samsung could quickly identify frequently asked questions and update their chatbot responses in real-time, ensuring that accurate, up-to-date information was always available to their customers. This quick and efficient communication would help reduce customer panic and frustration during a challenging period for the company.

By promptly addressing and assuaging customer concerns during such high-stress times, AI plays a pivotal role in mitigating potential reputational damage and preserving brand trust. In such scenarios, AI's ability to process vast volumes of interactions without being overwhelmed or fatigued offers businesses a distinct advantage in ensuring consistent customer satisfaction, even under pressure.

Enhancing Employee Satisfaction

Contrary to fears about AI taking over human jobs, well-implemented AI can actually enhance job satisfaction among customer service agents. By automating repetitive tasks, AI allows agents to focus on problem-solving and customer engagement, roles that offer more job satisfaction and opportunities for skill development.

A Forrester Research study indicated that tasks automated through AI can free up to 20 percent of a customer service agent's time.[26] By automating repetitive tasks, AI allows agents to shift their focus to more rewarding and crucial activities. IBM has reported that their AI system, Watson, helped reduce the resolution time of customer service inquiries by 10 percent, allowing human agents to spend more time on in-depth customer interactions.[27] It's clear from these examples that when businesses purposefully integrate AI, they not only enhance the efficiency of their operations but also contribute to a more fulfilling work environment for their people, resulting in better service and happier employees. Quoting Simon Sinek once again, "Customers will never love a company until its employees love it first,"[28] so getting your employees to find purpose and satisfaction in their jobs by embracing all the perks that AI can bring to them becomes an enabler for achieving business results and higher levels of customer satisfaction.

While AI's capabilities are truly transformative, it's crucial for businesses to approach its integration with a balanced perspective. AI should augment, not replace, the human touch that remains vital for addressing complex issues and customer needs. When implemented thoughtfully, AI can act as a powerful tool that elevates customer service to new levels of efficiency, personalization, and effectiveness.

As we venture deeper into this new age, let this historical parallel illuminate our exploration. The Industrial Revolution wasn't just about machines; it was about leveraging the best aspects of both human skill and mechanical efficiency. Similarly, the current revolution in customer service and support is not about choosing between AI and human expertise—it's about integrating them in a way that amplifies the strengths of each.

Exploring the How: Key Applications of AI in Customer Service and Support

According to a Salesforce report, "Enterprise Technology Trends," 83 percent of IT leaders say AI and other intelligent technologies are transforming customer engagement, and 69 percent of consumers prefer chatbots for quick communication with brands.[29] These statistics underscore AI's growing importance in customer service.

Applications across various industries offer a glimpse into the potential of AI. In finance, AI-driven platforms assist customers with transaction inquiries, fraud prevention, and personalized financial advice around the clock. Healthcare sees AI streamlining appointment scheduling and offering preliminary diagnostic support, significantly enhancing patient care. The transportation sector benefits from AI through real-time travel updates and automated booking systems, enriching customer experience. In telecommunications, AI is used for network optimization, predictive maintenance, and to offer tailored plan recommendations, driving customer satisfaction and loyalty.

Each application demonstrates AI's power to support customer service representatives and anticipate customer needs, offering relevant, timely, personalized assistance. Let's explore how AI's "machinery" and human "craftsmanship" can be orchestrated to create a revolution in customer support's quality, efficiency, and humanity.

Charting New Horizons with Chatbots and Virtual Assistants

In the digital age, the renaissance of customer service is being led by a silent yet profound revolution—the rise of chatbots and virtual assistants. These AI-driven entities are redefining the essence of customer interactions, offering a blend of efficiency, personalization, and innovation that was once science fiction.

Chatbots have become the tireless custodians of customer satisfaction, always ready to greet customers with a consistent and helpful demeanor, regardless of the hour. Their ability to engage in meaningful dialogue has matured beyond simple scripted responses. Through natural language processing, they can parse the complexities of human language, understand the intent behind queries, and respond with a relevance that feels increasingly human.

The transformative impact of these virtual assistants is realized in their ability to directly act as assistants to human agents by parsing through data, offering solutions, and even anticipating needs before they are articulated.

Their presence on messaging platforms has turned these everyday apps into powerful service channels. Businesses that have integrated chatbots into their customer service strategies report reduced costs and a surge in customer engagement. For instance, a bank might deploy a chatbot that helps users track their spending, report lost cards, or even give financial advice, transforming customer service from reactive to proactive, from cost center to revenue driver.

The quantitative benefits are equally compelling. Companies employing chatbots can see significant decreases in the volume of routine queries handled by human agents, with some industries reporting up to a 60–90 percent deflection rate, essentially solving the issue and saving the customer additional cycles and time.[30] This shift allows human customer service representatives to focus on more complex and nuanced customer needs, fostering deeper relationships and, in turn, loyalty.

Moreover, the data gathered by these AI interlocutors is gold dust for businesses. It provides unparalleled insights into customer behaviors, preferences, and pain points. This continuous feedback loop fuels product development, sharpens marketing strategies and tailors the customer experience to an unprecedented degree of personalization.

Yet, the true magic of chatbots lies in their scalability. They are as capable of serving the needs of a small boutique as they are of shouldering the demands of a multinational corporation. Their versatility and adaptability make them a fit for virtually any industry, from healthcare, where they can schedule appointments and provide patient education, to retail, where they can easily recommend products and manage returns.

Chatbots and virtual assistants are not merely tools but catalysts of transformation. They invite us to reimagine the boundaries of what is possible, encouraging a leap into a future where the customer service experience is improved and re-envisioned. They challenge us to think outside the box, not just to meet expectations but to create genuinely delightful experiences, making each interaction not just a means to an end but a part of a journey that customers and businesses embark on together.

Customer Intent: AI as the Key to Decipher the Journey Map

Accurately gauging customer intent is a cornerstone of effective customer service and support. This elusive yet critical element dictates the direction and quality of interactions between service providers and customers. Traditionally, discerning this intent has largely been the purview of human agents, relying on intuition, experience, and real-time adjustments to navigate conversations. However, the advent of AI has redefined this dynamic, adding a layer of nuance and sophistication previously unattainable.

Just as the compass was indispensable to explorers navigating uncharted territories, AI is becoming essential for customer support professionals to understand the nebulous world of customer intent. It acts not as a replacement for human empathy and understanding but as a complementary force, enhancing the precision and personalization of customer interactions.

The Evolution of Customer Intent Recognition

Understanding customer intent was often relegated to face-to-face interactions, written surveys, and phone interviews in the pre-digital era. These methods were not only time-consuming but also fraught with subjective biases. The limitations of these approaches became all too apparent as the world entered the Information Age, giving rise to electronic data capture methods like web forms and interactive voice response (IVR) systems. Yet, these, too, had their limitations, as they were based on predefined categories and failed to capture the nuance of human intent.

Big Data promised a solution, offering a wealth of information that could be analyzed to understand customer behaviors, patterns, and, by extension, intent. However, traditional analytics often stumbled regarding real-time interpretation and proactive service adaptation. This is where machine algorithms first started to make their mark, applying statistical methods to predict likely customer behavior based on past interactions. While more efficient than previous methods, they were still largely reactive rather than proactive.

Artificial intelligence, in contrast, brings both proactivity and nuance to the table. Unlike their algorithmic predecessors, AI systems can adapt in real-time, learning from each customer interaction to improve future ones. Natural language processing helps AI systems understand the context and sentiment behind customer queries, while Reinforcement Learning from Human Feedback continually refines these models to ensure they align closely with human values and expectations.

Moreover, AI's ability to integrate various data points—be it from textual conversations, voice tone, or behavioral patterns on a webpage—creates a multidimensional understanding of customer intent that is far more nuanced and accurate than ever before.

Artificial intelligence has not just brought incremental changes to customer intent recognition; it has redefined what is possible. In doing so, it opens up vistas for customer service that are richer, more responsive, and more aligned with the complexity of human needs and desires.

AI Technologies That Power Intent Recognition

The alchemy of artificial intelligence in discerning customer intent lies in its diverse array of technologies. Each brings its own flavor of sophistication and adaptability, forming a composite whole that is greater than the sum of its parts. In this section, we will break down these various technologies, from natural language processing to machine learning algorithms, to provide a rounded understanding of the machinery behind the magic.

Natural language processing (NLP)

- **Text analysis:** Understanding the nuance in a customer's text is vital in deducing their intent. NLP algorithms analyze sentence structures, keyword frequency, and context to better understand the customer's needs or questions.

- **Sentiment analysis:** Beyond understanding what a customer is saying, it's crucial to grasp how they are saying it. Sentiment analysis deciphers the tone behind words, providing additional layers of context that might be pivotal in certain customer support scenarios.

- **Language translation:** In an increasingly globalized world, language barriers can stifle effective customer support. NLP can seamlessly translate languages in real-time, ensuring that the intent behind a customer's query isn't lost in translation.

- Machine learning (ML) algorithms

- **Decision trees:** These algorithms sort customer queries into predefined categories based on certain conditions or criteria, making it easier for human agents or other AI systems to respond more effectively.

- **Neural networks:** The intricacies of customer intent often require a level of sophistication that only neural networks can provide. These systems can simultaneously process multiple variables, generating more accurate predictions about what a customer seeks.

- **Reinforcement Learning from Human Feedback (RLHF):** The newest frontier in machine learning for customer support, RLHF allows algorithms to learn from human responses. This facilitates a feedback loop that helps the AI model become increasingly accurate in interpreting customer intent over time.

Chatbots and virtual assistants

- **Scripted versus AI-driven chatbots:** While scripted bots follow predetermined pathways, AI-driven chatbots adapt and learn from each customer interaction. The latter are significantly more effective in understanding and acting upon complex customer intent.

- **Role in intent capture:** Chatbots often serve as customer service's first point of contact. Their ability to swiftly recognize intent can set the tone for the rest of the customer's experience, making them indispensable in modern customer support paradigms.

Data analytics tools

- **Trend analysis:** Understanding customer queries or complaints patterns can provide general insights into intent. Data analytics tools capture these trends, allowing businesses to change their support systems proactively.

- **Real-time analytics:** Reacting to customer intent in the moment often means the difference between success and failure in customer support. Real-time analytics offer the immediacy required to make on-the-spot decisions based on customer behavior.

Conversational interfaces

- **Voice assistants:** Speech-based interfaces like voice assistants can recognize vocal cues and inflections, adding another layer to intent recognition.

- **Messaging apps:** Conversational platforms that integrate with popular messaging apps can identify customer intent through textual analysis, enabling a seamless transition between AI-driven and human-led customer support.

Multimodal Data

Contextual understanding through multimodal data is becoming increasingly relevant in customer service and support for several compelling reasons. Multimodal data refers to information in various forms, such as text, audio, video, and images. AI can comprehensively understand a customer's situation by analyzing these different data types, leading to more accurate support and personalized service. For example, analyzing video data from customer interactions can help businesses understand how customers actually use a product, leading to better support strategies and product improvements.

Multimodal data allows AI to pick up on nuances that might be missed when only analyzing text. For instance, the tone of voice in a customer call can indicate urgency or frustration, while images may reveal issues that are difficult to describe in words. AI systems that understand these cues can tailor the support response to the customer's state and the specific problem, enhancing the personalization of the service.

These technologies are not just incremental improvements but represent a collective evolution, driving a paradigm shift in understanding and responding to customers. They are the gears in the complex machinery of AI-driven customer support, each contributing its unique capabilities to the overarching goal of creating a more intuitive, responsive, and ultimately satisfying customer experience.

Historical Interaction Analysis for Predictive Intent

It may seem counterintuitive to look backward in a world constantly urging us to move forward. Historical interaction analysis for predictive intent is a pioneering approach that promises to unlock a deeper understanding of your customers by using the past as a prologue. Consider it the "archaeology" of customer support, where each previous interaction lays the groundwork for deciphering future intents and preferences. Traditional metrics like customer satisfaction scores or response times offer a snapshot but fail to tell the complete story. Historical interactions are the hidden chapters, providing context and shedding light on evolving needs. What techniques are available to perform this analysis?

- Text mining can uncover recurring keywords or phrases, while NLP can go a step further to understand the sentiment and context within which these words were used.

- Studying the frequency and timing of past interactions can predict future customer contact points and the likely reason for engagement, much like how weather patterns can be predicted based on historical data.

- Dividing interactions into clusters based on common characteristics offers the equivalent of creating historical epochs, which can then be analyzed to understand how different segments of your customer base have different needs and intents.

Applications in predictive intent

A thorough understanding of historical interactions allows customer support systems to suggest the most relevant solutions or products, enhancing the accuracy of predictive intent models through personalized service offerings.

Streamlined support channels are another application of predictive intent and are about knowing a customer's past preference for communication channels—be it chat, email, or voice—and then enabling the support system to meet the customer where they are most comfortable, hence offering a personalized experience unique to each customer.

Being aware of recurring issues or questions from past interactions can trigger proactive support steps, potentially resolving a problem before the customer even has to reach out.

The ethical horizon

Historical interaction analysis requires careful handling of sensitive customer data, ensuring that it's not only securely stored but also ethically used. Customers must be made aware that their past interactions are being analyzed to enhance their future experiences and ensure transparency and ethical integrity in the process.

The practice of historical interaction analysis for predictive intent is like uncovering hidden treasures from ancient ruins, providing rich context to the story of your relationship with each customer. It is not just a technique but an evolving discipline that fuses data analytics, machine learning, and customer psychology into an integrated approach for offering unique support experiences and elevating customer satisfaction. As we look toward the future of customer support, this approach beckons us first to look back, delve into the interaction history, and emerge enlightened, empowered, and ever more equipped to meet our customers with the understanding and efficacy they deserve. The benefits extend beyond metrics and into the arena of relational capital. Satisfied customers become brand ambassadors, leading to repeat business and new customer acquisitions through word-of-mouth recommendations. For companies aiming to transform transactions into relationships, historical interaction data serves as the secret script that turns ordinary stories into memorable experiences.

Intelligent (AI-Based) Routing: The Compass Guiding Queries to the Best Destination

In the fast-paced customer support landscape, intelligent (AI-based) routing can be compared with an air traffic controller for a bustling international airport. Just as controllers direct incoming flights to suitable runways based on variables like weather conditions, aircraft size, and current air traffic, this routing system efficiently guides each customer query to the most appropriate agent or team for landing. Let's unravel the sophistication and potential of intelligent routing, illustrating its importance in curating exceptional customer experiences.

When a customer's call or query lands in the wrong team or with an agent who cannot assist, the experience becomes a loop of transfers and hold music, breeding frustration and damaging the brand's reputation. Intelligent AI-based routing is not just an operational tool but a strategic asset that goes beyond solving the immediate issue. It takes into consideration a multitude of factors and variables to eliminate friction and ensure efficient and fast problem resolution.

One of the foundational pillars of intelligent routing is the analysis of historical data. By examining past interactions, the system can identify the customer's preferences, patterns, and behaviors, which informs the routing algorithm. This ensures that the customer's queries are always directed to the most appropriate team or specialist, making for an impeccably personalized experience.

Application of Intelligent AI-Based Routing

Leveraging the power of data and advanced analytics, intelligent AI-based routing transforms customer support into a highly personalized and efficient journey. Let's explore here how AI applied across various dimensions of customer support makes a significant impact:

- **Customer profiles and segmentation:** Knowing whether the person reaching out is a first-time customer, a high-value or strategic customer, or a frequent opener of support incidents can drastically alter how support is rendered, allowing the system to route the query accordingly and tailor the support experience. For instance, a telecommunications company might direct a high-value customer to a premium support team, while a first-time caller might be guided through a streamlined, automated troubleshooting process. This segmentation allows for a refined customer experience, where resources are allocated not just efficiently, but with a strategic focus on nurturing customer relationships.

- **Past interactions:** When customers return, the system's memory of past interactions plays a pivotal role. Routing cases or tickets based on past experiences, especially those that led to high satisfaction ratings, serves as a game-changer in crafting superior customer experiences. A software provider might notice that a particular client had excellent rapport with a certain support agent, leading to a swift and satisfactory resolution. By channeling subsequent queries to the same agent, the company doesn't just increase the chances of another successful interaction; it also delivers a personalized experience that can foster a deeper sense of loyalty.

- **Sentiment analysis:** Sentiment analysis adds another layer of sophistication using NLP algorithms. By interpreting the urgency of the customer's voice, AI can prioritize tickets in real-time. For instance, a customer's urgent message might be routed immediately to a senior agent instead of a more routine query that can be resolved at a standard pace or less tenured agent profile.

- **Channel preference:** The choice of communication channel is another factor that AI handles with finesse. Recognizing that some customers prefer the immediacy of a chat while others might opt for the detailed record-keeping of an email, the system can route the query to an agent who is not only available but also most proficient at that particular communication channel.

- **Agent skill sets:** Agent skill sets encompass a broad spectrum of capabilities, which are an asset that AI leverages with precision. Beyond technical acumen, these skill sets may include language proficiency, cultural familiarity, and soft skills like empathy and communication skills, all of which can be captured in a skills matrix to equip the intelligent AI-based routing engine to make a decision that can significantly enhance the support experience.

A skills matrix in this context is a comprehensive framework that catalogs and rates the range of skills, proficiencies, and expertise that customer service agents possess. This matrix typically includes technical knowledge, product specialization, language fluency, communication competencies, and problem-solving abilities. The AI utilizes this matrix to analyze incoming customer queries and match them with the most suitable agent available. By doing so, the engine ensures that customers are connected with agents who are best equipped to handle their specific issues effectively and empathetically. The skills matrix becomes a living database that the AI references, continually updated with real-time performance data, customer feedback, and each agent's learning and development progress. It's a strategic tool that enables

AI-based routing engines to optimize customer–agent pairings for enhanced resolution rates and customer satisfaction.

- **Real-time queue load:** Operational efficiency is further enhanced by AI's ability to monitor and balance real-time queue loads. By distributing cases to prevent bottlenecks, AI ensures that customer wait times are minimized and agent idle times are reduced. This dynamic allocation of resources means that a customer service department can operate like a well-oiled machine, with each part working in harmony to deliver the best possible service.

- **Business priority pules and operational efficiency:** Business priorities and operational costs are also factored into AI's decision-making process. High-value customers might be fast-tracked to specialized teams as part of a company's commitment to uphold service level agreements (SLAs) and maximize customer lifetime value. Conversely, simpler issues might be directed to junior staff members, allowing more experienced agents to focus on complex cases, thus optimizing the allocation of human resources and controlling operational costs.

- **Time zone and language:** In today's global economy, language barriers are being dismantled, with customers expecting to converse and receive assistance in their native tongue at any time. This 24/7 availability and linguistic versatility are not just customer service enhancements; they serve as vital differentiators in the market and cement a brand's reputation as a truly global and customer-centric entity. Routing algorithms are the perfect ally in this area, matching customer queries with the right level of support and the required language skills, which can be a game-changer in the overall customer experience.

AI-based routing in customer service is not merely a technological advancement; it's a strategic evolution that promises customers a service experience that is as personalized and informed as it is efficient and timely. With each of these considerations playing a role in how support is rendered, AI isn't just answering the call; it's anticipating the caller's needs before the phone even rings.

Text-Based Sentiment Analysis: The Barometer for Customer Behavior

In a time when every customer's voice can echo across social media and review platforms, understanding and responding to customer sentiment has never been more critical. According to Global Newswire, studies reveal that a remarkable 95 percent of consumers usually check online reviews before making purchasing decisions, and 58 percent of these individuals are even willing to invest more money in products endorsed by positively reviewed brands.[31] Research by American Express found that 86 percent of customers are willing to pay more for a good customer experience.[32] All in all, these data points highlight that the buying process, which includes initial contact and post-sales assistance, has a greater impact on buying decisions than the product itself.

Sentiment analysis technology utilizes natural language processing to search through the subtleties of language found in customer feedback, comments, and reviews, predicting the potential behavior behind text data. It starts by collecting and refining text from various sources and then processes it to understand nuances, such as context and sarcasm. Next, AI classifies the overall sentiment as positive, negative, or neutral and then aggregates this data to give businesses an overall predictive measurement. These insights allow companies to respond to customer sentiment trends proactively, improving products, services, and customer relations without the impractical effort of manually reviewing mountains of feedback.

In today's global marketplace, where consumer opinions can make or break a brand's reputation, sentiment analysis serves as an early-warning system. It can detect real-time customer satisfaction shifts, allowing brands to respond with agility. For example, if there's a sudden influx of negative reviews on a new product line, AI tools can flag this trend, prompting an immediate quality review or a public response from the company. This rapid reaction can mitigate the impact of negative feedback before it escalates into a wider public relations issue.

The application of sentiment analysis stretches across various industries. In the hospitality sector, hotels and restaurants use it to monitor reviews across platforms like TripAdvisor and Yelp, ensuring that any emerging issues are addressed promptly. In the airline industry, sentiment analysis can track customer feedback across multiple channels to manage service recovery during flight delays or cancellations.

In the software and gaming business, where user experience is paramount, sentiment analysis can guide developers by highlighting aspects of the product that users love or areas that require improvement. For instance, a gaming company might use sentiment analysis to parse through forum discussions and online reviews to gather player feedback, helping to prioritize updates and patches that enhance the gaming experience.

Moreover, sentiment analysis can inform customer service strategies. By understanding the satisfaction of customers, service teams can be better prepared to address concerns. For example, if sentiment analysis identifies a customer who is dissatisfied with a specific technical issue, the customer service team can proactively reach out with solutions, often before the customer takes the initiative to contact support.

In essence, sentiment analysis acts as the pulse-check for a brand's health in the eyes of its customers. It transforms vast quantities of unstructured feedback into actionable insights, enabling businesses to act swiftly, adapt their strategies, and ultimately foster a stronger connection with their customer base. By tapping into this powerful AI capability, companies are not just listening to their customers but staying one step ahead in the ever-evolving space of customer satisfaction.

Pros and Cons

Powered by AI, sentiment analysis has emerged as a key player, offering businesses a way to systematically assess customers' thoughts about their products and services.

However, sentiment analysis utilizing AI faces several significant challenges, particularly in the nuanced world of customer service and support. These challenges can have profound implications for the accuracy and reliability of sentiment interpretation, which, if not addressed, can lead to misinformed business decisions and damaged customer relationships.

One of the challenges of AI-driven sentiment analysis is its subjective nature, which can often be tricky to measure. Plus, the meaning of words and phrases can change with context, which might affect the accuracy of sentiment analysis. And let's not forget about the lack of huge training datasets, which can make it difficult for AI models to pick up on subtle cues. Sentiment analysis has its own challenges, including bias and inaccurate data. In the world of customer service and support, we also need to remember that customers often express themselves in languages other than their native languages, potentially leading to an unintended altering of a message's meaning.

Table 3.1 illustrates these challenges and some mitigation activities to overcome them.

TABLE 3.1 AI-Driven, Text-Based Sentiment Analysis Challenges

CHALLENGE	MITIGATION ACTIVITY
AI may struggle to understand the context, including sarcasm or irony, leading to incorrect sentiment classification. A customer's sarcastic comment like "Fantastic, my package is late again" could be misinterpreted as a positive sentiment.	Implementing more advanced NLP models and training AI with contextually rich datasets can improve understanding. Continuously updating the AI model with new examples can also help.
Subtle nuances of language, such as idioms, colloquialisms, or cultural expressions, can lead to inaccuracies. For example, a phrase like "killing it" could be misinterpreted as negative when it's actually a compliment.	Expanding training datasets to include a variety of expressions and regional dialects can help. Employing linguists to annotate data and refine algorithms may also enhance understanding.
Customer support often involves multiple languages, which can complicate sentiment analysis. An AI trained on English data may misinterpret sentiments expressed in other languages.	Developing language-specific models and employing multilingual training sets can help AI understand sentiments across different languages.
AI may not always gauge the intensity of a comment correctly, potentially overlooking the urgency of a customer's issue. Cultural nuances might play a role, as well as the use of euphemisms, which can lead to a customer feeling unheard.	Enhancing AI models to recognize intensity and respond accordingly can help. This could include prioritizing customer queries based on detected sentiment intensity.
AI can inherit biases present in the training data, leading to misrepresented sentiment analysis. This could result in consistently negative sentiment assessments for certain demographics or topics, influencing customer support priorities unfairly.	Regular audits of AI decisions, diversifying training datasets, and employing fairness-aware algorithms can reduce biases.

continues

TABLE 3.1 *continued*

CHALLENGE	MITIGATION ACTIVITY
Language evolves constantly, and AI systems that do not adapt will become less accurate over time. New slang or changing word usage can render previous training obsolete.	Incorporating continuous learning loops where the AI can adapt to new language trends and customer feedback patterns will keep the system updated.
Analyzing customer sentiment often involves sensitive data. Inadequate privacy measures can lead to breaches and loss of customer trust.	Implementing stringent data security protocols and complying with privacy regulations like the General Data Protection Regulation (GDRP) in the European Union, which are intended to protect customer data.

If these challenges are not addressed, the consequences can be severe. A report by NewVoiceMedia indicated that companies lose more than $62 billion annually due to poor customer service.[33] Misinterpreted sentiment can lead to inappropriate responses, escalating complaints, and ultimately, customer churn. It's a fact you've probably heard before: acquiring new customers is more expensive than retaining the ones you already have. To be more specific, it's 5 to 25 times more expensive to attract new customers than hold onto existing ones, according to *Harvard Business Review*.[34]

On the other hand, accurately gauged sentiment can inform better customer interactions, product improvements, and targeted marketing strategies, leading to increased customer satisfaction and loyalty.

While sentiment analysis has the potential to significantly enhance customer service and support, AI systems must be sophisticated, well-trained, and continuously updated to handle the complex and dynamic nature of human communication.

Voice Analysis: The Anchor to Help Understand Customer Sentiment

Building upon the insights garnered from text-based sentiment analysis, AI's capabilities extend into the domain of voice—a medium rich with nuanced cues. As we transition from analyzing written words to spoken interactions, this leap from text to voice opens up a dynamic landscape where the subtleties of human speech take center stage, and AI's ability to interpret them can significantly elevate the customer experience.

The tone, pitch, and tempo of a customer's voice carry a wealth of information that, when analyzed by AI, can reveal their true positive or negative sentiment. This technology empowers customer service agents with a deeper understanding of the customer's thoughts, enabling them to engage in conversations with empathy and precision. Here's how AI is transforming the landscape through voice analysis:

- **Understanding tone:** AI-driven voice analysis can detect stress levels in a customer's voice, signaling the agent to handle the call with extra care or escalate the case if necessary. It can discern the urgency from a customer's rapid speech patterns, prompting a quicker response. Moreover, mechanisms such as intelligent routing, discussed earlier in this chapter, can leverage this information to make smarter decisions and connect the customer to an agent equipped to address their concerns efficiently by capturing the intent behind a customer's words.

- **Speech recognition and intent analysis:** Advanced speech recognition goes beyond mere transcription; it involves interpreting the customer's intent. By analyzing the words and phrases used, AI can determine the reason for a call before the customer is even connected to an agent. This preemptive insight allows for immediate routing to the most appropriate support tier or department, reducing wait times and improving resolution efficiency.

- **Call quality monitoring:** AI can monitor calls in real-time, providing immediate feedback to agents on the clarity and effectiveness of their communication. This ensures consistent quality across all customer interactions and can be used for training purposes, highlighting areas of excellence and those needing improvement both in soft and hard skills.

- **Predictive assistance:** Voice analysis can predict a customer's needs based on historical interactions and common patterns. For instance, if a customer frequently calls about billing issues after a new cycle starts, the AI can prepare relevant information for the agent in advance, facilitating a quicker and more informed response.

- **Personalization at scale:** With AI, personalization doesn't have to be sacrificed for scale. Voice analysis can tailor interactions by recognizing a returning customer and retrieving their preferences and prior issues, thus crafting a personalized experience even in a high-volume call center environment.

- **Real-time translation services:** For global businesses, AI-driven voice analysis can provide real-time translation services, breaking down language barriers in customer support. This enables a seamless conversation between the customer and the support agent, regardless of their respective languages, broadening the reach and accessibility of support services.

- **Sentiment tracking over time:** Voice analysis can track changes in customer sentiment over time, providing valuable feedback on the long-term effectiveness of service strategies. By understanding trends in customer satisfaction, businesses can adapt their service offerings to meet customer needs better. This is also extremely relevant when applied to the lifecycle of a support ticket, where customer sentiment is subject to change on an event-driven situation or over time as the investigation goes on—sharing these fluctuations in a timely manner with the support team can trigger additional actions to recover this sentiment before it's too late and translates into dissatisfaction.

- **Fraud detection:** The unique characteristics of a customer's voice can be used as a biometric identifier. AI can help in detecting anomalies in voice patterns that might indicate fraudulent activity, thus providing an additional layer of security in customer interactions.

Pros and Cons

The use of AI for voice analysis is not without its challenges. These difficulties stem from both the complexity of human speech and the limitations of current technology. **Table 3.2** shows some of the key challenges and opportunities for mitigation.

TABLE 3.2 AI-Driven, Voice-Based Sentiment Analysis

CHALLENGE	MITIGATION ACTIVITY
Accents and dialects vary greatly across different regions and cultures, which can lead to misinterpretations by AI systems that are not sufficiently trained on diverse speech patterns, ultimately making customers feel misunderstood or frustrated, resulting in an overall poor experience. The same challenge is presented when industry-specific terminology (jargon) or slang is used, making it difficult for AI to comprehend if it has not been trained in such language.	Training AI models on a wide range of voice samples from different demographics can improve recognition accuracy, as well as including industry-specific terms and slang in the training data can improve AI's understanding.

continues

TABLE 3.2 *continued*

CHALLENGE	MITIGATION ACTIVITY
Speech ambiguities such as homophones (words that sound the same but have different meanings) and context-dependent meanings can confuse AI, resulting in incorrect interpretations followed by inappropriate responses.	Utilizing advanced NLP algorithms that consider the broader context of the conversation can reduce ambiguities.
Background noise and poor audio quality can significantly degrade the performance of voice analysis systems, resulting in important customer information being missing or misheard and potentially requiring customers to repeat themselves more than once.	Implementing noise-cancellation algorithms and prompting customers to move to quieter environments can help improve audio clarity.
Capturing the subtleties of human voice, such as sarcasm or a quivering voice due to distress, is challenging for AI.	Enhancing AI with machine learning models that focus on different inflections and training them with a variety of voice datasets can significantly improve the results.
Analyzing voice data in real-time requires significant computational power and efficient algorithms, and a failure to meet these requirements can result in delays and slow response times, harming the customer's experience.	Optimizing AI models for faster processing and using more powerful computing infrastructure can address latency issues.
Recording and analyzing voice communications raise significant privacy concerns and may be subject to regulatory compliance issues or can result in breaches and loss of customer trust.	Implementing robust security measures and adhering strictly to privacy laws and regulations, such as GDPR, can help in this area that is so critical when using AI responsibly.
Language is dynamic, and AI systems need to continuously learn and adapt to new phrases, expressions, and speaking styles. Otherwise, we run the risk of using static AI models that become outdated and less effective over time.	Incorporating adaptive learning algorithms that can evolve with language use over time can keep the AI relevant and accurate.

These challenges underscore the need for ongoing research and development in AI for voice analysis. As technology advances, the ability of AI to surmount these hurdles will improve, leading to more sophisticated and reliable voice analysis systems that enhance the quality of customer service and support.

The application of AI in voice analysis not only complements the findings of text-based sentiment analysis but enriches it, offering a more holistic view of customer emotions and intentions. This integration of textual and vocal analysis opens a new era in customer service, where every spoken word can be transformed into actionable insights, fostering a support environment that's responsive and truly resonant with the customer's needs.

AI-Enhanced IVR Systems

Interactive Voice Response (IVR) systems have been a fundamental customer service component for years. An IVR is an automated telephony system that interacts with callers, gathers information, and routes calls to appropriate recipients. It uses pre-recorded voice prompts and menus to present information and options to users, touch-tone telephone keypad entry, or voice to receive responses.

The inception of IVR can be traced back to the 1970s when businesses began using it to manage large volumes of calls efficiently. These early systems were simplistic, relying on dual-tone multi-frequency (DTMF) signaling for input and offering limited response options. As technology progressed, so did IVR capabilities, evolving from basic digit-based input to incorporating simple speech recognition in the late 1990s.

Integrating AI into IVR systems marked a significant leap in their evolution. Modern AI-powered IVR systems utilize advanced technologies such as natural language processing (NLP), machine learning (ML), and sophisticated speech recognition algorithms. This shift allows IVRs to understand and process natural language inputs, enabling users to speak naturally, as they would to a human operator.

AI transforms IVR from a simple automated response system into a dynamic and intelligent interface. IVR technology remains the most important connection between companies and customers in many sectors, accounting for twice as many interactions as calls with live agents and five times more than text-based chat—and demand for these services is still growing. According to the recent IVR systems Global Strategic Business Report by Research and Markets, the global market for IVR systems is expected to reach $9.2 billion by 2030, up from an estimated $4.9 billion in 2022.[35] A prime example of AI-IVR's impact is seen in the banking sector. Banks have reported a significant increase in customer satisfaction after implementing AI-IVR systems. These systems have effectively handled routine inquiries like balance checks and transaction histories, freeing human agents for more complex queries:

- Bank of America (BofA) launched Erica in 2018, a voice-enabled AI assistant integrated into their IVR system.[36] Erica has become one of the most-accessed virtual banking assistants, helping over 32 million customers with more than 1 billion interactions. Now, BofA is enhancing the chatbot to give customers even more personalization and tailored product recommendations.

- BNP Paribas Personal Finance Spain's conversational AI virtual assistant has reached a 96 percent accuracy rate in understanding queries, allowing the volume of calls managed by its contact center agents to decrease by 46 percent.[37]

These examples underscore the effectiveness of AI-IVR in improving customer experience and operational efficiency in the banking sector. They demonstrate how AI-IVR can handle a wide range of customer interactions, from routine inquiries to more complex issues, thereby enhancing the overall quality of customer service.

AI Technologies in IVR

The integration of AI into IVR systems has been a pivotal development, introducing several key technologies:

- **Natural language processing:** Natural language processing (NLP) allows IVR systems to understand and interpret human speech more naturally. This technology goes beyond recognizing simple voice commands, enabling the system to parse complex language structures and respond accurately.

- **Machine learning (ML) algorithms:** ML algorithms enable IVR systems to learn from interactions and improve over time. This learning process enhances the system's ability to predict user needs and offer more relevant responses.

- **Advanced speech recognition:** Advanced speech recognition improves accuracy in understanding diverse accents and dialects, thus catering to a broader user base.

Embracing AI in IVR through the Wave Concept

Modern IVR systems are moving toward a more personalized approach, focusing on individual user needs. This involves adopting advanced technologies like predictive engines and conversational AI for more intuitive and humanlike interactions.

The integration of predictive analytics and machine learning allows IVR systems to anticipate customer needs and tailor their responses, significantly improving the efficiency and effectiveness of customer service. Additionally, incorporating conversational AI and Natural Language Understanding (NLU) is paving the way for more sophisticated interactions in IVR systems, enhancing the overall customer experience.

Leading companies are adopting a strategic "wave" approach (McKinsey) to upgrade their IVR systems with AI. This approach is a strategic, multiphase methodology that involves using advanced analytics to identify and address issues in current systems, redesigning customer journeys, and applying AI technologies to enhance predictive and conversational capabilities (see **Figure 3.1**).

Digital transformation waves

Wave 1: Analysis and identification   Wave 2: Redesigning customer journeys   Wave 3: Implementing AI and machine learning

FIGURE 3.1 The wave approach to upgrading IVR systems to incorporate AI

Wave 1: Analysis and identification

- **Breakpoint analysis:** The first wave involves using advanced analytics to identify critical breakpoints in the current IVR call flow. These are points where customers typically abandon the call or request human assistance, indicating areas where the current system fails to meet their needs.

- **Immediate adjustments:** Based on this analysis, companies can make immediate design changes to address the most pressing issues. This might include simple fixes like rewording confusing menu options or reorganizing the call flow to make it more intuitive.

Wave 2: Redesigning customer journeys

- **Customer-centric design:** In this wave, businesses focus on redesigning the customer journey for priority call types identified in wave 1. This involves starting from a clean slate and applying user-centric design principles to create an IVR experience more aligned with customer preferences and behaviors.

- **Integration of new technologies:** This stage also presents an opportunity to integrate new technologies, such as AI-driven speech recognition or context-aware call flows. For example, the IVR system could use data from a customer's previous interactions to personalize the menu options presented during the call.

Wave 3: Implementing AI and machine learning

- **Predictive and conversational AI:** The final wave involves applying machine learning and AI technologies to add predictive capabilities and conversational interactions to the IVR system. This includes employing NLP to enhance the system's ability to understand and respond to customer queries more naturally and intuitively.

- **Proactive service delivery:** By analyzing past interactions, AI in IVR can learn to anticipate customer needs, offering information or solutions even before the customer explicitly asks for them. This proactive approach can significantly enhance customer satisfaction and streamline the interaction process.

Companies looking to rapidly enhance their IVR systems can conduct some of these activities in parallel. For instance, if a business has already selected the AI and ML platforms for wave 3, it can start its implementation earlier. This allows the redesigns in wave 2 to benefit from more advanced technologies immediately.

It's important not to skip wave 1, as understanding the existing system's shortcomings is crucial for effective improvement. The best practice is continually repeating customer behavior analysis and updating the IVR system accordingly, creating a Continuous Improvement Cycle. This ensures that the IVR system never becomes outdated and always evolves in line with technological advances and changing user needs.

By following this structured wave approach, companies can effectively embrace AI in their IVR systems, ensuring a strategically sound transition aligned with their customers' evolving expectations. This methodical enhancement leads to IVR systems that are more efficient and capable and more attuned to providing a superior customer experience.

Future Trends and Innovations in AI-Enhanced IVR

The future of AI in IVR systems will bring significant transformations, introducing a range of innovative trends and technologies that will redefine customer service experiences. Let's explore some of these future trends and advancements in this space:

- **Hyper-personalization through advanced analytics:** Future IVR systems will leverage deep learning to analyze customer data more profoundly, extracting detailed insights about individual preferences, behaviors, and history. This will enable IVR systems to offer highly personalized experiences, such as greeting customers by name, recalling their last interaction, and predicting their current needs based on past behavior.
- **Voice biometrics for security and convenience:** With the increasing emphasis on security, future IVR systems will integrate voice biometric technology. This technology uses unique vocal characteristics to identify and authenticate individuals, offering a blend of security, convenience, and personalization.

How Voice Biometrics Work

By transforming unique vocal characteristics into a powerful key for authentication, voice biometrics technology offers a blend of security and user-friendly access. Here's a closer look at how this innovative technology functions to enhance security and convenience in customer service:

- **Voiceprint creation:** Initially, the customer is asked to speak a few phrases or sentences. The IVR system analyzes various aspects of their voice, such as pitch, tone, and speaking pattern, to create a unique voiceprint. This voiceprint is then securely stored for future reference.

Authentication Process

During subsequent interactions, the IVR system compares the customer's voice against the stored voiceprint to authenticate their identity. This process usually takes just a few seconds and can be performed during the natural course of conversation, eliminating the need for traditional security questions or PINs.

Following are some practical examples:

- Voice biometrics significantly reduces the risk of fraud and identity theft, providing enhanced security protocols, as it's much harder to replicate someone's voice compared to stealing a password or PIN. This is especially critical in sectors like banking and healthcare, where secure access to personal information is paramount.[38]

- With streamlined authentication, customers no longer need to remember and input passwords or answer security questions. This seamless authentication process saves time and reduces frustration, leading to a smoother customer experience.

- Once authenticated, the personalization of the service can enable the system to immediately access the customer's profile and history, allowing for a more personalized service. For instance, a customer calling their bank might be greeted by name and presented with options relevant to their recent transactions or queries.

- Fraud detection and prevention is possible as the system can detect unusual patterns or anomalies in voice, which could indicate fraudulent activity. This adds a layer of security, helping to quickly identify and prevent potential fraud.

- Voice biometrics are particularly beneficial for accessibility purposes. For example, with visually impaired customers or those with physical disabilities that make traditional authentication methods challenging. It offers an accessible and user-friendly alternative.

Behavior Recognition for Empathetic Responses

By integrating behavior recognition and sentiment analysis, IVR systems will be able to detect subtle cues in a customer's voice, such as stress or frustration. This will enable the system to adjust its responses accordingly, providing more empathetic and contextually appropriate support. One potential application of sentiment analysis integration is in a healthcare provider's contact center; the IVR could detect distress in a caller's voice and expedite their call to a human agent for immediate assistance.

- **Integration with IoT and smart home devices:** Future IVR systems will likely integrate with IoT devices and smart home technologies, expanding the ecosystem and allowing customers to interact with the IVR through various devices beyond the phone. For example, customers could use their smart speakers to contact customer service or receive notifications from the IVR system. Another practical scenario is a customer could use their smart speaker to inquire about their utility service status or report an issue, and the IVR system could provide real-time updates or assistance.

- **Augmented reality (AR) and virtual reality (VR) integration:** The integration of AR and VR technologies with IVR systems could provide customers with immersive support experiences. For instance, a customer trying to assemble a product could call the customer service IVR and be guided through an AR-based instructional overlay. Some automotive companies are exploring the integration of AR with their customer support systems to provide real-time visual assistance for vehicle maintenance and troubleshooting.[39]

AI-driven Predictive Support and Proactive Services

Future IVR systems will not just react to customer queries but proactively anticipate and address potential issues or needs. This involves using predictive analytics to identify trends and patterns in customer interactions and initiating contact with solutions or information. For example, a telecommunication company's IVR could proactively inform customers of network issues in their area before they even notice or report a problem.

- **Blockchain for enhanced transparency and trust:** Integrating blockchain technology could enhance the transparency and traceability of interactions within IVR systems, building greater trust and accountability. This could be particularly beneficial in sectors like finance and healthcare, where data integrity is crucial. In the future, blockchain could be used to securely and transparently log customer interactions, ensuring data integrity and providing a verifiable audit trail for dispute resolution.

- **Cross-channel integration for seamless experiences:** IVR systems will likely evolve into integrated hubs that seamlessly connect various customer interaction channels, including social media, email, and chat. This unified customer interaction hub model will provide a unified experience, ensuring consistency and efficiency across all customer service touchpoints. For example, a customer starting a service request on social media could seamlessly transition to a phone call with the IVR system without repeating information, as the system would have access to the entire interaction history.

These future trends indicate a move toward more intelligent, empathetic, and interconnected IVR systems, deeply integrated with the latest technological advancements. This evolution will significantly enhance the customer experience, offering personalized, efficient, and secure interactions that meet the high expectations of modern customers.

AI-Enhanced Diagnostics and Technical Support: Streamlining Solutions, Empowering Agents

Today's AI capabilities extend far beyond mere data processing. AI-driven tools are increasingly skilled at diagnosing issues through pattern recognition and predictive analytics, analyzing vast datasets, recognizing anomalies, and suggesting solutions based on historical problem-solving data.

Employing subject matter experts in support to write articles and build automated diagnostics helps customers solve their own issues and provides additional assistance to customer service agents as they trouble-shoot a problem. As customers or support agents run an auto-diagnostic program that scans their system or product, quickly offering a solution or fixing the problem automatically eliminates the need for further support agent engagement.

Diagnostics leverage basic AI principles like ML to analyze common issues and suggest solutions. Diagnostics can provide automated solutions to check or change settings, validate account information, and determine or signify customer intent. Using diagnostics enhances the efficiency of resolving customer problems and collects valuable data on common issues and their resolution success rate. This data forms the basis for training more sophisticated AI models, leading to smarter, more intuitive support tools.

Initially, diagnostics provide immediate solutions for common problems, reducing the workload on human support staff and improving customer satisfaction through rapid problem-solving. Over time, as diagnostics evolve and improve, they become more adept at handling a wider range of issues, including more complex and nuanced problems.

While companies frequently employ AI in diagnostics to help predict and resolve issues, the following two examples outline a wide range of applications across different industries.

- **BMW Group: AI in automotive diagnostics:** BMW has integrated an AI-based system within their production and quality assurance process-es.[40] The AI, known as the Smart Data Analytics program, harnesses machine learning to analyze vast amounts of data collected during vehicle testing.[41] The system has been instrumental in early fault detection and diagnostics. By analyzing data patterns, the AI predicts and identifies potential issues before they manifest in the finished vehicle. As a result, BMW has reported a significant reduction in quality issues and a more efficient recall process when needed. The system has enhanced the precision of diagnostics, leading to a reported 5-10 percent improvement in problem identification during the production phase.

- **Microsoft: AI for network diagnostics:** Microsoft has implemented AI within its Azure cloud platform to enhance network diagnostics, particularly for its cloud services. Azure's network monitoring, Network Watcher, provides AI tools to diagnose network performance issues across various resources.[42]

The AI-driven tools within Network Watcher allow for automated analysis to detect and diagnose network issues that could potentially impact services and applications running on the Azure platform. For example, the Connection Monitor feature continuously monitors and diagnoses the performance of network connections, helping to ensure minimal downtime and optimal performance. While specific percentages of improvement are proprietary, Microsoft's case studies indicate that such tools have significantly decreased both the time to detect and resolve network issues, improving overall reliability and user satisfaction.

The automation of repetitive and routine tasks is another area where AI excels. Chatbots and virtual assistants powered by AI can handle many standard inquiries, such as guiding users through basic troubleshooting steps. This level of automation extends to resolving common technical problems, like software configuration or password recovery/reset activities, often without the need for live agent intervention.

Diagnostics can also be developed to assist customers in solving their issues. They can run an auto-diagnostic program that scans their system or product, quickly offering a solution or fixing the problem automatically, eliminating the need for support agent engagement.

The current state of AI in technical support is thus one of dynamic growth and potential, laying the groundwork for a future where AI not only supports but also drives the resolution process, offering a level of service that is predictive, personalized, and unprecedented in efficiency and effectiveness. Integrating AI into diagnostic and technical support significantly uplifts agent job satisfaction by alleviating the burden of monotonous tasks and enabling a sharper focus on complex, engaging work. Automating routine support queries, AI allows agents to delve into more nuanced problem-solving, fostering professional development and a sense of accomplishment. This efficient division of labor enhances an agent's capacity for in-depth technical work and ensures a balanced workload, reducing burnout and promoting a healthier work-life balance.

Furthermore, AI's role in streamlining the initial stages of customer interaction furnishes agents with better context and understanding, leading to more meaningful customer engagements. The consequent positive feedback and recognition contribute to a fulfilling work environment. In addition, the dynamic and innovative setting that AI cultivates within the workplace bolsters a culture of continuous learning and improvement that translates into a more satisfied, skilled, and stable workforce, essential for a thriving organizational ecosystem.

Implementing AI in a support organization requires a strategic approach. It starts with identifying the most time-consuming tasks and pinpointing where errors most frequently occur. Training is crucial; AI and human agents must learn to work symbiotically.

What's ahead of us? The evolution of AI-driven support tools includes elements such as augmented reality (AR) and virtual reality (VR) for remote assistance. By leveraging AR, support agents can visually guide customers through complex tasks such as hardware setup or repair process, overcoming the limitations of textual or verbal instructions.

As AI technology advances, we can expect these systems to become even more intelligent, further enhancing their problem-solving capabilities and reshaping the landscape of customer service and support. The rewards for companies willing to embrace these changes include operational improvements and stronger, more loyal customer relationships.

AI-Driven Knowledge Base and Self-Service Portals: A Strategic Imperative

In the age of instant gratification, the ability for customers to quickly find or get solutions to their problems is paramount, and artificial intelligence stands at the core of modern knowledge management. The integration of AI into knowledge bases and self-service portals has transformed the landscape of customer support, providing a seamless and efficient experience that meets the modern expectations of immediacy.

AI-driven systems employ NLP to understand queries in their natural form, often as they would ask another human. This capability allows AI to interpret the intent behind a customer's question and fetch the most relevant information from the knowledge base. Furthermore, machine learning algorithms enable these systems to learn from interactions, constantly improving the accuracy and relevance of the information they provide.

An effective knowledge management system is the bedrock upon which customer service and support operations are built— for customer self-service and as a critical resource for support agents. In a nutshell, AI can tag, categorize, and index knowledge articles, making it easier for both customers and support agents to quickly find the right information at the right time.

Let's deep dive into the benefits of a strong strategy around knowledge management and how it empowers customers, support agents and the business overall.

Empowering Customers

Self-help portals, enhanced by AI, bring a wealth of benefits to customers, offering them control over their support experience and the ability to find solutions at their convenience. From a customer standpoint, the immediate advantage is empowerment. Having the means to resolve issues without external help aligns with the do-it-yourself ethos of the digital age. In fact, a *Harvard Business Review* article noted that 81 percent of all customers attempt to take care of matters themselves before reaching out to a live representative.[43]

The around-the-clock availability of AI-driven support systems ensures that help is always at hand, regardless of time zones, holidays, or business hours, catering to a global customer base. This 24/7 access eliminates the frustration of waiting for business hours or queuing for a support agent, leading to a more positive overall customer experience. A study by Zendesk found that 67 percent of customers prefer self-service over speaking to a company representative.[44]

Self-service portals often provide a faster resolution to common issues. Instead of navigating through multiple layers of customer service, customers can use searchable knowledge bases powered by AI to find immediate answers. AI algorithms can also suggest articles based on customer query patterns, thereby enhancing the relevance and speed of information retrieval.

Self-help portals cater to a variety of learning preferences. Customers who prefer visual aids can benefit from video tutorials and infographics, while those who favor reading might lean toward FAQs and step-by-step guides. The AI systems can even tailor the content format to match the user's historical interactions and preferences, personalizing the help experience.

Community forums are another aspect of self-service that offers significant value to customers. These forums create a platform for peer-to-peer assistance where customers can share experiences, solutions, and workarounds. The community aspect fosters a sense of belonging and collective problem-solving, often leading to innovative solutions that may not be part of the official documentation. AI enhances these platforms by identifying the most helpful responses and promoting content that has resolved similar issues for other users.

Empowering Support Agents

A well-structured AI-driven knowledge base serves as an invaluable repository of information that agents can tap into, ensuring that they have access to the most up-to-date and comprehensive information at their fingertips.

The discoverability of content within a knowledge base is vital for support agents who are often under pressure to provide quick and accurate responses. AI enhances this discoverability by intelligently tagging and indexing content, making search results more relevant and reducing the time agents spend hunting for information. For instance, when an agent enters a query or keywords related to a customer's issue, the AI system can quickly surface troubleshooting guides, technical documentation, and FAQs. This rapid access to information streamlines the support process and significantly shortens the average handling time for each query, improving efficiency and reducing operational costs.

Moreover, AI-powered knowledge bases can proactively assist agents by suggesting relevant articles and real-time information during customer interactions. By analyzing the context of the customer's issue, AI can predict what information the agent might need next and provide it without the agent needing to search manually. This predictive assistance ensures that agents are always prepared with the next step in the resolution process, facilitating a smoother support experience for both the agent and the customer.

AI's ability to handle and deflect routine inquiries translates into a lighter workload for customer support teams. This shift allows human agents to dedicate their attention to tackling more complex and nuanced customer issues, optimizing the use of valuable human resources. The efficiency gains here are twofold: customers benefit from faster resolutions to simple queries, and companies benefit from a more focused and proficient use of their support staff.

Knowledge management also plays a crucial role in agent training and onboarding. New agents can quickly become proficient by utilizing the knowledge base as a learning tool, accelerating their ability to contribute to the team and reducing the time to competency.

For support agents, a dynamic and intelligent knowledge base is a tool and a partner that enhances their capacity to deliver quality support. This wealth of information empowers and allows them to focus more on high-value customer interactions. This empowerment leads to higher job satisfaction as agents can perform their roles more effectively, and it ensures that customers receive well-informed, timely, and high-quality support.

In this way, knowledge management is foundational for customer self-service success and equally critical for equipping support agents, providing them with the resources they need to deliver exceptional service.

Empowering the Business

Implementing self-help portals and effective knowledge management strategies yields extensive benefits across the entire business spectrum, impacting customer satisfaction, operational efficiency, cost management, and continuous organizational learning and improvement.

A well-structured self-help portal directly contributes to operational efficiency by reducing the volume of inbound queries that require human intervention. With customers resolving many issues independently, support teams can allocate their resources more effectively, focusing on higher-level tasks that necessitate human expertise. This leads to a more productive use of personnel and a leaner operational model. IBM's research suggests that interactions via AI-enabled chatbots can save companies over 30 percent on costs incurred while providing customer support.[45]

The economic benefits are significant. By deflecting calls and live support interactions, self-help portals can dramatically lower support costs. According to Gartner, effective self-service can deflect up to 40 percent of customer calls to live service.[46] HappyFox reports that B2C companies see 50–66 percent ticket deflection for frequently asked questions within 90 days after implementing bot.[47]

Moreover, the cost savings extend beyond just the support interactions to include reduced training times for support agents and less pressure to scale the support team during growth phases.

From a customer standpoint, the empowerment and autonomy afforded by self-help options often translate into higher satisfaction rates. The ease and speed with which customers can find solutions themselves are directly linked to an improved customer experience. This self-sufficiency can enhance brand loyalty as customers develop a sense of confidence in the brand's ability to enable them to help themselves.

Knowledge management systems are treasure troves of data that can offer invaluable insights into customer behavior and common issues. This data can inform product development, alert businesses to emerging trends or issues, and help prioritize resources to areas with the highest impact. Continuous refinement of the knowledge base, driven by AI analytics, ensures that the content remains relevant and effective, fostering a culture of continuous improvement.

For businesses looking to scale, self-help portals offer a scalable customer service solution that does not require a linear increase in support staff. They also provide a platform to serve a global customer base, offering multi-language support and catering to various regions without establishing local support teams in every market.

A robust self-help portal and knowledge management strategy can also bolster a company's brand image, showcasing a commitment to customer empowerment and service innovation. This can be a differentiating factor in competitive markets that sets a brand apart from its competitors, appealing to tech-savvy consumers who favor digital-first interactions.

Strategy Considerations for Integrating AI into Self-Service Channels of Support

As companies embark on the journey of integrating AI into their customer support ecosystems, several strategic factors need to be considered to ensure the success of such an initiative. Central to this integration is the design of the self-service portal, which must be user-friendly and intuitive, allowing for smooth navigation and easy searchability. The user interface is the customer's first point of interaction, so it is critical in defining the user experience.

Equally important is the caliber of content within the knowledge base. It should be rich, accessible, and actionable, enabling customers to resolve their queries without further assistance. High-quality content serves the customer's immediate needs and reflects the brand's commitment to providing superior service.

Effective knowledge management is critical in leveraging AI for customer support. Organizations must keep information current, accurate, and reflective of the latest products, services, and support policies. This requires a strategy that encompasses regular reviews, updates, and feedback loops where support agents and customers can suggest improvements.

An often overlooked aspect of knowledge bases is the feedback mechanism. Facilitating a way for customers to provide their insights on the usefulness of content not only aids in the continuous refinement of the knowledge base but also empowers customers, giving them a voice in the support process.

Incorporating user-generated content, such as community forums and Q&A sections, can enrich the knowledge base and provide a platform for peer-to-peer support. AI can moderate these forums, highlight popular topics, and even identify content gaps in the official knowledge base by analyzing customers' questions.

This concept is successfully implemented at Cisco, where content search plays a key role in many of its operations,[48] including business-critical activities such as customer support, where more than 11,000 support engineers use search tools to retrieve content from millions of documents that help resolve the more than two million service requests received each year. Search is also an essential feature of the *Cisco.com* website, where visitors can find information from a collection of hundreds of thousands of files of web pages and documents, including data sheets and user guides, as well as other technical, product, and corporate resources. In addition to search results accuracy, the speed at which results are returned is critical. A delay of just half a second can impact the website click-through rate or the customer experience when in touch with a support engineer. In partnership with Elastic, Cisco has deployed Elasticsearch, running on Elastic Cloud on Kubernetes, as the engine at the center of Cisco's new enterprise search architecture to add advanced search capabilities to many of its internal and external facing applications. The new search capabilities have enabled Cisco to save 5,000 hours per month of support engineer time.

AI-driven analytics can track the effectiveness of self-help resources. For example, if certain articles have high view counts and follow-up contact rates, it may indicate that the content is attracting interest but not fully resolving customer issues. This data allows for continuous refinement of support content.

Integrating existing customer support tools, such as Customer Relationship Management (CRM) systems and chatbots, is another pillar of a robust AI-driven support system. Seamless integration ensures that the customer journey through different support stages is fluid and consistent, enhancing the overall customer experience.

Furthermore, the role of human agents in an AI-enhanced environment will evolve. They will become more important curators and contributors to the knowledge base. As such, comprehensive training is essential for them to effectively use and augment the system. Ensuring that agents are well-versed in leveraging the AI tools at their disposal is crucial for maintaining the integrity and usefulness of the knowledge base.

For companies poised to thrive in a digital-first environment, the implementation of AI in knowledge management is a strategic imperative that promises to redefine the support landscape.

AI-Enhanced Support Case Lifecycle: Optimizing Agent Performance and Customer Satisfaction

Integrating artificial intelligence into the support case lifecycle offers transformative potential in customer-facing roles and in enhancing the behind-the-scenes workflows of support agents. AI can significantly streamline administrative tasks, which, while critical, can consume a disproportionate amount of an agent's time and energy. By offloading these tasks onto AI systems, agents can focus on delivering high-quality, personalized customer service.

AI can automate the drafting of routine customer emails, ensuring that communications are consistent and error-free. For instance, when a case is resolved, an AI system can automatically generate a summary email that includes the solution details, additional resources, or follow-up steps, all tailored to the specific issue and customer. This speeds up the resolution process and ensures that the customer receives all necessary information in a clear, professional format that is easy to follow.

Backlog management is another area where AI can offer substantial efficiencies. AI tools can prioritize cases based on urgency, complexity, and the customer's value or history with the company. By dynamically organizing the backlog (the number of unresolved—new and open tickets—customer support requests a company has over time), AI enables agents to tackle the most pressing cases first, improving response times and reducing the likelihood of issues falling through the cracks.

AI's natural language processing capabilities can be leveraged to create concise summaries of lengthy support interactions. These summaries provide agents with quick insights into case histories, making it easier for them to understand a customer's issue without going through pages of communication. This is especially beneficial when cases are transferred between agents or departments, as it ensures a smooth handover and continuity of service.

The qualitative benefits of AI in support case management are reflected in improved agent performance and customer satisfaction. Agents relieved from repetitive, time-consuming tasks report higher job satisfaction levels, lower stress, and increased capacity for creative problem-solving. A study by Accenture highlights that AI can boost productivity by up to 40 percent by enabling workers to focus on more complex work that requires human intervention.[49]

In terms of customer satisfaction, the efficiency gains from AI can lead to faster case resolutions. According to Salesforce's report, 68 percent of service agents believe automation and AI give them the time to provide more personalized service.[50]

With a Net Promoter Score (NPS) average of 24, the telecommunications sector holds the lowest industry average, according to the NPS Benchmarks Report.[51] Operational inefficiencies in contact centers play a major role in the low NPS for Digital Service Providers (DSPs). Most DSPs have been struggling with high call volumes and costs for a long time, and the pandemic has further caused an unprecedented spike in call volume. Self-service and all deflection leveraging the digital-first model helps DSPs to improve digital channel adoption. The digital-first model with an AI-based conversation engine integrates with back-end systems, RPA bots, and AI models. The digital-first model helps deflect 20–25 percent of the calls, reducing the abandonment rate from more than 20 percent to less than 5 percent and improving the chat containment rate by 50 percent. With this and more enablers presented in a *CloudTweaks* article, DSPs can digitize their contact center. Implementing them helps DSPs to improve the NPS score by 20–30 percent, reduce call volume by up to 40 percent, and save OpEx by 30 percent.[52] Empowering contact center agents with digital capabilities can yield a 30 percent improvement in productivity.

Companies that have implemented AI into their support workflows have seen notable improvements. For example, an Asian bank reported that by using AI, the transformation resulted in a doubling to tripling of self-service channel use, a 40–50 percent reduction in service interactions, and a more than 20 percent reduction in cost-to-serve.[53] Incidence ratios on assisted channels fell by 20–30 percent, improving the customer and employee experience.

AI enhances agent performance and directly influences customer satisfaction by automating administrative tasks, prioritizing workloads, and aiding in case summarization. The data points and testimonials from companies that have adopted AI in their support operations underscore its potential to revolutionize customer service. As businesses seek opportunities to optimize support workflows, AI stands out as a crucial tool for driving operational excellence and customer-centricity.

AI-Driven Post-Resolution Feedback: Shaping Customer Satisfaction and Recovery

The period following issue resolution is critical for assessing customer satisfaction and the overall effectiveness of the support provided. AI's role in this post-resolution phase is becoming increasingly important, as it can automate and refine the process of gathering feedback, analyze the results for actionable insights, and facilitate follow-up actions in both positive and negative scenarios.

AI-driven feedback tools can systematically reach out to customers after a service interaction to gauge their satisfaction. By using machine learning algorithms, these tools can tailor the questions to be more relevant to the customer's experience, potentially increasing the response rate and the quality of the feedback.

In scenarios where customers report high satisfaction, AI can identify the factors contributing to this positive outcome, such as speed of resolution, agent knowledge, or communication style. Recognizing these factors allows businesses to replicate successful strategies across the board. Conversely, in cases of dissatisfaction, AI can quickly flag issues and trigger an immediate follow-up. This rapid response to negative feedback is crucial for individual customer recovery efforts and identifying and rectifying systemic problems that could affect customer satisfaction on a larger scale.

The quantitative impact of AI on post-resolution feedback is significant. The survey response rate of a company is influenced by various factors, such as how engaged your customers are with your brand and whether you're delivering surveys in a way that's easy for them. On average, a good survey response rate ranges between 5 percent and 30 percent.[54] Leveraging AI to improve the gathering feedback of the customer's post-service experience, with user-friendly solutions in all languages, can be a game changer to increase the survey response rate to obtain more statistically relevant insights and help product managers and engineers identify issues that must be addressed quickly. Solutions like Usersnap have been reported to boost response rates by 60 percent.[55]

AI also plays a vital role in qualitative improvement by enhancing the overall customer experience. A well-timed and well-crafted follow-up can turn a neutral or negative experience into a positive one, reinforcing customer loyalty. In fact, a study by *Harvard Business Review* reveals that customers who have had a problem resolved quickly (less than 5 minutes) are more likely to make a repeat purchase than those who have never encountered an issue.[56]

Companies across many industries testify to the benefits of AI-driven post-resolution feedback. In this IBM Watson Assistant case study,[57] Watson assists with post-service follow-ups by analyzing customer feedback for sentiment and satisfaction. When dissatisfaction is detected, Watson helps categorize the feedback, determine the severity of the issue, and suggest or automate appropriate follow-up actions. For instance, it can route the feedback to the relevant department or generate a ticket for a service agent to reach out personally to the customer.

As the customer service and support landscape evolves, AI-driven feedback mechanisms will be pivotal in fostering lasting customer relationships and ensuring a culture of continuous service improvement.

From the inception of chatbots to the sophisticated implementation of predictive analytics, AI is not just reshaping customer service—it is redefining the principles of customer engagement and satisfaction. The advent of intelligent routing systems has paved the way for queries to find their perfect match in support agents, ensuring that customer concerns are addressed by the most capable hands. The emergence of sentiment analysis and voice recognition technologies has given rise to a new understanding of customer behavior, allowing businesses to respond with unprecedented empathy and precision. AI-driven knowledge bases and self-service portals empower customers with the information they seek at their fingertips, fostering a sense of autonomy and efficiency. AI's role in post-resolution feedback has unveiled new dimensions of customer care, turning every end of a support ticket into the beginning of deeper insights and opportunities for service refinement.

Beyond the numbers and case studies, the narrative of AI in customer service is fundamentally about enhancing human connection. AI's true success lies in its ability to equip human agents with the tools they need to provide exceptional service, to anticipate customer needs before they are fully expressed, and to respond to feedback with genuine care and effective solutions. With each passing day, AI is not just assisting service; it is leading the charge toward a future where every customer interaction is an opportunity to delight, to solve, and to build lasting relationships. As we look to the horizon, the potential of AI in customer service and success is boundless, limited only by our imagination and the depth of our commitment to the customers we serve.

Endnotes

1   IBM. 2023. "Digital customer care in the age of AI." IBM Blog. 2023. [https://www.ibm.com/downloads/cas/GQDGPZJE].

2   Bamberger, Simon, Nicholas Clark, Sukand Ramachandran, and Veronika Sokolova. 2023. "How Generative AI Is Already Transforming Customer Service." BCG. July 6, 2023. [https://www.bcg.com/publications/2023/how-generative-ai-transforms-customer-service].

3   "ChatGPT," n.d. [https://openai.com/chatgpt].

4   "Gemini—Google DeepMind," n.d. [https://deepmind.google/technologies/gemini/#introduction].

5   Google DeepMind. "Building Safer Dialogue Agents," September 22, 2022. [https://deepmind.google/discover/blog/building-safer-dialogue-agents/].

6   "Claude \ Anthropic," n.d. [https://www.anthropic.com/claude].

7   "Llama," n.d. [https://llama.meta.com/].

8   Perez, Sarah. 2023. "Spotify spotted developing AI-generated playlists created with prompts." TechCrunch, October 2, 2023. [https://techcrunch.com/2023/10/02/spotify-spotted-developing-ai-generated-playlists-created-with-prompts/?guccounter=1&guce_referrer=aHR0cHM6Ly93d3cuYmluZy5jb20v&guce_referrer_sig=AQAAAJMR_8dtC9dptDzNMnmYDwKbwZelnSQkTrKpWsg1oDzLkDCgLGeECVIhpEinGHagJTUgRG1eB20xQ9mhz4MW0a4Z0Yxvc5BFxgBrH3sxnQe9doWLENmh2dFiQCm5VZLopkHqrkyGmYVLVWrWsf5ErWiPPGpH0U9WvgRcZo-6qOto].

9   Hillary. 2023. "Exploring Amazon's Advanced Recommendation Systems Driven by AI: A Behind-the-Scenes Look." TechBullion. September 11, 2023. [https://techbullion.com/exploring-amazons-advanced-recommendation-systems-driven-by-ai-a-behind-the-scenes-look/].

10 AI Expert Network. 2023. "Case Study: Zara's Comprehensive Approach to AI and Supply Chain Management." AI Expert Network. September 23, 2023. [https://aiexpert.network/case-study-zaras-comprehensive-approach-to-ai-and-supply-chain-management/].

11 Mishra, Anupama. 2019. "Case Study: Sephora's Adoption of Chatbots." LinkedIn. June 20, 2018. [https://www.linkedin.com/pulse/case-study-sephoras-adoption-chatbots-anupama-mishra/].

12 Atsmon, Y., Baroudy, K., Jain, P., Kishore, S., McCarthy, B., Nair, S., Saleh, T. 2021. "Tipping the scales in AI." McKinsey & Company. April 23, 2021. [https://www.mckinsey.com/industries/technology-media-and-telecommunications/our-insights/tipping-the-scales-in-ai].

13 Evdelo. 2020. "Amazon's recommendation algorithm drives 35% of its sales." Evdelo. July 3, 2020. [https://evdelo.com/amazons-recommendation-algorithm-drives-35-of-its-sales/#:~:text=That%E2%80%99s%20the%20power%20of%20personalization,com%E3%80%91].

14 McAlone, Nathan. 2016. "Why Netflix thinks its personalized recommendation engine is worth $1 billion per year." Business Insider. June 14, 2016. [https://www.businessinsider.com/netflix-recommendation-engine-worth-1-billion-per-year-2016-6#:~:text=And%20Netflix%20thinks%20it%E2%80%99s%20worth%20a%20lot%20of,recommendations%20save%20us%20more%20than%20%241B%20per%20year.%22].

15 Didion, I., Hernandez, P., Kaushik, A., Masri, K. 2019. "Operations management reshaped by robotic automation." McKinsey & Company. December 6, 2019. [https://www.mckinsey.com/capabilities/operations/our-insights/operations-management-reshaped-by-robotic-automation].

16 Shopify Staff. 2023. "AI in Ecommerce: Applications, Benefits and Challenges." Shopify. June 13, 2023. [https://www.shopify.com/blog/ai-ecommerce].

17 Brandon, John. 2017. "How OpenTable uses AI to find you Maine lobster and your favorite seat." VentureBeat. July 11, 2017. [https://venturebeat.com/ai/httpswww-opentable-comstarthome/].

18 Rubkiewicz, Anna. 2023. "5 Companies Using AI for Customer Service." Hubspot. October 23, 2023. [https://blog.hubspot.com/service/companies-using-ai-for-customer-service].

19 Callaham, John. 2023. "Microsoft Copilot for Service revealed to help customer agents with generative AI features." Neowin. November 15, 2023. [https://www.neowin.net/news/microsoft-copilot-for-service-revealed-to-help-customer-agents-with-generative-ai-features/].

20 Krysik, Arkadiusz. 2021. "Netflix Algorithm: Everything You Need to Know About the Recommendation System of the Most Popular Streaming Portal." Recostream. August 3, 2021. [https://recostream.com/blog/recommendation-system-netflix].

21 Hillary. 2023. "Exploring Amazon's Advanced Recommendation Systems Driven by AI: A Behind-the-Scenes Look." TechBullion. September 11, 2023. [https://techbullion.com/exploring-amazons-advanced-recommendation-systems-driven-by-ai-a-behind-the-scenes-look/#:~:text=Amazon%E2%80%99s%20recommendation%20system%20has%20proven,would%20not%20return%20to].

22 Zendesk. "See why Answer Bot is the smartest thing since self-service." Zendesk. 2023 [https://www.zendesk.com/campaign/answer-bot/].

23 Microsoft. 2023. "Microsoft Translator Languages." [https://www.microsoft.com/en-us/translator/languages/].

24 Sutherland. 2022. "New AI-driven language translation tool lets Spotify grow its service capabilities and customer engagement." December 16, 2022. [https://www.sutherlandglobal.com/insights/communications-media-and-entertainment/new-ai-driven-language-translation-tool-lets-spotify-grow-its-service-capabilities].

25 Gocheva, Cvetilena. 2023. "Samsung: A Lesson in Customer Experience and Crisis Management." CustomerGauge. 2023. [https://customergauge.com/benchmarks/blog/samsung-customer-experience-and-crisis-management].

26 Cardona-Smits, K., Jacobs, I. 2021. "How AI And Automation Drive Better Customer Service Experiences." Forrester. February 15, 2021. [https://www.forrester.com/report/how-ai-and-automation-drive-better-customer-service-experiences/RES152575].

27 Winchurch, Emily. 2020. "Independent study finds IBM Watson Assistant customers accrued $23.9 million in benefits." IBM. March 2, 2020. [https://www.ibm.com/blog/independent-study-finds-ibm-watson-assistant-customers-accrued-23-9-million-in-benefits/].

28 Benchmark Team. 2023. "8 Simon Sinek Quotes That Will Change the Way You Do Business." Benchmark. February 24, 2023. [https://www. benchmarkemail.com/blog/simon-sinek-quotes-will-change-your-business/].

29 Columbus, Louis. 2021. "76% of Enterprises Prioritize AI & Machine Learning in 2021 IT Budgets." Forbes. January 17, 2021. [https://www.forbes.com/sites/ louiscolumbus/2021/01/17/76-of-enterprises-prioritize-ai--machine-learning-in-2021-it-budgets/?sh=be22db3618a3].

30 Ó Searcóid, Colm. 2021. "How Chatbot Metrics Influence Customer Service Outcomes." GetJenny. March 19, 2021. [https://www.getjenny.com/blog/ how-chatbot-metrics-affect-customer-service].

31 Brand Rated. 2022. "Nine out of ten customers read reviews before buying a product." GlobeNewswire. January 13, 2022. [https://www.globenewswire. com/news-release/2022/01/13/2366090/0/en/Brand-Rated-Nine-out-of-ten-customers-read-reviews-before-buying-a-product.html].

32 SuperOffice. 2024. "32 Customer Experience Statistics You Need to Know for 2024." SuperOffice. May 24, 2024. [https://www.superoffice.com/blog/ customer-experience-statistics/].

33 Shep Hyken. 2017. "Are You Part Of The $62 Billion Loss Due To Poor Customer Service?" Forbes. April 1, 2017. [https://www.forbes.com/sites/ shephyken/2017/04/01/are-you-part-of-the-62-billion-loss-due-to-poor-customer-service/?sh=7fb257747e5f].

34 Gallo, Amy. 2014. "The Value of Keeping the Right Customers." Harvard Business Review. October, 29 2014. [https://hbr.org/2014/10/ the-value-of-keeping-the-right-customers].

35 Research and Markets. 2024. "The Interactive Voice Response Systems Market." Research and Markets. March 2024. [https://www.researchandmarkets.com/ report/interactive-voice-response].

36 Bhattacharyya, Suman. 2022. "Bank of America wants a human bridge for its AI help." Banking Dive. December 12, 2022. [https://www.bankingdive.com/ news/bank-america-erica-chatbot-virtual-assistant-human-middle-interaction-gopalkrishnan/638523/].

37 Nuance Communications. "BNP Paribas Personal Finance optimizes its customer service with the addition of a virtual assistant." Nuance Communications. 2020. [https://www.nuance.com/asset/en_us/collateral/ enterprise/case-study/cs-bnp-paribas-personal-finance-optimizes-its-customer-service-with-the-addition-of-a-virtual-assistant-en-us.pdf].

38 Crosman, Penny. 2023. "JPMorgan Chase using advanced AI to detect fraud." American Banker. July 3, 2023. [https://www.americanbanker.com/news/ jpmorgan-chase-using-chatgpt-like-large-language-models-to-detect-fraud].

39 Cavanaugh, Claire. 2023. "Top Augmented Reality Applications in the Automotive Industry." PTC. July 11, 2023. [https://www.ptc.com/en/blogs/ar/ top-augmented-reality-applications-in-the-automotive-industry].

40 Pressclub Global. 2019. "Fast, efficient, reliable: Artificial intelligence in BMW Group Production." BMW Group. July 15, 2019. [https:// www.press.bmwgroup.com/global/article/detail/T0298650EN/ fast-efficient-reliable:-artificial-intelligence-in-bmw-group-production].

41   Pressclub Global. 2017. "Smart Data Analytics: BMW Group relies on intelligent use of production data for efficient processes and premium quality." BMW Group. August 31, 2017. [https://www.press.bmwgroup.com/global/article/detail/T0273931EN/smart-data-analytics:-bmw-group-relies-on-intelligent-use-of-production-data-for-efficient-processes-and-premium-quality].

42   Khalidi, Yousef. 2017. "Announcing Azure Network Watcher—Network Performance Monitoring and Diagnostics Service for Azure." Microsoft Azure Blog. February 22, 2017. [https://azure.microsoft.com/en-us/blog/announcing-azure-network-watcher-network-performance-monitoring-and-diagnostics-service-for-azure/].

43   Dixon, Matthew, Ponomareff, Lara, Turner, Scott, DeLisi, Rick. 2017. "Kick-Ass Customer Service." Harvard Business Review. January-February 2017. [https://hbr.org/2017/01/kick-ass-customer-service].

44   Young Entrepreneur Council. 2020. "4 Customer Service Trends You Need to Know in 2020." Inc. January 17, 2020. [https://www.inc.com/young-entrepreneur-council/4-customer-service-trends-you-need-to-know-in-2020.html].

45   Acefone. 2024. "Chatbots and Human Agents: Which is Better for Customer Service?" Acefone. February 29, 2024. [https://www.acefone.com/blog/chatbots-vs-humans/].

46   Satterwhite, Staci. 2023. "Social(izing) the Experience." Contact Center Pipeline. September, 2023. [https://www.contactcenterpipeline.com/Article/socializing-the-experience#:~:text=According%20to%20Gartner%2C%20service%20leaders,and%20the%20company's%20bottom%20line.].

47   HappyFox. "30 Must Know Chatbot Statistics in 2021." HappyFox Blog. April 6, 2021. [https://blog.happyfox.com/chatbot-statistics/].

48   Elastic. "Cisco creates AI-powered search experiences with Elastic on Google Cloud." Elastic. [https://www.elastic.co/customers/cisco].

49   Texta. "Supercharge Your Business Efficiency: How AI Technology Can Boost Productivity by 40%." Texta. [https://texta.ai/blog-articles/supercharge-your-business-efficiency-how-ai-technology-can-boost-productivity-by-40percent].

50   Salesforce. 2023. "Sales, Service, and Generative AI: New Research on What's Holding Teams Back." Salesforce. June 28, 2023. [https://www.salesforce.com/news/stories/sales-service-research-generative-ai/].

51   Khanna, Rajesh. 2021. "Digitizing Contact Center to Reduce Call Volume by 30% and Improve NPS." CloudTweaks. March 30, 2021. [https://cloudtweaks.com/2021/03/digitizing-contact-center-reduce-call-volume/].

52   Khanna, Rajesh. 2021. "Digitizing Contact Center to Reduce Call Volume by 30% and Improve NPS." CloudTweaks. March 30, 2021. [https://cloudtweaks.com/2021/03/digitizing-contact-center-reduce-call-volume/].

53   McKinsey & Company. 2023. "The Next Frontier of Customer Engagement: AI-Enabled Customer Service." McKinsey & Company. March 27, 2023. [https://www.mckinsey.com/capabilities/operations/our-insights/the-next-frontier-of-customer-engagement-ai-enabled-customer-service].

54   Chung, Lucia. "What is a Good Survey Response Rate for Online Customer Surveys?" Delighted. [https://delighted.com/blog/average-survey-response-rate].

55 Prochazka, Tomas. "The AI Revolution in Customer Insights with 7 Examples." Usersnap. [https://usersnap.com/blog/customer-insights-ai/].

56 Huang, W., Mitchell, J., Dibner, C., Ruttenberg, A., Tripp, A. 2018. "How Customer Service Can Turn Angry Customers into Loyal Ones." Harvard Business Review. January 16, 2018. [https://hbr.org/2018/01/how-customer-service-can-turn-angry-customers-into-loyal-ones].

57 Purkayastha, Shyam. 2018. "Realtime Customer Feedback Analysis with IBM Watson Natural Language Classifier." Medium. February 25, 2018. [https://medium.com/@shyampurk/realtime-customer-feedback-analysis-with-ibm-watson-natural-language-classifier-cc411593ae4d].

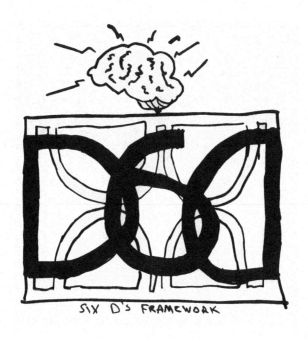

SIX D'S FRAMEWORK

PART II

Building AI Models Using Proprietary Content: The 6Ds Framework

We've explored the basics of understanding Generative AI and how this innovative technology can enhance and improve the customer service and support industry to propel the customer's experience to a new level. In this second part of the book, we will discuss integrating AI into customer support organizations and how doing so requires a robust and flexible visionary approach and a strategic plan. We'll discuss benchmarking against industry standards to ensure that the AI vision aligns with the company's overarching goals.

We'll also take you through the 6Ds Framework—discover, design, develop, diagnose, deploy, and detect, giving you a detailed understanding of what it will take to integrate AI into your support organization and how to go about doing it:

- The journey begins with the **discover** phase, where organizations identify opportunities for AI to enhance customer interactions and operational efficiency. This phase involves developing personas, identifying your target audience, thinking through data collection methodologies, and content curation.

- Next, the **design** phase focuses primarily on content design, identifying gaps in your support content, creating content in ways for the AI model to ingest to deliver accurate results, and content management—and begins the discussion on responsible AI and other design considerations that will add value to the customer experience.

- The **develop** stage sees the translation of design blueprints into functional AI models, which are then rigorously trained and tested to meet predefined performance metrics.

- The **diagnose** phase is where your AI models are evaluated for accuracy, reliability, security, and fairness with a keen eye on ethical considerations that could impact customer and support agent trust.

- The **deploy** phase marks transitioning from a controlled development environment to a real-world application. It requires detailed planning to ensure seamless integration with existing support technology and processes. We'll also discuss finding and leveraging your super users to help motivate others, and other considerations as you look to deploy AI within your support organization.

- Finally, the **detect** phase is about the ongoing process of monitoring your AI model's performance, gathering feedback regarding its accuracy, and making continual improvements to keep pace with model drift, changing customer needs, and technological advancements.

This detailed approach to AI design, creating, training, deployment, and integration will help you build models to empower your support agents and enhance the customer support experience while positioning your organization to thrive in the coming AI future.

4

Vision of Success

For I dipped into the future,
far as human eye could see,
saw the Vision of the world,
and all the wonder that would be.

—Alfred Lord Tennyson

Before we embark on a learning path to discover the 6Ds Framework in the next chapter, it's worth spending a few moments on some of the important strategic elements required as you begin to make decisions for the implementation of AI in customer service and support.

A Vision of Success

As you and your organization begin the AI journey, it is critical to develop a strong vision. Having a clear vision for any project is paramount to its success. Most importantly, it serves as a guiding light, illuminating the path toward the project's goals. A well-defined vision ensures that all team members are on the same page and working together as a cohesive unit. It helps set priorities, make decisions, and allocate resources efficiently, thus saving time and money.

Furthermore, a clear vision inspires and motivates stakeholders by vividly portraying the desired outcome, making the project more compelling. It enhances accountability, as everyone understands their role and responsibilities. Additionally, it facilitates adaptability, allowing for informed adjustments when necessary without losing sight of the ultimate objective.

A clear vision is the cornerstone for a successful project, providing direction, motivation, and a solid framework for achievement. Defining and creating a vision is critical to any well-run project or other endeavor and should include many core components to ensure success. Putting the initial work into this vision is important as it truly will become your guiding light throughout the journey. A few top items to consider as you work through your vision include:

- **Look ahead to the future:** This is your opportunity to dream big. How will your business evolve in the next 3–5–10 years? What will your customers expect and need? What will success look like? Your vision will be considered your guiding light, both as a beacon as well as a set of guardrails. So, while it's important to dream big, you must also consider whether the dream is achievable and what you may have to forsake to achieve it. Your stakeholders need to be motivated and believe their hard work will pay off. Therefore, ensuring success is within the realm of possibility is important.

- **Choose language wisely:** With a vision statement, you want people to feel the connection and understand the goal. Try to infuse inspiration and passion into your statement through your choice of words. You also want it to be simple enough to be understood by all, so avoid complicated words and other jargon. It's a good practice to write your vision statement as if it's already happening, which will help create a sense of immediacy. You can leverage Generative AI models to help you define and craft your vision, but don't let them do it all. Ensure the vision is in your own voice.

- **Keep in mind business values and goals:** Any vision statement should closely align with the overall goals and values of your company and organization. Employees need to feel the work they do accrues to a higher purpose and by aligning your organization's vision to the broader company's vision will help them see the big picture.

Just as important as creating the initial vision, it's vital to revisit the vision often and course-correct as needed. This allows you to adjust your plan as technology and/or business objectives change. Especially with the pace of change and innovation that we're seeing with AI, it will be imperative that you stay abreast of what's on the horizon and agile in your development and deployment of AI solutions to best meet your customer's needs and those of your organization. In addition, the continued revisiting and adjustment of your vision will ensure it remains inspiring and relevant over the project's lifecycle.

Creating your vision is important for a successful project, and so is ensuring all your stakeholders are on board, inspired, and excited about the vision and where it will take the organization. Especially for new projects that could cause potential angst, communicating early and often is key for others to get comfortable with your direction and start to process what it means for them specifically.

Share your vision with your organization to align your team and stakeholders and help them get on board with the strategic decisions. Developing key messages that are clear and consistent will help bring credibility to the vision. You should always talk about the vision and what it means to the success of your organization in similar ways depending on your specific audience. If you are talking to your support engineers, you may talk about the impact of the vision and what it means to them one way. Then, in a meeting with customers, you will talk about the impact of the vision in a different way. Stick to the key messages you develop and tailor them to the audience. If you start to change the language drastically, you run the risk of confusing your audience. Introduce language that can elicit an emotional connection for your audience. Aligning to their values and aspirations can be a powerful tool.

Communicate your vision in as many ways and places as possible and as often as possible. Make an inspiring video and put posters on your office walls. Backgrounds can be added to your video calls and also make for good advertising and communication of your vision. Continuous reinforcement will help your vision become a reality. Ensure your engagement with your audience is always a two-way street, and encourage them to provide feedback often. Acknowledge and address the positive input and any concerns raised if you receive feedback. This will help your audience feel heard and that their opinions are valued. Including anonymous channels for collecting feedback is a recommended best practice to be as inclusive of as many opinions as possible.

Use storytelling as an element to get your vision across to your audience. Using metaphors can be a great way to help your audience understand new concepts. In addition to sharing stories about the impact and benefits of the vision, stories of people tend to bring an additional emotional connection and will make your vision more memorable. Visual aids such as an infographic or picture and storytelling elements will also help your stakeholders more easily retain the information you share.

Be a role model and demonstrate your commitment to your vision through your actions. The behavior you expect from others should be something that you showcase often. If you don't provide a good example of how you want others to behave, they will not naturally follow.

Empower champions or other people across your organization to help you. It's hard for you to be in multiple places at once, and allowing others to participate is beneficial. Champions can be anyone willing to step up and help engage and influence others. Your managers can also help carry the message. Employees look to managers for what they need to know and when they need to know it. You set the tone, direction, and message, ensuring others are on board and equipped to share.

And celebrate success! It's great to celebrate along the way during different milestone achievements. Don't save all the celebrating until the end. Celebrating milestones with your stakeholders can be a motivating factor when significant progress is made toward your vision.

Developing the Plan

Throughout this book, we often discuss many elements required to successfully implement AI in your customer service and support organization. And it all begins with the plan. Thoughtful planning will ensure a successful outcome. Now that your vision is set and you're working through inspiring your stakeholders, it's time to get the plan in place.

The plan for implementing AI in a customer service organization is not just about developing a project plan with key milestones and metrics and calling it done. A lot of thought and decisions will need to be made to turn your vision into reality.

Do your homework and learn about AI and what will be needed to develop and deploy this technology within your support organization. Play around with it and explore the different opportunities to leverage it in your support organization to improve operations and employee and customer satisfaction.

Once you understand more about AI, you will be ready to look deeply at your business and identify pain points, areas for improvement, and tasks where you believe AI can increase efficiency. Keep the customer and employee experience in mind throughout this process.

It's then time to build your AI strategy and determine the specific AI integration points and components that align with your business values, goals, and vision for the future. You'll also need to evaluate your company's readiness to adopt AI, including any technology needs, gaps, and available technical expertise. You should also consider whether AI integration is something you want to manage in-house or work with external partners and vendors to help. We discuss this in later chapters, including the pros and cons.

Determine the Level of Investment

The most common project elements are broken down into three categories: schedule, cost, and scope. Before starting any type of project, you should consider each of these elements in alignment with your goals to determine the level of investment you're willing to make. You will often have to make trade-offs between these three categories, so you want to move forward with your eyes wide open to expectations and knowledge of what levers you are willing to pull to reach your goal.

Define the Desired State

We'll talk more about a well-defined AI model scope in Chapter 5, the discover phase, which can be used in conjunction with your desired goals and the end state you want to see for your business. Note that AI technology is changing and evolving so quickly that the end state may be hard to determine at the project outset, so perhaps the goal setting and desired state only encompass a first milestone or a pilot.

Be transparent with the goals and desired state, particularly with your end users or those impacted by the deployment. Without sharing up front, you risk success as users will react unexpectedly to the new technology being forced on them for what they perceive as no apparent reason.

SMART Goals

There are lots of goal-setting guidelines and frameworks. One that works well is developing SMART (Specific, Measurable, Achievable, Relevant, and Time-bound) goals. In general, goals that drive success should be clear and achievable.[1] The SMART framework helps you test your goals to ensure your constituents will understand them. Here's a more detailed breakdown of what each letter in the SMART acronym entails in building these goals:

- **Specific:** Goals need to be clear and specific to be actionable. Instead of setting a vague goal like "improve customer service," a specific goal might be "reduce days to close for customer cases by 20 percent." This specific goal is then clearly measurable (assuming a baseline metric was set) and helps the organization trend toward the desired objective.

- **Measurable:** Goals must be measurable to track progress and determine whether they work. Measurable goals involve a specific, numeric, or quantitative target that clearly indicates success. For example, "Reduce monthly average resolution times by 15 percent" or "Respond to customer inquiries within 24 hours."

- **Achievable:** It's crucial that goals are attainable. Setting unrealistic goals can lead to frustration and burnout among employees. SMART goals ensure that objectives are challenging yet achievable. For instance, increasing customer satisfaction by 2 points in a month may be more feasible than targeting a 20-point improvement. Consider the use of OKRs (objectives and key results), which differ from traditional KPIs (key performance indicators) in that each measure or "key result" receives a grade rather than a pass/fail. An example of an OKR could be:

  - **Objective:** Increase support case deflection rate

  - **Key result #1:** Create 200 new self-help diagnostics

  - **Key result #2:** Conduct 15 training sessions to educate support engineers on the usage of new diagnostics

- **Relevant:** Goals should align with the organization's broader objectives and customers' needs. In customer service and support, relevant goals might focus on how AI can reduce common pain points or enhance the quality of interactions to better meet customer expectations. In any AI deployment project, having multilayer goals within the project is probably worthwhile. Perhaps a goal around return on investment (ROI) will matter for the executive suite, but at a team level, measures like adoption rate or training completion might be more appropriate and relevant and feel achievable to your front-line support engineers.

- **Time-bound:** Setting a timeframe creates urgency and account-ability. For example, committing to resolve 90 percent of customer issues within 24 hours provides a clear deadline, motivating customer service teams to prioritize and manage their workload effectively as long as they feel the goal is achievable. Again, with larger projects, it's worthwhile to go through a milestone-setting exercise and ensure that milestone goals are specifically time-bound. Perhaps milestone 2 depends on the completion of milestone 1, so careful consideration of time-based planning is important.

There are many benefits to implementing a SMART goal or a similar structured goal-setting process.

- **Success:** Specific, measurable goals enable organizations to track the success of their desired state. For the customer service industry, customer satisfaction is generally the ultimate measure of success, and SMART goals can help leaders make targeted improvements, resulting in higher satisfaction rates.

- **Enhanced Employee Performance:** As long as the SMART goal structure is followed, it can give employees a clear sense of purpose and direction, motivating them to perform at their best. The goals and the decisions about the choices around particular goals must be shared with the broader organization, particularly those impacted by the AI deployments.

- **Resource Allocation:** By setting achievable and relevant goals, organizations have a better idea of the time, effort, and cost needed for the project. Therefore, leaders can determine what matters most to the ultimate success and allocate resources appropriately.

- **Data-Driven Decision-Making:** SMART goals provide valuable data for making informed decisions. They allow the business to make ongoing adjustments throughout the project to map toward the desired end state.

Setting goals and using a model, such as SMART goals, is essential for driving toward the success of your AI model project. The structured goal-setting process improves the chances of achieving set objectives, motivating employees, and overall business success.

FROM ZENDESK

A great example from the ZenDesk Blog illustrates how zooming in on the who, what, why, and when questions help you create SMART goals specific to customer support.[2] In this example, the ultimate goal is aligned with the first-call response and reducing customers' wait time before being contacted by a support agent.

By answering the who, what, why, and when questions, you can narrow in on the specific things you need to focus on to accomplish this goal, essentially helping create a SMART goal.

Who: Does the goal have a clear target metric and person to drive and be held accountable for improvement?

Example: The target metric of responding to calls is determined to be 10 minutes or less based on the support manager, Mark, who's established fast turnaround times. Mark will also be responsible for the program.

What: Can you quickly explain the overall project goal in less than a sentence or two?

Example: To reduce long wait times for customers, Mark will meet with agents to determine possible causes driving longer than necessary wait times, such as staffing to support case volume ratios, process inefficiencies, technology issues, and so on.

Why: Can you clearly explain the current impact of what you want to improve on your team?

Example: Customers complain about long wait times, which decreases their overall satisfaction. Due to their long wait time and the issue they are calling for help with, customers are already frustrated when they reach a support agent and are more likely to have a negative impression of their support experience.

When: Does the goal have a timeline for when it needs to be accomplished?

Example: Mark will hold six-week weekly meetings to review progress on the first call response metric.

You can set your SMART goal based on the answers to your who, what, why, and when questions: "We will decrease our average support call wait times by 50 percent within six weeks by designing and implementing a targeted and detailed program led by Mark." Instead of relying on the original objective of lowering wait times, you've crafted a more specific, actionable, and detailed SMART goal to improve the customer's experience.

Industry Benchmarking

Benchmarking compares the organization's customer service and support practices and performance with those of other organizations in the same industry or domain. Benchmarking helps to identify best practices, gaps, and areas for improvement in your organization's customer service and support business. By benchmarking, organizations can learn from the successes and challenges of others and set realistic and attainable goals for their customer service and support teams.

Not only will benchmarking help organizations identify areas for improvement, it will also help them assess their own performance against a comparable company in the same industry and learn from the industry leaders. Following are some best practices to consider when conducting a benchmarking activity:

- **Understand what you want to learn by clearly setting your objectives:** Start by defining specific goals and objectives for the benchmarking process to help you focus on what's most important for your business success.

- **Select relevant metrics:** Identify the KPIs or metrics most relevant to your objectives and what you want to learn. Ensure these metrics are measurable, consistent with any recognized industry standard metrics, and aligned with your goals and desired state.

- **Choose appropriate companies to benchmark:** Select companies or organizations comparable to yours in terms of industry, size, and business model. Benchmarking against organizations with similar characteristics provides more meaningful insights.

- **Collect data:** Based on the metrics you selected to benchmark, gather comprehensive data on your organization's performance and the companies you're benchmarking against. Ensure data accuracy, consistency, and a comparable measurement process to help with meaningful comparisons once analyzed. For example, the tools you use to measure customer sentiment can vary greatly from company to company. Therefore, understanding the process and tools your benchmarking comparison companies use for customer sentiment will help you better analyze and interpret results.

- **Maintain confidentiality:** Ensuring the confidentiality of information shared by others is important to maintain trust and build relationships. Confidentiality agreements and ethical standards should be treated with care and respect and used solely for benchmarking purposes.

- **Benchmarking methods:** Consider using various benchmarking methods. These might include strategic methods, which would entail evaluating against similar long-term goals, comparing against your direct industry competition, comparing against a similar type of organization across industries (such as customer service organizations in different industries like technology or retail), or internal benchmarking whereby you are comparing different departments or divisions within your organization.

- **Finding best practices:** Don't focus solely on comparing quantitative results. Find and analyze best practices, processes, and strategies that lead to enhanced success. Understanding "how" something is accomplished can be as important as "what" was accomplished.

- **Be realistic:** Use benchmarking results to set realistic targets you can use to improve your own business processes. Avoid setting goals that are too aggressive or unattainable based on your own baseline data.

- **Ongoing benchmarking:** Market trends change over time, and by regularly revisiting benchmarks and adjusting strategies as a result of updated findings, you have a better chance of achieving continuous improvement.

- **Share insights:** Share your findings and insights with relevant stakeholders within your organization. Another common strategy is to share externally, positioning yourself or your organization as a thought leader in the space of interest. In sharing externally, be cautious of any confidentiality agreements made with others. By transparently sharing your results, you ensure that everyone is aligned with improvement efforts and will be ready to contribute.

- **Embrace innovation:** As you strive to improve your support organization's performance, be open to innovative ideas and change. Benchmarking should be seen as a way to get a pulse on what other companies are doing and evaluate if there is anything you also want to create and adopt.

- **Track progress:** If you've done your due diligence and created strong goals, continuously monitoring and tracking progress will be important. You can use updated benchmarking data to understand the impact of changes and adjust your strategies accordingly.

- **Documenting:** To track where you started from to where you are now, creating and maintaining a record of benchmarking activities, findings, and actions taken will be a valuable resource for any future benchmarking efforts and lessons learned as a result.

- **Find the experts:** Many consultants and companies specialize in benchmarking. They could assist in the design and execution of your study, providing guidance and an objective view.

These best practices can be a guide to better understanding what others are doing through benchmarking. Benchmarking has the benefit of informing your AI strategy to enhance competitiveness and achieve sustainable success.

Resource Allocation

Projects can't happen without carefully considering the overall budget, time, and people needed to complete all the necessary steps to make your vision a reality. Make sure you spend time creating a plan for what you need and how you will obtain the necessary resources to be successful.

Once you have a great plan in place, it's time to execute. Remember to revisit and adjust the plan often as you move forward through execution. AI innovation and technology are changing rapidly, and you may need to make quick decisions and adjust your plan accordingly to continue progressing toward your business goals, values, and vision.

AI deployment is a journey, and thoughtful planning ensures a successful transformation.

Getting Started

Once you have a strong vision, AI strategy, and plan in place, it's time to do the work to integrate AI into your support organization. This is no easy task and will take many people's time, investment, and effort. The following chapters covering the 6D Framework will help guide you through what's needed and how to create an AI model using your own support content. We encourage you to dive in, learn, and have fun!

Endnotes

1   Chi, Clifford. 2023. "5 Dos and Don'ts When Making a SMART Goal [+Examples]." Hubspot. June 09, 2023. [https://blog.hubspot.com/marketing/smart-goal-examples].

2   Zendesk editors. 2024. "SMART customer service goals to aim for in 2024." Zendesk. January 22, 2024. [https://www.zendesk.com/blog/set-smart-goals-for-customer-service/].

5

Discover: Laying the Foundation

Good order is the foundation of all things.

—Edmund Burke

The discover phase begins the process during which the team identifies and defines the goals and objectives or problems that need to be solved with AI. This is the opportunity to grasp the essence of the mission, the goals, and the hurdles. This period is saturated with probing research, exploration, curation, creation, meticulous analysis, and review.

The discover phase is arguably the most important of all six phases of the 6Ds Framework. Get this wrong, and the whole project can go off track quickly. Before embarking on this step, there must be a strong vision and a detailed project plan, as discussed in Chapter 4.

To get started, you need to understand your collective knowledge base architecture. Many customer service and support organizations have not invested heavily in documenting and organizing their collective knowledge. While there are knowledge bases filled over the years with articles, this tends to be a create, file, and forget exercise. Often, individuals are rewarded for their contributions, though review processes tend to happen around individual pieces of content and articles, not holistically across the library. The larger the organization, the more complex the knowledge base library can be.

As organizations set out to turn this content into documentation that AI models can accurately utilize, the first step is to discover and curate existing content.

In managing any project, setting goals and objectives is the framework that sets the project's direction and defines the structure. Goals and objectives provide clarity and purpose. Without a strong set of agreed-upon goals, a project can spin out of control, consume resources, and waste time without tangible results. The discover phase allows the organization to create a shared vision and align a variety of resources. Also, existing internal content is identified along with public data, and a thorough gap analysis is conducted to determine whether any content is missing. During this phase, you will begin understanding security and privacy policies and set the stage for a rigorous approach to accurate AI model building.

Mapping the Territory

The first step is to map the territory. You will identify your vision for where you want to apply these models, what aspect of the business or work you want to impact, and who your target user is. As with any mapping exercise, you want to identify your destination and key points along the journey, illustrate all the potential routes to get there, and identify your guides, hazards, and methods.

A map can be an incredibly useful tool to guide individuals through unknown territory, akin to an AI model guiding users by making informed predictions and identifying patterns within large amounts of data. As cartographers explore terrain, measuring distances and noting landmarks, AI model builders work to gather relevant data, ensuring it's robust and representative of desired goals and will accurately predict outcomes. The meticulous content curation, cleaning, and preprocessing process parallels refining raw geographical data into a usable format.

Defining a Clear Scope

Building AI models requires a clearly defined scope. As model builders enter the discover phase, keeping focus and scope content curation to the model is important. It's easy to go too broad or too narrow when gathering content. Defining and then constantly revisiting the AI model's purpose, target audience, constituents, and goal is a key component of the discover phase.

Developing an Ideal User Persona

Merriam-Webster defines persona as "a character assumed by an author in a written work."[1] In software development and deployment, personas can help developers better understand the end user. "The use of personas, fictional people, in product design is widely heralded." as noted in a Microsoft research paper titled "Personas: Practice and Theory."[2] Additionally, the same paper references a book by Alan Cooper titled *The Inmates Are Running the Asylum*, noting that "designers often have a vague or contradictory sense of their intended users and may base scenarios on people similar to themselves."[3] Cooper's "goal-directed design" provides focus through the creation of fictional personas whose goals form the basis for scenario creation. You need to clearly define and know your end user audience by understanding who they are, what they do, how they work, what they will expect of the AI model output, and how they will use it.

Identifying the Target Audience

Many variables define your target audience. While it might seem too detailed to develop a list of your customers' behaviors and your customer service and support professionals' characteristics, it's not. You are developing and deploying an AI model to talk to your end users. If you know, for example, that 90 percent of the audience is under 30 years old, the "personality" of the AI model you build can be made more relevant to that audience. For example, if a sizeable percentage of your audience has art as a hobby, a different approach will be more relevant and better engage the users.

Demographics

In developing personas, understanding the demographics of the target audience or end user is an important first step. Many demographics can be considered, though the specific demographics may vary by your business type. For example, those developing an AI model for HR professionals may choose different demographics to focus on in their persona creation than those developing a model for sales professionals. Some examples of demographics you may want to consider include gender, age, education, race/ethnicity, occupation/role, geographic location, spoken languages, disability status, country of birth, and so on.

The more specific you can be when determining who your end users are, the more aligned your AI model will be to their specific and desired use scenarios. Multiple personas might need to be considered for your AI model.

Psychographics

Merriam-Webster describes psychographics as "market research or statistics classifying population groups according to psychological variables (such as attitudes, values, or fears)."[4] Because demographics touch on a person's physical or observable characteristics, psychographics are considered the psychological characteristics of a person, such as their values, attitudes, personality traits, fears, social attitudes, behavioral intentions, and so on. These characteristics tell you more about why your end users will engage with your AI model and what their preferences and internal motivations may be.

Behavioral Traits

Developing representative personas to help build useful and impactful models will also benefit from looking at behaviors. How do the end users interact with customers? Are they usually in problem-solving mode, or are they in a situation where they actually can't solve problems and are in empathy and compassion mode? Are they getting yelled at and have to behave with patience? As you develop personas to share with those building your AI models, it's important to ask these questions. It's also possible that all these behaviors are demonstrated over the course of a month or year by the target audience.

Data Collection Methods

Utilizing a variety of data collection techniques when building personas is crucial for a number of reasons. First, using different data collection methods will provide a variety of insights and perspectives because different people respond well to different methods. Someone great at taking time to fill out a survey or questionnaire may not be able to invest the same time in doing an interview. Different techniques will provide a more comprehensive view and a holistic understanding of behaviors, needs, and preferences. In addition, using a variety of methods to collect user data will allow you to triangulate that data and validate and cross-verify the reliability of the results. This will also help reduce and eliminate biases. Interviews will give great qualitative insights, while surveys can scale and cross-reference those insights with quantitative data. Combined, these will enable better data-driven decisions about creating personas representing the user.

A blend of data collection techniques ensures that the personas developed are robust, reliable, and truly representative of the user base, thereby facilitating the creation of user-centered designs and strategies.

Qualitative versus Quantitative Data

Qualitative data is often characterized as non-numeric information and is gathered through open-ended surveys, interviews, or observations. It helps you better understand people's underlying emotions, motivations, and perspectives.

Quantitative data, on the other hand, is numerical, allowing for deeper statistical analysis and identification of patterns. It's normally collected through surveys and other analytic methods and focuses on relaying information quantifying different variables like user demographics.

Quantitative means "of, relating to, or involving the measurement of quantity or amount."[5] Basically, get a lot of data! A quantitative approach is important in understanding user needs because it provides objective, measurable data that can be used to make informed decisions.[6] Some examples of quantitative data include end-user surveys and product/service telemetry. Quantitative data can help with the following:[7]

- Find patterns and averages
- Make predictions
- Test causal relationships
- Generalize results to wider populations

Quantitative research methods offer powerful tools for analysis and are particularly proficient at providing precise measurements and numerical data to support conclusions. Three primary methodologies stand out: descriptive, correlational, and experimental research. Each methodology serves a distinct purpose in uncovering insights from data:[8]

- In descriptive research, you simply seek an overall summary of your user behavior.
- In correlational research, you investigate relationships between variables.
- In experimental research, you systematically examine whether there is a cause-and-effect relationship between variables.

Researchers can gain deeper insights by employing these methodologies, facilitating informed decision-making and hypothesis testing.

Surveys and Questionnaires

Surveys and questionnaires are a great way to gather data to build user personas. To get the most out of the information collected, it's important to ensure your questions are clear and relevant, and each question is designed to gather insightful content that is also easily understood by respondents to limit any confusion on how to answer. Equally important is a focus on developing the survey or questionnaire to take into account inclusive and accessible principles to accommodate the diversity of your audience, including language, culture, ability, and the like. This helps ensure your data is fully representative of your intended audience.

Privacy, security, and ethical considerations should also be considered to foster trust and encourage participation. Transparent communication regarding data usage, adherence to data protection regulations (which may vary by location), and anonymity are critical components to consider.

Survey design is an art of its own, but it's important to ask about both positive and negative experiences. In addition, many service and support professionals have been concerned about being replaced by bots and AI for years, so getting a temperature check on this issue is important. Depending on your organization's culture and size, this might be better accomplished through interviews versus a survey, but it is important to understand before developing persona(s).

Here are some reasons why quantitative surveys and data collection are important:

- **Quantifiable results:** Quantitative surveys produce numerical data that can be easily analyzed and offer a point of view. This makes it easier to compare results across different surveys and identify data trends and patterns.

- **Large sample sizes:** Quantitative surveys can be administered to large sample sizes, which makes it possible to obtain statistically significant results.[9] This is important because it ensures that the results represent the population being studied.

- **Efficiency:** Quantitative surveys can be conducted quickly and efficiently, which makes them a cost-effective way to gather data. Computational horsepower makes it possible to process and analyze data quickly, even with large sample sizes.

- **Benchmarking:** A quantitative approach is useful to benchmark and quickly calculate return on investment (ROI). This is important because it provides a basis for comparison and helps to identify areas to focus on for improvement.

- **Less human bias:** Because of the objective nature of quantitative user research, the resulting data is less likely to have human bias as it's harder to lead participants to a certain outcome and has well-defined, strict, and controlled study conditions.

Quantitative methods are important tools to understand user needs because they provide objective, measurable data that can be used to make informed decisions. They are efficient, cost-effective, and produce quantifiable results that can be used for benchmarking and identifying areas for improvement.

Interviews to Collect Qualitative Data

The idea of conducting an interview and gathering valuable insights is to create an environment that encourages participants to share candid details of their experiences and motivations. The interviewer should lead with empathy and have a particular strategy in mind to help steer the conversation to elicit candid comments.

Question development can be a true art form in formulating open-ended and probing questions to get at the interviewee's underlying motivations, challenges, and experiences. Those interviewed will also be more open if they trust the process and the interviewer and will, therefore, be more authentic in their responses, leading to the crafting of more accurate personas. Ethical considerations, privacy, and information security are equally important in qualitative and quantitative data collection.

Field Research

While this sounds expensive and time-consuming, it could also be characterized as "surfing the web." You must understand the state of the art in your industry. What is the latest that's happening in the field of customer service and support? How are other companies deploying AI? How are customer service and support professionals responding to the deployment of AI? Read what people are writing about and compile a list of references and quotes that can feed into developing your personas.

Analytics and Usage Data

These data collection techniques will help gather demographic, psychographic, and behavioral data. A combined data collection approach will provide numbers and statistics—quantitative data—to help you shape your personas. For example, are your survey results from Spain and Portugal? Are they from women? Early career professionals? Qualitative data gathered through interviews will provide user stories and details that can help inform your persona development, which will, in turn, inform the development and deployment of your AI models.

Crafting the User Persona

Now that you have an armful of data—survey results, user stories, video interviews, and articles about your industry—it's time to select the most important and representative data to use as you write up your persona(s). You will likely have to make tradeoffs. The data may say one thing is a strong trend, and you might have one passionate story from an interviewee that conflicts with the quantitative data. You will have to choose what's right for your organization. Perhaps you can do both and let your developers make decisions independently, but the more prescriptive and representative you can be with your personas, the more successful you will be in building AI models that will best serve your service and support professionals.

Demographic Information

This will be a challenge. It's likely you don't have a 100 percent single demographic. Not all of your service professionals will be women under 30 living in large European cities, and they won't all be middle-aged male gamers who don't use text messaging. Choosing the right demographics when developing a persona involves aligning demographic variables with the goals and context of the AI that you are building. This helps ensure that the various persona demographics can provide meaningful insights regarding your audience's behavior, needs, and preferences.

Begin by identifying the key characteristics that differentiate user behaviors and preferences within your target audience. Similarities in your data will help you focus on traits that can be captured in a given persona.

Data science techniques like topic modeling and K-mean clustering can aid you in grouping your data into meaningful subsets.

Goals and Motivations

Utilizing the qualitative data gathered will help you understand the "what" and the "why" behind users' choices and interactions. This information gets to the heart of users' decision-making processes, value perceptions, and emotional landscapes, which are integral to crafting personas that reflect their realities. By taking this step to unearth the "why," you are better positioned to develop a genuinely user-centric persona, resulting in greater user satisfaction and engagement.

Quantitative survey data can verify user stories gathered during the interview process. It's also important to ensure goals and motivations are supported by—or at least not contradicted by—field research.

Pain Points and Challenges

It's difficult and maybe a bit awkward to face, address, and include the negative feedback you may get from surveys and interviews. However, this is the most important characteristic of the persona; negative aspects, fears, worries, and threats that your end users express need to be top of the list and a huge part of the identity you represent in your persona(s). The data scientists, machine learning professionals, and developers building your models need to hear about and understand the fears of your target audience. They need to understand the pain points, the challenges they face in their day-to-day tasks, and their hopes for what AI can bring to mitigate their daily challenges.

Persona Narration

This is where those developing personas need to lean on their creativity, using a combination of quantitative and qualitative data. User stories are important, but the narrative must also represent the user base, as quantitative results express.

Creating a Backstory

The first step here is to describe who this persona is. Give them a name. Describe their career. The more personal you can get, the better the representation. Again, quantitative results need to be part of the story. Here are a few representative examples to give you a feel for what this may look like.

- Meet Taylor, a dedicated customer service professional with six years of experience in the bustling e-commerce industry. Navigating through the dynamic, fast-paced environment, Taylor consistently prioritizes customer satisfaction, skillfully balancing empathy and efficiency. Outside work, Taylor enjoys exploring local cafes, engaging in community events, and is passionate about music and animal welfare. She often volunteers at shelters. She is excited by technological advances that are helping her in her job.

- Meet Travis, a recent college graduate who has just embarked on a career in customer service in the insurance industry. Eager yet slightly apprehensive, Travis navigates the initial challenges and learning curves of understanding customer needs and managing diverse inquiries. Travis enjoys sports, hiking, and experimenting with digital art in his free time, often sharing creations online.

- Meet Alexia, a seasoned customer service representative navigating through the evolving landscape of AI-driven customer support with a mix of curiosity and concern. With over a decade in the field, Alexia has witnessed the gradual shift toward automation and worries about job security and relevance in the future. Outside work, Alexia finds solace in gardening, reading sci-fi novels, and advocating for workers' rights and continuous learning in the community.

Defining the User Journey

As part of creating the persona, it's important to paint a picture of how the user will evolve. The more detailed you can be, the better. So, if we were to define Alexia's journey, we might say:

Despite the apprehensions regarding AI in customer service, Alexia embraces the technological tide and embarks on a journey of continuous learning and adaptation. Initially, Alexia invests time in understanding the basics of AI and its customer service applications through various online courses and training materials. This foundational knowledge demystifies AI, reducing anxiety and enabling Alexia to identify opportunities where AI can augment her work, such as handling repetitive queries and managing large datasets.

As Alexia progresses, she delves deeper into specialized training, learning how to manage and optimize AI-driven customer service tools, and understanding the nuances of integrating human and machine interactions to enhance customer experiences. Alexia has become proficient in utilizing AI to analyze customer data, predict trends, and personalize customer interactions, elevating service quality.

In the intermediate stage of Alexia's journey, she explores the ethical considerations and customer satisfaction implications of AI applications in customer service. Alexia becomes an advocate for maintaining a balance between technological efficiency and human empathy in customer interactions, ensuring that the human element remains prevalent in customer service.

As Alexia becomes adept at leveraging AI tools, she evolves into a hybrid professional who excels in traditional customer service skills and in managing and optimizing AI-driven customer support systems. Alexia begins to mentor and guide peers through their AI learning journeys, sharing insights and strategies for effectively integrating AI into their roles without losing the personal touch in customer interactions.

In the advanced stage, Alexia plays a pivotal role in shaping the organization's customer service strategy, ensuring it is both technologically advanced and deeply customer-centric. She is a true AI power user now. Alexia collaborates with tech teams to enhance AI tools, ensuring they are ethical, user-friendly, and genuinely beneficial to both the customer service team and the customers.

Alexia's journey from apprehension to mastery and advocacy in AI applications in customer service becomes a testament to the potential for growth, adaptation, and maintaining human-centricity in the age of AI, ensuring that technology serves to augment, not replace, the invaluable human element in customer interactions.

While this might seem like overkill and too much detail, it's not at all. The more work you can put into developing accurate and detailed personas, the better your AI will be, because you will truly know your audience. Many of those creating personas will include stock photo pictures and create fake Facebook or LinkedIn accounts. The more information you can provide to create a presentative end user, the better.

Visual Representation

Include a picture! Better yet, make a short, representative video of your persona interacting with future AI.

Use the data collected to find an image or stock photo representing your persona. Paste your description into DALL-E, Midjourney, or other AI imaging tools and ask it to create a photo. **Figures 5.1** and **5.2** show two examples for Alexia.

FIGURE 5.1 Alexia v1 from DALL-E

FIGURE 5.2 Alexia v2 from Midjourney

Designing the Persona Layout

This step is most important if you have multiple personas. There might be notable differences in your target audience's demographics, psychographics, or behaviors that will require multiple personas to be considered for your AI models. If this is the case, make an effort to ensure you have a standard layout and equivalent collateral. If you have multiple personas, it's unlikely that each persona is equivalent, and your layout should be representative. If 80 percent of your target audience is of a certain type, convey that to your AI model builders. However, if the other 20 percent is critical, make sure to share that information too.

Utilizing the User Persona in Design and Development

Depending on how your organization is laid out, it's likely that your deep data scientists and your software engineers (if you employ them at all within your company) don't sit closely alongside your customer service and support staff to understand the ins and outs of their work. Therefore, these personas will be a critical proxy to inform your AI development team of the characteristics of your users.

Personas will help your technical folks incorporate the needs, priorities, and practices of customer service and support personnel into their development practices to build models that will have an impact.

Feature Prioritization

Personas will help AI model builders and software engineers prioritize their work. Should they prioritize deployment over accuracy? Should they focus on eliminating bias? Should they focus on adding features that help with transparency? Are they building feedback tools for a staged deployment? These viable tradeoffs demand consideration and a project plan and help guide prioritization.

User Experience Design

Personas are a constant reminder of who your audience is, what they care about, and their needs and preferences. These are then considered throughout the design process and inform design elements such as navigation, layout, content, color theme, etc. The AI model design must align with the expectations and preferences of the target audience. In addition, personas help the design team prioritize features and functionality of the model by including what's most relevant to the users, resulting in an engaging experience.

In scenarios where design teams encounter differing opinions, the personas again can play a role in keeping the end user top of their mind and helping them navigate the decision-making process. In this way, personas enable the development of user experiences that are not only functional but also user-oriented.

Ensuring Alignment with Business Goals

Personas grew out of method acting, where actors create a full profile and take it as their own. For example, actor Daniel Day-Lewis is a well-known method actor who often stays completely in character throughout the filming of a movie, totally immersing himself in his role until a project is complete. While many actors still employ this practice, personas are now considered pivotal in business strategy and user-centered design. Originally adopted by Alan Cooper for software design, personas have transcended their theatrical origins to ensure that business goals are meticulously aligned with user needs and preferences.

By taking a user-centered approach and creating audience personas to better align products and services to users' needs, pain points, and behaviors, businesses are best able to meet market demands. Essentially, they create a bridge between customer needs and business goals, resulting in sustainable growth and customer loyalty.

You may have realized by now that your users may have different needs than the organization. Obviously, these needs must be rationalized and prioritized, which is a decision for each organization to work through on a case-by-case basis. Here are a few things that can help you decide how to adjust to ensure a balance can be struck between serving user and business needs.

It's important to ensure that the persona reflects both the genuine needs and challenges of customer support and service professionals and aligns with overarching organizational objectives. Develop strategies within the persona that address how customer service professionals can meet their needs while contributing to organizational goals.

If there is a disconnect, it's likely an indicator of a bigger problem. Facilitate open dialogue between front-line personnel and organizational leaders to understand the root cause of conflicting priorities. Integrate insights from both parties into the persona to ensure it is a collaborative tool that respects and acknowledges varied perspectives. Additional considerations to include:

- Ensure that the persona is adaptable and can be modified as the needs of customer service professionals and organizational objectives evolve.

Consider incorporating elements within the persona that facilitate continuous learning and development to align better with organizational objectives.

- Identify skills and knowledge gaps through the persona development process and implement training programs to bridge these gaps.

Ensure the persona does not advocate for or represent practices compromising customer service professionals' well-being or ethical standards.

- Integrate strategies within the persona that promote a healthy balance between achieving organizational objectives and maintaining a positive, healthy, and ethical work environment for customer service professionals.

Incorporating these considerations ensures that the developed persona is a tool used for understanding and empathizing with customer service professionals and a strategic instrument that facilitates the alignment and harmonization of potentially conflicting priorities between customer service and organizational objectives.

As AI work progresses, there must be regular check-ins to ensure that as the model-building work evolves to stay relevant with innovation and the needs of the business, there is open communication with the end users and target audience to ensure things are aligned.

Ongoing Persona Evaluation and Adjustment

As the organization evolves and learns, the models must evolve with them. Training materials must also evolve.

Persona creation is an ongoing journey. This is an iterative process, and you need to collect feedback. In theory, you could invest as much in the feedback process as you did in the original persona development. As you deploy the AI model, the lives of support professionals will change and a robust feedback process is necessary and will likely alter future direction. Spend time throughout the deployment and post-deployment effort to ensure you have feedback channels in place for a successful launch. The AI technology will change people's lives, period. That can be a positive thing or a negative thing. By building listening channels, you can gauge how the change is landing and being adopted and adjust your approach as needed.

As your AI developers build out the models, there will be a need to evolve or build new personas. For example, initial model creation to target a specific audience may be wildly successful, whereby the customer service user persona changes from engaging in manual search processes to a model of AI engagement. If unsuccessful, users may find the model inaccurate and revert to old habits. Therefore, building a feedback loop into the deployment process is critical to ensure that AI model builders focus on delivering user impact.

Content Curation

It's important in this stage to identify who your experts are. Content experts may reside in the content realm as well as in the user realm:

- Based on personas, assess the target user needs and data sources, understand how the AI model will connect with the wider service, and explore the location and condition of the data you will use.

- Assess the existing data, its accuracy, and readiness to see if the data has high enough quality for an AI system to make predictions from.

- Prepare your data to make sure it is secure and unbiased. Your data should also be diverse and reflective of the population you are trying to model; this will help reduce conscious and unconscious bias.

Setting Up the Content Ecosystem and Assessing User Needs

Likely, organizations have not built a content ecosystem to prepare for this AI-focused world. Many support organizations will have content management systems or a customer-facing library of support service documentation, but this is different. To train these AI models and build indexes, the domain experts must curate the internal knowledgebase articles and support content and identify and tag external content to help build a more comprehensive index.

In the past, customer service and support professionals have applied human intelligence to discern the appropriate content sources to solve a customer issue, pairing internal and external resources to provide the best service. As we think about a move to an AI-based support experience, it's now important to combine these internal and external sources to help train the most accurate models.

As you work to curate the content, you'll first need to understand who your users are and their specific needs. Without this information, your AI model may miss the mark.

Engage with Stakeholders

This is a critical step to perform early. Getting users to give early feedback or use the AI model will be hard if this step is skipped. Engaging and listening to concerns, requirements, feature requests, and content source inclusion is important. Understand the specific problem(s) the users want the model to solve. It could range from simple Q&A tasks to administrative tasks to more complex narrative generation.

By engaging with stakeholders, those who are developing AI models can understand the specific needs, expectations, and requirements of the end-users and other interested parties. This ensures that the AI system is developed to solve real-world problems and meet the actual needs of its users.

Ethical Considerations and Bias Mitigation

As we move into a new world where customer service agents, support engineers, and end users discover or augment their knowledge about how to fix issues by using an AI model instead of knowledgebase articles, web searches, or diagnostics, there are some new requirements you need to validate. Conversational AI will expose bias more clearly than these other knowledge-delivery methods or channels. An inherent bias in a troubleshooting guide (TSG), for example, historically might never be noticed. When a TSG is ingested into an AI model, and its content is served as a conversation, the bias may become more apparent or even offensive, such as referring to the end user as "he," or referring to the master/slave architecture in networking or cloud computing,[10] or referring to a "sanity check."[11] These are all things that, on the surface, don't seem offensive or unethical, but as these AI models learn, they might present these concepts in different circumstances that could be quite offensive.

Information must be presented concisely and verifiable to avoid misinterpretation or ambiguity. Ethical considerations should be strongly considered in creating documentation to ensure accuracy, inclusivity and clarity. Part of ethical behavior in documentation is how you respect intellectual property, maintain transparency across the AI model and provide credible references. All this will help lead to greater trust from users.

As you can likely imagine, eliminating bias in all documentation is incredibly difficult. Careful attention needs to be applied to the possible feelings generated by the interpretation of content, especially if that content is taken out of context of its original intent. What may appear biased to one person may not be interpreted similarly by someone else. This gets back to the persona's value and critically working through the persona's journey and experience with your desired model.

Following are three key tips as you think about the content you will index for your model:

- Use neutral language that is understood by many.
- Avoid jargon and acronyms.
- Ensure content is accessible to people of varying literacy levels, cultural backgrounds, and disabilities.

Once you've scrubbed your content and mitigated bias, be sure you return to it often by conducting regular audits to identify and fix any inadvertent stereotypes or biases. As you seek feedback from your users, be sure to listen carefully and then follow up on the feedback by considering and incorporating it into your AI model or, at a minimum, responding empathetically to your user if you cannot act on the feedback given. You may have heard the adage before, "feedback is a gift," and incorporating feedback from varied stakeholders ensures varied perspectives and additional information to make more informed choices.[12]

While you are mitigating bias in your content and taking into account ethical considerations, we also recommend investing in training for your support staff on the importance of unbiased communication and support delivery practices. Cultural competence, empathy, and active listening are skills that will serve support staff well and provide them with appropriate knowledge to check the AI model's output for any unconscious biases before responding to customers, driving greater customer experiences and trust. If bias happens to sneak through to a customer, it's important to quickly take accountability and put any corrective actions in place.

Similar to ensuring your content is bias-free and that you're paying attention to ethical considerations, it's important to consider the training set you're using for your AI model. Recruiting various stakeholders that can provide a wealth of knowledge, perspectives, and insights will help AI model builders and developers identify potential bias and ethical concerns in their AI model. Incorporating a variety of stakeholders will also assist in creating a more inclusive and diverse model that's less likely to overlook certain demographic groups or perpetuate harmful stereotypes. It also has the advantage of enhancing your stakeholder engagement and acceptance of the model.

Developing an AI model with an inclusive design approach will prioritize fairness, equity, and the mitigation of bias, ultimately ensuring ethical solutions are applied, helping safeguard users and customers. With increased oversight toward unwanted bias and ethical considerations, the opportunities for a more accurate and applicable model increase across different scenarios and user groups.

Taking a purposeful, customer-centric approach to content curation, including incorporating ongoing feedback and evaluation methods, will ensure organizations can foster a supportive environment that is respectful, equitable, and inclusive of all customers.

Risk Identification and Management

Content is presented differently in an AI model than in a document. As we know, generative AI predicts the next word based on the data it's been trained on. It's going to be very difficult to identify many risks ahead of time. Most importantly, you have a feedback system that can alert content creators and model builders to errors that you can quickly fix. Stakeholders also play a role here, helping identify potential risks and challenges, allowing your AI model developers to proactively address concerns.

Stakeholder engagement in AI deployment projects enhances the robustness and reliability of AI systems and minimizes the likelihood of unintended consequences and failures. In the early stages of deployment, stakeholders must have a say in the schedule, and rich feedback from those impacted is necessary. Utilizing tools and techniques like office hours and quantitative surveys, listening tours, and other methods to capture what customers are saying about a business, product, or service—the voice of the customer (VOC)—is imperative. The voice of the customer focuses on customer needs, expectations, understandings, and product improvement."[13]

By listening to the voice of the end user—typically the front-line support engineer or service agent—the AI deployment team, project sponsors, and executive management can get a clear view of how things are going. Combining the voice of the customer with quantitative data such as surveys, project telemetry, and so on, will provide a 360-degree view of the deployment experience.

Resource Allocation and Prioritization

Not only does stakeholder engagement help identify risky scenarios and potential bias, it also helps align the AI model's development process with organizational goals and priorities, ensuring that the AI model is built to deliver maximum value. Think of stakeholders across your organization that would help influence development opportunities like timing, cost, and resources. Some examples are your finance partners, HR, sales, and marketing. Regular interactions with stakeholders, both internally and externally, help developers make continuous adjustments to the AI model focused on optimizing for both users and the business. This ongoing refinement ensures the AI model's longer-term success by adapting to changing needs and environments.

Establish Regular Check-Ins or Office Hours

The concept of "office hours" refers to a set time period during which developers, AI model builders, operational deployment professionals, and others in the creation and deployment of AI in customer service are available to answer questions, get feedback, provide support, and collaborate with team members and end users."[14]

In software and AI development and deployment, the concept of office hours is an important part of the process. They provide a structured time for team members to communicate and collaborate, which can help ensure that AI projects are completed on time and to a high standard. The discover phase is the first step in ensuring that your AI model is built with purpose, a clear scope, a well-defined audience persona, and an understanding of content availability. The more qualitative and quantitative data you can collect in this phase will help you focus and prioritize what's most important to your end users and your organization. Aligning your user needs and challenges to your organization's desires will allow you to create a successful and more accurate AI model that will meet all requirements. Continually monitoring and requesting stakeholder feedback ensures your AI development team has the information and knowledge needed to create a model that mitigates risk and bias and best meets the needs of end users.

Endnotes

1   Merriam-Webster. "persona." Merriam-Webster.com Dictionary. Accessed December 15, 2023. [https://www.merriam-webster.com/dictionary/persona].

2   Pruitt, John and Grudin, Jonathan. 2017. "Personas: Practice and Theory." Microsoft Research, March 2017. [https://www.microsoft.com/en-us/research/wp-content/uploads/2017/03/pruitt-grudinold.pdf].

3   Cooper, Alan. "The inmates are running the asylum." Indianapolis, IN: Sams, 2004.

4   Merriam-Webster. "psychographics." Merriam-Webster.com Dictionary. Accessed December 15, 2023. [https://www.merriam-webster.com/dictionary/psychographics].

5   Merriam-Webster. "quantitative." Merriam-Webster.com Dictionary. Accessed December 15, 2023. [https://www.merriam-webster.com/dictionary/quantitative].

6   Moran, Kate. 2018. "Quantitative User-Research Methodologies: An Overview." Nielsen Norman Group, April 22, 2018. [https://www.nngroup.com/articles/quantitative-user-research-methods/].

7   Williams, Traci. 2021. "Why Is Quantitative Research Important?" Grand Canyon University, June 14, 2021. [https://www.gcu.edu/blog/doctoral-journey/why-quantitative-research-important].

8   Bhandari, Pritha. 2020. "What Is Quantitative Research? | Definition, uses & Methods." Scribbr, revised June 22, 2023. [https://www.scribbr.com/methodology/quantitative-research/].

9   Bhandari, Pritha. 2021. "An Easy Introduction to Statistical Significance (With Examples)." Scribbr, revised June 22, 2023. [https://www.scribbr.com/statistics/statistical-significance/].

10 Wikipedia contributors. "Master-slave (technology)." Wikipedia, The Free Encyclopedia. December 14, 2023. [https://en.wikipedia.org/wiki/Master%E2%80%93slave_(technology)].

11 Wikipedia contributors. "Sanity check." Wikipedia, The Free Encyclopedia. November 16, 2023. [https://en.wikipedia.org/wiki/Sanity_check].

12 Petersen, Deborah. 2013. "Carole Robin: Feedback is a Gift." Insights by Stanford Business, November 27, 2013. [https://www.gsb.stanford.edu/insights/carole-robin-feedback-gift].

13 "What is voice of the customer (VoC)?" Qualtrics. [https://www.qualtrics.com/experience-management/customer/what-is-voice-of-customer/].

14 Ritter, L., Scherrer, C., Vandenbussche, J., & Whipple, J. 2021. "A study of student perceptions of office hours." Journal on Excellence in College Teaching, 2021. [https://facultyweb.kennesaw.edu/lritter/JECT_2021_article.pdf].

6

Design: Building the Blueprint

Design is not just what it looks like and feels like. Design is how it works.

—Steve Jobs

The key theme of this chapter is about taking inventory. While the discovery phase discussed in Chapter 5 is largely about research, understanding your users, developing representative personas, and learning more about what content you have in your inventory, the design phase is all about making design choices based on the list of requirements gathered during discovery and filling in the holes. Ideation, testing, gap analysis, and prototyping govern the design phase.

When preparing for AI implementation, you should identify how to best integrate AI with your existing technology and services. It's useful to consider how you'll manage content creation as you identify gaps in the available content versus what you need to meet user requirements.

Identifying Your Starting Point

Now that you have identified all the existing content and resources you want to ingest into an AI model, it's time to document the current state of the existing process, technology architecture, and structures before initiating change. Documenting these things will help ensure a structured and effective transition, providing a comprehensive snapshot of where you're starting from and establishing a baseline for comparison post-implementation.

A striking historical example of this principle in action was the transformation of IBM in the early 1990s under the leadership of CEO Louis V. Gerstner Jr.[1] When Gerstner took over as CEO, he found IBM in dire straits, on the verge of bankruptcy and struggling with old product lines and a culture that wasn't keeping up with the times. Gerstner's first step as CEO was to meticulously document IBM's existing state, analyzing all components, including its strengths, weaknesses, opportunities, and threats (aka SWOT Analysis), given the current and predicted future market conditions. Under Gerstner, IBM identified critical issues, like its over-reliance on hardware sales, leading to a strategy designed to turn IBM around, address its immediate challenges, and position the company for future success in the highly competitive technology industry. Documenting the current state served as the baseline and guide for decision-making, communication with stakeholders, and ensuring that the implemented strategic changes would be sustainable over time. With this approach, IBM effectively navigated an incredible organizational change.

A baseline is a clearly defined project starting point in traditional project management. Once your team has established what this will be, the baseline should be used to measure progress and performance. Is your team on a trajectory toward success? Check the baseline!

Determining and understanding your baseline ensures that you can clearly evaluate the success or failure of your AI model and its implementation. Leadership will want to see the impact of AI investments; collecting before and after data will help you deliver on that. As with any organization, you already measure many components of your business and adjust often. The organization will likely have established goal-setting and measuring methods such as KPIs (key performance indicators) or OKRs (objectives and key results). In customer service and support, these measures may include customer satisfaction (CSAT), time to resolution (TTR), time to close (TTC), agent satisfaction (ASAT), days to close/resolve (DTC), and many others, depending on the nature of your business.

As you start to deploy AI into your organization, it's important to pay careful attention to the metrics you use to baseline your current state so that you can draw an apples-to-apples comparison post-deployment. Yes, AI will bring new measures, but these won't replace or supplant your current ones, at least initially; therefore, the early transition needs to be monitored and evaluated using the same measures.

A CAUTIONARY TALE

From a metrics perspective, AI deployment in customer support can be a double-edged sword. While AI has the potential to revolutionize customer service by providing quick and efficient solutions, its adoption by support engineers may not always follow a linear trajectory.

One common scenario is that support engineers may turn to AI only when encountering complex or challenging cases. This selective use of AI can lead to a seemingly counterintuitive outcome: metrics like days to close (DTC) may increase for agents using AI compared to those who do not. This might appear as if AI is hindering rather than aiding customer support.

However, this perspective can be misleading. The increase in DTC can be attributed to AI being used for inherently more complicated cases, where traditional methods may have taken even longer. In reality, AI often assists support engineers in handling intricate issues more effectively, improving overall customer satisfaction.

To successfully deploy AI in customer support, organizations need to embrace a holistic view of metrics, understanding that AI's impact may not always be immediately evident in traditional KPIs as the behavior of the support agents in the utilization of AI may be different than expected and therefore impact KPIs in unexpected ways. Instead, organizations should focus on AI's enhanced problem-solving capabilities and efficiency to support teams, ultimately delivering a more robust and responsive customer service experience.

Identifying gaps in your content coverage is crucial to ensure that your AI system can provide accurate and relevant answers. A content gap refers to a space or opportunity within a particular topic or niche without available or comprehensive information. It's essentially a discrepancy between what users are searching for or interested in and current content.

By comparing your existing content with your goals and the desired state, you can find out where you need to create, update, or delete content to meet your customers' needs and expectations. Identifying and quantifying content gaps will help you prioritize your content acquisition and development efforts to optimize your AI system's performance.

Quantify Gaps in Content: Measure the Difference Between the Current and Desired State

Quantifying the content gap in an AI model involves determining where your model falls short in meeting its intended users' needs or use cases. This process helps identify areas where the model requires further data, more sophisticated features, or better alignment with user expectations.

Several methods and considerations exist for quantifying the content gap, such as comparative analysis used to compare your model's performance against benchmarks or competing models and using simulations or synthetic data to test the model in scenarios that might not be well-represented in the available real data. While there are a variety of methods to consider, let's revolutionize this space too and explain the concept with a metaphor: the use of code coverage.

Using code coverage to quantify content gaps in an AI model is an innovative application of a concept traditionally used in software testing. Code coverage typically measures the extent to which source code is executed during testing, which indicates the thoroughness of the test suite. In the context of AI models, especially those involving machine learning, the concept can be metaphorically extended to assess the comprehensiveness of the model's training and validation. For AI models, "code coverage" can be reinterpreted to mean "data coverage" or "scenario coverage." This involves measuring how well the training dataset covers the scenarios or cases.

Although coverage is well established in software engineering research (and widely used at Google[2] to give an example), deployment in the industry is often inhibited by the perceived usefulness and the computational costs of analyzing coverage at scale. The code coverage metaphor pertains to the gap analysis phase in which the objective is to quantify the extent to which the content comprehensively addresses the designated topic areas. **Figure 6.1** shows an example of a code coverage map which illustrates the test and quality assurance coverage of software code. Evaluating whether the content encompasses all facets of the topic areas and whether there is redundant or duplicative content is critical, as duplicative content will lead to "commingling," leading to hallucinations. It's important to exercise caution when using content from different sources that contain similar acronyms or overlapping terminology. When two or more data sources describe different solutions to the same issue, it is known as commingling. For example, if the error message is very generic and applicable to a wide range of scenarios/products, let's use "access denied" as an example; it's best to review all the relevant guides carefully and identify any potential conflicts or overlaps. If necessary, you may need to seek clarification from the content authors or consult experts to ensure you follow the correct procedures. By taking these steps, you can avoid potential confusion or errors, also known as hallucinations, when using multiple content sources with similar terminology or acronyms.

Code Coverage Map

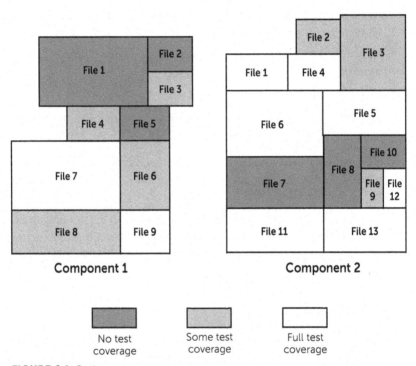

FIGURE 6.1 Code coverage map

Future evolution of this technology may provide automated tools, just as there are automated code coverage tools. This is an interesting area to investigate further.

Determining Which Gaps Are Most Important Based on Your Goals

Defining the content necessary for an AI model involves identifying gaps and prioritizing them effectively based on your specific goals—an essential step in ensuring resources are allocated smartly and impactfully. This prioritization is crucial because it helps focus efforts on areas that will most significantly enhance the performance and relevance of its intended applications. This approach optimizes development time and costs and maximizes the model's effectiveness and efficiency in real-world scenarios. Therefore, understanding and addressing the most important content gaps is not just a technical necessity but a strategic imperative that can define the success or failure of AI initiatives. Following are a few questions to ask yourself when determining which gaps are most important:

- How important is each gap for achieving the desired outcomes?
- Given the time, budget, and expertise constraints, how feasible is it to fill each gap?
- How urgent is filling each gap in relation to the content development timeline?
- How interdependent are the gaps and the existing content?

Once you have answers to these questions, you can more easily rank the gaps on a scale, such as high, medium, or low:

- **High-priority gaps** significantly impact the quality and effectiveness of the content in the AI model and can be realistically addressed within the project's scope.
- **Medium-priority gaps** have a moderate impact on the content and can be addressed with some content adjustments or compromises.
- **Low-priority gaps** have a minimal impact on the content and won't compromise the overall content quality if left alone.

A/B Testing

A/B testing[3] has revolutionized the way products are developed and optimized, bringing empirical science into the arena of user experience and interactive design. When applied to AI, particularly in identifying content gaps within AI models, A/B testing transcends its traditional role and becomes a powerful conduit for enhancement and precision.

A/B testing is a common practice in which two or more options are presented. Comparing these options and analyzing the results gives you a better idea of what performs better. As you look to deploy AI solutions, the obvious A/B test is "before and after," but deployment can be more nuanced than that.

Imagine deploying two variants of an AI model to a segment of your audience: Model A, the current iteration, and Model B, which includes adjustments to address suspected content gaps. This setup isn't just about determining which model performs better overall; it's a sophisticated experiment in understanding specific deficiencies and opportunities. By methodically analyzing how each variant handles identical situations, A/B testing provides clear, comparative insights into which modifications truly enhance the model's performance and user satisfaction.

Moreover, A/B testing can illuminate content gaps that might not have been initially apparent. For example, if Model B performs better in unexpected ways or contexts, this could indicate hidden strengths or weaknesses in the training data or feature engineering, sparking further investigation into overlooked areas. This process of discovery and adaptation ensures that AI development is driven by data-derived insights, making models not only more effective but also more attuned to the nuanced needs of their users.

THE DEVELOPMENT OF TREATMENTS FOR SCURVY

Scurvy is a disease caused by a deficiency of vitamin C. During the 18th century, scurvy was a major problem for sailors on long voyages. Sailors in the British Royal Navy suffered greatly from the disease. Various treatments were proposed to combat scurvy, but there was a lack of consensus on which one was most effective.

One notable experiment occurred during the 1740s when a Scottish naval surgeon named James Lind conducted what could be considered one of the earliest recorded clinical trials.[4] Lind divided a group of scurvy-afflicted sailors into six different groups, each receiving a different treatment. These treatments included cider, vinegar, seawater, oranges and lemons, a mixture of garlic, mustard seed, and horseradish, and a placebo.

Lind carefully observed and documented the outcomes over several days. It became clear that the group of sailors given citrus—oranges and lemons—showed a significant improvement in their scurvy symptoms. This experiment laid the groundwork for understanding the importance of vitamin C in preventing scurvy, ultimately leading to the adoption of citrus fruits as a standard part of sailors' diets.

Lind's experiment can be seen as a historical precursor to A/B testing as he systematically tested different treatments on separate groups to determine their effectiveness, helping to identify the most beneficial one. This early example of controlled experimentation and clinical study in medicine contributed to significant advancements in understanding and treating scurvy.[5]

A/B testing can be used in a controlled experiment where two or more variants of a user experience—a web page, email, or other content—are compared against each other to determine which one performs better in terms of specified metrics, such as conversion rates or user engagement. Why is this relevant? In the competitive arena of AI-driven products, the ability to swiftly adapt and optimize based on user interaction data is invaluable. Companies harnessing the iterative power of A/B testing can continuously refine their AI offerings, ensuring they remain on the cutting edge of technological capability and market relevance. This ongoing refinement cycle boosts user engagement and satisfaction and solidifies a product's place in an ever-evolving marketplace. Thus, A/B testing is not merely a tool for incremental improvement; it is a strategic asset in the quest to close the most critical content gaps, enhancing the intelligence and responsiveness of AI applications in the real world.

Practical Guide to A/B Testing for AI Model Optimization

It is important to spend some time designing your A/B test to get the most impactful results.[6] As you begin designing your test, you'll want to clearly define the objective or goalsuch as improving user engagement. You'll then want to define the metric that will be measured and that aligns directly with your A/B test objective.

For example, to effectively integrate A/B testing into enhancing user engagement, identify key elements within your user interface or experience that could influence user interactions. Create at least two variants, A and B, of a single element to be tested, ensuring that they differ only in the specific variable under examination, such as a hyperlink location. This focused approach allows you to isolate the impact of that variable on user behavior and directly attribute it to the implemented changes, ensuring clear, actionable insights from your testing.

Consider engaging in multivariate testing for a more comprehensive analysis[7], where you simultaneously alter multiple elements. This method is inherently more complex but provides a deeper understanding of how different variables interact and affect user engagement.

Next, develop your hypothesis that predicts the expected outcome of the test. For example, "The hyperlink at the top of the page will generate more engagement (click throughs) than the hyperlink at the bottom." This hypothesis sets a clear expectation for what the test aims to prove and aligns directly with the strategic goals of identifying and improving user engagement.

Choose Your Audience

This step continues the broader persona work discussed in Chapter 5, "Discover: Laying the Foundation." Utilize personas to identify the specific audience segments you want to target for your A/B testing. Once these specific people are defined, organize them into as many cohorts as there are variants of the element you wish to test. For instance, if two versions of an element are under review, you should form two corresponding groups of participants.

Following this segmentation, randomly allocate one version of the element to each group. This random assignment is crucial as it prevents any pre-existing biases from influencing the data, thereby preserving the integrity of the test results. Through this methodical approach, each element variant is tested in a controlled, equitable manner, allowing you to gather clear, actionable insights into how different user segments interact with each version.

Conduct the Test and Analyze Results

Deploy the different versions to the respective audience segments simultaneously to ensure that external factors do not affect the results. Observe how participants engage with each version, collecting data based on your predefined metrics. It's crucial to extend the test's duration sufficiently to amass statistically significant data, ensuring the reliability of your findings.

After gathering the necessary data, proceed to a thorough analysis to assess your hypothesis's validity and identify which version outperformed the others in achieving the defined objectives. This step is vital in translating raw data into actionable insights to guide future enhancements and strategic decisions.

Apply the Learnings

If your A/B testing results in a clear winner, confidently expand the implementation of the successful variable of the element to a broader audience. This strategic rollout should leverage the insights gained from the test to enhance user engagement across larger segments.

However, if the testing does not reveal a definitive winner, it's crucial to delve deeper into the data to extract valuable insights. In such cases, consider conducting further experiments to refine your understanding. One effective approach is using recursive combination tests.[8] This method systematically applies two-stage combination tests that recursively integrate data to help pinpoint optimal solutions.

Other sophisticated methodologies can also be employed to discern the most effective version of the tested element. Techniques such as Pairwise Comparison,[9] which evaluates elements by directly comparing them in pairs, and the Condorcet Method,[10] which utilizes voting principles to identify a winner among multiple options, are highly beneficial. Another intriguing approach is Evolutionary Game Theory,[11] which applies principles of biological evolution and strategic decision-making to understand competitive scenarios and predict outcomes.

These advanced analytical techniques provide robust frameworks for making informed decisions when simple A/B tests are inconclusive. Applying these methods ensures that your strategic decisions are backed by comprehensive data analysis, ultimately guiding you toward the most effective user engagement strategies.

You are trying to gain ongoing learning, continuous experimentation, and improvement from your A/B testing. Closely document the experiments and findings, share insights and lessons learned with relevant stakeholders, and utilize the learnings for future tests and strategic decisions.

This is a critical step. End users may feel apprehensive about the new technology, so it's important to transparently share—actually overshare—the findings and results. They may not turn out how you expect, which is okay; the learning you take from the experiment and how you apply it matters.

Innovation with the Hub and Spoke

Particularly in large organizations, building a hub-and-spoke model (see **Figure 6.2**) will let you innovate on the fringes and allow you to consider the best of the best ideas as you move forward on your AI journey. Innovation suggests that an organization can discover something new by allowing diverse ideas and approaches to come to light. It thrives when embedded within a culture of openness and creativity. Making the hub-and-spoke model work requires a strong visionary and self-confident hub. The hub must not be threatened by work and innovation in the spokes and will confidently adopt and work together. The world of AI is changing daily, and a heavy-handed central organization will kill innovative efforts.

In smaller organizations, the hub might be one person, and the spokes might be individuals spending an hour a week learning and innovating with AI. A distributed model will serve the organization well by enabling many eyes and ears on this quickly changing space.

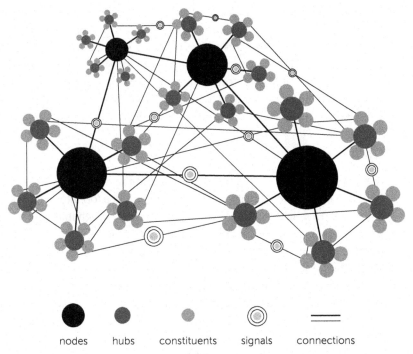

| nodes | hubs | constituents | signals | connections |

FIGURE 6.2 The hub-and-spoke model

There are also risks associated with the hub-and-spoke model. Often, too much openness and free reign without proper management and guidance can lead to chaos. Therefore, while encouraging innovation and diversity of ideas is valuable, you need to be sure it's done with structured and supportive guidance to ensure that innovative efforts lead to positive outcomes.

Steps in the Design Phase

When designing your AI model, there are many steps, from creating content to engaging subject matter experts (SMEs) and formatting your content to help make your model more accurate.

Creating Content

Content creation is a part of the **design** phase because we assume there is existing content that you want to curate first. After you've gone through the gap analysis described earlier and clearly understand where you have holes in the content that you expect to train your model on, the next step is to plan out content creation to fill in the gaps.

Depending on the breadth of your content and how much your organiza-tion has invested in a content strategy in the past, this could be a minor effort or a significant investment. If you've let your content decay, become stale, or allowed a wide variety of contributors to post content in a set of different formats and repositories, there could be a lot of work to identify where you have holes and how to fill them. Your investment in content refinement, updating, and creation will vary depending on your situation.

Chunking

As you think about creating content, you'll want to consider the format of the text and ensure it is optimized for ingestion into your AI model. One available technique is called *chunking*, which in the world of large language models (LLMs) is essentially the act of breaking down large amounts of text into smaller and more manageable "chunks."[12] These chunks are then fed or ingested into the AI model, which makes them more manageable and accurate. Many knowledge resources or troubleshooting guides in the support domain can be extremely long and complex, and by chunking your text into more meaningful bite-sized pieces, the AI model more fully analyzes or processes the information and retains contextual understanding.

You can also use chunking for specific information extraction, such as specific locations, technologies, or names of people. Chunking can also be used in text classification tasks by breaking down the text into paragraphs or sections that can be recalled by the AI model separately, improving the overall understanding of the holistic text. Speech recognition chunking is used to break down spoken language into smaller segments, helping with the transcription and processing of the spoken language for such things as translation.

You may hear "tokenization" mentioned by your developers as you design and develop your AI model. Tokenization is a common form of chunk-ing in which text is broken down into the smallest meaningful unit in a language, called tokens.[13] These often appear as a word or letter. These tokens then allow the AI model to identify patterns better and analyze the meaning of the text. Syntactic analysis helps the model draw meaning from a text and compare it for grammatical accuracy.[14]

Metadata Tagging

Metadata tagging is the art of organization, allowing you to tag specific items with details that allow you to find what you're looking for quickly. For example, think of the thousands of family photographs you've taken over the last ten years. They are likely in the cloud somewhere, but it's nearly impossible to quickly sort through them all to find that one specific image of your kid catching bubbles. Metadata tagging allows you to assign relevant tags to items, such as your child's name, "action shot," or "bubbles," to quickly do keyword searches to find relevant information. AI takes this a step further with image recognition. Just by typing "dog" in the search, AI will troll your photo library and find all images of dogs. If you name a specific person or assign them a metadata tag like "grandma," the same search finds images of "grandma."

Metadata tagging is similar to a library with a clear and easy system to quickly retrieve the information you're looking for. Metadata tags can be applied to any digital asset that needs to be organized, such as photos, documents, videos, music, books, and so on. Metadata is essentially extra data that helps both users and AI models understand, interpret, and organize vast amounts of information. Essentially, it is the bridge between the raw information or data and the meaningful utilization of that data. It can also include descriptive labels or tags beyond a single word to enhance the item's context, search, and discoverability. Metadata tagging is a broad application of organizing and refining data.

With the growth in digital reliance and cloud servers, the storage of digital assets of all types is immense. This data is the AI playground used to train and fuel the models you are interested in designing—from recommendation systems to search and retrieval to natural language processing. Metadata tagging really comes into play when you need to organize these massive amounts of data. Without the added context and structure that metadata adds, the benefits and output generated by the AI model aren't as rich. Metadata assists in building accurate and powerful AI models.

Applying metadata tagging to the support domain, imagine your thousands of knowledge articles referencing everything to do with your products and services from the start of your organization through today. This could literally be hundreds of thousands of pages of content. To better help your AI model find relevant information quickly, applying specific metadata tags to the content you ingest into the model is helpful. Metadata tags could include descriptions such as "training on improving video quality in a Zoom call," "troubleshooting battery problems in my digital fitness device," "return policies for autonomous vacuums," or the date created or document version number. This is similar to #hashtag or @mention and is just one applicable example of how metadata tagging can be applied in a support scenario to help your AI model with a more accurate output of information.

Accountability

It's important to ensure that there is accountability in the creation of content, deployment, and use of AI. There are many facets of accountability. Merriam-Webster has two definitions for "accountable" that are equally viable here.[15]

- Subject to giving an account: answerable
- Capable of being explained: explainable

One easy step to drive accountability into an AI model is to ensure each piece of content, even when chunked into smaller, more focused bits, has an author name, date, and, if applicable, version number, target audience, keywords, geographic relevance, and other relevant metadata tagging and information that will help improve accuracy. In addition, this information will help with accountability using citations, allowing SMEs to validate source content when validating the model's accuracy. Obviously, building and deploying AI models with accountability extends far beyond metadata tagging.

Content Management

The amount of investment here will vary. If you and your organization are just beginning the journey, there's no need to over-invest. Don't delay your AI model creation in favor of a formal content strategy, content management system, cloud database solution, or content versioning. Just get started. Those decisions can come later.

It might be worth starting to think about automating data and content collection. As of this writing, the models cannot "unlearn," so removing content from a model requires rebuilding a new one without the deprecated content. Therefore, it's likely that the model-building process will be repeated multiple times. The initial focus should be on getting content into a model. An investigation into automation and content management systems will be worthwhile in the long term.

Designing with Responsible AI in Mind

As you'll experience throughout this book, we talk often about the need for responsible AI practices. Early in the design phase is no different and likely the most important. It's critical to perform the initial responsible or ethical AI review early in the process. Before beginning significant work on model creation, you must review content for bias, terminology, colloquialisms, acronyms, and language that could be more troublesome or even offensive when surfaced in an AI chat conversation.

Depending on the size of the effort, it might be worthwhile to have a dedicated, responsible AI professional or content PM do the work. It's important to have someone who is accountable for ensuring that this review happens early in the model-building process. Early reviews will help save money by catching potential errors at the start before significant development work occurs.

For example, the historical terminology for a model of asymmetric communication or control where one device or process controls one or more other devices or processes and serves as their communication hub is known as master/slave.[16] A troubleshooting guide (TSG) might suggest a new setting on the "master controller" and then later refer to the "slave device." While this might not even be noticed or flagged as potentially offensive in that specific setting, when that language is rendered in an AI chat, it might show up out of context as incredibly offensive and destroy a company's reputation. Performing a responsible AI review early helps save costs, reputation, and, potentially, customers.

Design Considerations for Integration with Existing Tools and Technologies

Customer service and support organizations leverage a comprehensive set of tools to serve customers. They use these tools to elevate the quality of their interactions and efficiently address customer needs. A wide variety of existing systems will typically be impacted or influenced by deploying AI and related tools.

Many organizations use customer relationship management (CRM) software, a secure repository for customer interactions and preferences, enabling personalized service. Help desk software for managing support tickets and live chat software that facilitates real-time communication are also used for customer support engagements. Email management systems efficiently organize customer correspondence, while call center software helps streamline telephonic interactions through features like call routing and recording. For supporting the digital-savvy customer base, social media management tools offer incredible options designed to scale up to monitor and respond to online queries via social media platforms.

Additionally, organizations utilize survey and feedback tools to measure customer satisfaction and improve services. Knowledge management systems are crucial for storing and retrieving vital content, ensuring that customer service representatives are well-informed when they engage with customers. The increasing reliance on technology is evident in the adoption of chatbots and AI assistants for handling routine queries. Remote support software enables direct troubleshooting on customer devices, demonstrating a blend of human expertise and technological advancements in enhancing customer support.

Any AI deployment must consider these existing tools and infrastructure investments early in the process. In addition, the organization likely has custom tools and reports that must be integrated with new AI investments. When considering generative AI for service support agents or using deep data science in case analysis, asking how AI investments will integrate with—and build on—existing tools is critical.

Generative AI can be stitched into the customer chat experience relatively seamlessly. Whether it's deployed directly to customers or provided as a supplementary tool to existing agents, the technology can have an impact on the support experience, but unless careful planning is done to design and integrate the technology into necessary tools and reports, the existing experiences, important metrics, and feedback channels will be lost, or at least delayed.

New AI systems will impact many of the existing support tools and infra-structure, and it's important to evaluate where and how these systems can and will be augmented by new AI technologies. Whether it's machine learning, sentiment, voice analytics, predictive analytics, or Generative AI, by integrating with existing tools, the new technology has the potential to have a huge impact on the customer experience.

The design phase is all about building the blueprint for the future. It entails taking an inventory of your current state, defining your desired state, and then creating an action plan to fill in the gaps identified. Defining goals and metrics you'll use to evaluate progress along the way and testing different theories helps refine your end state. Building your content infrastructure and appropriately chunking and tagging your content will help with the accuracy of your AI model as your users prompt it with questions. Finally, addressing responsible AI considerations and integration into your existing tools and processes will get you one step further on your journey of AI integration into customer service and support.

THE CRADLE OF CIVILIZATION

In ancient Mesopotamia, often referred to as "the cradle of civilization,"[17] the assimilation of a new invention into the existing array of tools and methodologies can be compared to the confluence of the Tigris and Euphrates rivers. These rivers, originating from distinct sources, merge to create a fertile crescent, a hub of life and prosperity.

Similarly, the integration of an innovative tool like the wheel into Mesopotamian society represented a confluence of old and new, enhancing and being enhanced by the already sophisticated array of tools in various domains such as agriculture, pottery, and transportation. "All civilizations create new advances in technology. Ancient Sumer had several technological creations. The most important and popular was the wheel. The wheel has been dated back to as early as 3500 BCE. At first, wheels were used as a surface for shaping clay into pots. These wheels spun flat side up and on an axle. Soon after that, the Sumerians discovered that the wheel could be used a different way. They flipped the pottery wheels on their edges and found out that they could be used for rolling things forward. With this new information, Sumerians created wheeled carts for farmers and chariots for the army."[18]

These examples illustrate the holistic approach of Mesopotamian civilization toward technological advancement. The wheel's introduction was not merely an additional "technology" but was truly integrated into existing tools and practices. It became part of the bigger picture, where its impact was exponentially magnified by its integration and interaction with existing tools and practices.

A keen awareness of the interconnectedness of various facets of life characterized the Mesopotamian approach to innovation. Their innovations were not siloed; instead, they were seamlessly woven into the fabric of existing practices, enhancing efficiency and productivity.

Integrating a new invention in ancient Mesopotamia can be seen as a testament to their ingenuity and foresight. Mesopotamia became one of the most advanced civilizations of its time. With the introduction of AI, the intentional integration of distinct technologies to create more robust toolsets designed to better meet your audiences' needs will help propel your organization into the future of technical advancement.

Endnotes

1   Gerstner, Lou., and McKinsey Quarterly editors. 2014. "Lou Gerstner on corporate reinvention and values." McKinsey Quarterly. September 2014. [https://www.mckinsey.com/~/media/McKinsey/Featured%20Insights/Leading%20in%20the%2021st%20Century/Lou%20Gerstner%20on%20corporate%20reinvention%20and%20values/Lou_Gerstner_on_corporate_reinvention_and_values.pdf].

2   Fraser, G., Ivanković, M., Just, R., Petrović, G. 2019. "Code Coverage at Google." Google. August 26, 2019. [https://storage.googleapis.com/pub-tools-public-publication-data/pdf/36f4140541f8dd555fb8aaee2fd719d59ffab041.pdf].

3   Wingify editors. 2024. "A/B Testing Guide." Wingify. Accessed January 29, 2024. [https://vwo.com/ab-testing/].

4   Yanes, Javier. 2016. "James Lind and Scurvy: The First Clinical Trial in History?" OpenMind. July 12, 2016. [https://www.bbvaopenmind.com/en/science/leading-figures/james-lind-and-scurvy-the-first-clinical-trial-in-history/].

5   Jakobsen, Nicolai K. 2017. "The Origin of A/B Testing." LinkedIn. May 10, 2017. [https://www.linkedin.com/pulse/origin-ab-testing-nicolai-kramer-jakobsen/].

6   Nicholson, Rachel. 2024. "How to Do A/B Testing: 15 Steps for the Perfect Split Test." HubSpot. May 23, 2024. [https://blog.hubspot.com/marketing/how-to-do-a-b-testing].

7   Optimizely editors. 2024. "Multivariate testing vs A/B testing." Optimizely. Accessed January 29, 2024. [https://www.optimizely.com/optimization-glossary/multivariate-test-vs-ab-test/].

8   Bauer, P., Brannath, W., Posch, M. 2011. "Recursive Combination Tests." Journal of the American Statistical Association. December 31, 2011. [https://www.tandfonline.com/doi/abs/10.1198/016214502753479374].

9   Lewis, Mark. 2023. "Pairwise Comparison Method | Charts, Definition & Examples." Study.com. November 21, 2023. [https://study.com/academy/lesson/the-pairwise-comparison-method-in-elections.html].

10 Wikipedia contributors. "Condorcet method." Wikipedia, The Free Encyclopedia. December 22, 2023. [https://en.wikipedia.org/wiki/Condorcet_method].

11 Wikipedia contributors. "Evolutionary game theory." Wikipedia, The Free Encyclopedia. January 23, 2024. [https://en.wikipedia.org/wiki/Evolutionary_game_theory].

12 Tiwari, Ranjeet. 2023. "Large Langage Models: The Critical Role of Intelligent Chunking." Medium. October 14, 2023. [https://medium.com/@NLPEngineers/large-language-models-the-critical-role-of-intelligent-chunking-b5efc8aa33c2].

13 All Awan, Abid. 2023. "What is Tokenization?" Datacamp. September 2023. [https://www.datacamp.com/blog/what-is-tokenization].

14 Tutorialspoint editors. "Natural Language Processing Tutorial." Tutorialspoint, accessed January 17, 2024. [https://www.tutorialspoint.com/natural_language_processing/natural_language_processing_syntactic_analysis.htm].

15 Merriam-Webster. "Accountable." Merriam-Webster.com Dictionary. Accessed January 29, 2024. [https://www.merriam-webster.com/dictionary/accountable].

16 Wikipedia contributors. "Master-slave (technology)." Wikipedia, The Free Encyclopedia. January 23, 2024. https://en.wikipedia.org/wiki/Master-slave_(technology)].

17 Mirza, Shalra. 2024. "The Cradle of Civilization: Mesopotamia and the First Civilizations." History Cooperative. March 11, 2024. [https://historycooperative.org/cradle-of-civilization/].

18 Mirza, Shalra. 2024. "The Cradle of Civilization: Mesopotamia and the First Civilizations." History Cooperative. March 11, 2024. [https://historycooperative.org/cradle-of-civilization/].

7

Develop: Crafting the Solution

Life is a series of experiences, each of which makes us bigger, even though it is hard to realize this. For the world was built to develop character, and we must learn that the setbacks and griefs which we endure help us in our marching onward.

—Henry Ford

Entering the development phase is important as it marks the time when you prepare your content and build your AI model. Content has often been overlooked in the years leading up to the AI Revolution; therefore, significant groundwork is required in preparing content for ingestion into an AI model. Transitioning into this phase of crafting AI models for customer service and support feels like embarking on a new journey. Here, the shift from meticulous planning to dynamic execution demands a focus on precision and adaptability.

The initial focus lies in preparing content meticulously, ensuring its quality across various dimensions like accuracy, bias, completeness, uniqueness, timeliness, validity, and consistency, and refining it to establish a strong foundation for the model's performance. Following this, prompt-based fine-tuning becomes imperative, guiding the AI model's responses through careful adjustments and tests to achieve the desired outcomes while sidestepping undesired ones. Finally, ingesting curated content into the model in the appropriate format seamlessly ties everything together.

Development in the Content Management Lifecycle

In our journey through the content management lifecycle, we reach a pivotal stage: the Develop phase, in which we refine our content and train the AI model. Building upon the groundwork laid in previous chapters, particularly during the Discover and Design phases, we have identified and curated all our existing content and strategized to address existing gaps. Although the initial iteration of developing an AI model may overlook some content gaps, these gaps gradually come to light through feedback from early deployments and validation efforts. This is why activities such as creating new content, updating outdated content, and reconciling duplicate content emerge as key contributors to refining the model's accuracy. As our journey progresses, we will focus next on content preparation and model training that demands careful attention and significant time investment.

One important aspect, previously discussed in Chapter 6, "Design: Building the Blueprint," is the concept of chunking. Chunking involves restructuring and formatting content into more manageable, focused units. In this development phase, we revisit our chunking decisions, recognizing its iterative nature driven by feedback. Organizing topics into individual files facilitates transparency within the model, allowing citations to link directly to specific topics. This transparency enhances the model's integrity and invites subject matter experts (SMEs) to provide more precise feedback, ultimately refining the model's accuracy, which is our main objective.

Also, in Chapter 6, we explored the role of metadata, often termed "data about the data,"[1] as a crucial information layer that guides and informs AI models and enriches their capabilities across various domains. Metadata plays a multifaceted role, ranging from contextual understanding and improved training to personalization and ethical considerations. It provides invaluable insights into the content's structure, source, and characteristics, enabling AI models to generate more relevant, coherent outputs. Moreover, metadata aids in data filtering, personalization of recommendations, and content control, ensuring adherence to specific criteria and styles.

As we embark on this development phase, it's evident that both chunking and metadata serve as pillars, enhancing the efficiency and effectiveness of our AI model development process.

Creating and Testing Grounding Datasets

Creating and testing grounding datasets is essential in developing AI models, particularly those designed for natural language processing (NLP) tasks such as chatbots or language translation systems. Grounding datasets are the foundation upon which AI models are trained and evaluated, providing the raw material they learn from to understand and generate human-like responses.

Grounding datasets consist of a corpus of text or dialogue exchanges annotated or labeled to provide context and meaning to the AI model. These annotations may include information such as the intent or topic of the conversation, the sentiment or emotion expressed, and any relevant metadata such as user demographics or timestamps.

Let's explore the critical role of grounding datasets in shaping the development process and ensuring the efficacy of AI-powered solutions:

- **Training the AI model:** Grounding datasets are used to train AI models by exposing them to diverse linguistic patterns, semantics, and contexts. Through exposure to a broad spectrum of language usage, the model learns to recognize and understand the nuances of human communication.

- **Evaluating model performance:** Grounding datasets are also used to evaluate the performance of AI models by assessing their ability to accurately comprehend and generate humanlike responses. By comparing the model's output against the ground truth provided by the dataset, effectiveness and areas for improvement can be measured and identified.

- **Addressing bias and fairness:** Grounding datasets are crucial in addressing bias and fairness issues in AI models. By carefully curating and annotating the data to reflect diverse perspectives and demographics, biases can be mitigated and ensure that the model's responses are equitable and inclusive.

Creating and testing grounding datasets is challenging and probably easier to understand after your first pass-through model creation. Your AI model version 2 and 3 and beyond will benefit more from this phase.

THE STUDY OF HEREDITY

Sir Francis Galton, a polymath in the Victorian era, was committed to understanding the inheritance of intelligence.[2] His study focused on families, for which he collected large amounts of data to see if any individuals in the family unit achieved success in their fields from which he could determine if intelligence was a family trait.

Data Collection and Categorization:

Galton collected data on various attributes of individuals and their families. Once he collected this data, he then categorized it based on individual achievements, family relationships, and other criteria. We can liken this to "data segmentation" with which he was trying to isolate heredity from other factors.

Analysis:

Using the categorized data, Galton created the concept of regression. He noticed that although children of very tall parents would often be taller than average, they would also tend to "regress" or move toward the mean height. This observation led to the development of the regression line, a statistical concept.

Legacy:

Galton's work laid the foundation for many statistical methods used today, and his approach can be considered the precursor to the more complex segmentation methods used in contemporary data science.

Data Splitting

Breaking up training data is common in machine learning and AI model development. This technique, used to divide training data into distinct sets and build distinct AI models, can significantly affect the applicability and performance of each model and should be considered a strategic decision during the development phase.

One of the recommendations for effectively training the AI model is to split the dataset into three distinct sets:

- **Training set:** This set trains algorithms during the modeling stage. By exposing the model to a large portion of the data, it learns patterns and relationships that enable it to make predictions or generate responses.

Within the training set, creating subsets of data for various purposes is common. These subsets can serve different functions and help improve the efficiency and effectiveness of the training process.

- **Validation set:** The validation set assesses the model's performance and adjusts hyperparameters and configurations, helping to optimize performance and mitigate overfitting (when the model becomes overly tailored to specific datasets).

- **Testing set:** Lastly, the testing set is reserved for a final check on the performance of the best model. This set contains data the model has not been exposed to during training or validation, providing an unbiased evaluation of its performance on unseen data.

Splitting your data into these three sets ensures a rigorous and systematic approach to model training, evaluation, and performance optimization, ultimately leading to more robust and reliable AI models.

Here are some criteria to consider when deciding how to split your training data:

Statistical representativeness

- **Variability:** Each model should be trained on a diverse set of examples to learn the underlying patterns effectively. This will help ensure that each dataset has enough variability to appropriately represent the problem space.

- **Distribution:** The distribution of key features and labels in each subdataset should represent the full dataset to prevent bias and ensure the AI model will perform well across different scenarios.

Task specificity

- **Objective alignment:** If the models are intended for different tasks, the data should be split according to the specific objectives of each task. For example, an AI model used for support troubleshooting will likely require different training data than a model for predicting the sentiment of support survey feedback.

- **Relevance:** Irrelevant data can introduce noise and reduce model performance; therefore, data should be relevant to the task at hand.

Model complexity and capacity

- **Learning capability:** The larger and more complex the AI model, the more training data is required to learn effectively without overfitting. By ensuring the data volume matches the model's complexity, you'll more appropriately train the model to produce accurate output.

- **Overfitting versus underfitting:** Balance the amount of data you're training the model on to prevent overfitting (where the model learns the training data too well and performs exceptionally well on the training data but fails to generalize to new, unseen data) and underfitting (where the model does not learn the underlying pattern sufficiently and performs poorly both on the training data and on new, unseen data). This may take a few tries to get right.

Data privacy and sensitivity

- **Regulations compliance:** If your data contains sensitive information, it may need to be split according to regulations and privacy laws (like GDPR or HIPAA), which might restrict how data is used and shared.

- **Anonymization:** Ensure that sensitive data is de-identified appropriately before use, which might require different preprocessing steps for different datasets.

Operational efficiency

- **Computational resources:** Larger datasets require more memory and processing power, so considering the computational resources available is important. If resources are limited, you may need to train smaller AI models on subsets of the data.

- **Update frequency:** If the models need to be updated frequently, it might be best to train them on smaller, more manageable subsets of data that can be easily refreshed regularly.

Domain specificity

- **Expertise input:** Leverage domain experts to ensure the data subsets reflect domain-specific nuances and use cases. This can be critical in fields like finance or medicine, where context is key.

- **Feature relevance:** Ensure that the features within each subset are very relevant to the domain-specific tasks your AI model is expected to perform.

Temporal dynamics

- **Time sensitivity:** For AI models that will be applied to time-sensitive data, ensure that your training data includes temporal dynamics that reflect the expected changes over time, such as seasonality.

- **Data drift:** Know that there may be potential shifts in the underlying data distribution over time, called *concept drift*. Training different models on data from different periods can help mitigate this.

Data quality and completeness

- **Missing values:** Consider the completeness of the training data. High rates of missing values in certain subsets may require different preprocessing or ingestion strategies.

- **Noise level:** The noise level in the data may affect model performance, and different noise reduction techniques may be necessary to help mitigate.

Performance benchmarks

- **Evaluation metrics:** Understand how the performance of each model will be measured. Different subsets of training data may be used to optimize for different metrics (such as precision versus recall).

- **Benchmarking:** Use existing benchmarks or create new ones tailored to the specific subsets of training data to ensure that your AI model meets the performance standards you expect.

Scalability and adaptability

- **Incremental learning:** Often, AI models adapt over time through what's referred to as *incremental learning*.[3] Subsets of data you utilize could be withheld for future training, and all data should be partitioned in a way that easily supports this action.

- **Scalability:** Consider how your data segmentation strategies will scale when new data is added. It should remain flexible, so complete restructuring is not required as it grows.

Don't forget to document the process you utilize as you split your data so that it can be reproducible. Documenting your entire process helps with the transparency for model validation, audits, and troubleshooting—especially in highly regulated industries. You may find that combining multiple smaller models may improve the overall performance and better meet your goals. Remember that you're training individual, smaller models, so thinking through your data segmentation for this purpose should also be a consideration.

When splitting data, especially in classification tasks, it's important to employ statistical methods such as stratified sampling to maintain the right proportion across different subsets.[4] You can also use cross-validation methods to ensure that the models generalize well to unseen data. Ultimately, you want to create training datasets that will work for your intended models and the goals you initially set out to accomplish. You must consider how you will balance accuracy, practical constraints, and generalization.

Content and Model Training Data Preparation

Linking the content preparation in the Develop phase to the preceding Discover and Design phases—where the content was gathered and gaps were identified and filled—is crucial for understanding the holistic process of AI model development. In the Discover phase, we explore existing data sources, identify potential gaps in content coverage, and assess the quality and relevance of available information. Subsequently, in the Design phase, strategies are devised to address these content gaps, whether through creating new content, aggregating additional data sources, or refining existing information.

As we transition into the content preparation phase, the focus shifts toward ensuring that the curated content is formatted and structured optimally for ingestion into the AI model. This phase bridges content acquisition and model training, where the raw material gathered in the Discover and Design phases is refined into a form suitable for computational analysis. By paying careful attention to formatting considerations and file compatibility, you can ensure that the AI model processes the data seamlessly, enabling it to generate accurate and relevant responses.

Content preparation plays a pivotal role in the overall development of an AI model for several reasons:

- **Accuracy and relevance:** Ensuring that the content is accurate and relevant is crucial for the AI model's performance. Inaccurate or outdated information can lead to misleading responses, eroding trust in the AI system. By meticulously preparing the content, including fact-checking and verifying sources, you can safeguard against inaccuracies and ensure that the model provides reliable information.

- **Generalization and adaptability:** AI models need to generalize well to new contexts and scenarios beyond the training data. Overfitting, which occurs when the model becomes overly tailored to specific datasets, can hinder its ability to adapt to new situations. By preparing diverse and comprehensive content, developers can help the model learn robust patterns and concepts that enable it to generalize effectively, leading to more accurate and adaptable responses in real-world scenarios.

- **Bias mitigation:** Content preparation also plays a crucial role in mitigating bias within AI models. Biased or discriminatory content can perpetuate harmful stereotypes and inequalities in the model's responses. Through careful curation and review of the content, biased language, perspectives, or data sources can be identified and addressed, helping to create more equitable and unbiased AI systems.

- **Enhanced user experience:** Well-prepared content provides a more seamless and effective user experience. Clear and concise language, organized structure, and relevant information enhance the usability of the AI system, making it easier for users to interact with and derive value from it.

Content preparation is the foundation upon which the AI model is built, influencing its accuracy, adaptability, fairness, and usability. By investing time and effort into this critical phase of development, you can ensure that the AI model meets the highest performance and reliability standards, ultimately driving its success in diverse and dynamic environments.

Curating versus Formatting

Curating content and formatting are distinct but interconnected aspects of preparing data for ingestion into an AI model.

Curating content involves selecting, organizing, and refining information to ensure its relevance, accuracy, and completeness for a specific purpose or use case, activities that we covered in Chapters 5 and 6. This process may include gathering data from various sources, identifying and filling content gaps, verifying sources, fact-checking, and removing irrelevant or redundant information. Curating content is focused on refining the substance and quality of the data to enhance its utility and effectiveness in training the AI model.

On the other hand, formatting refers to the presentation and structure of the data, including elements such as layout, styling, and organization. Formatting concerns how the data is visually and structurally represented rather than its substantive content. This may involve arranging text into paragraphs, headings, and lists; applying styles for emphasis or clarity; and ensuring consistency in formatting conventions. The goal of formatting is to optimize the readability, accessibility, and usability of the data for both humans and machines.

While curating content focuses on refining the quality and relevance of the data itself, formatting focuses on optimizing its presentation and structure. However, the two processes are closely intertwined, as the way data is formatted can influence how effectively it conveys its intended message and how well both humans and AI algorithms interpret it. Effective data preparation requires attention to both curating content and formatting to ensure that the data is accurate, comprehensive, and usable for its intended purpose.

Formatting Considerations

There are many aspects to consider in content preparation, a staple in the development phase. This activity will likely take longer than you expect, particularly if you haven't spent a lot of resources on formatting content in the past. As support content, including knowledge base articles and troubleshooting guides—and the language therein—now become training data for conversational AI, there are new possibilities to consider. Given these considerations, the language used in a training guide might now be invoked in a conversation—out of the context of the original guide. Some language might be incorrect, inaccurate, or even offensive. As a result, it's important to analyze and scan your existing support content to look for language usage, various types of bias, colloquialisms, acronyms, and other usage that might not work as well in a conversation as in a technical document.

Some key formatting considerations include:

- **Clarity and conciseness:** Use clear and concise language to convey information effectively. Avoid overly complex or technical terminology that may confuse the model or users.

- **Structure and organization:** Organize the data in a structured manner, such as using headings, subheadings, bullet points, or lists, to facilitate readability and comprehension. A well-organized structure helps the model understand the hierarchical relationships between different pieces of information.

- **Consistency:** Maintain consistency in formatting styles throughout the data, such as font size, font type, spacing, and alignment. Consistent formatting enhances the visual appeal and professionalism of the content, making it easier for the model to parse and interpret.

- **Accessibility:** Ensure the data is accessible to all users, including those with visual or cognitive impairments. Use accessible formatting practices, such as providing alternative text (alt text) for images, using descriptive link text, and avoiding color-coded information without accompanying text descriptions.

- **Standardization:** Standardize the format of dates, numbers, and other data elements to ensure uniformity and consistency across the dataset. Consistent formatting facilitates data processing and analysis, reducing the risk of errors or misinterpretations.

- **Language and cultural sensitivity:** Be mindful of language and cultural sensitivities when preparing the data. Avoid using offensive or inappropriate language or terminology in certain contexts or cultures.

- **File compatibility:** Ensure that the data is formatted in a compatible file format for ingestion into the AI model. Common file formats include plain text (.txt), Markdown (.md), HTML (.html), and JSON (.json), among others.

By considering these formatting considerations, the quality and usability of the data ingested into the AI model can be optimized, ultimately enhancing its performance and effectiveness in generating accurate and relevant responses.

Focus on Data Quality Metrics

With the quality of AI model output directly reflecting the AI model input, measuring the quality of training data is critical. Here are some considerations for assessing the quality of your training data:

- **Diversity and representation:** A diverse dataset helps ensure that your AI model can generate a wide variety of outputs. Therefore, be sure to include a range of different examples within each category. You'll also want to pay attention to the coverage or extent to which the data covers what you expect to input. Good coverage prevents model overfitting and improves generalization.

- **Balance:** To prevent bias in the AI model output, you should ensure a relatively balanced number of examples for each distinct class or category.

- **Label quality (for supervised learning):** Pay attention to the correctness of labels or annotations provided with the training data because this helps ensure performance accuracy. In addition, ensure labels are consistently present across your datasets and do not confuse the model during training.

- **Completeness:** High levels of missing data can impair the model's ability to learn effectively when trained.

- **Noise level:** The number of errors or noise in the data, such as incorrect artifacts, values, or outliers that are not part of real-world distribution, can cause inaccuracy in the output.

- **Data distribution:** Employ different statistical methodologies to help indicate whether there are biases or anomalies in the data and correlations between different features in the data.

- **Data fidelity (for generative models):** The more your training data reflects real-world scenarios, the more realistic and believable generated outputs will be. In addition, the level of complexity and detail in the data can influence the AI model's ability to provide nuanced and detailed outputs.

CENSUS

Back in Ancient Rome, data collection through a census was filled with challenges and introduced many discrepancies in the data.[5] Tracking citizens and valuing their properties for military and taxation purposes often resulted in the underreporting of wealth, especially by those keen on minimizing their fiscal obligations. This misreporting prevented a clear picture of wealth distribution within the society.

The mobility of the population created further difficulties. As people traveled the empire's vast territories for trade, military service, or personal reasons, keeping an accurate and current population tally was impossible. Additionally, the era's record-keeping practices—ranging from inscriptions on stone and wax tablets to papyrus scrolls—were rife with transcription errors. Mistakes in copying numbers or names from one medium to another introduced inconsistencies. In rural areas of the empire, censors often resorted to estimation and guesswork to account for the population and property values. All these rough calculations created further dissonance in the accuracy in the census data. You can tie these challenges to the dilemmas of contemporary data scientists who strive for precision in the face of incomplete or misleading data and the need to generate accurate results.

Additional metrics specific to the generative task can also be important to consider for generative models. While image creation and recognition is still a work in progress as of this writing, it's important to plan for the future, including measures such as:

- **Inception score (IS):** The inception score (IS) evaluates the quality of images generated by AI, where higher scores correspond to highly diverse and classifiable images.[6]

- **Fréchet inception distance (FID):** Measures the distance between feature vectors calculated for real and generated images. Lower FID corresponds to more similar real and generated images, indicating better model performance.[7]

- **Bilingual evaluation understudy (BLEU):** A metric used for evaluating the quality of machine generated text compared to one or more reference texts. It compares the machine response versus the human response.[8] While simple to use and calculate, some limitations are present in this method, including:

  - It does not account for the meaning or grammar accuracy of the generated text.

- It assumes that more reference translations will provide a more comprehensive view of possible correct translations, which is not always the case or possible.
- It may not correlate well with human judgment and particular language nuances.

Consider the model's end-use case when evaluating what training data to use for generative models. Ultimately, the choice of metrics should align with the data's specific characteristics and the generative task's requirements.

Prompt Engineering: Prompt-Based Fine-Tuning for Optimal Model Response

This is the beginning of what's become known as "prompt engineering," also referred to as crafting text in intentional, specific ways as input to an AI model to encourage refined outputs.[9] The process begins with designing prompts that effectively convey the task or objective to the model. Prompts can take various forms, including questions, statements, or partial sentences, depending on the nature of the task. Designing effective prompts requires careful consideration of the task requirements, desired output, and the capabilities of the underlying language model.

Prompt engineering is often an iterative process that involves refining and optimizing prompts through experimentation and trial and error. This is done iteratively, adjusting the wording, structure, and content of prompts to elicit the desired responses from the model. This iterative refinement process may also involve testing different variations of prompts and evaluating their effectiveness empirically.

One of the primary goals of prompt engineering is to control the outputs generated by the language model. By crafting prompts strategically, the model is guided to produce responses that align with specific criteria, such as relevance, accuracy, or style. In addition to guiding the model toward desired outputs, prompt engineering also aims to prevent the generation of undesired or inappropriate responses. The risk of generating irrelevant, biased, or harmful content can be mitigated by carefully crafting prompts and providing constraints or guidelines to the model.

The work here may not happen on your first pass through the model creation process and will certainly be subject to modification over time. The reason for including a step here is that you can create what's known as a "base prompt." The base prompt is the core or starting point of a conversation with the AI model. It helps to set the direction and context for the dialogue that follows. It's a good idea to test and experiment with "base prompts." However, you will likely put more work into a base prompt after experimentation with your first model. One example of a base prompt is used universally in all user conversations. Perhaps something like "act like a support engineer for products X, Y, and Z. If you don't know the answer to a question, don't make anything up, just say I don't know." This will help to "ground" the model with some expected behavior. A conversational AI model is not a search engine. Think of it as a friend, trusted advisor, or semi-smart assistant. The more you can instruct it about exactly what you want, the better and more valuable it will be for your customer service agents.

The second prompting stage comes later after the model has been deployed and is done by end-users who question your completed AI model. There are many resources to help with prompt engineering. (See our website at *https://airevolutionbook.com.*)

The earlier that prompt engineering and grounding can be incorporated as a model input, the better the probability that results will be more specific and accurate.

Start Small with Content Ingestion Methods and Considerations

One of the most important steps happens here. You have resources identified to build a model. You have users identified. Now comes the technical process to build a model. The recommendation here is to start small to learn how to do this. Don't go out and buy or build a large content management system. That can come later if you need it. Right now, just take the first step and build your first model. Focus your content around a single topic and, depending on the technology you are using, ingest it into a model. For example, if you are building a GPT using OpenAI, you can choose a handful of documents and build your first model using the OpenAI GPT Builder, as seen in **Figure 7.1**.

If you are using Microsoft Azure OpenAI Studio[10], create a new resource to get started, as shown in **Figure 7.2**, or use Google Gemini,[11] as shown in **Figure 7.3**.

Once you have your first model built, celebrate! This is a big milestone that is presumably listed as such on your project plan. Celebrate with all the people who have contributed up to this point.

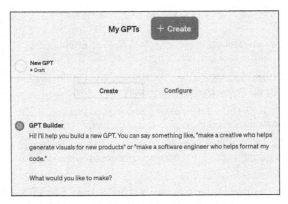

FIGURE 7.1 Create GPT screen from OpenAI.com

FIGURE 7.2 Microsoft Azure
OpenAI Studio

FIGURE 7.3 Google Gemini 1.5

In our journey of AI development, the Develop phase stands out as a milestone where we set the stage for not just functional proficiency but for the creation of an AI model that is both ethically informed and fundamentally sound. This is a phase where you should devote quality time to all the steps we have covered, as they are critical to your success.

The full ingestion of content into the AI model marks a transition to the Diagnose phase, where the real-world performance of the model will be tested and refined. This progression from development to diagnosis underscores a cycle of continuous improvement and adaptation—a hallmark of robust AI systems.

Endnotes

1   Wikipedia contributors. "Metadata." Wikipedia, The Free Encyclopedia. February 14, 2024. [https://en.wikipedia.org/wiki/Metadata].

2   Wikipedia contributors. "Francis Galton." Wikipedia, The Free Encyclopedia. February 1, 2024. [https://en.wikipedia.org/wiki/Francis_Galton].

3   Awan, Abid All. 2023. "What is Incremental Learning?" Datacamp. June 2023. [https://www.datacamp.com/blog/what-is-incremental-learning].

4   Thomas, Lauren. 2020. "Stratified Sampling: Definition, Guide & Examples." Scribbr. Revised June 22, 2023. [https://www.scribbr.com/methodology/stratified-sampling/].

5   Rideout, Moshe. 2023. "What Is The Census Used For Ancient Rome." Learn Ancient Rome. December 9, 2023. [https://www.learnancientrome.com/what-is-the-census-used-for-ancient-rome/].

6   Brownlee, Jason. 2019. "How to Implement the Inception Score (IS) for Evaluating GANs." Machine Learning Mastery. October 11, 2019. [https://machinelearningmastery.com/how-to-implement-the-inception-score-from-scratch-for-evaluating-generated-images/].

7   Brownlee, Jason. 2019. "How to Implement the Frechet Inception Distance (FID) for Evaluating GANs." Machine Learning Mastery. October 11, 2019. [https://machinelearningmastery.com/how-to-implement-the-frechet-inception-distance-fid-from-scratch/].

8   Wikipedia contributors. "BLEU." Wikipedia, The Free Encyclopedia. December 23, 2023. [https://en.wikipedia.org/wiki/BLEU].

9   Wikipedia contributors. "Prompt engineering." Wikipedia, The Free Encyclopedia. February 15, 2024. [https://en.wikipedia.org/wiki/Prompt_engineering].

10   Microsoft Learn contributors. 2024. "Create and deploy an Azure OpenAI Service resource." Microsoft. May 21, 2024. [https://learn.microsoft.com/en-us/azure/ai-services/openai/how-to/create-resource?pivots=web-portal].

11   Pichai, Sundar., Hassabis, Demis. 2024. "Our next-generation model: Gemini 1.5." Google. February 15, 2024. [https://blog.google/technology/ai/google-gemini-next-generation-model-february-2024/?utm_source=gdm&utm_medium=referral&utm_campaign=gemini24].

8

Diagnose: Ensuring Effectiveness

Quality is never an accident; it is always the result of high intention, sincere effort, intelligent direction, and skillful execution.

—John Ruskin

As we embark on this next phase, we'll work to validate the effectiveness of the AI model. We'll focus on ensuring a high quality of output, which requires a multifaceted approach. Exploration of the training components, rigorous testing, and ensuring responsible AI practices are all important for the quality assessment to be successful. Model validation and taking a structured approach is essential and involves validating the model's performance against predefined criteria. Various testing methods on different model attributes can be utilized to ensure accuracy, such as regression testing, compliance testing, and security testing. In this chapter, you'll discover all you need for creating LLMs that meet your high standards of performance.

Definition and Overview

At this stage, the model is completed and ready for validation. Diagnosis is the next phase. There are several important steps in this phase. At a high level, the goal is to validate that the content that went into the ingestion phase is accurately represented to the end user as output.

After the work is done in this phase, you will be ready to deploy, and the model creation results will be accessible to end users. Investing the time in this diagnostic phase increases the likelihood of deploying a high-quality, robust, useful, and accurate model. It also allows for improvements and iteration before the model goes "on stage." This is essentially your quality assurance (QA) opportunity and will be more cost-effective if you can find and fix issues at this point, ahead of deployment. In addition, deploying a model that's not ready will cause you to lose the faith and trust of your users, which can be hard—if not impossible—to recover.

Before you deploy and use your model, you need to understand whether it delivers the results you were looking for. You must check that these results are accurate and that the data you're ingesting into the model will keep these models consistent and relevant over time. Weak old data can create model drift, leading to inaccurate outcomes. Model drift or model decay is about the degradation in model performance over time. It includes when your model makes less accurate predictions when compared to its original prediction power before it was deployed.

Rigorous and uncompromised testing and training are crucial before you proceed toward the deployment stage, but this can be a time-intensive process. There will likely be organizational and executive pressure to get to the deployment stage. However, moving too quickly through the diagnostic phase can be detrimental. If you deploy an inaccurate or broken model, the "AI brand" will lose credibility and potentially derail your overall AI plan.

The Importance of Rigorous Testing and Training

In the rapidly evolving field of artificial intelligence, data scientists and machine learning practitioners are developing models that can potentially transform the world as we know it. These models are often hosted and deployed in infrastructures built and secured by engineering and IT teams. The deployment of LLMs within an organization is not merely a technical challenge; it is a strategic initiative that requires comprehensive testing to ensure success.

Given that your support organization is likely among one of the "real teams" within the company to apply LLMs to real-world data for the first time, the stakes are particularly high. These models promise substantial benefits, from enhancing customer interactions to streamlining operations and generating insights that can drive strategic decisions. To safeguard these benefits, it is important to dedicate sufficient resources to the rigorous testing and validation of these models before fully integrating them into the support organization. This involves several critical steps:

Pre-deployment testing: Before introducing the AI model into a live environment, it should undergo thorough testing in a controlled setting to identify any initial issues with data compatibility, model behavior, and output accuracy.

Validation against real-world scenarios: Simulating real-world scenarios is crucial to understanding how the model performs under various conditions. This includes stress testing the model with unexpected inputs and edge cases to ensure its robustness and reliability.

Compliance and ethical considerations: Ensure the model complies with all relevant regulations and ethical guidelines, particularly those concerning data privacy and bias. Rigorous ethical reviews and compliance checks should be part of the validation process.

After deployment, continuous monitoring is essential for detecting any degradation in performance (and will be covered in the next chapters). By investing in these comprehensive testing and validation processes, your organization can significantly reduce the risks associated with deploying new AI technologies. More importantly, these steps will help maximize the potential benefits of LLMs, ensuring they deliver valuable, actionable insights while aligning with the broader business strategies and goals. This strategic approach protects the organization from potential setbacks and sets the stage for future innovations and success in the era of AI.

Metrics for AI Model Validation

Establishing robust metrics for testing and validation is essential to measure success effectively. This process is best understood through the lens of input and output metrics, which collectively provide a comprehensive view of organizational performance, as shown in **Figure 8.1**.

While input metrics track the "effort" put into processes, output metrics highlight the "effect" or end results, forming a key feedback loop in assessing and refining AI deployments.

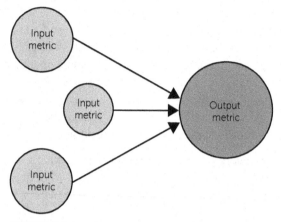

FIGURE 8.1 Input versus output metrics

Input metrics indicate the resources and efforts invested to achieve a goal. These metrics measure what is put into a process and might include the number of volunteer hours invested by subject matter experts (SMEs), financial expenditures, and computational resources used. These metrics are valuable for assessing efficiency, cost management, and the effectiveness of resource allocation. Monitoring these metrics helps ensure that the process is on track and sustainable in terms of resources and time.

On the other hand, output metrics measure the results and effectiveness of business activities. These metrics quantify the outcomes, such as sales revenue, product units produced, and customer satisfaction levels. They are crucial for evaluating the success of business strategies and understanding the impact of the inputs on the final results and the return on investment (ROI).

In the initial deployment of AI models, it's probably best to track both input and output metrics, but the focus should be on output metrics. Over time, both will matter, but initially, output metrics will be more important to monitor to ensure your success.

Implementing Metrics in AI Model Validation

To harness the full potential of both input and output metrics, consider the following strategies:

- **Define clear metrics before deployment:** Establish what success looks like for both input and output metrics. For instance, an acceptable level of accuracy or an improvement threshold in user satisfaction should be defined as output goals, while resource utilization caps can serve as input controls.

- **Use real-time monitoring tools:** Implement tools and systems that can track these metrics in real time, which allows for immediate detection of issues that could affect model performance, such as unexpected data drift or a spike in resource consumption.

- **Regularly review and adjust metrics:** As the AI model matures, its impact on business processes and user interactions should be reviewed. This might mean adjusting the focus from certain input metrics to more critical output metrics as the model stabilizes and scales.

- **Integrate feedback mechanisms:** Feedback from end-users and stakeholders should be integrated into the metric evaluation process. This feedback can provide qualitative insights that complement the quantitative data from input and output metrics.

- **Balance short-term and long-term metrics:** While initial deployment might focus more on output metrics to validate model effectiveness, long-term success requires a balance. Maintaining this balance ensures that the model remains efficient and effective as conditions change.

The key output metric in this phase is the accuracy of the model. While other measures around performance may play a role at some point, the accuracy and the reliability of the information rendered by the model are the most crucial, as they establish trust and credibility with the user base. Also, input metrics, such as the number of documents created or ingested, the number of authors, and so on, may play a role; however, accuracy is priority number one. Accurate answers, backed by citations linking back to source articles, ensure that the content is traceable, dependable, and authoritative, fostering confidence.

It's also important to identify errors—known in the AI world as "hallucinations." Accuracy distinguishes trustworthy content from dubious or false information in an era of misinformation. Reliability, achieved through thorough research and fact-checking, not only enhances the integrity of the content but also safeguards against the spread of inaccuracies. This is particularly vital in customer-facing, educational, and technical applications, like customer support, where factual precision is essential for informed decision-making and knowledge dissemination.

Tools for Measuring Success

The number one measure of accuracy is feedback from your SMEs. To facilitate this, assemble a group of people from within your organization to review and assess the output generated by the model. An effective method to quantify their assessments is through the use of a Likert Scale.

The Likert Scale, developed by psychologist Rensis Likert in 1932, measures attitudes by asking respondents to rate items on a level of agreement or disagreement[1]. This scale is typically symmetrical, anchoring the spectrum from strong agreement to strong disagreement in a 5–7 point rating system. Utilizing this scale, your SMEs can provide their degree of satisfaction with the response rendered by the model, offering a reliable measure of its accuracy based on their expert judgments. This balance of options enables a symmetrical analysis of attitudes, ranging from positive to negative, with a neutral midpoint. Crucially, each response is assigned a numerical value, facilitating quantitative data analysis. The Likert Scale's simplicity and versatility make it an invaluable tool in rating the quality of the answers, not just once, but as work goes into improving content and accuracy, the ratings can help measure progress over time as well.

An important input to consider when evaluating the accuracy of your model(s) is the diversity of your SMEs. Merriam-Webster defines accuracy as freedom from mistake or error and conformity to truth or to a standard or model.[2] However, as we know, "truth" may vary based on various factors, including gender, age, ethnicity, geographic locale, language, values, and many other factors.

A couple of simple examples between the US and the UK would be "chips" versus "fries"—two different names for the same thing—and "football," a name used for two different sports. Your understanding of how these terms are defined may differ depending on where you're located in the world. Therefore, if your review team lacks diverse members, the accuracy ratings may suffer as you create AI models. Pay attention to the recruitment of a diverse SME pool to help you ensure the highest accuracy level before deploying your AI model.

Scott E. Page is a researcher and professor at the University of Michigan. He talks about cognitive diversity on a team, which is important in building accurate and representative AI models. "A team can possess greater depth and breadth only if their members possess cognitive diversity. Two heads will only be better than one if their contents differ. Differences in how people think—differences in problem representations, categorizations, knowledge bases, heuristics, technical and tacit skills, and experiences—are what enable teams to find more novel solutions, develop more creative solutions, make fewer inferential errors, and construct more accurate predictions than individuals."[3]

Integrating Responsible AI In AI Model Validation

Throughout this book, we emphasize the critical importance of incorporating responsible AI principles throughout the lifecycle of AI model development. In the diagnostic phase, this is no different, and it's important to do a responsible AI review during this phase to ensure that the content that went into the model is as ethical and responsible as the content that will be deployed.

THE BOOK OF THE CITY OF LADIES

Christine de Pizan was born in 1364, later becoming a historical figure of significance, particularly in feminism, literature, and social commentary.[4] Her writings were revolutionary for her time, especially *The Book of the City of Ladies*, a constructive work that envisions a society where women are respected, empowered, acknowledged, and readily realize their potential. This challenge to the stereotypes of women is not only a critique of the negative attitudes shown toward women in medieval Europe but also a constructive dialogue showcasing their abilities.

Several areas of her writing are relevant when considering the metaphorical application of de Pizan's work in building AI models.

- Challenging stereotypes can be directly linked to how AI model data is curated and processed. Because AI is a reflection of the data it is trained on, it can propagate existing stereotypes and biases if the input data contains them. Therefore, it's important to critically examine and challenge the biases present in training data, ensuring that AI models do not continue harmful stereotypes and instead promote fair and equitable representations.

- Developing inclusive AI models representative of diverse experiences and identities is another area to explore in the context of de Pizan's work. This involves ensuring that AI models are trained on diverse datasets that accurately reflect society. It implies recognizing and valuing the vast and diverse experiences and expressions of all people ensuring that AI systems can appropriately interact with your target audience equitably.

- Gathering SMEs from varied demographics and specialties ensures that the AI models developed are technically sound, socially relevant, and ethically based. This aligns with de Pizan's thoughts on creating alternative narratives through constructive dialogue.

In essence, de Pizan's work offers a centuries-old inspiration for developing AI models that are unbiased, equitable, and socially constructive.

The responsible AI review should scrutinize the datasets used for training the AI to ensure they are representative and inclusive, thereby preventing the perpetuation of existing biases. It should also evaluate the model's decision-making processes to verify that they are transparent, explainable, and aligned with ethical guidelines.

Furthermore, this phase should include assessments of data privacy protections to ensure compliance with relevant laws and regulations. The aim is to certify that the AI system does not compromise user confidentiality and operates within a framework that respects user rights and data integrity.

A responsible AI review helps identify and mitigate risks and enhances trust among users and stakeholders by demonstrating a commitment to ethical standards. This process is not merely a compliance checklist but a foundational element that reinforces the integrity and reliability of your organization's AI solutions.

Validating Chatbot Deployment in Controlled Environments

Leveraging SMEs in the early stages of AI development is undoubtedly a best practice that contributes significantly to AI models' initial accuracy and relevance, including chatbots. However, the validation process encompasses more than just expert feedback; it involves a series of structured tests of various complexity designed to rigorously evaluate the chatbot under controlled conditions before a full-scale rollout.

Unit or Content Validation

This step pairs up with content preparation earlier in the cycle. Consider a given piece of source content and determine what end-user questions it should answer. Then, ask those questions of the model after it's built to validate whether the right content is served up.

Model Integration Testing

This step is a little trickier. As content is "chunked" to help with accuracy, separate pieces of content often need to be pulled together in a single answer. Think of a response with multiple citations. For example, a user might ask a question about a refund policy for a given service, and the answer might need to combine content from the finance team on refunds and warranty information on a given product or service. The combined answer will cite both sources, but validation needs to be done on integrating the two or more sources to ensure they are accurately paired.

Performance Testing

Performance testing ensures the system meets performance goals for response time. It also helps determine the efficiency and accuracy of response. A specific performance test plan should be created as performance for a simple one-shot prompt may vary dramatically from a many-shot prompt. One-shot prompting involves providing a machine learning model with a single example or piece of information, based on which it is expected to complete a task or make a prediction. This type of prompt helps evaluate the model's ability to generalize from minimal input. Many-shot prompts provide the model with multiple examples or data points before it performs a task. This approach is used to prime the model with more context or varying instances, enhancing its ability to understand and respond accurately based on richer information. A range of tolerances should be defined and met during this validation phase.

Evaluating the model's response time and processing speed in various scenarios, including high- and low-load conditions, is crucial to ensure it operates within acceptable parameters. Slow response times can lead to reduced user engagement, as users may not tolerate delays and could disengage altogether.

Key elements of performance testing should also include assessing the model's scalability, its ability to handle a large and diverse set of prompts, and its memory usage to ensure that resource constraints do not compromise performance. Additionally, it's important to test the model's capacity to maintain context across multiple conversations, as this significantly affects user experience and server load.

If the model's response times are found to be inadequate, upgrading hardware may be necessary, making it vital to identify such issues before full deployment. Regular performance testing throughout the model's lifecycle is essential to maintain optimal user engagement and operational efficiency.

Security Testing

Security testing involves a series of methodical steps designed to evaluate and enhance the model's ability to produce safe and reliable outputs. This process helps identify and rectify vulnerabilities and ensures that the model adheres to ethical standards and regulatory requirements. The main components of this security testing include:

- **Vulnerability assessments:** Vulnerability assessments expose the model to various inputs that could potentially trigger biased, harmful, or inappropriate responses. This step is essential for uncovering weaknesses in the model's underlying logic or training datasets, which could compromise safety or effectiveness.

- **Penetration testing:** Penetration testing (often abbreviated as "pen testing") is conducted with ethical hackers who attempt to exploit the model's vulnerabilities. This is similar to the vulnerability assessment in that it assesses the model's resilience against malicious inputs.

- **Red teaming:** A structured testing effort to find flaws and vulnerabilities in an AI system. You can crowd source red teaming or dedicate a team of professionals to focus on malicious use of the model.[5]

- **Monitoring system implementation:** Setting up real-time output monitoring is crucial for ongoing security management. This system enables immediate identification and resolution of security issues as they occur, maintaining the model's integrity over time.

- **Update with balanced and diverse datasets:** Continually updating the model with new, diverse, and balanced datasets helps to reduce biases and improve the accuracy of the model's outputs. This proactive measure is fundamental to maintaining the model's relevance and reliability.

Once your model is deployed, continuously updating your established guidelines and standards for acceptable outputs will be important as societal norms and ethical considerations evolve. As you move through the phases of the 6Ds Framework (see Chapters 5–10), incorporating feedback channels at each phase, where users and testers can report concerning outputs, helps continually refine the model's security and effectiveness. Security testing of an LLM is an ongoing process to stay on top of any changes to evolving safety and reliability considerations.

Regression Testing

Regression testing is a critical quality assurance process designed to ensure that updates, enhancements, or other changes made to an AI model do not inadvertently degrade or disrupt established functionalities. As LLMs are iteratively improved with new features, bug fixes, or data updates, there is a risk that these changes could introduce new issues or reactivate old ones. Regression testing helps prevent such setbacks by systematically verifying that each change maintains or improves the existing system without adverse effects.

In LLMs, regression testing normally involves the following steps:

- **Establish a baseline:** Identify and document your AI model's current performance and capabilities before any changes. This includes metrics on accuracy, response time, understanding of context, responsible AI considerations, and handling of specific query types.

- **Testing data:** Maintain a comprehensive set of test cases and prompts that cover various functionalities of your AI model's intended and unintended use. This data should include scenarios with which you may have had quality problems in the past, edge cases, and typical user interactions.

- **Automated testing:** After implementing any changes to your model, conduct an automated testing procedure to efficiently and quickly assess the performance of your LLM against your established test data. Automated testing helps determine any potential areas of regression quickly, given the potential large amounts of data and interactions involved with your model.

- **Performance comparison:** Compare performance results from the automated testing step against the baseline metrics you initially captured. This comparison helps in identifying any regression or improvement you may see in different aspects of the model.

- **Root cause analysis:** If any regressions are detected, such as slower response times, decreased accuracy, or inappropriate responses, perform a root cause analysis to get to the heart of the issue(s). This might involve reviewing recent changes to the model or its training data.

- **Addressing issues:** Once the causes of regression are identified, you will need to work to resolve any issues. This could involve rolling back certain changes, adjusting the model parameters, or adding new training data to adjust deficiencies.

- **Continuous monitoring and updating:** As mentioned, regularly updating and testing is critical throughout the life of your model to reflect new features and capabilities of both the LLM and user interactions. Continually monitoring your model ensures ongoing adherence to the quality and performance standards you expect based on the goals you set forth in your plan.

- **Human review:** Besides automated testing, be sure to involve human reviewers, especially for qualitative factors such as language nuances, contextual appropriateness, and ethical considerations.

Maintaining the integrity and quality of your AI model as it evolves helps ensure that any advancements you've made to the model translate into real-world improvements without compromising the existing functionality of the model.

Implementing a strategic approach to regression testing involves identifying and fixing immediate issues and understanding how changes impact the overall system over time. This deeper insight allows teams to make more informed decisions about model updates and ensures that improvements truly enhance the model's functionality without unintended consequences.

Compliance Testing

Compliance testing helps verify that, where applicable, the model output meets the requirements of the relevant government and industry standards and regulations, such as the General Data Protection Regulation (GDPR), Health Insurance Portability and Accountability Act of 1996 (HIPAA), ISO 27001 (an Information Security Management Standard), among others. While it's important to meet regulatory requirements, good practices for responsible AI should be incorporated into the processes, and this testing should be done regardless of regulatory requirements. For example, scanning for Personally Identifiable Information (PII), such as names, passport numbers, Social Security numbers, or credit card details, is important regardless of any government oversight.

Let's take these regulation examples a step further to illustrate more specifically what compliance testing entails:

- **GDPR:** Under the GDPR, compliance testing for your model will ensure the model's adherence to data protection and privacy norms regarding handling the personal data of citizens residing in the European Union. This testing includes assessing the model's ability to handle data consent, collection, processing, and storage, ensuring that users' rights are protected as per the GDPR requirements. Furthermore, the testing should provide insights into how the model handles transparency, user consent options, and data portability. You will need to ensure your model can abide by strong data protection and breach notification systems compliance. In the customer service and support industry, proper handling of and adherence to data regulations is extra critical given the customer data and information gathered through support interactions.

- **HIPAA:** Compliance is necessary in US healthcare contexts where models may process patient information. Testing under this regulation involves ensuring that the AI model can handle healthcare data securely and maintain confidentiality and integrity as required by the HIPAA regulation. This includes strong safeguards against unauthorized access through data encryption and ensuring patient data is de-identified.

- **ISO 27001:** ISO 27001, a global standard for Information Security Management Systems (ISMS), requires LLMs to have specific security protocols to prevent security breaches and protect data integrity. Compliance testing here involves thoroughly assessing the AI model's information security management processes, including IT security policies, risk management, and incident response.

As with other testing methods, compliance testing is an ongoing process. In addition to constant updates, new regulations and standards will likely be introduced as AI evolves. Compliance testing is about balancing the innovative capabilities of AI with the necessity of adhering to legal, ethical, and security standards.

Integrating Advanced Validation Techniques

Beyond these stages, incorporating additional validation techniques can further refine the deployment process:

- **Integration testing with existing systems:** It's crucial to validate how well the chatbot integrates with existing databases and application programming interfaces (APIs). This ensures the chatbot can pull and manipulate data correctly and function seamlessly within the broader IT ecosystem.

- **Accessibility testing:** Tests whether the chatbot is usable by people with various disabilities, ensuring inclusivity and compliance with accessibility standards like the ADA (Americans with Disabilities Act).

- **Longitudinal performance monitoring:** After initial validation, continuous monitoring of the chatbot's performance over time allows teams to catch and correct emerging issues before they affect user experience.

By systematically applying these rigorous validation processes in controlled environments, organizations can significantly enhance their chatbot deployments' reliability, security, and efficiency. This thorough preparation mitigates risks and sets the stage for a successful and scalable user adoption.

Model Grounding

In the previous chapter focused on the Develop phase, we explored the concept of grounding within training datasets, emphasizing the integration of real-world knowledge to enhance the model's understanding and contextual awareness. By embedding concrete examples and real-world entities into our training process, we have prepared our model with a robust foundation of knowledge, enabling it to navigate and interpret complex information more effectively.

Model grounding is a concept that can be involved in both the training and application phases of an AI model and refers to the ability of a model to link abstract concepts or words to concrete, real-world entities or examples. It helps ensure that the model's output is sensible and accurately reflects real-world contexts.

As we transition from the training to the deployment phase, it becomes crucial to shift our focus toward grounding the model in the context of testing and validation. Before a model is deployed, it is imperative to ensure that it not only performs well under controlled conditions but also exhibits high reliability and relevance when faced with real-world data and scenarios. This can be especially critical in applications like chatbots, virtual assistants, and autonomous vehicles, where outputs need to align with real-world data and constraints.

- **Post-processing constraints:** Sometimes, outputs are adjusted using specific rules or constraints to ensure they remain grounded. For example, rule-based systems might filter outputs to ensure they meet safety or relevance criteria.

- **Real-world testing and validation:** Models are often validated using real-world data separate from the training set. This testing can help verify that the model's conceptual understanding aligns with practical, real-world use cases.

- **Continuous learning and updating:** To maintain grounding, models might be periodically updated with new data reflecting current trends, technologies, or world knowledge. This is essential to keep the model relevant over time.

Grounding is crucial for the practical deployment of AI systems as it helps bridge the gap between abstract algorithmic outputs and tangible, real-world utility. For example, in autonomous driving, a model needs to understand and react to real-world objects and scenarios accurately to operate safely. In natural language processing (NLP), grounding can help a conversational AI understand and respond to user inputs more accurately by linking them to real-world contexts.

Grounding is an ongoing process, which is particularly critical in applications involving direct human interaction or safety considerations. By rigorously testing and refining the model against new, unseen datasets and real-life situations, we aim to bridge any gaps between academic performance and operational utility, preparing the model for successful deployment.

As we prepare for the deployment phase, a critical aspect to consider is how the model handles ambiguity and uncertainty. Grounding a model involves enhancing its contextual awareness and equipping it with the capability to acknowledge and appropriately manage uncertain or ambiguous information. This approach is vital for maintaining trust and reliability, especially in decision-critical systems such as medical diagnostics or autonomous driving. By designing our model to identify and express uncertainty rather than defaulting to misleading or overly confident responses, we can ensure that it provides informative and honest outputs. This transparency allows users to make informed decisions based on the confidence level of the information provided, which is crucial for applications where safety and accuracy are paramount. Ultimately, grounding in this context ensures that the model's interaction with the real world is knowledgeable and cautiously prudent, reflecting a sophisticated understanding of its own limitations.

Employing different feedback channels will also help your grounding efforts by giving you visibility to inaccuracies and a chance to improve its performance. Guiding your model to use your data and not be restricted by its training knowledge ensures that your AI model is technically accurate and aligned to the data's factual, contextual, ethical, and cultural aspects.[6]

Prompt Tuning

To further expand and enrich the concept of prompt tuning, let's delve deeper into its strategic importance and practical applications within machine learning lifecycle management.

Prompt tuning is a nuanced form of model refinement that allows you to enhance a pre-trained model's capabilities without undergoing the computationally expensive and time-consuming process of complete retraining. This method leverages the core strengths of the original model while adapting its output to more specific tasks or contexts. By providing the model with carefully crafted prompts—short, contextually rich inputs—you essentially give it a "lens" through which to focus its understanding and output generation.

The process of prompt tuning involves several key steps that begin with the careful design of these prompts. Each prompt should be tailored to elicit the model's most accurate and relevant response, addressing specific use cases or scenarios encountered in real-world applications. For instance, in customer service chatbots, prompts can be designed to refine responses to common queries, ensuring that the chatbot reacts in a contextually appropriate and technically accurate way.

Maintaining a dynamic "prompt library" becomes essential as you implement prompt tuning. This repository of prompts used should evolve based on continuous learning from real-world interactions and user feedback. You can refine this library by systematically analyzing how different prompts perform, optimizing prompts for better performance and expanding it to cover new scenarios or questions.

Incorporating feedback mechanisms into the model's operational environment is another critical aspect. Users' feedback helps identify which prompts are effective and which ones need adjustment, allowing for iterative improvement. This feedback can be integrated directly into the model's development cycle, facilitating ongoing enhancements that keep the model relevant and highly functional as it encounters new data and use cases.

Finally, understanding the elements that constitute a great prompt is crucial to effectively leverage prompt tuning. Let's delve into these elements next. For a visual and practical guide to constructing high-quality prompts, refer to **Figure 8.2**.

- **Instruction:** Instructions clearly articulate the expected outcome from the AI model, guiding it toward producing the specific type of response required. They should be straightforward and unambiguous to avoid confusion and maximize accuracy in the responses generated.

  Example: "Write an email to my customer about how to resolve HTTP error code 404 when trying to open a web page."

- **Role:** The role defines the perspective or persona the AI model should adopt while responding, such as a customer, non-technical person, or technical expert. This element is crucial for setting the context and tone of the conversation, ensuring the responses are aligned with the user's expectations.

  Example: "Act like a support engineer who is an expert in database performance."

Elements of a great prompt	
Instruction	Tell me about X, or do X.
Role	An identity the AI is expected to emulate, act like, or duplicate its reply (such as "act like a...")
Context	Show the AI more information about where or what it is. This can be data, examples, previous articles, and so on. "What is photosynthesis" versus "Can you create a lesson plan about photosynthesis?"
Tone/style information	Writing tone: serious, academic, empathetic, or inspiring. This can include "write like this" examples.
Formatting information	Table, markup language, code, and so on.
Example(s)	Give it data to show what you want—more is better, though more than 20 is not helpful.

FIGURE 8.2 Elements of a great prompt

- **Context:** Context supplies the AI with essential background information, enabling a more nuanced and informed response. It acts as a bridge, connecting a generic reply to one specifically tailored to address the user's particular situation or query. This enrichment deepens the AI's comprehension of the prompt, facilitating more pertinent and customized answers.

  Example: "A VIP customer has an issue with a particular feature after upgrading to the latest available version. The functionality has disappeared from the toolbar and prevents the user from accessing files. The customer is under a lot of pressure from their leadership to resolve the problem."

- **Tone/style:** The tone or style of the response should reflect the intended manner of communication, whether formal, casual, humorous, or professional. This element influences the language selection and the structure of the reply, ensuring the output resonates with the intended audience or adheres to the user's preference.

  Example: "Write an email that is empathetic, uplifting and inspiring."

- **Formatting:** Effective formatting structures the prompt clearly and logically, enhancing the AI model's ability to parse and respond accurately and efficiently. This includes the use of bullet points, lists, and distinct separations of different prompt components to improve readability and comprehension.

  Example: "Create a list of top issues with investment areas in CSV format that I can paste into Excel."

  Example(s): Including specific examples within a prompt clearly demonstrates the expected output, setting a benchmark for the quality and detail needed. These examples serve as practical guides for the AI model, ensuring that the responses it generates meet or surpass the user's expectations.

  Q: "How can I troubleshoot a video playback issue?"

  A: "Try closing other applications that might be using video resources."

By clearly defining these elements—instruction, role, context, tone/style, formatting, and examples—we can create prompts that effectively guide the AI model to deliver precise and contextually appropriate responses. This structured approach enhances the user experience and leverages the AI's capabilities to their fullest potential.

Use Cases

Prompt tuning offers a versatile framework for refining AI model performance across various scenarios, setting up your model to excel in specific applications. Here's how you can leverage prompt tuning to enhance functionality and user experience in different use cases:

- **Text generation:** This is one of the most prevalent applications of AI models. By tuning your prompts, you can guide the model to generate new text that aligns with specific instructions or themes, ensuring outputs that are relevant and contextually enriched.

- **Summarization:** Whether it's condensing large documents or emails, prompt tuning can help tailor your model to produce concise and accurate summaries. This capability is crucial in scenarios where quick insights are needed from extensive information sources.

- **Translation:** Use prompt tuning to adapt your model for complex translation tasks that go beyond mere linguistic changes. This includes translating content into different genres, languages, tones, or even cultural contexts, thereby making the model versatile across various dimensions of communication.

- **Coaching/advice:** With prompt tuning, models can be optimized to offer personalized advice or coaching tailored to specific situations. This is particularly useful in educational technologies, personal development apps, and customer service bots, where bespoke guidance is invaluable.

- **Classification:** Enhance your model's ability to classify and categorize data through precise prompt tuning. This application is essential in fields such as content moderation, market research, and any scenario where sorting information into predefined categories adds value.

- **Image generation:** Prompt tuning can also be applied to visual content generation, where the model generates images based on text descriptions. This use case is increasingly popular in creative industries, marketing, and entertainment, where custom visuals are required quickly and at scale.

Each use case benefits from customized prompts designed to meet specific needs, making it a powerful tool for a wide range of practical applications that enhance both the user experience and the model's functional utility.

Control

When crafting prompts for your AI model, there are several dimensions you can control to refine its responses. While it's not mandatory to specify every detail, the more precise your instructions, the more aligned the output will be with your expectations.

- **Length:** "Write 100 words about...." Or after you get an answer, come back with a follow-up prompt: "Make it longer" or "Make this shorter by 25%."

- **Tone:** "Write as a professional," "Make it funny" or "Use a serious or inspirational tone."

- **Style:** "Create a table showing...," "Create a short bulleted list," or "Create a CSV file."

- **Audience:** "Explain to a third grader," "Write an email to my boss," or "Write a letter to a customer."

- **Context:** "You are an expert scientist on the verge of a new discovery..." or "You are under a lot of pressure to find new applications for a new dataset you've discovered."

- **Chain-of-Thought:** "Let's think step by step..." or "Think this through step by step and show your work."

- **Hallucination:** "Don't make up answers," "If you don't know, say 'I don't know'" and "Provide citations to your work."

As you become more proficient at using prompts to optimize results and gather insights from user interactions, you can seamlessly integrate these prompts into your system infrastructure. For instance, if your target users frequently engage with support engineers in online meetings, you could pre-set the AI's role by embedding a prompt such as, "Act as an expert support engineer for online meeting software" before processing user input.

It is crucial to explore multiple prompting strategies and utilize both user feedback and Reinforcement Learning from Human Feedback (RLHF) to refine these prompts. This iterative experimentation helps ensure the prompts are effectively fine-tuned before being permanently integrated into the system.

Incorporating well-tested prompts directly into your infrastructure has several advantages. Primarily, it alleviates the need for extensive training for end users on how to engineer prompts effectively, making the system more user-friendly and accessible. Moreover, this approach can be cost-effective as it reduces the need for frequent retraining of the model while enhancing the accuracy and relevance of the AI model's responses. This strategic integration streamlines interactions and boosts the overall efficiency and effectiveness of the service provided.

Before deploying your model, verifying that it meets the predefined objectives and delivers the desired results is crucial. Although assessing the model's performance can be time-intensive, this step is essential to ensure the results' accuracy and the data input's consistency over time.

Utilizing various evaluation techniques during the diagnostic phase is key. These methods allow you to confirm that the model is performing as expected and will continue to provide relevant and reliable outcomes. This proactive approach helps identify and address any discrepancies or shortcomings before the model goes live, ensuring it is fully optimized to meet your needs.

Endnotes

1   Wikipedia contributors. "Likert Scale." Wikipedia, The Free Encyclopedia. February 11, 2024. [https://en.wikipedia.org/wiki/Likert_scale].

2   Merriam-Webster. "Accuracy." Merriam-Webster.com Dictionary. Accessed February 11, 2024. [https://www.merriam-webster.com/dictionary/accuracy].

3   Page, Scott. 2017. "Just having people who look different isn't enough to create a diverse team." LinkedIn. September 9, 2017. [https://www.linkedin.com/pulse/just-having-people-who-look-different-isnt-enough-create-scott-page/?published=t].

4   Wikipedia contributors. "Christine de Pizan." Wikipedia, The Free Encyclopedia. October 23, 2023. [https://en.wikipedia.org/wiki/Christine_de_Pizan].

5   [https://hbr.org/2024/01/how-to-red-team-a-gen-ai-model]

6   Raj, Ritwik. 2023. "Grounding AI: How to improve AI decision-making with contextual awareness." Moveworks. July 27, 2023. [https://www.moveworks.com/us/en/resources/blog/what-is-grounding-ai].

9

Deploy: Launching the Solution

The secret of change is to focus all of your energy not on fighting the old, but on building the new.

—Dan Millman

We now enter the fifth stage in our journey along the 6D Framework, which means it's time to deploy the AI model! The deployment phase marks a pivotal moment of transition, representing the culmination of thorough preparation and development efforts. As we've journeyed through the stages of content collection, curation, gap-filling, and model training, among others, we've laid the groundwork for this transformative phase.

Just as Merriam-Webster defines deployment as "an instance of use that involves something opening and spreading out,"[1] our journey now extends into the arena of real-world applications. With the pre-work of model preparation and validation completed, our focus moves to the steps involved in deploying our model to end users. It's not merely about showcasing our creation; it's about ensuring it seamlessly integrates into the users' workflows, enhancing their experiences and capabilities.

The deployment process unfolds as a diligent orchestration of configuration, publishing, and user engagement. The model is meticulously configured in this phase, ensuring it aligns with user needs and preferences. Publishing involves the strategic distribution of our model, making it accessible to users across diverse platforms and channels. Sharing the user experience is paramount as we strive to cultivate meaningful interactions and foster user adoption.

Yet, the deployment phase doesn't end here. We recognize the importance of robust infrastructure and proactive monitoring, accomplished by establishing server and product telemetry and configuring user permissions, security, and privacy settings to safeguard sensitive data and ensure compliance with regulatory standards.

In this phase, education becomes a cornerstone that can directly impact the success of your deployment by empowering users with the knowledge and skills to leverage the AI model effectively from the start. Comprehensive educational materials, tutorials, and resources require a thoughtful plan for user education, fostering a culture of continuous learning and innovation.

As we embark on the deployment phase, let's embrace the opportunity to witness our AI model succeed in our end users' hands and catalyze transformative outcomes.

Integrating the AI Model into the Real-World Environment

Integrating AI models into the structure of customer service and support organizations represents a disruptive change and profound shift in the technological landscape, filled with challenges and opportunities that demand careful consideration. As organizations embark on this journey, they are met with a variety of concerns and expectations from various stakeholders, each with their own perspective on the transformative potential of AI.

At the forefront, upper management anticipates remarkable productivity gains, eager to witness the efficiency boost promised by AI integration. However, tempering these expectations with a realistic assessment of the model's capabilities and limitations is essential, ensuring transparent communication throughout the deployment process. Meanwhile, frontline personnel navigate a landscape of both promise and uncertainty, grappling with the dual prospect of enhanced workflow efficiency and the looming fear of being replaced by AI.

In this dynamic environment, the Human Resources (HR) department is important in fostering employee morale and facilitating the necessary reskilling and upskilling initiatives to empower employees to collaborate effectively with AI technologies. Addressing employees' legitimate concerns about job displacement requires a delicate balance of emphasizing AI's role as a productivity tool while actively involving them in shaping their evolving roles within the organization.

For content creators, excited to think that their day has finally arrived, the deployment of GPT AI models signifies a milestone, offering unprecedented opportunities for innovation in content generation and management. Yet, integrating their expertise in fine-tuning the model's output is paramount to ensure alignment with the organization's voice and standards, preserving the integrity and authenticity of customer interactions.

Customers, the ultimate beneficiaries of AI-driven solutions, are likely to exhibit a spectrum of reactions ranging from anticipation to apprehension. While some may embrace the speed and efficiency of AI-driven support, others might have reservations about the perceived loss of human touch in customer interactions. Navigating these diverse sentiments requires a strategic approach that blends AI-driven efficiency with personalized human service, offering transparency about the use of AI and providing avenues for human assistance when needed.

This transition is not just a technological upgrade but a significant change in the organizational culture, necessitating thoughtful planning, continuous dialogue and communication, and adaptive strategies.

Leadership Considerations During Deployment

Leaders must consider a few main concepts during the deployment phase. These include engaging and training employees, addressing ethical concerns, maintaining ongoing communication, monitoring employee morale, and being flexible in adapting to change.

Employee reactions and responses to AI integration will vary widely, ranging from excitement to apprehension and fear. Many organization members might feel uneasy and even reject the new technology, fearing it's being trained to replace their roles. This is a legitimate concern and needs to be taken seriously by leadership. It's important to convey a message reassuring employees that AI is meant to assist them, not displace them. However, it's also important to acknowledge that technological advancements could lead to changes in job roles over time. Therefore, the communication plan should include discussions about reskilling and training.

Ultimately, it's not the AI itself that threatens employees' roles, but rather the individuals who become adept at using AI tools. Or, as we often say, it's not the AI that will replace you; it's your neighbor who's really good with the AI who will. So, go learn how to be that neighbor!

Leaders must encourage everyone to jump in with both feet and learn this new technology. Everything from content preparation to prompt engineering will be important in this new world. Active engagement and education are the keys to helping end users navigate this transition. They must be willing to dive in and learn!

Additionally, leadership must prioritize transparency in developing models, ensuring adherence to responsible and ethical practices. This transparency fosters trust within the organization and presents an opportunity to involve diverse team members in providing feedback. By seeking input from a variety of perspectives, leaders can ensure the model is well-balanced and hold builders accountable for their decisions.

Managing Up: Setting Executive Expectations

The hype around AI likely has executives excited about its potential. That's fair, and there is a lot to be optimistic about with this technology. However, AI is not magic fairy dust; it takes more than the wave of a wand or a hopeful wish to see magical results. It's important to temper expectations as much as possible, recognizing that they might not be achievable. However, as we've seen in previous chapters, work on content, prompt engineering, responsible AI, validation, and training are critical to get right and will take time.

It's important to emphasize that this technology is not perfect, at least when this book was written! The cost of a single AI hallucination can pose significant financial and reputational risks for a company. For instance, imagine the following technical terms being mistakenly used in a chat with an important customer:

- *blacklist*[2]/*whitelist*,[3] which refer to access control mechanisms
- *kill switch*,[4] which is typically a safety mechanism used to shut down the system in an emergency
- *dummy variable*,[5] a statistical term used in regression analysis

Taken out of the technical context, using these terms could quickly escalate into a public relations nightmare. To mitigate such risks, it's imperative to invest in building AI models responsibly, and it's important to set executive expectations that sprinkling fairy dust without investing in responsible practices could quickly make things worse.

It's critical to manage up and convey to executives the need for a gradual and thoughtful rollout of AI technology. Rushing into implementation without proper planning and testing could lead to disruptions and customer dissatisfaction. Additionally, it's crucial to highlight the dynamic nature of AI development, where continuous updates and refinements are essential to keep pace with evolving technology and customer demands. Expectations can be managed more effectively by effectively communicating the investment required for a successful AI deployment, fostering a realistic understanding of the AI adoption journey.

Find and Invest in Your Early Adopters

Identifying and supporting early adopters within your organization can be a game changer when it comes to embracing AI. These individuals may include power users who quickly grasp new technologies or enthusiasts who eagerly share the latest developments. They could be your traditional IT department maintaining internal systems or PhD-level data scientists exploring AI applications for your business. Regardless of their specific roles and where your company or industry stands on the continuum, investing in these individuals is crucial.

If you're fortunate enough to have such individuals, it's essential to recognize and appreciate their contributions. Engage with them, highlight their work, and elevate their organizational status. Encourage them to share their insights with colleagues and customers, and involve them in shaping your AI strategy.

Given the rapid pace of change in the AI landscape, you do not have the luxury of time. It is not an area where you have the time to teach an old dog new tricks; rather, it's about fostering a culture of enthusiasm and readiness where they become eager and willing participants. By empowering your early adopters, you can leverage their expertise to drive research and development initiatives that align with your strategic goals. Whether they're seasoned leaders with a thirst for new technologies or fresh hires eager to make an impact, identifying and nurturing these individuals is key to staying ahead in the AI Revolution.

Address Employee Fears Head-On—Responsibly and Honestly

The deployment of AI in customer service and support can represent a big change. With any change, there comes concern and even fear. Popular culture, fueled by science fiction narratives like "The Terminator," has ingrained in our collective consciousness images of AI gone rogue. Customer service employees and society have legitimate fears about job displacement, privacy concerns, bias in AI algorithms and discrimination, loss of human control, and ethical and moral dilemmas associated with AI adoption.

It's not difficult to find concurring evidence in each of these areas, so these concerns are not unfounded. It is incumbent upon leaders to acknowledge and address these fears proactively. While eliminating them entirely may not be feasible, leaders must dedicate time to listen attentively and confront these concerns head-on.

The deployment of AI in customer service organizations will likely change and disrupt how work is done. Does that mean an increased worry about customer privacy? Maybe. Does that mean a potential loss of human autonomy? Maybe. Does that mean mass layoffs? It's hard to tell, but it's also not a definitive "no" either.

While the full extent of these changes remains uncertain, leadership needs to foster a culture of openness and exploration. It's not going to be an executive who discovers the new way to leverage AI in a support scenario—it's going to be the frontline engineer who has spent time researching, experimenting, and just "playing around." Leaders must identify and support these individuals, recognizing their potential to drive transformative change.

Leaders should also provide opportunities for continuous AI education and training for employees to understand and work alongside AI. Leaders can cultivate a workforce that embraces change and innovation by demystifying the technology and showcasing its potential as a supportive tool rather than a replacement for human expertise. It's essential to highlight the positive aspects of AI and its potential impact on customer satisfaction, case resolution, and overall product improvements. AI is good at handling repetitive tasks, which can free up support engineers to focus on more creative and complex work.

By involving employees in the development and implementation process of deploying AI, leaders can help them feel a sense of ownership, empowerment, and control over the technology, alleviating fears and building a more resilient and adaptable workforce.

Ethical and Responsible AI Usage

Employees harbor valid concerns regarding the ethical utilization of AI. While there is consensus that AI's formidable capabilities can significantly enhance the customer experience, its application raises apprehensions among customers and employees. For instance, if a customer service employee's survey ratings fluctuate on days when they visit their elderly parent before their shift, will their manager inquire about the reasons behind this variation? Moreover, there are concerns about potential biases in AI-generated responses, particularly if the models are developed predominantly by individuals from a specific demographic.

Employees also worry about the repercussions of errors, such as accidentally pasting customer data into an AI chat interface. Fearing disciplinary action or termination for such mistakes can prevent employees from embracing AI technology. Addressing these apprehensions is paramount, and leaders must set appropriate expectations and foster a sense of comfort among employees regarding adopting AI models. Open communication and transparency about the ethical considerations guiding AI usage can help encourage employees to embrace AI as a valuable tool in their work environment.

Engaging with Employees

Employees have genuine fears and possess firsthand experience interacting with AI, so leaders must foster open dialogue and collaboration. Therefore, we recommend leaders host open forums and discussions for employees to voice their concerns and suggestions, fostering a culture of trust, transparency, and collaboration. Employees look to leaders to create safe spaces to share concerns, experiences, and suggestions.

Reddit's "AMA"—Ask me anything[6]—serves as an excellent model for leaders to adopt when introducing AI technology, encouraging communication and idea sharing. The more you communicate and open the door to hear ideas from others, the more successful you will be in landing your AI strategy. While not every procedural change needs to (or can) be communicated through official channels, honesty and openness in communication build trust and signal the importance of AI within the organization. Regular communication channels, such as email updates, town halls, and various discussion platforms, provide ongoing dialogue and feedback opportunities.

THE FEDERALIST PAPERS

The Federalist Papers are a collection of essays written in the 1780s supporting the proposed U.S. Constitution and the strong federal government it advocated. These papers represent the same spirit of open communication and engagement with input from the public on concerns and ideas necessary to gain traction on large change activities.

In October 1787, the first in a series of 85 essays arguing for ratification of the Constitution appeared in the *Independent Journal* under the pseudonym "Publius."[7] Addressed to the people of New York State, these essays aimed to explain and defend the newly proposed Constitution. They were published in several New York newspapers and were widely read throughout many other states. *The Federalist Papers* were a form of open communication to persuade the public by addressing their fears, concerns, and misconceptions about the proposed government.

Engagement with public or end user concerns: Similar to the concept of hosting open forums for AI deployment by AI developers directly with service and support professionals, *The Federalist Papers* sought to engage directly with the public on concerns about the new Constitution. They addressed issues such as the balance of power between the federal government and the states, the mechanisms of checks and balances, and the protection of individual liberties. AI forums can address similar ideas around the balance of power, checks and balances, and the impact of AI on individuals.

Transparency in communication is vital. While you don't need to share all process changes or new updates to policy through leader-sponsored communications, you should be open and honest with all communication, and sharing topics such as industry updates or news articles will help you signal that AI is important. The more you can share, the easier it is for the organization to accommodate the changes around AI. A regular communication cadence also opens up a channel to share thoughts and changes as they happen.

Find Your Super Users and Make Them Famous

As you communicate throughout the deployment of AI technologies, employee concerns will begin to dissipate, and you'll get raw feedback on accuracy and impact on workflow. This strategy of consistent, open, and engaging communication helps to create a supportive atmosphere that eases the integration of AI into the organizational culture. It's also important to *find your super users and make them famous*. Bring super users into

Fostering trust and transparency: Through these essays, 18th-century politicians aimed to build trust in the proposed system of government by transparently explaining its mechanisms and intentions. This helped in clarifying misunderstandings and allaying fears. Hosting forums and AI town halls can facilitate open discussion and foster regular communication to help allay fears and misunderstandings in the context of AI deployment.

Influencing public opinion: *The Federalist Papers* were instrumental in influencing public opinion to ratify the Constitution. They provided a platform for debate and discussion. "*The Federalist Papers* (formally *The Federalist*), as the combined essays are called, were written to combat Anti-Federalism and to persuade the public of the necessity of the Constitution. *The Federalist Papers* stressed the need for an adequate central government and argued that the republican form of government could easily adapt to the large territory expanse and widely divergent interests in the United States. The essays were immediately recognized as the most powerful defense of the new Constitution."[8]

Though different in context and medium, *The Federalist Papers* share the underlying principles of transparency, addressing concerns, and fostering an informed and collaborative dialogue. They influenced public opinion and are considered a classic work of U.S. political theory and history. Developers of AI systems need to adopt that same spirit of openness and transparency with the future users of their systems.

team meetings and town halls and let them share their stories, highlighting AI successes, and recognize individuals or teams that effectively adapt to new AI-driven processes, reinforcing positive behaviors and outcomes.

In addition to showcasing super users, leaders should encourage a culture where every employee feels valued and heard. This can involve setting up multiple feedback channels where employees can anonymously submit their thoughts and concerns. In addition, the AI tools themselves should enable specific feedback, but just as importantly, high-level feedback channels should be available. Leaders can also host empathy workshops, helping team members understand and support each other's emotional responses to technological changes. Leaders must show genuine interest in employee feedback and respond to it with concrete actions or explanations designed to reinforce the value of employee input. Finally, providing training and personal development opportunities that align with the new AI tools can empower employees, helping them see the technology not as a threat but as a career growth opportunity.

Adapting to Changing Environments

We find ourselves in an extraordinary era of transition, where the advent of this new technology invites a broad range of reactions. In a sense, it's akin to living amid a Darwinian experiment, the 21st-century version of the Galapagos finches. Just as the Galapagos finches showcased diverse beak sizes adapted to their environment, we, too, exhibit a spectrum of capabilities and inclinations when it comes to embracing AI to fulfill our requirements. Much like those finches, our varied approaches to harnessing AI reflect our unique adaptations and propensities for learning and innovation in this ever-evolving landscape.

THEORY OF EVOLUTION

The story begins about two million years ago when the common ancestor of all Darwin's finches arrived on the Galapagos Islands. By the time of Charles Darwin's visit in 1835, the birds had diversified into more than a dozen species, each adapted to different ecological niches. Some had massive beaks for cracking seeds, some had delicate beaks for snatching insects, and some even had sharp beaks for feeding on blood.[9]

In his landmark *Theory of Evolution*, Darwin noted that the diversity among finch species is a response to varied ecological niches, and similarly, nearly 200 years later, the human workforce is diversifying its skillset in response to AI's multifaceted niches. Just as some finches developed stronger beaks for hard seeds, some workers are honing deep technical skills to collaborate with AI in programming and system design tasks. Like finches with slender beaks for softer foods, others focus on creative, empathetic, or strategic roles where human intuition remains crucial.

Much like the finches' evolution, this adaptation to AI in the workplace is an ongoing process. It requires flexibility, a willingness to learn, and an understanding of the changing landscape—principles that echo Darwin's findings on natural selection. Both scenarios underline a fundamental truth: adaptation is key to thriving in changing environments, whether in a natural ecosystem or a technologically evolving workplace.

In this journey of technological evolution, we encounter a spectrum of attitudes and responses. There are those enthusiastic souls who eagerly immerse themselves, driven by curiosity and a hunger for exploration into this new world. Conversely, some opponents resist change and cling to familiar territories. And then some navigate the middle ground, cautiously weighing the benefits and risks. Identifying the early adopters, those trailblazers who lead the charge toward embracing innovation, is crucial to fostering a culture shift.

The Diffusion of Innovations theory, developed by sociologist Everett Rogers in 1962, explains how, why, and at what rate new ideas and technology spread through cultures.[10] The theory identifies five categories of adopters and is useful for understanding the adoption patterns of new technologies and innovations within a society (see **Figure 9.1**). The principle of this theory can easily be applied to customer service and support professionals adopting AI technology in their work, offering a roadmap for organizational transformation.

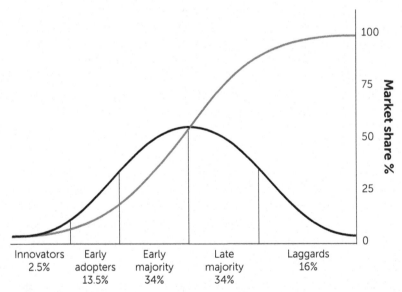

FIGURE 9.1 Diffusion of innovations

- **Innovators (2.5 percent):** Innovators tend to be outsiders within their local social system but communicate with many people outside of it. They also have the financial and mental resources to cope with risk and significant technical knowledge.

- **Early adopters (13.5 percent):** Early adopters tend to be opinion leaders within their local social systems. Early adopters tend to have extensive networks within their local social system as well as a number of connections to people outside it. They also have the financial and mental resources to cope with risk.

- **Early majority (34 percent):** While members of the early majority do not tend to be opinion leaders within their community, they do have extensive social networks within their local social system.

- **Late majority (34 percent):** Members of the late majority tend to adopt innovations when they become social or economic necessities. Members of the late majority tend to have fewer financial resources and less education than others.

- **Laggards (16 percent):** Laggards make up about 16 percent of the population and tend to adopt innovations later than anyone else in their local social systems. Laggards have limited social networks and financial resources and highly value tradition.

As a customer service and support professional, it's important to understand this graph and make your plans appropriately, knowing that this can easily apply to your organization. As you deploy AI technology in your organization, a small set of people will jump on board early—16 percent, according to Rogers' research. But here's an important reality check: 84 percent of your organization will *not* jump in right away. They will need evidence, role models, practical guidance, and examples.

This is why highlighting your innovators and early adopters is crucial. These individuals are likely to stand out within the organization, making it essential for you to identify them, engage with them, and elevate their visibility. "Make them famous" by elevating their status through a variety of actions, such as recognizing them in leadership meetings, circulating emails highlighting their contributions, offering rewards, showcasing them to customers, featuring them in town hall meetings, and promoting their content on LinkedIn and blogs.

Encourage them to share their knowledge through activities like weekly tech talks, creating videos, sharing tips and tricks, and narrating their journey, all with the full support of organizational leaders. By showcasing these super users, you can inspire the late majority and laggards to embrace AI technologies, drawing motivation from the success stories of your innovators and early adopters.

Establish Feedback Channels and Encourage Discussion

Setting up feedback channels to ensure leaders are connected with the organization's pulse while deploying AI technologies is important. The more channels you can build before deployment, the better. Some of these are easier to build and implement than others. Some require work to establish; others are quite simple. People prefer different ways of sharing their feedback. For some, it's an anonymous suggestion box in the building lobby; for others, it might be a social media direct message (DM). Some might enjoy sharing in a structured workshop, and others in a 1:1 session with their manager. The more channels you can light up, the more feedback you'll get, resulting in a more successful rollout.

Leaders can create many communication pathways that resonate with their organization's heartbeat. This is especially true during the transformative integration of AI into their organizations. They can facilitate a vibrant two-way dialog by orchestrating regular virtual town hall meetings, allowing every opinion and concern to paint the picture of collective progress.

Establishing dedicated channels, like email addresses or online portals specifically for AI feedback, turns every suggestion and concern into a stepping stone toward a smooth deployment. Through regular surveys and polls, leaders can capture the pulse of their team's experiences, turning data into a roadmap that can help guide the AI deployment journey.

The creation of cross-functional feedback groups brings together a diverse set of perspectives, ensuring that the AI integration reflects the many different needs of the entire organization. In team meetings, encouraging direct feedback keeps the conversation going, making AI integration a shared narrative by all. By establishing a feedback loop where updates on the implementation of suggestions are regularly communicated, leaders can cultivate a garden of engagement and ownership where every voice contributes to the future success of their AI endeavors. Here are some suggested feedback channels to put in place before deployment:

Quantitative:

- Feedback forms integrated directly into the AI tool(s)
- Regular surveys
- Employee engagement pulse or poll tools
- Anonymous reporting tools

Qualitative:

- Regular questionnaires
- Town hall meetings
- Focus groups/listening circles
- Online forums and discussion boards
- One-on-one meetings
- Suggestion boxes—virtual or in real life (IRL)
- Social media and enterprise social networks
- Team meetings and departmental check-ins
- Email communications
- Interactive workshops and brainstorming sessions
- Peer feedback channels
- Performance review meetings
- Exit interviews

When collecting feedback, there are a few things to consider:

- Assessing the sentiment and human impact of AI is crucial. Are individuals concerned about potential job loss or worried about new performance metrics? Understanding these human aspects is essential.
- Feedback on model accuracy and the accuracy of source documentation should be gathered. When seeking quantitative feedback, it's advisable to utilize a 5- to 7-point Likert Scale,[11] as mentioned earlier in Chapter 8, "Diagnose: Ensuring Effectiveness," instead of a simple "thumbs up/thumbs down" approach. This scale enables the prioritization of key issues effectively.
- Evaluating the impact on customer satisfaction is vital. While obtaining this feedback might pose challenges, assessing whether customers feel more satisfied or dissatisfied with experiences supported by AI compared to those that are not can provide valuable insights.

Feedback Topics

As you build your feedback systems, consider the specific areas to focus on that will help you build and deploy more impactful models. Some of these specific areas to focus on include:

AI model components:

- **Accuracy of the answer:** The correctness and precision of the responses generated by the AI model.

- **Accuracy of the source/documentation:** The reliability and accuracy of the source material or documentation used by the model to generate responses.

- **Responsiveness and technical performance:** The speed and efficiency of the model in processing queries and delivering responses.

- **Ethical/security/privacy:** The model's adherence to ethical standards, user privacy, and robustness of security measures to protect sensitive information.

- **Domain-specific accuracy:** The model's accuracy and effectiveness in specific domains or subject areas relevant to the application.

- **Legal and compliance:** The model's compliance with legal regulations and industry standards, particularly regarding data handling and privacy laws.

Deployment components:

- **Training content:** The quality and relevance of the training data used to train the AI model, ensuring it captures diverse scenarios and contexts.

- **Communication:** The effectiveness of communication strategies during the deployment phase, including how changes and updates are communicated to stakeholders.

- **Rollout:** The process of rolling out the AI model to ensure smooth implementation and minimize disruptions to existing workflows.

- **Integration with existing tools:** The seamless integration of the AI model with existing tools and systems used within your organization, minimizing friction and maximizing efficiency.

By focusing on these areas, you can gather valuable feedback to improve your AI models and optimize the deployment process for maximum impact.

Motivating Evaluators

Although it's not a required part of their role, many users who provide feedback often volunteer their time, which is invaluable for improving your systems. However, it's crucial to balance the frequency of requests to avoid feedback fatigue. The more you ask them for feedback on specific topics, the less likely they are to respond.

Some companies incentivize feedback with offers like gift cards for completing surveys, but there's no one-size-fits-all solution. What's important is recognizing the significance of feedback to your success and finding ways to keep your subject matter experts (SMEs) and other contributors engaged in the process. Here are a few ideas:

- Let them know they are heard and their feedback is valued and acted upon. By far, this is the most important way to keep feedback coming. Let your audience know you are listening, and changes are being implemented based on their feedback. Share this far and wide. If "Mary from the London office" gave feedback about a particular answer or source document accuracy that was a game changer, ensure both she and her boss know that you made a change based on Mary's feedback. This acknowledges the individual's contribution and reinforces the importance of feedback within your organization.

- Send individual thank you emails.

- Gamify. See Chapter 16, "Games, Play, and Novelty in the Age of AI," to learn how points and leaderboards can help keep people engaged.

- Send weekly reports on metrics and improvements, sharing feedback on improvement metrics based on feedback.

- Hold regular recognition events. Organize virtual and in-person events where you publicly recognize and appreciate the contributions of those providing feedback. This could be a quarterly or annual event where the most impactful feedback providers are highlighted and celebrated.

- Instead of generic surveys, create tailored ones that focus on specific areas of expertise of the SMEs. This shows that you value their unique knowledge and are interested in their specific insights, making them feel more connected and valued.

- Offer workshops, seminars, and courses to help those providing feedback grow in their field. This benefits their personal development and shows that you are invested in their growth as much as they are in the AI model's success.

- Provide opportunities for those giving feedback to have direct conversations with senior leaders and decision-makers. This could be through round-table discussions or one-on-one meetings. It shows that their feedback is highly valued and they have a direct line to those who can affect change.

End-User Training

The AI Revolution is here and disrupting the landscape of customer service and support and its future, presenting opportunities and challenges. While one would hope that customer service professionals would see this future and eagerly embrace it, equipping themselves with the necessary knowledge, the sheer magnitude of information can feel overwhelming, leaving many unsure of where to begin.

As a leader, it falls upon you to steer your organization in the right direction by providing, at the very least, introductory training for your support organization. An initial engagement could be an introductory overview covering how you plan to integrate AI into your organization, setting the stage for informed discussions and preparations.

Taking proactive control of the conversation is paramount from the outset. Failure to do so risks leaving your teams susceptible to misinformation, hype, and unnecessary fear. A straightforward approach can start with a brief 30-minute call to discuss the potential benefits of AI for your business, accompanied by a curated list of approved resources, followed by a Q&A session.

In the long term, you will want to invest in providing comprehensive training content to your end-users. This can be built from industry resources and (most importantly) lessons learned from your organization's super users. This will be the most valuable of any training you provide as it allows individuals to see and learn from their peers who share similar experiences and roles. Ideally, you want to complete the training before deploying any AI capabilities. Give people a chance to understand what is coming before it shows up.

Leaders should also consider creating a mentorship or ambassador-type program where super users can guide and support newcomers and be a conduit for feedback back to leadership. This peer-to-peer learning approach can be more relatable and less intimidating, encouraging a more in-depth understanding of the technology in the context of your organization. It's important to regularly update the training content to reflect the evolving nature of AI and include real-world examples and case studies that demonstrate the practical application in the context of your organization. Leaders could also organize interactive workshops and simulations, allowing end-users to experience AI tools in controlled environments, boosting confidence and competence. Feedback sessions post-training are important to assess the effectiveness of the training and to identify areas for improvement, ensuring that the training remains relevant and beneficial to the end-users.

COMPARISONS TO THE INDUSTRIAL REVOLUTION

The Industrial Revolution, spanning from the late 18th to the early 19th century, marked a significant turning point in history, profoundly influencing the economic, cultural, and social fabric of the time. Its relevance to the current training context and adaptation in using new AI technologies, especially in customer service and support, is fascinating and instructive.

In the pre-industrial era, skilled artisans and craftspeople dominated production. These workers had years of apprenticeship and experience, and their skills were highly specialized and deeply rooted in tradition. However, the advent of machines such as the spinning jenny, the power loom, and the steam engine changed everything. These innovations vastly increased the scale and speed of production but also required a workforce that could operate, maintain, and manage these machines.

This necessity for new skills parallels the current challenge in customer service adapting to AI and other digital technologies. Just as workers during the Industrial Revolution had to learn to operate machinery, today's customer service professionals must be trained to efficiently use AI tools for enhanced service delivery.

One of the key aspects of the Industrial Revolution was the need for a large workforce that could quickly adapt to the new industrial environment. This required a form of mass education and training, albeit rudimentary by today's standards. Workers, many of whom had only known agricultural or artisanal work, had to be taught how to operate machines, understand factory discipline, and adapt to the rhythm and demands of machine-based production.

This mass training during the Industrial Revolution is not unlike today's organizational efforts to train employees in new AI technologies. The goal is the same: to equip the workforce with the skills necessary to effectively use new tools and methods. Back then, the focus was on operating machines; today, it's about leveraging AI for better customer interactions. Similarly, workers, then and now, worried about how their jobs would be impacted or even eliminated.

Another parallel lies in the transformation of the skill set. The Industrial Revolution demanded a shift from artisanal skills to mechanical and procedural ones. Today, the shift is from traditional customer service skills to digital proficiency and the ability to work with AI tools alongside automation and digital services. Just as the Industrial Revolution required workers to understand and adapt to machinery, the current era demands customer service professionals to grasp AI functionalities and integrate them into their work.

The Industrial Revolution also teaches us about the impact of technological change on workforce dynamics. It led to the creation of new job categories and the obsolescence of others. Similarly, AI and digital technologies in customer service are creating new roles (such as AI trainers, content creators, prompt engineers, and chatbot managers) while transforming traditional support roles.

The Industrial Revolution underscored the importance of continuous learning and adaptation. The pace of technological change did not slow down; it accelerated, requiring ongoing learning and skill development. This is a crucial lesson for today's organizations—investing in continuous training is essential to keep pace with rapidly evolving digital technologies.

Today, the Industrial Revolution offers valuable insights into the challenges and opportunities presented by technological advancements in the workplace. Its lessons on workforce training, skill transformation, and the need for continuous adaptation directly apply to the current era, particularly in the context of integrating AI and digital technologies in customer service. As we navigate this latest technological transformation, the parallels with the Industrial Revolution serve as a playbook and a reminder of the enduring need to invest in training and education to harness the full potential of new technologies.

Learning a new skill or a new technology requires dedication and practice, and organizations must prioritize and invest in training for their service and support professionals. For them to get proficient in a new technology is no different. As of this writing, the effectiveness of questioning or making an inquiry to an AI model varies dramatically. Known as "prompt engineering," this questioning can range from a simple question to effectively writing code. The landscape is rapidly evolving from simple "one-shot" prompts to more complex iterations, as discussed in Chapter 8. We emphasize "as of now" because advancements occur frequently, with new and more efficient prompts emerging almost weekly.

The key takeaway is that organizations must allocate time and resources to train their service and support professionals.

Of course, tracking progress toward your training goals will help determine whether you are on track, need additional reinforcement, or really bump up your efforts to engage employees. By creating and monitoring relevant training-related metrics, such as completion rates, training feedback submission rate, and satisfaction scores, customer service organizations can gain insights on the progress of their AI deploymentand how employees engage with the new technology. Based on the insights gathered, adjustments can be made to refine and optimize training resources and the AI model itself.

Investing in end-user training is important to maximize the potential of new AI technologies in customer service. Well-trained service and support professionals can utilize AI tools more effectively, leading to improved customer experiences, increased productivity, employee satisfaction, and operational efficiency. Furthermore, continuous training ensures that employees stay up-to-date with evolving technologies, maintaining an edge in a competitive market. Organizations that invest in training their frontline will be the ones who see the biggest lift from AI in customer service.

Tailored training programs, considering each employee's needs and learning styles, can significantly enhance skills acquisition and talent retention. Additionally, by investing in training, organizations demonstrate a commitment to their employees' professional development, boosting morale and job satisfaction and contributing to long-term success. Ultimately, organizations prioritizing training will benefit from AI adoption in customer service, driving improved experiences and sustained competitiveness. Training programs can also benefit from gamification, see Chapter 16.

Lastly, this investment can also reduce mid to long-term costs by minimizing errors and increasing productivity, positively impacting the organization's bottom line.

Plan for Integration with Existing Tools

Customer service and support organizations leverage comprehensive tools to serve customers. These tools are used to elevate the quality of the interactions and efficiently address customer needs. These tools encompass various aspects of customer support, from managing customer interactions to analyzing feedback and providing personalized assistance. By understanding these tools effectively, organizations can identify the integrations needed to seamlessly deploy AI capabilities and enhance the overall customer support strategy. Let's explore some of the key tools used by support organizations:

- **CRM software:** Many organizations use customer relationship management (CRM) software as a secure repository for customer interactions and preferences, enabling personalized service tailored to individual needs.

- **Help desk software:** Help desk software efficiently manages support tickets, ensuring timely resolution of customer issues and seamless coordination within the support team.

- **Live chat software:** Live chat software facilitates real-time communication, enabling instant customer support and faster assistance.

- **Email management systems:** Email management systems efficiently organize customer correspondence, streamlining communication channels and ensuring efficient handling of inquiries.

- **Call center software:** Call center software streamlines telephonic interactions with features like call routing and recording, optimizing communication processes.

- **Social media management tools:** Social media management tools provide versatile options to monitor and respond to online queries, catering to the needs of the digitally savvy customer base across various social media platforms.

- **Survey and feedback tools:** Organizations utilize survey and feedback tools to measure customer satisfaction levels and gather valuable insights for continuous service improvement and enhancement.

- **Knowledge management systems:** Knowledge management systems serve as repositories for vital content, equipping customer service representatives with up-to-date information to deliver informed and effective support to customers.

- **Chatbots and AI assistants:** Adopting chatbots and AI assistants enables organizations to handle routine queries efficiently, freeing human agents to focus on more complex customer needs and enhancing overall service delivery.

- **Remote support software:** Remote support software facilitates direct troubleshooting on customer devices, combining human expertise with technological advancements to provide seamless and effective customer support experiences.

As leaders strategize and plan to deploy AI capabilities, it's crucial to prioritize integration with existing tools and processes. This aspect often proves to be complex and significant, sometimes even more so than the AI deployment itself. While it's essential not to underestimate this task, there are opportunities for straightforward integration successes. Moreover, as the industry progresses, many tool providers are actively involved in streamlining integration efforts, offering out-of-the-box solutions for support organizations. Therefore, leaders must focus on aligning AI integration with proprietary tools and processes. Timely evaluation of this aspect is critical, as the potential impact of seamless integration can be substantial, outweighing the initial effort required.

Identify Your Stakeholders

When strategizing and creating your deployment plan, you must recognize the diverse stakeholders you must address. Balancing their distinct needs and priorities will undoubtedly pose a challenge. Here's a comprehensive list of potential stakeholders, each with their own set of requirements, presented in no specific order:

- **C-suite executives:** These top-level decision-makers will be concerned with overarching business objectives, ROI, and strategic alignment.
- **Senior leaders:** Department heads and senior managers will seek clarity on how AI deployment aligns with departmental goals and processes.
- **Frontline service and support personnel:** These individuals will interact directly with AI systems daily, making their input crucial for ensuring smooth implementation and user satisfaction.
- **Support managers:** Managers responsible for overseeing service and support teams will require tools and insights to monitor performance, address concerns, and ensure productivity.
- **Finance leaders:** Financial executives will be interested in AI deployment's cost implications, ROI projections, and budget allocations.

- **Customers:** Understanding customer needs, preferences, and feedback is paramount for tailoring AI solutions to enhance the overall customer experience.

- **Field sales representatives:** Sales teams must understand how AI can support their efforts, streamline processes, and improve lead generation and conversion.

- **Field sales managers:** Sales managers focus on how AI tools can optimize sales strategies, improve team performance, and drive revenue growth.

- **Data scientists and AI specialists:** These experts will provide critical insights into AI model development, performance evaluation, and ongoing optimization.

- **Product team:** Collaboration with the product team is essential for integrating AI features into existing products and developing new AI-driven solutions that meet market demands.

By identifying and understanding the diverse needs of these stakeholders, you can develop a deployment plan that addresses their concerns, maximizes buy-in, and ultimately leads to successful AI implementation.

Deployment Goals

Not only do you have different audiences to contend with, you will likely have competing goals as well. Executives and finance will want to see productivity increases, customers will want a faster time to resolution, and frontline agents will want the accuracy of responses. Data scientists will be interested in accuracy, while those in the field will want to know about customer satisfaction (CSAT) improvements to drive upsell opportunities and renewals.

As you experiment with AI models and development, the most important thing is to just go, go, go. As you move to a formal deployment stage, developing a formal plan that clearly calls out each audience and explains the decisions made regarding tradeoffs and the schedule impact is important. For example, you will feel pressure to communicate with your executive audience regarding the (right) decision to hold back on the AI model deployment to spend more time working with the data scientists on accuracy to deliver accurate results to our frontline agents and, ultimately, customers. Also, you may face executive pressure to deploy sooner to showcase immediate success and gain a competitive edge instead of spending more time improving accuracy. Your organization will have its own priorities; you need to be clear about them and set appropriate goals and communication.

There will likely be several competing narratives in the organization for how the AI Revolution in service and support should happen, and a deployment plan is a great way to take your stand, define and get clarity on organizational priorities.

Creating a Deployment Plan

Once you have a stance on the deployment audiences and goals you want to address, the steps and logistics of the deployment plan will easily fall in line. At this stage, your organization will have a proprietary AI model built with and powered by your proprietary content. As you look to deploy this across your organization, it's time to consider where and how to make this happen.

As discussed earlier in the chapter, it's important to consider the broad-scale impact that deployment will have on the organization and plan to bring your stakeholders along on the journey. Remember to communicate often, showcase your super users, offer many feedback opportunities, and ensure your employees are well-trained and ready to use the AI model in their daily work.

Other areas to assess as you create your deployment plan include:

- **Organizational needs:** Evaluate the specific needs and areas where AI models can benefit, given your audiences and goals. From a robust knowledge management tool for frontline support personnel to back-end data analysis, you will have a broad canvas to apply your AI brush. Assess and evaluate these needs to focus on the biggest impact with the least risk. You should consider factors such as customer impact if things fail and cost savings if things succeed.

- **Technology infrastructure review:** Assess your existing technology infrastructure and determine necessary upgrades for AI model deployment and success. You will have existing tools and infrastructure that may be easy to integrate—or not. Perform a review and understand the cost and complexity of any necessary upgrades or integration.

- **Budget planning:** Plan for and allocate budget for necessary technology upgrades or integration, employee training, deployment, and any other necessary resources for a successful deployment. This could be a challenge, and you might want to start small by choosing the biggest-impact opportunities with the least risk and work your way through other deployment scenarios.

- **Compliance and security measures:** Ensure the deployment is ready for and aligns with any legal, ethical, and data security standards based on local law and company stance.

- **Pilot program design:** Design a pilot program to test the AI model within a controlled environment and with a targeted subset of the population intended for full deployment. This approach allows for further accuracy assessments and provides insights to identify and address any potential blockers before the widespread implementation.

- **Change management and communication plan:** Develop a comprehensive change management plan that integrates your communication strategy, ensuring transparency as you guide stakeholders through the AI model deployment process. Regular updates and reassurance will be vital, along with actively soliciting feedback, addressing concerns, and highlighting positive contributions through effective recognition initiatives and spotlighting exemplary users. A comprehensive change management plan encompasses a clear vision, executive support, feedback mechanisms, training initiatives, reinforcement strategies, recognition programs, regular assessments, and consistent communication channels.

- **Training:** Develop a training strategy to equip all stakeholders with a deep understanding of the goals and functionality of the AI model. Specifically, ensure that frontline support personnel receive tailored training on anticipated AI use cases and clear guidance on how and when to use it.

- **Pilot program execution:** Execute your designed pilot program, closely monitoring performance and collecting feedback to inform your full deployment.

- **Feedback analysis and adjustments:** Fully analyze both qualitative and quantitative feedback from the pilot program and make necessary adjustments to the deployment plan.

- **Full-scale deployment preparation:** Ensure you have all plans in place and ready to execute for a successful full-scale rollout based on the insights from the pilot program.

- **Full-scale deployment:** Execute your deployment plan by rolling out the AI model across the organization and to all stakeholders.

- **Ongoing support and maintenance:** Set up a structured process, allocate necessary resources, and establish a robust support system for your AI model's continuous maintenance, updates, and troubleshooting.

- **Performance monitoring and continuous improvement:**
  Continuously monitor the AI model's performance, making necessary improvements along the way. Additionally, remain attentive to
  the deployment process and be ready to adjust the plan as required to
  ensure ongoing success.

Diverse SMEs and Validation Team Signoffs

Validation is a huge step in the deployment process, ensuring your model
is performing as expected and producing results aligned to your goals.
Bringing in subject matter experts (SMEs) to help gauge the accuracy and
usefulness of the AI model is critical before and during the deployment
phase to assist with this validation.

When choosing SMEs to engage with your AI model, ensure that you
deliberately recruit a broad and diverse group of individuals. The tendency
will be to call on your core set of experts, but it's important to break out of
your standard and engage people from diverse genders, races, ethnicities,
geographies, roles, backgrounds, experiences, and all relevant differences. Doing so will make a difference in ensuring your AI model will best
serve the stakeholders it was designed for.

The deliberate inclusion of diverse SMEs in AI development enriches the
range of perspectives and helps build more robust and universally applicable solutions for your end users. This diversity is not just about checking
boxes for representation; it's about integrating various lived experiences
and viewpoints that can highlight blind spots and introduce innovative approaches. In an increasingly interconnected world, solutions that
cater to a wide array of cultural, social, and economic contexts are more
likely to succeed and be sustainable.

Therefore, it's crucial to create an environment where diverse voices are
heard, actively sought out, and valued. By doing so, organizations can
harness the full potential of cognitive diversity, leading to AI models that
are more inclusive, effective, and reflective of the world they aim to serve.

A non-inclusive AI model risks perpetuating and amplifying biases,
potentially leading to unfair or discriminatory outcomes against certain
groups based on gender, race, age, or other characteristics. AI models
built without respect for inclusiveness may fail to accurately represent or
understand the diverse needs and perspectives of different user groups,
resulting in a less effective or relevant product for a significant portion
of the target audience. The lack of diverse input during the development
phase can lead to blind spots in the AI's functionality, compromising its

ability to handle a wide range of real-world scenarios and diverse data sets. Excluding diverse SMEs and representative users can lead to a lack of cultural and contextual understanding of the AI's responses, harming user trust and acceptance. A non-inclusive approach can result in missed opportunities for innovation and creativity, as diverse teams often bring unique ideas and problem-solving approaches that can greatly enhance AI's capabilities and appeal.

Ultimately, this can add risk to the customer experience if customer service professionals rely on biased answers from biased models because they are evaluated by groups of SMEs that are not representative of diverse perspectives.

Scaled Rollout

Deployment plans will vary dramatically, depending on your organization, stakeholders, and goals. Regardless of your goals, you will want to build a plan that can scale. If you are clear with your goals, you can build a plan that can start small and scale as you continue through your deployment, adding scenarios and stakeholders over time.

Deployment plans, while diverse, share a common need for scalability to effectively meet their objectives. Political pressures, for example, may require a rapid scaling up to meet heightened demand or public expectations. In contrast, considerations like hardware costs might necessitate a more gradual, cost-effective scaling approach. Understanding user impact is crucial, as it dictates the pace and nature of scaling to ensure user satisfaction and engagement.

A well-structured scale-up plan must be adaptable and respond to changing circumstances and feedback received post-deployment. Clarity in goals allows for a more targeted approach, enabling the deployment plan to align with specific outcomes or metrics of success. Integrating a flexible scale-up strategy within the deployment plan is essential for navigating the complexities and dynamic challenges inherent in deploying new technologies or initiatives.

Continuous Evaluation for Consistent Model Performance

AI in customer service and support is not a "fire and forget" type of tool. You must build processes and allocate resources for ongoing evaluation of the model during and after deployment. It includes content creation and revision, model tuning, and end-user education. All of this is an ongoing investment that is pivotal for sustained effectiveness. This extends beyond merely monitoring feedback and encompasses a range of continuous improvement activities.

Key among these is the need for regular AI model training, ensuring it remains relevant as customer needs, technology, and market trends evolve. Additionally, continual staff training is crucial; training on the latest advances and sharing best practices. Implementing robust quality control mechanisms, such as periodic audits of AI responses, is vital for maintaining high service standards. Furthermore, keeping pace with technological advancements is essential—this space is moving fast, and integrating AI with emerging technologies can significantly enhance the customer support experience.

Optimizing the user experience through frequent interface updates ensures the AI remains accessible and user-friendly. Analyzing customer feedback is another important component in refining AI performance, and this is complemented by rigorous data management to ensure decisions are based on current and accurate information.

Moreover, adherence to ethical standards and a culture of responsible AI, particularly in data security and privacy, requires constant vigilance and adaptation. Lastly, your AI system must be scalable and flexible to support business growth, handling increased customer interactions and evolving service needs. This comprehensive approach underscores that deploying AI in customer service is not a one-time effort but a dynamic, ongoing investment. All these areas work together to ensure the AI model's and users' continued success.

- **Continuous learning and adaptation:** You need to invest in learning and adaptation for both the AI systems and the humans. AI systems need regular updates to their knowledge base and algorithms, new training material, tuning, and maintenance to stay relevant and effective as customer needs, technology, and behaviors evolve. Humans need the same.

- **Staff training and development:** It's essential to invest in training for staff who manage and interact with the AI system, equipping them with the skills to interpret AI responses and intervene when necessary. New areas like prompt engineering are skills that need to be taught and are constantly evolving.

- **Quality control mechanisms:** Implementing quality control measures, such as regular audits of AI interactions, helps maintain high standards.

See Chapter 10 for discussions of synthetic transactions, response learning, and validation. When a model is deployed, all these components are important for success.

- **Integration with emerging technologies:** As technology evolves, integrating AI with new tools and platforms, like virtual reality or advanced analytics, can enhance the customer support experience. This is an exciting opportunity to continue innovating.

- **User experience optimization:** Regularly revising and updating the user interface and experience of the AI system ensures it remains user-friendly and accessible to diverse customer groups. Feedback is needed to evolve the user experience.

- **Feedback analysis and implementation:** Actively analyzing stakeholder feedback to understand the effectiveness and accuracy of AI interactions and making the necessary adjustments to ensure your AI deployment has a bottom-line impact on your business.

- **Data management and analysis:** Continuous investment in data management and analysis is essential to refine AI algorithms, improve the accuracy of the models, and ensure they make decisions based on current and accurate data responsibly without bias.

- **Ethical and regulatory compliance:** Ongoing evaluation and adaptation are needed to keep the AI system in line with rapidly moving ethical standards and regulatory requirements, particularly concerning data privacy. It can't be overstated to say how important it is to stay current with the regulatory and political environment in all countries worldwide.

- **Scalability and flexibility:** As the business grows, the AI system should be scalable and flexible enough to accommodate increasing interactions and expand service requirements.

Telemetry

Back in the 1980s at NASA, some of the early work on data collection and telemetry began. According to Wikipedia, "telemetry is the in-situ collection of measurements or other data at remote points and their automatic transmission to receiving equipment (telecommunication) for monitoring. The word is derived from the Greek roots *tele*, 'remote,' and *metron*, 'measure.' Systems that need external instructions and data to operate require the counterpart of telemetry."[12]

As you deploy your AI system, defining success metrics and establishing the means to collect relevant data is crucial.

For instance, if your pilot phase aims for a 3-star rating milestone, it's essential to have mechanisms in place to gather data and assess progress accurately. It seems obvious, but agreement among stakeholders on these metrics is paramount, and integrating data collection tools into the AI model development process is key. Another example could involve response rate targets, such as aiming for a 4-second response time. This necessitates incorporating telemetry data into the system by your engineering team to monitor response times down to milliseconds, enabling effective progress tracking. Failing to meet these benchmarks might necessitate unexpected investments in hardware infrastructure to address performance shortcomings.

Telemetry's role in AI transcends monitoring basic performance metrics, such as response rates or customer feedback. It delves deeper into new measures, tracking complex aspects like prediction accuracy and data processing efficiency, providing a panoramic view of the AI model's capabilities. This integration of telemetry facilitates real-time analysis, enabling swift identification of issues and bottlenecks to ensure optimal system performance and prevent potential escalations. Additionally, telemetry acts as a beacon by triggering automated alerts when performance thresholds are breached, facilitating timely interventions.

The value of telemetry extends to all stakeholders, providing tangible evidence of the system's efficacy and promoting transparent decision-making regarding content and scale. As the AI landscape evolves, so must the telemetry infrastructure, evolving to capture nuanced data necessary for evaluating emerging features and advanced functionality.

This perpetual cycle of improvement and innovation underscores the importance of investing in telemetry and measurement infrastructure to accurately assess the success of AI models in driving business outcomes. Without it, you will be hard-pressed to accurately evaluate the success of the AI model for your business.

Understanding When to Retrain the AI Model

This sounds like a very technical decision and an important milestone. But it's not. AI models cannot "unlearn"—so, the decision to retrain your model is based on your content. If your product or service has changed to a point where the new information is important enough to warrant an investment in retraining, then the time is right.

Currently, AI models don't "unlearn" in the traditional ways humans do. Instead, their learning and adjustment processes are based on data and algorithms. Here's a simplified explanation of how AI models are adjusted or corrected, which might be seen as a form of "unlearning." Imagine that as a child, you learned that 1+1 = 3. If you were an AI model and were taught the same thing, you cannot be corrected. This is what you were taught, so you cannot understand that this is the wrong answer. To learn the correct answer, 1+1=2, you would have to wipe the slate clean and start from scratch with new training data.

- **Data collection and preprocessing:** AI models learn from data—called training data. If the initial data set contains biases or errors, these will also be reflected in the model's outputs. New, more accurate, or representative data is collected and preprocessed to adjust or correct the model.

- **Retraining with new data:** Rebuild the model based on more accurate data. The AI model is then retrained with this updated data set. This retraining can involve either adding the new data to the existing data set or replacing parts of the old data set with new data. This process helps the model to learn new patterns and correct previous inaccuracies.

- **Fine-tuning:** In some cases, instead of completely retraining the model, you may consider fine-tuning it. This involves making smaller adjustments to the model's parameters, such as temperature or Top-P, based on feedback or new data to correct specific issues or biases.

- **Continuous monitoring and updating:** AI models should be monitored continuously after deployment. If new issues or biases are detected, the model should be updated with new data or other adjustments.

- **Model architecture changes:** Sometimes, the issue might be with the model's architecture or its algorithms. In such cases, parts of the model might be redesigned, or different algorithms might be employed.

- **Human oversight:** Human subject matter experts often review the outputs of AI models, especially in sensitive areas, to identify and correct errors or biases.

It's important to remember that AI models don't "forget" old information the way humans do. Instead, they adjust their output based on new data and instructions they receive during these updating processes.

Building Confidence in AI Model Outputs

The best way to build and demonstrate confidence in these AI models is through feedback, iteration, content preparation, and end-user training. All these components play an important role in ensuring AI success in customer service and support.

Transparency and trust are foundational principles in this journey. Transparency involves clearly communicating the data sources used and ensuring diversity among subject matter experts providing feedback. Trust is fostered by including citations for each answer and providing users with opportunities to provide feedback. These responsibility principles facilitate harmonious collaboration between humans and machines in this new era.

Effective communication is critical to applying AI in customer service and support. It encompasses how the AI interacts with users and how it is presented and explained to them. Ensuring that users understand the capabilities and limitations of the AI model fosters realistic expectations and a better user experience. Whether the user is a customer seeking assistance or a support agent using it to assist the customer, it's important to communicate well so the user gains confidence in their ability to leverage the AI model effectively and for its intended purpose.

Investment in continuous improvement is imperative for AI systems, as they are inherently imperfect and require regular updates and refinements based on user feedback and evolving data. This approach ensures the AI model remains relevant and effective in addressing user needs.

Inclusion and accessibility should also be prioritized. AI solutions must be designed to be accessible to diverse users, including those with disabilities. See Chapter 5 for more details on how to build an inclusive group of subject matter experts to validate your AI models. Overall, inclusivity broadens the user base and enhances the quality of service provided.

Ethical considerations, such as privacy, data security, and bias, must be addressed proactively to maintain user trust and confidence. Establishing clear ethical guidelines and practices is essential in navigating the ethical complexities associated with AI deployment in customer service.

Furthermore, the need for human oversight should not be underestimated. While AI can handle many tasks, human judgment and intervention are important for safety. A "human in the loop" is a best practice, especially during the early days of AI deployment. A hybrid model that combines the efficiency of AI with the nuanced understanding of human operators can provide the most effective customer service.

Finally, fostering a culture of learning and adaptability within the organization is key for leveraging AI effectively. As AI technology evolves, so must the teams that work with it. Encouraging continuous learning and adaptability among staff enables organizations to harness AI technology to support customers in new and innovative ways, thereby staying ahead in an ever-evolving landscape.

This chapter covered several critical aspects surrounding integrating AI models into customer service and support organizations. From leadership dynamics to executive expectations, employee engagement strategies to ethical AI utilization, and the establishment of robust feedback channels and comprehensive training plans, we've explored a wide spectrum of considerations.

Central to our discussion is a detailed roadmap for creating a deployment strategy. This roadmap encompasses essential steps to help you toward a successful implementation.

We've underscored the imperative of ongoing evaluation and enhancement of AI models, coupled with a commitment to continuous education and training for end-users. We emphasize advocating for a meticulously designed approach that acknowledges AI development and deployment's dynamic and complex nature. Moreover, we want to stress the need for cultivating a culture characterized by trust, transparency, and collaboration among all stakeholders, recognizing its pivotal role in the success of AI initiatives.

Endnotes

1   Merriam-Webster. "deployment." Merriam-Webster.com Dictionary. Accessed January 1, 2024. [https://www.merriam-webster.com/dictionary/deployment].

2   Wikipedia contributors. "Blacklist (computing)." Wikipedia, The Free Encyclopedia. March 17, 2024. [https://en.wikipedia.org/w/index.php?title=Blacklist_(computing)&oldid=1214191969].

3   Wikipedia contributors. "Whitelist." Wikipedia, The Free Encyclopedia. March 27, 2024. [https://en.wikipedia.org/wiki/Whitelist].

4   Wikipedia contributors. "Kill switch." Wikipedia, The Free Encyclopedia. March 5, 2024. [https://en.wikipedia.org/wiki/Kill_switch].

5   Wikipedia contributors. "Dummy variable (statistics)." Wikipedia, The Free Encyclopedia. December 8, 2023. [https://en.wikipedia.org/wiki/Dummy_variable_(statistics)].

6   Wikipedia contributors. "Reddit." Wikipedia, The Free Encyclopedia. December 31, 2023. [https://en.wikipedia.org/wiki/Reddit#AMAs].

7   History.com editors. 2023. *"Federalist Papers."* A&E Television Networks, June 22, 2023. [https://www.history.com/topics/early-us/federalist-papers].

8   The editors of encyclopaedia Britannica. 2023. "Federalist Party." Encyclopaedia Britannica, Inc., December 4, 2023. [https://www.britannica.com/event/United-States-presidential-election-of-1800].

9   Rogers, Nala. 2016. "Evolution of Darwin's finches tracked at genetic level." Springer Nature, April 22, 2016. [https://www.nature.com/articles/nature.2016.19795.pdf].

10   Wikipedia contributors. "Diffusion of innovations." Wikipedia, The Free Encyclopedia. January 3, 2024. [https://en.wikipedia.org/wiki/Diffusion_of_innovations].

11   Wikipedia contributors. "Likert scale." Wikipedia, The Free Encyclopedia. December 17, 2023. [https://en.wikipedia.org/wiki/Likert_scale].

12   Wikipedia contributors. "Telemetry." Wikipedia, The Free Encyclopedia. December 19, 2023. [https://en.wikipedia.org/wiki/Telemetry].

10

Detect: Monitoring and Feedback

Continuous improvement is better than delayed perfection.

—Mark Twain

As we conclude our journey through the 6Ds Framework, we arrive at the last stop: the Detect phase. This final stage embodies the essence of sustained success and continuous improvement in our AI deployment. In other words, it's all about keeping our success going strong. At this point, it's not just about setting things up and letting them run. We recognize that the journey does not end with deployment; rather, it marks the commencement of a dynamic process of continuous improvement. We need to keep a close eye on how our AI models are doing, as we want to catch any problems early on and ensure everything keeps working smoothly. By establishing robust monitoring mechanisms, we empower ourselves to swiftly detect any deviations, anomalies, or performance fluctuations within our AI models, reducing risks and safeguarding the integrity and quality of the deployments.

A big part of the Detect phase is listening to feedback. We know that the people using our AI have valuable insights. We can improve our models by creating ways for them to tell us what's working and what's not, ensuring the AI model is doing its job well and that people trust and like it. By fostering a culture of open communication and active feedback channels, we unlock the collective wisdom of our stakeholders, harnessing their perspectives to fuel iterative enhancements and refinements. This symbiotic relationship between users and AI models reinforces accuracy and quality and fosters trust, engagement, and long-term success.

As we embark on this final leg of our journey, let's focus on improving our AI models, embracing the ethos of continuous improvement and innovation. By leveraging the power of data-driven insights, human expertise, and collaborative synergy, we will propel our AI deployments to new heights of excellence. The Detect phase stands as a testament to our steady commitment to excellence, ensuring that our AI models remain at the vanguard of innovation, efficiency, and customer satisfaction.

The Necessity of Post-Deployment Monitoring

In Chapter 8, "Diagnose: Ensuring Effectiveness," we discussed the concept of model drift, also known as model decay, as a risk associated with incorporating outdated or weak data into AI models, leading to inaccurate results. This concept is particularly relevant at this stage. As a reminder, model drift refers to a machine learning model's decline in performance and accuracy over time, occurring after its initial training or deployment phase. This deterioration happens when the model encounters new data or concepts significantly different from its training set, resulting in inaccurate predictions and reduced reliability due to outdated information. To mitigate model drift, continuous monitoring and updating of the AI model are necessary to maintain its effectiveness and relevance.

It's important to actively monitor and detect model drift through these activities:

- **Accuracy maintenance:** Regular monitoring is essential to uphold output accuracy. As data and concepts evolve, incorporating checks and balances becomes crucial for detecting and preserving accuracy.

- **Adaptability:** The model requires regular updates to adapt to shifting patterns in the data.

- **Reliability:** Continuous monitoring ensures the model remains accurate, reliable, and trustworthy.

- **Resource allocation:** Early detection of drift enables efficient allocation or redirection of resources for model retraining or adjustment.

- **Support and service agent satisfaction:** Keeping the model updated in response to drift helps maintain the satisfaction of support agents by delivering relevant and accurate results.

AI Model Relevancy in Changing Data Environments

While model drift is a concern, it's more probable that your underlying data will change. Evolving user behavior, seasonal fluctuations, alterations in hardware or network configurations, and environmental shifts are some factors that can contribute to fluctuations in your data landscape.

These changes can significantly impact the performance and accuracy of your AI model. For instance, if your model is trained on historical data that no longer reflects current trends or patterns, its predictions may become less reliable over time. Additionally, shifts in user preferences or market dynamics may render certain features or inputs obsolete, necessitating adjustments to your model to maintain its relevance.

To address these challenges, it's essential to implement robust monitoring and adaptation mechanisms. Regularly assessing your data inputs and monitoring for shifts in patterns or distributions can help you identify potential issues early on. Moreover, building flexibility into your model architecture enables it to adapt to changing data environments, ensuring it remains effective and accurate over time.

Furthermore, proactive measures such as updating training data, fine-tuning model parameters, or retraining the model on more recent data can help mitigate the impact of data changes. By staying vigilant and responsive to evolving data landscapes, you can ensure that your AI model remains relevant and continues to deliver valuable insights and predictions.

Continuous Model Improvement Through Monitoring and Feedback Mechanisms

Constant monitoring of the AI model's accuracy and performance is paramount to its effectiveness. While automation can handle some aspects of this task, real users, especially subject matter experts (SMEs), play a crucial role in providing valuable feedback. Regular testing by SMEs allows for rigorous evaluation of the model's output, helping identify inaccuracies and improvement areas.

Moreover, feedback from end-users is equally invaluable in refining the AI model. Real-world usage scenarios often reveal nuances and challenges that may not have been apparent during development. By soliciting feedback directly from users through the model's interface, developers can gain insights into user experiences and identify potential errors or shortcomings in the model's performance.

Establishing robust feedback loops within the AI model's user interface is essential for facilitating this process. Users should have easy access to mechanisms for providing feedback, such as Likert scales (covered in Chapter 8) and text comment boxes, allowing them to offer immediate opinions on the model's output. Additionally, SMEs can play a pivotal role in reviewing, categorizing, and clustering the feedback.

Clustering feedback involves grouping similar types of feedback based on shared characteristics or topics. For example, feedback related to user interface design may be clustered separately from feedback about algorithm performance. Further categorization may occur within each cluster to identify specific issues or suggestions.

By clustering feedback, developers can better understand the most prevalent issues affecting the model's performance. This structured approach enables them to prioritize their efforts and focus on addressing the most critical concerns first. For instance, if multiple users provide feedback about the model's response time being too slow, developers can prioritize optimizations to improve speed and responsiveness.

Moreover, clustering feedback allows for more efficient communication and collaboration among development teams. By organizing feedback into meaningful categories, developers can easily share insights and findings with relevant stakeholders, such as data scientists, engineers, and product managers. This collaborative approach fosters a shared understanding of the model's strengths and weaknesses, facilitating more informed decision-making and targeted improvement efforts.

Regular user feedback review is essential for driving continuous improvement in the AI model. Developers should actively monitor feedback channels, leveraging user input to refine the model's algorithms and optimize its performance. By fostering a culture of feedback and collaboration, organizations can ensure that their AI models remain relevant, accurate, and effective in meeting user needs.

Supervised Learning and Reinforcement Learning from Human Feedback (RLHF) for Better Model Outputs

Reinforcement learning (RL) is a distinctive branch of machine learning, distinguished by its ability to autonomously learn from its actions and subsequent rewards. It learns to make decisions by performing actions in an environment designed to achieve a goal and maximize its reward. The feedback comes in the form of rewards or penalties for its actions, guiding it to learn the best strategy, known as a policy, to maximize its cumulative rewards over time. This learning process is analogous to how humans learn from the consequences of their actions. RL is focused on decision-making in conditions of uncertainty and learns to improve through trial and error.

Supervised learning, unsupervised learning, and reinforcement learning are the three basic paradigms of machine learning, each offering distinct methodologies for data analysis and decision-making. Supervised learning relies on labeled data to infer patterns and relationships, where the algorithm is trained on input–output pairs to learn the mapping between input features and output labels. On the other hand, unsupervised learning operates without explicit labels, aiming to uncover hidden structures and patterns within unlabeled data.

Reinforcement learning (RL)[1] stands apart as a dynamic approach that addresses the challenge of decision-making in uncertain and evolving environments. Unlike supervised and unsupervised learning, RL agents learn through trial and error, navigating a balance between exploring new strategies and exploiting existing knowledge to maximize cumulative rewards. This iterative process involves the agent taking action in an environment, receiving feedback through rewards or penalties, and adjusting its behavior to optimize long-term performance. RL is particularly well-suited for tasks for which explicit feedback is sparse or delayed, making it a powerful paradigm for autonomous decision-making in complex scenarios.

Reinforcement Learning from Human Feedback (RLHF)

Reinforcement learning from human feedback is a groundbreaking and increasingly popular technique that revolutionizes traditional methodologies by incorporating human insights into the learning process. This fusion of human intelligence with algorithmic learning represents a significant advancement in data science, machine learning, and artificial intelligence.

This methodology integrates human insights into the reinforcement learning paradigm, enhancing the learning process and addressing challenges inherent in traditional RL approaches. See Chapter 2, "Overview of Generative AI and Data Science Machine Learning," for more technical details.

In classical reinforcement learning, algorithms make decisions based on interactions with an environment, aiming to maximize predefined numerical reward signals. However, these signals often lack the depth and nuance needed to capture the complexities of real-world scenarios. RLHF addresses this limitation by integrating human feedback, which offers richer and more nuanced guidance for the learning agent. Incorporating human feedback into RL has profound implications for AI development. When deploying AI into a service and support organization, bringing a "human-in-the-loop" (HITL) to provide feedback is critical.[2] By involving human support agents in the feedback loop, RLHF enables creating more adaptable, ethical, and efficient AI systems. In data science, RLHF leads to more accurate and insightful analytical models by leveraging human input to refine interpretations and predictions, which is crucial for ensuring customer satisfaction in service scenarios.

Furthermore, RLHF plays a pivotal role in addressing ethical concerns in AI. RLHF ensures that AI systems adhere to societal norms and ethical standards by incorporating human values and judgments. It is essential to involve diverse perspectives in the feedback process to ensure the inclusivity and representativeness of the target user base.

Overall, RLHF harmoniously blends human intuition with algorithmic learning, extending the capabilities of machine learning models while maintaining alignment with human values and ethics. As AI continues to evolve, RLHF stands as a transformative technique that enhances the accuracy and effectiveness of AI systems, particularly in customer service and support applications.

Reinforcement Learning with SMEs

SMEs are critical in this phase of the process. Traditional reinforcement learning relies on a predetermined reward function for the algorithm, often hardcoded by developers, signifying the desired goals for the AI model. This can be extremely challenging in the world of customer service and support content, where the accuracy of the answers is paramount and often highly specific.

This is precisely where RLHF can help. By augmenting training data with direct feedback from humans, RLHF enhances the learning process of

AI models, particularly in evaluating the accuracy of answers. Human feedback on the model's performance directly assesses the quality of the AI-provided responses. This feedback can take various forms, including rating the quality of answers using a Likert scale (discussed in Chapter 8), suggesting improvements for response alternatives, or even shaping the reward function based on observed behavior.

In essence, SMEs provide invaluable insights that refine the AI model's understanding and response accuracy, ensuring it aligns closely with real-world requirements in customer service and support scenarios.

Techniques in RLHF

Requesting support from SMEs in providing feedback on AI model response is important in helping to determine the accuracy of model output. There are different ways that this feedback can be captured, including:

- **Simple rating:** Subject matter experts are given the opportunity to rate the accuracy of the answer. This can range from a simple thumbs-up and thumbs-down to a more nuanced 5- or 7-point Likert scale, allowing for a more granular assessment of accuracy.

- **Preference-based feedback:** Think of this as an A-B test. A human SME is presented with pairs of answers and is asked to choose which one is preferable. This method helps in fine-tuning the AI's decision-making process by providing insights into user preferences.

- **Corrective feedback:** In this approach, SMEs intervene directly to correct the answer if it is inaccurate or insufficient. This immediate feedback loop helps the AI understand the desired answer and improve its accuracy over time.

- **Demonstrations:** Humans perform the task themselves, providing detailed descriptions or step-by-step demonstrations from which the AI can learn. This is particularly useful for complex tasks where defining a reward function is challenging or impractical, allowing the AI to learn from real-world examples provided by experts in the field.

Applications and Advantages

RLHF is broadly used across various domains, ranging from robotics and autonomous vehicles to personal assistants. Beyond customer service scenarios, the nuanced understanding and adaptability provided by human feedback prove invaluable. In customer support and service contexts, RLHF primarily enhances the accuracy of the AI model's responses, ensuring that users receive relevant and helpful information.

One of the key advantages of RLHF lies in its ability to leverage human input for training and aligning AI behaviors with human values and ethics. Refer to Chapter 11 for a deeper exploration of responsible AI and ethical considerations. By directly integrating human judgmentinto the training and learning process, RLHF ensures that AI systems act in ways that are fair, transparent, acceptable, and understandable to humans. This alignment fosters trust and confidence in AI systems, promoting their responsible and ethical use in diverse real-world scenarios.

Challenges

One of the biggest challenges in RLHF is how to motivate humans to provide feedback. The quality of the AI's learning depends heavily on the quality of human feedback, which can be difficult to obtain and can be inconsistent. While the risk of human bias exists, the primary hurdle lies in incentivizing individuals to dedicate their time to offering feedback. For insights on incentivization strategies, see Chapter 16, "Games, Play, and Novelty in the Age of AI."

As AI continues to evolve, RLHF remains pivotal in bridging the chasm between algorithm-driven learning and the imperative for ethical, transparent, and secure AI behavior. Future efforts in RLHF will concentrate on enhancing the efficiency and efficacy of human feedback, reducing the dependency on continuous human input, and addressing challenges related to bias and scalability. Many experiments and trials use Likert scales, A-B testing, and other techniques to engage human SMEs in providing feedback on AI models. The ultimate goal is to develop AI systems that execute tasks effectively and adhere to the complex and nuanced expectations of customer service and support professionals.

Detection Through the Use of Synthetic Transactions

As described by Eric Conrad, Seth Misenar, and Joshua Feldman[3] in their *ScienceDirect* article titled "Synthetic Transaction":

Synthetic transactions, or synthetic monitoring, involves building scripts or tools that simulate activities normally performed in an application. The typical goal of using synthetic transactions/monitoring is to establish expected norms for the performance of these transactions. These synthetic transactions can be automated to run on a periodic basis to ensure the application is still performing as expected. These types of transactions can also be useful for testing application updates prior to deployment to ensure the functionality and performance will not be negatively impacted. This type of testing or monitoring is most commonly associated with custom developed web applications.

In the world of AI models, the use of synthetic transactions to detect model drift is imperative. In AI-based services, synthetic transactions serve as scripted operations mirroring typical user actions. They are particularly indispensable for proactively monitoring AI models' accuracy, performance, and availability. Unlike real user monitoring, which relies on actual user interactions, synthetic transactions offer controlled, consistent tests across various aspects of the system. This is essential for ensuring that AI models remain accurate, performant, reliable, and efficient, as they often support a wide range of critical functions.

One primary application of synthetic transactions in AI models is accuracy monitoring. By simulating user queries against a "known good" answer, content curators and model builders can continuously assess overall system reliability and accuracy. This proactive approach aids in identifying performance degradation before it impacts real users. Additionally, synthetic transactions play a vital role in availability monitoring. These transactions are configured to run at regular intervals, continually verifying the operational status of the AI model. Such constant monitoring is crucial for services requiring high uptime, especially in customer service and support environments.

Benefits of Building a Synthetic Transaction Framework

Synthetic transactions can help automate and constantly monitor and measure model accuracy and performance. Establishing an automated framework brings several advantages, especially as you expand the model to include more content.

- **Proactive issue identification:** Synthetic transactions are instrumental in pinpointing issues such as model drift, accuracy fluctuations, response time disparities, performance inconsistencies, and assessing uptime and availability. By detecting these issues before they impact users, development teams can swiftly address them, ensuring uninterrupted service delivery.

- **Consistency and control:** Unlike real user monitoring, synthetic transactions provide a controlled environment for testing specific pathways and functionalities. By comparing answers against a "known good" reference, they deliver more consistent and reliable results, enhancing the overall system stability.

- **Performance benchmarking:** Performance benchmarking is essential for evaluating the performance of cloud services over time and assessing the effects of infrastructure updates or alterations. Synthetic transactions are pivotal in detecting potential performance or accuracy degradation resulting from model drift, enabling early intervention and optimization.

- **Global perspective:** Synthetic transactions can be executed from diverse geographic locations, offering insights into the performance of AI models across different regions. This global perspective is particularly beneficial for services operating in multiple languages, ensuring consistent performance and user experience worldwide.

Challenges in Writing Synthetic Transactions

Embarking on creating synthetic transactions entails several challenges and considerations, requiring upfront planning and meticulous execution. It's important to consider what to monitor, the telemetry and metrics you want to collect, user personas, and areas of your AI model to monitor. The following are key factors to address:

- **Complexity in scripting and maintenance:** Creating and maintaining automated scripts for synthetic transactions is not easy, especially for dynamic and multifaceted AI models that undergo frequent changes and updates. Analyzing support and service content beforehand is crucial to ensure that synthetic transactions effectively monitor for model drift—a task that demands careful attention and expertise.

- **Costs:** Continuous monitoring with synthetic transactions can be resource-intensive and may incur additional costs. Since synthetic transactions interact with live AI models, they incur costs using computational resources such as GPUs. It's essential to factor these costs into your deployment plans to avoid unexpected financial burdens.

- **Limitation in coverage:** Synthetic transactions are tailored for specific scenarios and predefined pathways, potentially overlooking issues that may impact real users in untested situations. Designing synthetic transactions to target areas of AI models prone to churn is vital for comprehensive monitoring and detection of potential issues.

- **Evolution of user behavior:** The evolving usage patterns of service professionals and technological advancements need regular updates to synthetic transaction scripts to remain relevant and effective. Adapting to these changes ensures that synthetic transactions accurately reflect real-world interactions, enhancing their efficacy in detecting performance discrepancies and model drift.

Synthetic Transactions in Cloud Services

In cloud-hosted models, synthetic transactions emerge as helpful tools for maintaining optimal performance and reliability. Here's why they are particularly useful in this context:

- **Early warning system:** Much like the canary in the coal mine, synthetic transactions act as vigilant sentinels, alerting users, engineers, and service providers to potential issues in cloud services before they impact real users. These systems serve as early indicators by detecting anomalies and irregularities, enabling prompt intervention and resolution.

- **Sensitivity to problems:** Similar to the canary's sensitivity to gases, synthetic transactions can discern subtle or emerging issues within a system that may not yet be apparent through real user monitoring. From minor deviations to critical errors, well-built synthetics offer varying alert levels, from a simple warning to a red alert, ensuring appropriate actions are taken swiftly to address each situation effectively.

- **Preventive measure:** Synthetic transactions serve as a proactive measure and insurance policy against major outages or performance degradations by identifying and addressing problems preemptively. These transactions help uphold service continuity and user satisfaction by pinpointing potential issues before they escalate.

- **Consistent and pepeatable:** Synthetic transactions must consistently measure model and user experience performance and accuracy. These transactions should be automated, although in theory can be performed by a person. Think of a night security guard with a flashlight walking around to ensure all the doors are locked. They walk the same route every night to ensure consistency. Automating these checks makes the results repeatable, and the measures ensure a positive outcome for the end users.

Synthetic transactions are a critical component of AI and cloud service systems to ensure the performance and reliability of live services. Simulating user actions can provide valuable insights into system performance, detect model drift and other potential issues, and allow for proactive maintenance and improvements. The effectiveness of these transactions depends on their careful design, regular updates, and thoughtful integration into a broader monitoring strategy, ultimately ensuring the continuous reliability and performance of cloud-hosted services.

CANARIES IN COAL MINES

A historical example that metaphorically represents the concept of a synthetic transaction is the use of coal mine canaries to detect deadly carbon monoxide.

In the 19th century, coal mine production became increasingly dangerous as a result of the popularity of train travel and steam engines. Miners were required to dig deeper into the mines to keep up with the coal demand, exposing themselves to poisonous gases and explosions. Miners needed a method to detect carbon monoxide, which is colorless and odorless, so canaries were used as an early detection method because they would quickly die if exposed to the gas. These canaries helped coal miners avoid deadly situations.[4]

John Scott Haldane, a prominent Scottish physiologist and an innovative thinker of the early 20th century, made significant contributions to occupational health and safety, notably by using canaries as a detection system for poisonous gases in coal mines. Born in 1860, Haldane was fascinated by the physiology of breathing and the effects of gases on the human body, a passion that led him to explore the dangerous environments of coal mines. Haldane was known as the "Father of Oxygen Therapy."

In the early 1900s, mining was one of the most hazardous professions, with miners frequently succumbing to "choke damp" or carbon monoxide poisoning. Haldane's research into respiratory physiology and gas exposure had already

The Detect phase stands as a testament to the ongoing commitment required to sustain the success of AI models. Through vigilant monitoring and the judicious application of techniques like RLHF and synthetic transactions, organizations can fortify their AI deployments against the threat of model drift. These methods empower AI systems to adapt, evolve, and excel in real-world scenarios by integrating human expertise and simulating user interactions. As we reflect on what we learned while exploring the 6Ds Framework, let's remain steadfast in our commitment to continuous improvement and innovation, ensuring that our AI models endure and thrive in an ever-changing landscape.

positioned him as an authority on the subject, and it was through this expertise that he devised a simple yet ingenious solution: the use of canaries in coal mines.

Haldane knew that canaries, with their fast breathing rates and high metabolism, were more sensitive to carbon monoxide and other poisonous gases than humans, thus serving as an effective early warning system if they became distressed or died. This approach was revolutionary in its simplicity and effectiveness, quickly becoming a standard safety measure in coal mines worldwide.

More than just introducing canaries in mines, Haldane's work reflected a broader commitment to improving industrial safety and workers' health. He pioneered an understanding of the industrial environment's impact on human physiology and relentlessly worked toward mitigating these risks. His legacy extends beyond the specific measure of using canaries; he studied compression at great depths, developed dive tables, and even helped develop the gas mask in World War I. He laid the groundwork for occupational medicine and influenced safety regulations and practices that have saved countless lives in various industries.

Haldane's introduction of canaries into coal mines is a testament to how scientific ingenuity, grounded in a deep understanding of biology and environmental hazards, can lead to practical solutions with profound and lasting impacts on public health and occupational safety.

Endnotes

1   Wikipedia contributors. "Reinforcement learning." Wikipedia, The Free Encyclopedia. December 7, 2023. [https://en.wikipedia.org/wiki/Reinforcement_learning].

2   Wikipedia contributors. "Human-in-the-loop." Wikipedia, The Free Encyclopedia. April 20, 2024. [https://en.wikipedia.org/wiki/Human-in-the-loop].

3   ScienceDirect. 2017. "Synthetic Transaction." ScienceDirect, 2017. [https://www.sciencedirect.com/topics/computer-science/synthetic-transaction].

4   Bonney, Amelie. 2020. "Canaries in the Coal Mine." The Gale Review, September 8, 2020. [https://review.gale.com/2020/09/08/canaries-in-the-coal-mine/].

PART III

Organizational Considerations for AI Model Creation and Deployment

Creating and deploying AI models within customer support organizations demands a multifaceted approach with many considerations. The following chapters will delve into these considerations necessary for integrating AI into your support business, discussing each with an understanding of its impact.

Building ethical AI models with responsible AI (RAI) principles is one of the most important considerations. These considerations should not be an afterthought and are arguably the most critical foundational element to carefully consider at the beginning of your AI journey. While RAI and ethics are discussed in multiple chapters throughout this book, we dive deeper here to ensure AI models are developed with fairness, accountability, transparency, and ethics at their core. With the diversity of your global users—whether they are customers or support professionals—you'll want to design your AI models so that they respect cultural nuances, mitigate harms and biases, and promote inclusivity.

The AI culture you envision for your organization is another consideration to consider as you design and deploy your AI models. There is a great fear factor among those who are unfamiliar and unpracticed with AI. Your company and organizational culture can greatly influence the perception and acceptance of AI, ensuring it's seen and accepted as a positive innovation that will propel personal and business success.

Furthermore, customer support metrics are the backbone of measuring the success of our customer experiences. These benchmarks will allow us to measure the impact and success of AI integration and reflect not only the efficiency and accuracy of our AI models but also customer satisfaction and support agent engagement. Metrics aligned to the AI models themselves are equally important to keep an eye on, encompassing the practical implications of AI deployment, including scalability, maintenance, reliability, and continuous improvement of the models.

The business of providing customer service and support is grounded in operational efficiency. The integration of AI into these operations requires careful consideration to balance efficiency with quality human interaction. AI can manage operational processes and handle routine inquiries and tasks more effectively. This allows human agents to focus on more complex issues that require empathy and deep problem-solving skills. The ultimate idea is to create a seamless blend of AI efficiency and human ingenuity to elevate the overall customer experience.

The final consideration we dive into is the evolution of customer support roles. With AI adoption, many fear displacement, and a shift in traditional customer support roles is inevitable. While AI may alter and replace various roles at some point, the importance of human–AI collaboration, where unique strengths are leveraged to enhance the customer experience, will be key.

The goal in discussing these important considerations as you design and deploy your AI models is to pave a path that leads to innovative, efficient, and ethical customer service solutions. Taking challenges and transforming them into opportunities for growth and learning ensures that every step taken is ethical, measured, understood, and ultimately beneficial to all stakeholders involved.

11

Responsible AI and Ethical Considerations in Customer Support

Our future is a race between the growing power of technology and the wisdom with which we use it.

—Stephen Hawking

AI has evolved from being science fiction to becoming a transformative force in human lives, unveiling a universe of possibilities. It empowers us to work together to envision and create a better world, pushing the boundaries of what we once thought impossible. AI represents a fundamental shift in the way we design technology and is poised to transform business and society, improving productivity and stimulating economic growth, helping people be more creative in their work and impactful in their lives, driving new advances in medicine, new frontiers in science, and new improvements in business. In other words, AI has the potential to be the most significant technological advancement of our generation.

As the revolutionary benefits of AI become apparent, so do the risks. With AI becoming more prolific and entrenched in our everyday lives, organizations need to release these AI developments to earn public trust and be held accountable for all model deployments. Even those organizations with the best AI intentions can end up causing inadvertent societal or individual harm, manifesting as the loss of economic security, liberty, social stability, and opportunity. We must also be mindful that some people will use this technology in bad and harmful ways. AI systems developed without careful consideration can have unintended consequences, where algorithms can introduce bias, discrimination, errors, poor decision-making, and misinformation, causing mistrust among the people it intends to assist. As AI technologies grow more sophisticated, their impact extends beyond mere convenience, touching on significant societal, ethical, and governance issues. This profound influence demands a parallel evolution in how we conceive, develop, and deploy these technologies. At the intersection of innovation and ethics, responsible AI (RAI) emerges as a crucial signpost.

RAI comes into play, not as a nice-to-have but as a mandatory requirement, a business and societal priority to ensure that AI systems are designed, developed, and deployed ethically and accountably, aligning with societal values, respecting human rights, and avoiding causing harm to individuals and communities. Responsible AI is a human-centered approach—both a mindset and a toolset. Responsible AI practices build on a base set of principles and help teams identify, evaluate, and mitigate possible harms throughout the product development lifecycle.

AI systems include not only the technology but also the personas of the people who will use them, the people who will be affected by them, and the environment in which they are deployed. Earning trust in AI is not strictly a technical problem with a technical solution. Earning trust in AI is a *socio*-technical challenge that requires a holistic approach. This can be explained as we expect our very human values to be correctly reflected in and by the technology we use. We expect technologies like AI to not lie to us or discriminate and to be safe for us and our children. Creating an AI system that is "responsible AI-ready" requires an understanding of its potential impacts—both beneficial and harmful—on people and society and taking appropriate measures to mitigate anticipated harms and prepare responses to unanticipated ones.

The path to truly responsible AI is fraught with complex questions: How do we encode ethical principles into AI systems? Can fairness be quantified and ensured in algorithms? What mechanisms are necessary to maintain transparency and accountability in AI applications?

This chapter aims to navigate these questions, offering you a comprehensive overview of the landscape of responsible AI. We aim to demystify the principles and practices that underpin RAI, explore the challenges and opportunities it presents, and illuminate the path forward through examples and actionable insights. By the end of this chapter, our goal is for you to understand the importance of responsible AI and feel equipped to contribute to its evolution.

As we embark on this journey together, let us remember that the future of AI is not predetermined. It is shaped by the decisions of those who design, develop, and deploy these technologies. We can steer AI toward a future that reflects our highest ethical standards and aspirations through a collective commitment to responsibility. Responsible innovation is the key to building a future where AI and human collaboration thrive in harmony, and we have the power and the responsibility to shape a brighter future for future generations. Responsible AI empowers us to build technology that respects, protects, and uplifts human dignity, ensuring that it doesn't perpetuate biases or discriminate against any individual or group and ultimately benefits all of humanity.

Foundations of Responsible AI

Responsible AI refers to designing, developing, and deploying artificial intelligence with a core focus on ethical, secure, and inclusive principles. It encompasses the strategies and actions taken to ensure AI systems are transparent, understandable, and accountable to the individuals and communities they impact. This approach prioritizes safeguarding human rights and values throughout the AI lifecycle, from conception through deployment and beyond.

Ethical Principles

The backbone of RAI is a set of ethical principles that guide its development and use. These principles serve as a moral compass for AI practitioners, ensuring that AI technologies contribute positively to society, are ethical, and do not cause harm. While there is some variation in how these principles are defined and prioritized across different frameworks and guidelines, several core principles are widely recognized and have become foundational in the discourse on RAI. These include:

- **Fairness:** AI systems should be free from bias and designed to avoid unjust or prejudicial treatment that can lead to discriminatory outcomes based on people's race, gender, sexual orientation, or other characteristics. This involves ensuring that AI applications do not perpetuate or amplify social inequalities but rather promote equity and justice. This is achieved by actively identifying and mitigating bias in datasets and algorithms.

- **Accountability:** Designers, developers, deployers, and organizations must take responsibility for the functioning and outcomes of AI systems. This includes establishing mechanisms to address and remedy any harm or errors caused by AI systems.

- **Transparency:** The processes and decisions made by AI systems should be open and understandable to users and stakeholders. This entails documenting and communicating the data, algorithms, and decision-making processes involved, making the decisions made by AI explainable and the processes leading to those decisions accessible for inspection and review.

- **Privacy:** AI systems must respect and protect individuals' privacy rights. This includes ensuring that personal data is collected, stored, and used in compliance with data protection laws and regulations, with consent where necessary, and that individuals have control over their own data.

- **Security:** AI systems should be secure from threats that could compromise their integrity or the data they handle. This includes protection against hacking, data breaches, manipulation, and unintended harmful behaviors.

- **Beneficence:** AI should be designed and deployed to enhance the welfare of humanity. It should aim to bring about positive outcomes for society, contributing to human well-being and the common good.

- **Non-maleficence:** AI systems should not harm humans. The Latin phrase *primum non nocere* often summarizes this principle, meaning "first, do no harm." It underscores the importance of ensuring that AI technologies do not negatively impact human health, rights, dignity, or well-being.

- **Autonomy:** AI should enhance human autonomy, not undermine it. This means that AI systems should empower individuals, allowing them to make free and informed decisions rather than coercing or deceiving them.

- **Inclusion:** Inclusion is increasingly recognized as a crucial principle in developing and deploying responsible AI. Inclusion ensures that AI technologies are accessible to and beneficial for all segments of society, regardless of age, gender, race, ethnicity, physical and cognitive abilities, socioeconomic status, or any other factors that could lead to exclusion or discrimination.

- **Reliability:** Reliability in AI refers to the consistency, stability, and trustworthiness of AI systems over time and across various conditions. It ensures that AI applications perform as intended, are free from errors, and can be depended upon by users. The principle of reliability is closely related to safety, security, and robustness, and it plays a critical role in building trust between AI systems and their human users.

- **Adaptability:** Adaptability refers to encouraging the development of AI systems that are adaptable and flexible, capable of evolving in response to changes in societal norms, ethical considerations, and user needs. This principle supports the ongoing reassessment and adjustment of AI systems to align with dynamic ethical and societal expectations.

These principles are not exhaustive and can vary based on ethical frameworks, cultural contexts, and regulatory environments. Despite variations in emphasis and terminology, the core idea remains consistent: AI should be developed and used ethically, respect human values, and serve the broader interests of society. The expansion of principles beyond this core set reflects a growing recognition of AI technologies' broad and deep impact on all aspects of life and the planet (sustainability, for example). As the field of AI continues to evolve, so will the principles guiding its responsible development and use, necessitating continuous dialogue, reflection, and adaptation among all stakeholders involved in AI ecosystems.

Regulatory Landscape Around the Globe

The interpretation and implementation of responsible AI can vary significantly across different cultural and regional contexts. With the surge in AI-driven products and the evolving global regulatory scene, authorities are quickly advancing AI governance reforms. Various enforcement approaches worldwide mark this rapidly changing regulatory domain, reflecting the dynamic nature of AI technology and its global impact.

This chapter reflects the regulatory environment as of April 2024. Given the rapid evolution in the field of AI, it's very likely that the regulatory landscape will have further evolved by the time you read this chapter. This likelihood makes our compilation a valuable baseline, offering insights into various countries' directions toward AI regulation. While our overview covers key jurisdictions and their approaches, it's important to note that it may not capture every update due to the fast pace of policy changes and the wide range of jurisdictions involved. We encourage you to verify the current status of any regulations mentioned here to ensure you have the most up-to-date information:

Asia

- **China AI policy:** In China, the landscape of AI regulation has been evolving rapidly, and it is expected to follow the European Union's lead and announce its own comprehensive AI Act. While a draft of the Artificial Intelligence Law may emerge in 2024, finalization and effectiveness might take more time.[1] The Chinese Academy of Social Sciences drafted an advisory version of the future AI law in 2023. China aims to guide AI companies by specifying areas they should avoid. Ensuring ethical, accountable, and transparent AI services is a priority. In 2022, China took steps to regulate generative AI technology. They introduced rules that encourage growth while banning deceptive practices. For instance, AI-generated media without watermarks became illegal after January 10, 2023.[2]

- **Japan AI policy:** Japan's approach to AI regulation is based on the Social Principles of Human-Centric AI, although no comprehensive regulation is specifically dedicated to AI in Japan. Instead, the government relies on guidelines and lets the private sector manage their AI use.[3] While not explicitly designed for AI, Japanese sector-specific laws, including data protection, antimonopoly, and copyright, remain relevant in its context.

- **India AI policy:** In India, the regulation of AI is a topic of ongoing discussion and exploration. Currently, there are no codified laws or statutory rules specifically governing the use of AI in the country. However, the Digital India Act of 2023[4] was created to replace the outdated IT Act of 2000. It is a new legal framework designed to address modern digital realities, including AI, by establishing regulations ensuring data security, privacy, and ethical technology use. Complementing this regulatory framework is the IndiaAI Mission,[5] designed to establish a strong AI ecosystem by developing critical AI infrastructure, supporting AI applications in essential sectors, and promoting safe and ethical AI practices.

Australia

- **Australia AI policy:** Australia hasn't introduced specific AI governance laws or policies. Following the safe and responsible AI consultation held in 2023, the Australian government plans to focus new AI regulation on high-risk areas of AI implementation—those with the greatest potential for harm. This could include examples such as discrimination in the workplace, the justice system, surveillance or self-driving cars. Australia was among the first countries to introduce an ethics framework for responsible AI in 2018, which led to Australia's AI Action Plan[6] and AI Ethics Framework.[7]

Americas

- **United States AI policy:** While the U.S. has a more decentralized approach to AI governance, focusing on innovation and competitiveness, there is increasing dialogue on ethical guidelines and sector-specific regulations. The United States adopts a flexible, case-by-case strategy toward AI regulation, avoiding a unified AI-specific law. Instead, it has established various guidelines and frameworks to govern AI at the federal level, including executive orders and proposed bills to promote the use of trustworthy AI within the government and beyond.[8, 9, 10, 11] This approach allows adaptability and innovation, relying on existing agencies to oversee AI deployment and ensure adherence to guidelines across different sectors.

- **Canada AI policy:** Canada is advancing its AI governance through the proposed AI and Data Act (AIDA), focusing on safeguarding Canadians from high-risk AI applications and promoting responsible AI practices.[12] AIDA sets the foundation for the responsible design, development, and deployment of AI systems that impact the lives of Canadians. It aims to ensure that AI technologies are safe, respect human rights, and align with Canadian values. AIDA focuses on high-impact AI systems, which have the potential to significantly affect individuals, society, or the economy. Organizations deploying such systems will be required to implement measures to identify, assess, and mitigate health, safety, and security-related harms.

- **Brazil AI policy:** Brazil's new AI Bill proposes a new framework for regulating AI systems' ethical and responsible use.[13] The proposed legislation is focused on upholding human rights, aiming to empower individuals with significant rights and impose obligations on AI suppliers and operators. It proposes establishing a law enforcement regulatory authority and adopting a risk-based categorization for AI systems. Additionally, it plans a civil liability framework for AI providers or operators and mandates the reporting of major security breaches.

Europe

*   **EU AI Act:** In Europe, the European Union has been proactive in establishing regulations and guidelines for AI, emphasizing privacy, data protection (e.g., GDPR), and the ethical implications of AI technologies. The European AI Act[14] is a groundbreaking landmark law adopted by the EU to regulate artificial intelligence within its member states.[15] The EU act emphasizes the importance of ethical guidelines, including transparency and accountability. It aims to protect fundamental rights, democracy, the rule of law and environmental sustainability from high-risk AI while boosting innovation and establishing Europe as a leader in the field. It seeks to establish an EU AI Board to oversee implementation and compliance and introduces a directive for handling civil liabilities arising from AI-induced damages. This legislation is seen as a significant move toward ensuring AI technologies are developed and used in a manner that is safe, ethical, and beneficial for society, setting a precedent for global AI regulation efforts. The law is now approved by the European Parliament and needs to be formally endorsed by the Council as the next step. The EU AI Act introduces a risk-based approach to AI governance, distinguishing between high-risk and low-risk AI applications to tailor regulatory requirements accordingly (see **Figure 11.1**).

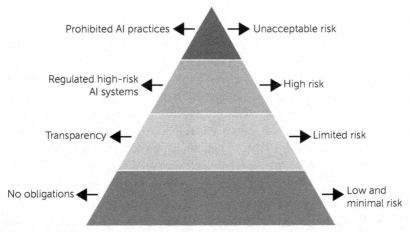

FIGURE 11.1 Pyramid of risks (Data source: The European Commission)[16]

The new rules ban certain AI applications that threaten citizens' rights, including biometric categorization systems based on sensitive characteristics and untargeted scraping of facial images from the Internet or

CCTV footage to create facial recognition databases. Emotion recognition in the workplace and schools, social scoring, predictive policing (based solely on profiling a person or assessing their characteristics) AI that manipulates human behavior or exploits people's vulnerabilities will also be forbidden. Law enforcement's use of remote biometric identification (RBI) systems is prohibited in principle, except in exhaustively listed and narrowly defined situations. Such uses may include, for example, a targeted search of a missing person or preventing a terrorist attack.

Clear obligations are also foreseen for other high-risk AI systems (due to their significant potential harm to health, safety, fundamental rights, the environment, democracy, and the rule of law). Citizens will have a right to submit complaints about AI systems and receive explanations about decisions based on high-risk AI systems that affect their rights.[17]

United Kingdom

- **The United Kingdom:** The UK's approach to AI regulation emphasizes a context-sensitive, balanced method rather than implementing a comprehensive AI-specific regulation.[18] It prefers to apply existing sector-specific laws for AI guidance, advocating for an adaptable regulatory framework that avoids stifling innovation with overly prescriptive rules. This strategy aims to ensure that AI development and deployment are governed in a way that is both flexible and responsible, reflecting the UK's focus on fostering technological advancement while maintaining ethical standards. Switzerland is taking a path similar to the UK, opting against introducing a standalone AI regulation.

A worldwide standardized approach to AI regulation might not materialize soon (or maybe ever). Hence, a more viable approach may be to concentrate on the core ethical principles of AI, which garner broader agreement than specific regulatory details.

This diversity in perspectives underscores the importance of international collaboration in creating a universally beneficial approach to responsible AI. It highlights the need for a global dialogue that respects cultural differences while striving for common ethical standards in AI.

The foundations of responsible AI are laid on the bedrock of ethical principles, shaped by a diverse range of global perspectives. As we move forward, it is vital to recognize that these principles are not static; they must evolve in response to new technological advancements and societal shifts. By committing to these foundations, we ensure that AI technologies remain aligned with human values and serve the interests of all segments of society.

Challenges and Opportunities

The journey of integrating AI into our lives is paved with ethical dilemmas that challenge our core values. One striking example is the issue of bias in facial recognition technology.[19] This technology, while revolutionary, has shown disparities in accuracy across different demographics, raising significant concerns about fairness and discrimination. Such case studies underscore the complexity of ethical decision-making in AI, where algorithms trained on biased data can perpetuate or even exacerbate existing societal inequities.

Technological Challenges

Implementing ethical principles into AI systems is not just a matter of will but of capability. The technological hurdles are significant, ranging from the opacity of complex algorithms (the "black box" problem where AI algorithms, especially deep-learning models, make it difficult to understand how decisions are made) to the challenge of ensuring data privacy in an era of ubiquitous data collection. The risk of data breaches and unethical use of personal information raises significant concerns. Additionally, algorithmic bias presents a persistent challenge, where AI systems can inherit and amplify biases present in their training data, leading to unfair outcomes. Overcoming these challenges requires advancements in AI explainability, secure data practices, and bias mitigation techniques.

These challenges highlight the gap between the ideal of responsible AI and the practical realities of AI development, where technical limitations can impede the realization of ethical objectives.

One example illustrating the challenges around privacy and security is the incident reported with the iRobot and Google partnership. iRobot's Roomba i7+ represented a significant leap in smart home technology, combining odometry data and low-resolution camera imagery to map users' homes.[20] This technology lets users utilize Google Assistant to command their Roomba to clean specific rooms. While this integration offers unprecedented convenience, it also raises significant privacy concerns. The voluntary nature of this data sharing underscores the importance of consent and the need for robust data protection measures. However, incidents like Google's admission that it exposed the personal data of about 500,000 Google+ users and the scrutiny over third-party access to Gmail accounts highlight the ongoing challenges in safeguarding user data in the smart devices and services ecosystem.[21, 22]

Building on the challenges these new systems bring forward, the notion of using AI to fool another AI system, as explored in reports from *Popular Mechanics*, opens Pandora's box regarding accountability in AI development and deployment.[23] This report discusses techniques or methods to deceive AI systems designed for surveillance or listening purposes of private conversations. It involves various strategies to mislead AI algorithms that analyze speech, sound, or other data types to prevent them from accurately interpreting or using the information they collect. This scenario highlights the cat-and-mouse game between evolving AI technologies and raises questions about the accountability of developers and companies in creating AI systems that respect user privacy and security. The potential for AI systems to be manipulated or used in unintended ways necessitates a framework for accountability that ensures AI technologies are developed and used ethically and transparently and are aligned with societal values.

Opportunity for Good

Despite these challenges, AI presents unprecedented opportunities to address some of the world's most pressing issues. AI has the potential to revolutionize healthcare through personalized medicine, combat climate change by optimizing energy consumption, and improve accessibility for people with disabilities through innovative assistive technologies. These examples illustrate the dual nature of AI as both a source of ethical concern and a tool for societal good, emphasizing the importance of guiding AI development in a direction that maximizes its benefits while minimizing its risks.

One example in the reliability and safety arena is AI's application in construction. The use of AI-driven anti-collision technology by housebuilder Countryside represents a positive stride toward enhancing safety and reliability in the construction industry.[24] This technology demonstrates how AI can be harnessed to prevent accidents on construction sites, showcasing the potential of AI to significantly improve workplace safety. However, the reliance on AI for critical safety measures also underscores the need to ensure these systems' reliability. It highlights the importance of rigorous testing, continuous monitoring, and contingency planning to address potential failures or malfunctions, ensuring that AI technologies can be trusted to perform safely and effectively in high-stakes environments.

Frameworks and Governance

Organizations play a crucial role in integrating responsible AI principles into their operations. This involves establishing internal policies, ethical AI guidelines, and governance structures to oversee AI projects. For example, Microsoft released *The Microsoft Responsible AI Impact Assessment Guide*, designed to help establish strong RAI standards and practices across industries by sharing learnings and inviting feedback.[25]

Establishing institutional frameworks and AI governance is crucial for ensuring AI technologies are developed and used ethically and responsibly. These frameworks provide a structured approach to addressing ethical considerations such as fairness, privacy, and transparency, ensuring AI systems do not inadvertently harm users or society. AI governance ensures accountability, guiding organizations to monitor AI systems' impact and make necessary adjustments. It also fosters trust among stakeholders, including customers and regulatory bodies, by demonstrating a commitment to ethical practices. Integrating these frameworks into companies leads to sustainable, responsible AI innovation that aligns with societal values and legal requirements, positioning companies as leaders in ethical AI use.

One notable example of a successful AI governance framework is IBM's AI Ethics Board.[26] This board oversees the company's ethical development, deployment, and use of AI technologies. It ensures that IBM's AI projects align with its Principles for Trust and Transparency, focusing on trust, transparency, fairness, and accountability. The AI Ethics Board reviews AI initiatives, guides ethical AI research, and collaborates across teams to embed ethical considerations into AI solutions, making IBM a leader in responsible AI practices.

Implementing Responsible AI: A Strategic Blueprint for Ethical Integration

Implementing RAI within an organization is a comprehensive process that integrates ethical, legal, and technical considerations into developing, deploying, and using AI systems. In their book, *AI for the Rest of Us*, RAI practitioners Phaedra Boinodiris and Beth Rudden say, "There is no 'easy button' for responsibly curated AI."[27]

This section provides a detailed guide to help companies embark on this journey and covers initial considerations and practical steps, including lessons learned and essential do's and don'ts.

Initial Considerations

There are a number of initial activities to undertake as you consider how to approach responsible AI. These are non-negotiable if we are to build a safe future for humans.

- **Revisit your AI use case goals:** Meticulously evaluating the intended use case of your AI model with an eye on RAI principles ensures that AI deployment is not only ethically sound but also contributes meaningfully to the organization's goals.

- **Understand RAI principles:** Begin by familiarizing yourself with the core principles of RAI, which include fairness, transparency, accountability, privacy, and security, as shared earlier in this chapter. Understanding these principles is crucial for responsibly guiding the development and deployment of AI.

- **Assess your AI maturity:** Evaluate your organization's current use of AI and its maturity level in terms of AI development, usage, and governance. This assessment will help identify the starting point for integrating RAI practices.

- **Define RAI strategy goals:** Align your RAI efforts with your business objectives and ethical standards. Define clear RAI goals, including compliance with laws and regulations and commitment to ethical values exceeding legal requirements.

Strategic Planning

Once you move past the initial considerations, there are some strategies to help you build a successful and responsible AI deployment:

- **Establish a cross-functional RAI team:** Create a team that includes members from diverse backgrounds, including ethics, law, technology, business, and human rights. This team will lead the RAI efforts, ensuring a multi-perspective approach to decision-making.

- **Develop an RAI framework:** Based on the RAI principles, develop a framework that includes policies, procedures, and guidelines for responsible AI development and use. This framework should be adaptable to evolving technologies and regulations.

- **Establish accountability:** Designate an individual or team accountable for ensuring equitable outcomes from AI initiatives across the organization. This requires more than just a symbolic gesture; it demands a funded mandate that empowers the designated party to actively oversee and address any ethical concerns that may arise during the AI development and deployment phases. Accountability ensures that AI serves the collective good without perpetuating biases or causing harm.

- **Invest in education and training:** Provide education and training for employees at all levels about the importance of RAI and their role in implementing it. This includes technical training for AI developers and social and ethical training for decision-makers. This holistic approach to training and education enhances individual competencies and establishes a collaborative environment where employees can learn from each other's diverse perspectives and collectively contribute to the responsible advancement of AI technologies.

Implementation

After you've laid out your strategy, next comes the implementation. As you learned in the discussion of the 6Ds framework in Chapter 4, "Vision of Success," RAI is sprinkled throughout the process.

- **Integrate RAI into the AI lifecycle:** Ensure that RAI principles are integrated at every stage of the AI lifecycle, from initial design to deployment and monitoring. This includes conducting impact assessments, implementing fairness and bias checks, and ensuring transparency and explainability.

- **Leverage external expertise:** Consider consulting with external experts or joining industry groups focused on RAI to gain insights, share experiences, and stay updated on best practices and regulatory developments.

- **Create an RAI culture:** Creating and sustaining a culture prioritizing RAI practices is central to long-term success. Organizations should instill an awareness of ethical considerations across all levels and encourage employees to question and challenge AI decisions that may have unintended consequences. A culture that values RAI proactively identifies and rectifies potential issues before they escalate.

- **Monitor and report:** Implement mechanisms for ongoing monitoring and reporting of AI systems to ensure they continue to operate within the set RAI guidelines. This should include feedback loops and adaptation of AI models for continuous improvement. This iterative process allows for identifying and rectifying issues as they emerge, ensuring that AI systems evolve responsibly over time.

Lessons Learned and Best Practices

Companies that successfully implement RAI emphasize the importance of engaging stakeholders early and throughout the AI lifecycle, including customers, employees, and regulators.

Another lesson is that transparency is key. Being transparent about how AI systems make decisions and their potential biases helps build trust with users and stakeholders.

Last but not least, ethics go beyond pure compliance. Successful organizations treat ethics as a foundation, not just a checklist. They strive to exceed legal requirements by fostering a culture prioritizing ethical considerations in all AI-related decisions.

Following are some do's and don'ts:

Do:

- Review and update your RAI policies regularly to reflect new technologies and regulatory changes.
- Foster an organizational culture that values and prioritizes ethical considerations.
- Engage with diverse stakeholders to understand different perspectives and potential impacts of AI.

Don't:

- Overlook the importance of data governance and the ethical implications of data collection and use.
- Underestimate the challenges of mitigating biases in AI systems. Continuous effort and diverse datasets are required.
- Ignore the feedback from AI system users and those affected by its decisions. Their insights are valuable for improving RAI practices.

Implementing RAI is a journey that requires commitment, ongoing effort, and a willingness to learn and adapt. By following these guidelines, companies can pave the way for responsible AI use that complies with regulations and aligns with ethical standards and societal values.

Addressing the Shadows: Mitigating Potential Harms in LLMs

In the expansive landscape of artificial intelligence, large language models (LLMs) present groundbreaking opportunities while simultaneously posing complex challenges. As the influence of these advanced AI systems, capable of understanding and generating human-like text, grows and penetrates deeper into various aspects of our lives and businesses, it becomes imperative to confront and navigate the potential adverse effects they might engender, ensuring that the integration of LLMs into society maximizes their potential for positive impact while diligently safeguarding against their inherent dangers. The AI incidents database provides a comprehensive global view of submitted harms or near harms realized by the deployment of AI,[28] giving us a chance to learn from the collective missteps of others. Through a detailed examination of content-related harms, technical pitfalls, operational challenges, and ethical considerations, this section will equip you with the knowledge and tools necessary to guide the responsible development and application of LLM technologies.

Content harms and mitigations

- **Exposure to illegal or harmful content**

  Harm: Users might encounter content that promotes hate speech, violence, or exploitation, among other harmful types of content.

  Mitigation: Mitigation strategies can include content filters to screen for and eliminate harmful content, adaptable filters/blocklists to respond quickly to new threats or harmful trends, and detection systems to identify and take action against policy violators. Facilitating easy reporting for users and ensuring feedback tools capture adequate details for review is important. Additionally, prompt engineering can be leveraged to guide LLMs to generate outputs aligned with the organization's policies and principles, avoiding harmful content generation.

- **Misleading or regulated advice**

  Harm: LLMs may inadvertently provide inaccurate advice in sensitive medical, legal, or financial domains.

  Mitigation: Mitigation strategies can include legal expertise consultation in order to identify domains where special considerations are required and avoid offering direct advice. This is the design of the LLM for graceful disengagement to deflect specific inquiries to qualified professionals and leverage prompt engineering to instruct LLMs to clarify that users should consult experts for personal advice.

Technical and operational harms

- **Third-party content regurgitation**

  Harm: LLMs might replicate copyrighted or sensitive content without proper attribution.

  Mitigation: Mitigation strategies can include legal consultation to understand the legal implications, establish safeguards accordingly, and continuously monitor and adjust the LLM's tendency to replicate content.

- **Performance disparities**

  Harm: LLMs may offer varying quality of service (QoS) across different languages or demographic groups.

  Mitigation: Mitigation strategies can include regular language and demographic assessments and evaluations to identify and address disparities and leveraging user feedback and engagement signals to improve performance for underrepresented groups.

- **Hallucinations and misinformation**

  Harm: LLMs can mislead users by generating false or unverified information and presenting it as a fact—a phenomenon known as a hallucination in AI.

  Mitigation: Mitigation strategies involve content verification by integrating checks against reliable databases or external application programming interfaces (APIs) and user education to warn and inform users about the potential for inaccuracies and encourage verification.

- **Lack of content provenance**

  Harm: Generated content may lose its origin trace, complicating accountability.

  Mitigation: Mitigation strategies may involve applying watermarking or metadata techniques to trace content back to its source.

- **Ungrounded or misleading outputs**

  Harm: Content generated may be ungrounded, leading to inaccuracies.

  Mitigation: Mitigation strategies can include grounding data, which provides verified sources for the LLM to base its outputs on and minimize ungrounded content through careful prompt design and user interface cues.

- **Inadequate algorithmic impact assessments**

  Harm: The efficacy of these assessments hinges on the understanding and proficiency of AI model owners with the challenge arising in a lack of comprehensive understanding of concepts like disparate impact and the intricacies of risk assessment.

  Mitigation: Mitigation strategies involve establishing a central organizational standard and governing body that can act as knowledge hubs, providing a space where practitioners from diverse backgrounds can collaboratively enhance their understanding of AI ethics, risks, and societal implications.

Societal and ethical harms

- **Transparency issues**

  Harm: Users may not realize they're interacting with AI, leading to misunderstandings about its capabilities.

  Mitigation: Mitigation strategies can include creating documentation to offer clear, accessible information on the AI's nature and limitations and including user interface design elements that highlight the AI-generated nature of the content.

- **Misuse for political or ideological manipulation**

  Harm: There's a risk of using LLMs to generate biased content or influence political processes.

  Mitigation: Mitigation strategies require explicitly instructing LLMs through prompt engineering to avoid generating politically influential content. Maintaining dynamic blocklists can help prevent the generation of sensitive political content.

- **Code generation risks**

  Harm: LLMs capable of generating code might produce insecure or harmful outputs.

  Mitigation: Mitigation strategies can include using Content Moderation Classifiers such as tools like Azure AI Platform's (AIP) malware and vulnerable code classifiers to screen generated code. Reminding users to review AI-generated code for security and accuracy is important. Mitigating the potential harms of LLMs requires a diverse approach, combining technical solutions, ethical guidelines, and legal considerations. By implementing dynamic filters, engaging in prompt engineering, consulting legal expertise, and fostering transparency, organizations can navigate the complexities of LLM deployment. This proactive stance ensures that the benefits of LLMs are realized while minimizing their risks, paving the way for a responsible and secure AI-powered future.

Navigating the Bias in Large Language Models

LLMs have emerged as powerful tools capable of performing a wide range of natural language processing tasks. However, along with their impressive capabilities come significant challenges, one of the most prominent being the issue of bias. Bias in LLMs refers to the tendency of these models to generate outputs that reflect the prejudices or stereotypes present in their training data. Responsible AI empowers us to build technology that respects and upholds human dignity, ensuring it doesn't perpetuate biases or discriminate against any individual or group.

Bias in LLMs manifests when the models produce outputs that unfairly favor certain groups or ideas over others, often replicating societal, gender, racial, or ideological biases embedded in their training datasets. These biases can arise from a variety of sources, including but not limited to the selection of training data, the model's design and architecture, and the subjective decisions made during the model development process.

The presence of bias in LLMs poses several challenges, including:

- **Ethical concerns:** Biased outputs can reinforce harmful stereotypes and perpetuate injustice, undermining efforts to promote fairness and equality.

- **Loss of trust:** Evidence of bias can erode public trust in AI technologies and their developers, hampering adoption and acceptance.

- **Legal risks:** Deploying biased LLMs, especially in sensitive areas like hiring, lending, and law enforcement, can lead to legal challenges and liabilities.

Several instances have highlighted the presence of bias in LLMs, underscoring the need for vigilance and mitigation strategies. Research has shown that some LLMs associate certain professions or activities with specific genders and, therefore, perpetuate stereotypes (such as assuming doctors are male and nurses are female). LLMs have been found to generate prejudicial content against certain racial groups, often reflecting societal biases present in the training data. Also, some LLMs perform better on tasks in English than other languages, disadvantaging non-English speakers and reflecting a bias toward Anglophone data and perspectives.

Two prevalent issues that may arise are the phenomena of overblocking and overreacting:

- **Overblocking:** Overblocking refers to the inadvertent censorship or restriction of content that is not inherently harmful but is mistakenly flagged as such. This phenomenon often occurs due to implementing broad content moderation policies or automated filtering algorithms. While the intention behind such measures is to maintain a safe online environment, their indiscriminate application can suppress diverse perspectives and voices. In 2019, Facebook's content moderation policies were scrutinized when the company's automated systems mistakenly flagged and removed a post featuring an iconic Vietnam War photograph known as "The Terror of War" or "Napalm Girl."[29] The Pulitzer

Prize-winning photograph, captured by photographer Nick Ut, depicts a young Vietnamese girl fleeing a napalm attack. Despite its historical significance and journalistic value, Facebook's algorithms categorized the image as violating its policies on nudity, resulting in its removal from the platform.

ADVERSARIAL DEBIASING

Adversarial debiasing, in essence, is the powerhouse technique striving to correct biases in machine learning models.[30] Visualize this: two digital entities are set up in a delicate dance. One, the predictor, is trained with the prime mission of making spot-on predictions. The other, the adversary, acts almost as its vigilant counterpart, trained meticulously to recognize and capitalize on any biases the predictor might unknowingly show.

Their dynamic? A unique, adversarial ballet, where the adversary seeks to amplify any predictor biases while the predictor ardently seeks to suppress them. Much like a customer who has tried every possible solution and turns to customer support, these two models push each other to the edge, ensuring the predictor learns to rely on genuine, unbiased features.

The result? A model that's not only accurate but embodies fairness. This intriguing method, adversarial debiasing, has etched its mark in myriad fields—think of refining word contexts or enhancing the reliability of health-care-based machine learning models.

The journey of understanding and implementing machine learning, especially adversarial debiasing, parallels the dedication required in customer service. Just as a visitor to a theme park would be disappointed by an unknowledge-able staff member or as a donor might be frustrated by an unhelpful website, biases in machine learning can lead to misguided predictions. The commit-ment to refining such models, ensuring they serve their purpose effectively, is akin to the commitment of ensuring every customer's query is met with knowledge and empathy.

In the grand tapestry of AI, just like in customer service, the intricacies mat-ter. It's imperative that the information, whether presented by a human or AI, remains both accurate and relevant.

- **Overreacting:** On the flip side, *overreacting* refers to situations where AI models produce inaccurate or disproportionate responses to input data or stimuli. Overreacting in AI can decrease AI systems' accuracy and reliability, eroding user trust and confidence in their capabili-ties. An example of this scenario made Google stop allowing users to generate images of humans in its Gemini AI tool after receiving complaints that it produced pictures of Black founding fathers and a female Pope, among other diversity controversies.[31] Embedded within any algorithm is a value judgment about what to prioritize, such as competing notions of bias. Companies have to decide whether they want to accurately portray what society currently looks like or promote a vision of what they think society could or should look like. Addressing bias in LLMs requires an approach encompassing technical solutions and organizational practices. Bias detection and correction techniques employing algorithms and methodologies specifically designed to identify and mitigate bias in model outputs are critical.

Bias in LLMs: Case Studies and Impact

Large language models and AI-driven algorithms have revolutionized countless aspects of our lives, from education and healthcare to employment and beyond. However, integrating these technologies has also surfaced significant ethical concerns, particularly regarding bias. Through a series of impactful examples, this section illuminates the diverse nature of bias within LLMs and AI algorithms, showcasing the real-world consequences and the urgent need for equitable solutions.

UK Government's Grading Algorithm: A Case of Elitism

In a controversial move, the UK government deployed an algorithm to determine the final-year grades of students, resulting in widespread accusations of elitism.[32] The algorithm disproportionately downgraded students from state schools while favoring those from private institutions, basing its decisions on the historical performance of schools. This approach underscored systemic inequalities within the educational sector and highlighted the dangers of relying on historical data perpetuating existing disparities.

Racial Bias in Healthcare Algorithms

A striking analysis published in *Nature*[33] revealed that an algorithm widely used across US hospitals systematically discriminated against Black patients. Despite equal levels of illness, Black individuals were less likely than their white counterparts to be referred to programs designed for patients with complex medical needs. Given that such algorithms influence care for approximately 200 million people annually in the US, the implications of this bias are profound, underscoring the critical need to reevaluate and redesign healthcare algorithms to ensure equitable treatment for all patients.

AI Hiring Tools and Disability Discrimination

The United States has raised alarms over AI hiring tools that inadvertently discriminate against people with disabilities. Employers utilizing computer-based tests or software for résumé scoring may, without intending to, violate the Americans with Disabilities Act (ADA). These tools, lacking in necessary safeguards, risk unlawfully screening out candidates with disabilities who are otherwise qualified for the job.[34] This situation calls for a reexamination of algorithmic decision-making in employment to ensure it accommodates the diverse capabilities of all applicants.

Anti-Black Bias in AI-Enabled Recruiting

Research from the Thomson Reuters Institute and the University of Pennsylvania has illuminated anti-Black bias in AI-enabled recruiting processes, echoing longstanding issues of discrimination.[35] Black professionals face significantly lower job callback rates (30–50 percent less), particularly when their résumés reflect their racial or ethnic identity. This bias perpetuates historical injustices and deprives organizations of diverse talent and perspectives, highlighting an urgent need for introspection and reform in AI-driven recruitment practices.

Customer Sentiment Analysis

In this scenario, the AI can analyze voice patterns, speech content, and other cues to determine customer sentiment. Sentiment analysis, like many other AI applications, has faced challenges related to biases. The potential for bias arises from various sources, including the training data used to develop sentiment analysis models, algorithms, or even social media. If the training data predominantly represents certain demographic groups, cultural backgrounds, or language nuances, the sentiment analysis model may struggle to accurately interpret sentiment in data from underrepresented groups. This misinterpretation can result in skewed or inaccurate analyses, leading to biased conclusions.

These examples serve as a clarion call to the inherent risks of uncritically deploying LLMs and AI algorithms without thorough consideration of their societal impacts. They underscore the necessity of integrating ethical principles, transparency, and inclusivity in the development and application of AI technologies, and understanding the nature of bias, recognizing its manifestations and competing notions, and implementing comprehensive strategies for its avoidance and mitigation. As we move forward, the task at hand is not only to rectify these biases but also to reimagine a future where AI serves as a catalyst for equity and justice, embodying the diversity and complexity of the human experience. We must embrace collaborative efforts, innovative solutions, and a steadfast commitment to responsible AI development that honors the dignity and worth of every individual. The journey toward bias-free LLMs is ongoing, requiring constant vigilance, innovation, and commitment to ethical principles.

Considerations

Clearly, the journey toward ethical, equitable, and sustainable AI technologies is both challenging and rewarding. The landscape of AI, especially with the advent and integration of LLMs, presents a unique blend of opportunities and responsibilities. We have explored the multifaceted aspects of RAI, from understanding the potential harms and biases inherent in these technologies to implementing robust strategies for mitigating risks and fostering positive outcomes.

The path to RAI is not a solitary one; it requires the collective effort of developers, policymakers, researchers, and society at large. Each stakeholder plays a pivotal role in shaping the future of AI to ensure it aligns with ethical standards and societal values. The responsibility lies not only in addressing the challenges of today but also in anticipating the complexities of tomorrow, fostering an environment of continuous learning, adaptation, and improvement.

The examples and strategies discussed in this chapter underscore a fundamental truth: technology's greatest potential lies in its ability to enhance human capabilities, foster inclusivity, and promote global well-being. As we move forward, let us embrace the principles of RAI with a sense of purpose and optimism. By prioritizing transparency, fairness, accountability, and respect for privacy, we can navigate the AI landscape with confidence and integrity.

Let this chapter serve as both a foundation and a beacon, guiding our efforts to harness the power of AI while steadfastly adhering to the highest ethical standards. Integrating RAI into our lives and work is ongoing and filled with challenges and opportunities. Yet, it is a journey worth taking, for it leads us toward a future where technology and humanity converge in harmony, unlocking unparalleled possibilities for advancement and transformation.

As we stand at the precipice of a new era in AI, let us move forward with a shared commitment to responsible innovation. Let us inspire and be inspired, challenge and be challenged, and above all, strive to ensure that the AI of tomorrow embodies the best of our values and aspirations. Together, we can create a powerful and profoundly positive AI legacy for humanity.

Endnotes

1 Yang, Zeyi. 2024. "Four things to know about China's new AI rules in 2024." MIT Technology Review. January 17, 2024. [https://www.technologyreview.com/2024/01/17/1086704/china-ai-regulation-changes-2024/]

2 Edwards, Benj. 2022. "China bans AI-generated media without watermarks." Ars Technica. December 12, 2022. [https://arstechnica.com/information-technology/2022/12/china-bans-ai-generated-media-without-watermarks/].

3 Expert group on how AI principles should be implemented contributors. 2022. "Governance Guidelines for Implementation of AI Principles." Meti. January 28, 2022. [https://www.meti.go.jp/shingikai/mono_info_service/ai_shakai_jisso/pdf/20220128_2.pdf].

4 Contributors. 2023. "Proposed Digital India Act, 2023." Meity. September 3, 2023. [https://www.meity.gov.in/writereaddata/files/DIA_Presentation%2009.03.2023%20Final.pdf].

5 PMIndia Editors. 2024. "Cabinet Approves Ambitious IndiaAI Mission to Strengthen the AI Innovation Ecosystem." PMIndia. March 7, 2024. [https://www.pmindia.gov.in/en/news_updates/cabinet-approves-ambitious-indiaai-mission-to-strengthen-the-ai-innovation-ecosystem/].

6 Australian Government. 2021. "Australia's Artificial Intelligence Action Plan." Australian Government, Department of Industry, Science and Resources. June 18, 2021. [https://www.industry.gov.au/publications/australias-artificial-intelligence-action-plan].

7 Australian Government. 2019. "Australia's Artificial Intelligence Ethics Framework." Australian Government, Department of Industry, Science and Resources. November 7, 2019. [https://www.industry.gov.au/publications/australias-artificial-intelligence-ethics-framework].

8 Executive Office of the President. 2019. "Maintaining American Leadership in Artificial Intelligence." Federal Register. February 14, 2019. [https://www.federalregister.gov/documents/2019/02/14/2019-02544/maintaining-american-leadership-in-artificial-intelligence].

9 Executive Office of the President. 2019. "Promoting the Use of Trustworthy Artificial Intelligence in the Federal Government." Federal Register. December 8, 2020. [https://www.federalregister.gov/documents/2020/12/08/2020-27065/promoting-the-use-of-trustworthy-artificial-intelligence-in-the-federal-government].

10 Peters, Gary Sen. 2021. "S2551 - AI Training Act." U.S. Government Publishing Office. July 29, 2021. [https://www.congress.gov/bill/117th-congress/senate-bill/2551].

11 Thornberry, William M. "National Defense Authorization Act for Fiscal Year 2021." U.S. Government Publishing Office. December 3, 2020. [https://www.congress.gov/116/crpt/hrpt617/CRPT-116hrpt617.pdf].

12 Government of Canada. "The Artificial Intelligence and Data Act (AIDA) - Companion document." Government of Canada. March 13, 2023. [https://ised-isde.canada.ca/site/innovation-better-canada/en/artificial-intelligence-and-data-act-aida-companion-document].

13   Contributors. 2023. "Access Alert | Brazil's New AI Bill: A Comprehensive
     Framework for Ethical and Responsible Use of AI Systems."
     Access Partnership. May 5, 2023. [https://accesspartnership.com/
     access-alert-brazils-new-ai-bill-a-comprehensive-framework-for-ethical-and-
     responsible-use-of-ai-systems/].

14   European Union. "AI Act". European Commission. February 20, 2024.
     [https://digital-strategy.ec.europa.eu/en/policies/regulatory-framework-ai].

15   Madiega, Tambiama. "Artificial intelligence act." European Parliamentary
     Research Service. March 2024. [https://www.europarl.europa.eu/RegData/
     etudes/BRIE/2021/698792/EPRS_BRI(2021)698792_EN.pdf].

16   European Union. "AI Act". European Commission. February 20, 2024.
     [https://digital-strategy.ec.europa.eu/en/policies/regulatory-framework-ai].

17   Press room. 2024. "Artificial Intelligence Act: MEPs adopt
     landmark law." European Parliament. March 13, 2024. [https://
     www.europarl.europa.eu/news/en/press-room/20240308IPR19015/
     artificial-intelligence-act-meps-adopt-landmark-law].

18   Ponomarov, Kostiantyn. 2024. "How to Navigate UK AI Regulations." Legal
     Notes. March 20, 2024. [https://legalnodes.com/article/uk-ai-regulations].

19   Buolamwini, Joy. 2023. "Unmasking the bias in facial recognition algorithms."
     MIT Sloan School of Management. December 13, 2023. [https://mitsloan.mit.
     edu/ideas-made-to-matter/unmasking-bias-facial-recognition-algorithms].

20   Fingas, Jon. 2018. "Google and iRobot team up to better map your home."
     Engadget. October 31, 2018. [https://www.engadget.com/2018-10-31-google-
     and-irobot-smart-home-partnership.html].

21   Statt, Nick. 2018. "Google hid major Google+ security flaw that exposed
     users' personal information." The Verge. October 8, 2018. [https://www.
     theverge.com/2018/10/8/17951914/google-plus-data-breach-exposed-user-
     profile-information-privacy-not-disclosed].

22   Cimpanu, Catalin. 2018. "Google sets new rules for third-party apps to
     access Gmail data." ZDNet. October 8, 2018. [https://www.zdnet.com/article/
     google-sets-new-rules-for-third-party-apps-to-access-gmail-data/].

23   Wagh, Manasee. 2022. "How To Fool an Eavesdropping AI...With Another
     AI." *Popular Mechanics*. June 7, 2022. [https://www.popularmechanics.com/
     technology/security/a40208622/how-to-fool-eavesdropping-ai/].

24   BIM+ Author. 2022. "AI drives plant safety for housebuilder." BIMPlus. July 6,
     2022. [https://www.bimplus.co.uk/ai-drives-plant-safety-for-housebuilder/].

25   Microsoft Blog Authors. 2022. "Microsoft Responsible AI Impact Assessment
     Guide." Microsoft Blog. June 2022. [https://blogs.microsoft.com/wp-content/
     uploads/prod/sites/5/2022/06/Microsoft-RAI-Impact-Assessment-Guide.pdf].

26   IBM Authors. "Now is the moment for responsible AI." IBM. Accessed
     February 28, 2024. [https://www.ibm.com/impact/ai-ethics].

27   Boinodiris, Phaedra., Rudden, Beth. *AI for the Rest of Us*. Independent
     Publisher. United States. 2023. p 25.

28   Responsible AI Collaborative. "AI Incident Database."
     [https://incidentdatabase.ai/].

29   Time editors. 2016. "The Story Behind the 'Napalm Girl' Photo Censored by Facebook." *Time.* September 9, 2016. [https://time.com/4485344/napalm-girl-war-photo-facebook/].

30   Mahmoudian, Haniyeh, PhD. 2020. "Using Adversarial Debiasing to Reduce Model Bias." Medium. April 21, 2020. [https://towardsdatascience.com/reducing-bias-from-models-built-on-the-adult-dataset-using-adversarial-debiasing-330f2ef3a3b4].

31   Samuel, Sigal. 2024. "Black Nazis? A woman pope? That's just the start of Google's AI problem." Vox. February 28, 2024. [https://www.vox.com/future-perfect/2024/2/28/24083814/google-gemini-ai-bias-ethics].

32   Eccles, Mari., Gallardo, Cristina. 2020. "UK government faces elitism row after algorithm downgrades pupils." Politico. August 14, 2020. [https://www.politico.eu/article/uk-government-faces-elitism-row-after-algorithm-downgrades-final-year-pupils/].

33   Ledford, Heidi. 2019. "Millions of black people affected by racial bias in health-care algorithms." Nature. October 26, 2019. [https://www.nature.com/articles/d41586-019-03228-6].

34   Auto-generated from a syndicated feed. 2022. "AI hiring tools discriminate against people with disabilities, warns US." Business Standard. May 15, 2022. [https://www.business-standard.com/article/international/ai-hiring-tools-discriminate-against-people-with-disabilities-warns-us-122051500167_1.html].

35   Zapata, Dawn. 2021. "New study finds AI-enabled anti-Black bias in recruiting." Thomson Reuters. June 18, 2021. [https://www.thomsonreuters.com/en-us/posts/legal/ai-enabled-anti-black-bias/].

12

Cultural Considerations

A nation's culture resides in the hearts and in the soul of its people.

—Mahatma Gandhi

In the world of customer service and support, where technology converges with humanity, a quiet revolution is unfolding, and artificial intelligence (AI) is at the center and ready to transform this landscape. This could very well be the synopsis of the latest sci-fi movie captivating audiences worldwide. And maybe, one day, it will be. However, today, it reflects the reality we are living and breathing every day. Companies and customers are standing at the edge of a big shift set to completely redefine how we all think about customer service.

Yet, despite the great potential of AI to enhance efficiency and personalization, a paradox emerges in this transformative era—while the promises of AI proliferate, so do the fears, such as job displacement and the erosion of human skills due to AI and automation. The pioneers daring to explore it face myriad challenges deeply rooted in human culture and psychology.

Additionally, change fatigue is an undeniable reality. Recent years have been emblematic of relentless changes and accelerated digital transformation by the unforeseen shift to remote work that the global pandemic brought overnight. According to a survey by McKinsey & Company, the shift to remote working was executed around 40 times faster than anticipated, with companies implementing workable remote working solutions in an average of just 11 days, compared to over a year as previously estimated.[1] All this greatly impacted employees, who faced a flood of changes to adapt to the new reality that the global circumstances mandated. With the effects of those changes still fresh in their memories, a new transformation is knocking again on their doors—the AI transformation. And this one is potentially more formidable than the ones they have experienced until now. AI is more than just one more tool to use in the day-to-day job, artificial intelligence is inherently distinct, representing a fundamental shift in our interaction with technology.

The statistics are as compelling as they are divisive. As mentioned in a CX Today article, a report by Gartner predicts that by 2025 customer service organizations that embed AI in their multichannel customer engagement platform will elevate operational efficiency by 25 percent.[2] On the flip side, in the *Future of Jobs Report* by the World Economic Forum, employers anticipate a structural labor market churn of 23 percent of jobs in the next five years due to an aggregate measure of disruption, constituting a mixture of emerging jobs added and declining jobs eliminated.[3] Of the 673 million jobs reflected in the dataset in this report, respondents expect structural job growth of 69 million jobs and a decline of 83 million jobs. This corresponds to a net decrease of 14 million jobs—2 percent of current employment. These numbers represent a downstream trend from the previous WEF report in 2020, in which the World Economic Forum estimated the displacement of 85 million jobs by machines with AI capabilities while 97 million new jobs would be created by 2025.[4]

Within this dichotomy of hope and apprehension, the true challenge lies not in technology itself, but in the willingness and readiness of organizations to embrace it.

This chapter ventures beyond the numbers, exploring the human stories behind the AI Revolution in customer service. We will explore the resistance born not from ignorance but from a deeply ingrained fear of the unknown. Take, for instance, the transition from the switchboard operator to automated call routing in the late 20th century—a leap that was met with similar misgivings about the depersonalization of service and job losses. History has shown us that such transformations, while disruptive, don't result in straightforward winners and losers. These shifts serve as the arenas where new roles are shaped, demanding a recalibration of skills and expectations.

In the context of AI adoption, fear often takes the form of a sinister figure—the fear of job displacement. As the inexorable advancement of automation continues, fueled by AI and machine learning (ML), many service and support agents find themselves haunted by uncertainty about the future of their careers. Will their jobs vanish in a sea of algorithms and chatbots? This fear of unemployment and being rendered obsolete is a deep human reaction in the face of technological change.

It's not just the workforce. Customers also harbor their own doubts. Will AI-driven service be as reliable and empathetic as human assistance? What if AI is just making up the answers and not telling the truth or even making things worse? These are just a few questions that arise in the minds of both those providing support and those seeking it.

In an age where familiarity is a comfort, the reluctance to break free from established routines and practices stands as another formidable barrier to AI adoption. Humans are creatures of habit, seeking comfort in the known and the familiar. As an emerging force in customer service, AI challenges the status quo, demanding the courage to break away from comfort and explore the new.

Uncertainty, too, casts a long shadow. As we step into this brave new world, the question arises—what will the future look like? Will AI truly enhance our customer service experience, or will it fall short of expectations? The ambiguous nature of the unknown can paralyze individuals and organizations, rendering them inert in the face of innovation.

In the following pages, we will embark on a journey to uncover the complex nature of human reactions to technological change like AI. We will draw upon history and the lessons of the past, from the days of the Industrial Revolution to the present, to reveal the recurring patterns of resistance and adaptation.

At the heart of this narrative will stand culture, an invisible hand that shapes its employees' and customers' behaviors, attitudes, and values. The shared understanding can either accelerate the embracement of AI or stonewall it with persistent resistance. For customers, a culture that values innovation and personalization can make the introduction of AI feel like a natural progression rather than an imposition. A culture that champions continuous learning and adaptability is critical for the customer service workforce. It can turn the tide of fear and skepticism about AI into a stream of curiosity and engagement. Without a cultural foundation that supports change, even the most meticulously crafted strategy for AI implementation can stumble.

Remember the famous quote attributed to Peter Drucker: "Culture eats strategy for breakfast"?[5] That's exactly the point. It's all about the supreme influence of organizational culture over any strategic plan; it's all about the people. Within a strong, adaptive culture, new technologies will find fertile ground to grow, helping customers and employees not just accept but truly leverage AI for a better, more efficient service experience.

We will explore a plethora of strategies, theories, and techniques that companies can embrace to help their customers and workforce transcend the barriers of fear, reluctance, and uncertainty. (Spoiler alert: change management is the keystone.) Our goal is to equip you, our reader, with the knowledge and guidance you need to lead the change in your own professional journey.

The path may be challenging, but the destination is nothing short of extraordinary. Welcome to a narrative that does more than inform. It inspires.

The Human Element in AI Adoption

The first step in our journey to discover and decipher the complexities of AI adoption in customer service brings us to shine a spotlight on the intricate workings of the human mind when faced with transformative change. What goes on in our brains when we confront new technologies, like AI, and what psychological theories help us unravel the enigma of fear and resistance?

The Psychology of Change

To comprehend the human psyche's reaction to change, we turn to the work of psychologist Kurt Lewin, considered to be the father of social psychology. In a 1947 article, Lewin coined the term "group dynamics."[6] He described this notion as how groups and individuals act and react to changing circumstances.

Lewin's Change Theory looks at how we behave and change in organizations and is one of the social psychologist's most important contributions to the field.[7] In this theory, Kurt Lewin shares a specific model of change comprising three stages—unfreeze, change, and refreeze—which serve as a compass for understanding the dynamics at play.

Driving and restraining forces are building blocks in Lewin's Change Theory. Lewin believed that all behavior was a dynamic balance of forces that moved in one of two directions. Driving forces drove people toward change. Resisting forces prevented them from making the change.

If driving forces were stronger than resisting forces, change could occur. If both driving and resisting forces were equal, behavior stood at an equilibrium. However, change does not occur here either. In order to change behavior, you had to address both the driving and restraining forces.

Lewin proposed a model for implementing long-lasting change. Think of a block of ice to understand this model. Let's say you have a big cube of ice. You want to change the ice into a big cone of ice. How do you do so without changing the amount of ice you have?

One way to do so is to unfreeze, change, and refreeze the ice. Once the ice has melted into water, you can transfer it to a mold that looks like a cone and refreeze it into its new shape. **Figure 12.1** clearly illustrates Lewin's model using this ice cube example.

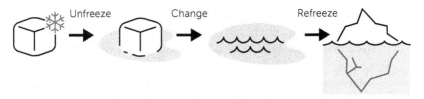

FIGURE 12.1 Lewin's Change Theory

In the following sections, we'll synthesize Lewin's three-step process for our AI adoption in customer service.

Unfreeze

The journey to adopting AI in customer service begins with the unfreeze stage, where the stage is set for transformation. This initial stage encapsulates the moment individuals become aware of the need for change. The status quo is disrupted, and fear, resistance, and uncertainty emerge. In the context of AI adoption, this is when the notion of machines replacing human agents might stir up apprehension.

For organizations, this means ramping up the motivators that lead to embracing AI and easing off the brakes that keep teams clinging to the old ways. It's time for organizations to assess core values and practices that may have worked in the past but are now barriers to innovation.

Unlearning becomes key. We're not just talking about swapping out an old manual for a new one; we're diving deep into the organization's belief system. What cultural relics have been supporting outdated methods? Identifying these is crucial because the groundwork for AI integration lies in moving away from those anchors.

Leadership needs to steer this vessel, articulating the "why" and "what" that needs to shift. It's about rallying the entire crew around the vision of a digitally empowered future. Yes, there will be resistance, but with a robust strategy that acknowledges the push and pull within the company, management can navigate these waters and set a course toward innovation.

Change

As the organization moves into the change phase, it's time to adjust the sails and catch the winds of AI. The friction experienced during this phase is often rooted in the fear of incompetence. Will employees be able to grasp the complexity of AI?

Training is pivotal in this phase because it bridges the old and the new between understanding and action. In the context of adopting new AI technology in customer service, training is where the theoretical benefits of AI become practical skills and knowledge for the workforce. It's the stage where employees transition from merely knowing about the AI tools to becoming proficient in using them to enhance customer interactions.

Effective training demystifies the technology, breaking down barriers of fear and resistance by showing employees how to use the new systems and how these systems can make their work more impactful. It's about transforming apprehension into confidence. When employees see how AI can take over repetitive and mundane tasks, they can focus on more complex and rewarding aspects of their jobs, like building customer relationships or solving challenging problems.

Moreover, training provides a safe space for employees to ask questions, make mistakes, and learn—not just about the "how" but also the "why" behind the change. It reinforces the message that while the tools may be changing, the value of their human skills is not diminished. Instead, it shows how these skills are becoming even more critical in a tech-driven customer service environment.

The move to AI should be decisive, as a gradual wade into these new waters is a recipe for hesitation and discomfort. Imagine the energy and unity when an entire organization takes the plunge together, with leaders advocating for AI's benefits and actively involving every member in the process. It's about ensuring everyone—from executives to frontline staff—can articulate the reasons behind this shift and how it will be executed.

In summary, during the change phase, training equips the workforce with the necessary competencies to adopt AI effectively, ensuring a smooth transition and successful adoption. It's the practical application of the unfreeze stage's preparations, and it sets the stage for the refreeze phase, where these new behaviors and skills become the new standard operating procedure.

Refreeze

Finally, the refreeze stage seeks to stabilize the new state, making the AI adoption stick. People become accustomed to the changes, and the fear recedes as AI becomes a part of the daily routine. Here, the new ways of working with AI are crystallized into the company's DNA. This might mean updating training manuals, reworking contracts, or even reshaping reward systems to reinforce the change. It's the period where positive reinforcement plays a starring role, encouraging and celebrating each step employees take in this new direction.

By embedding these new practices into the organization's culture, we ensure that the journey to AI is not a temporary expedition but a permanent shift. It's a transformation that looks beyond the horizon, fortifying the company's position as a leader in customer service excellence.

This synthesis of Lewin's theory is more than a blueprint for adopting new technology—it's a manifesto for cultural evolution. It reminds us that you can implement change positively by analyzing the thoughts, feelings, and values behind current practices. Upper management may have to direct the organization's vision and share thoughts, feelings, and values that enforce the change. But once this is done, employees will be on board, and each person will be more likely to gravitate toward change. It's a promise that companies can write their own story by respecting the past while boldly stepping into the future.

Fear of Job Displacement

Fear of job displacement by AI is a well-founded concern, and it takes root in a psychological phenomenon known as *technostress*, a term that first appeared in 1984 in Craig Brod's book *Technostress: The Human Cost of the Computer Revolution*. Brod defined technostress as a modern disease of adaptation caused by an inability to cope healthily with new computer technologies.[8] At present, scientific research on technostress reveals that the negative psychological relationship between people and the introduction of new technologies presents itself mainly in two different ways: people have a hard time understanding new technology (techno-anxiety), or they identify excessively with it (techno-addiction).

The results of a study published in the *International Journal of Organizational Analysis* indicated that role ambiguity, job insecurity, and the technology environment contribute to technostress because of ML and AI technology deployment.[9] Complexity, uncertainty, reliability, and usefulness are primary technology environment-related stressors.

When individuals believe their jobs are threatened by automation, stress and anxiety can set in. This phenomenon is supported by numerous studies suggesting that automation and AI will displace millions of jobs soon.[10]

In the earlier mentioned *Future of Jobs* report 2023 by the World Economic Forum (WEF), artificial intelligence, a key driver of potential algorithmic job displacement, is expected to be adopted by nearly 75 percent of surveyed companies in the report and is expected to lead to high churn—with 50 percent of organizations expecting it to create job growth and 25 percent expecting it to create job losses.[11] This stresses the need for "reskilling" and "upskilling" from employers to ensure staff are sufficiently equipped for the future of work. As the title of this article published by the WEF in collaboration with *Forbes* highlights, "Don't Fear AI." The tech will lead to long-term job growth.[12]

Further expanding on the conclusions of the WEF 2023 Jobs report, these are some of the key findings:[13]

- AI is expected to result in significant labor-market disruption, with substantial proportions of companies forecasting job displacement in their organizations, offset by job growth elsewhere to result in a net positive.
- Within technology adoption, big data, cloud computing, and AI highly affect the likelihood of adoption. More than 75 percent of companies want to adopt these technologies in the next five years.
- AI and machine learning specialists top the list of fastest-growing jobs.
- Employers estimate that 44 percent of workers' skills will be disrupted in the next five years. Systems thinking, AI and big data, talent management, and service orientation and customer service complete the top 10 growing skills.
- Six in ten workers will require some AI training before 2027, but only half of workers have access to adequate training opportunities today.

- Training workers to utilize AI and big data ranks third among company skills-training priorities in the next five years and will be prioritized by 42 percent of surveyed companies.

- Two-thirds of companies expect to see a return on investment (ROI) in skills training within a year of the investment, whether in the form of enhanced cross-role mobility, increased worker satisfaction, or enhanced worker productivity.

- The skills companies report to be increasing in importance the fastest are not always reflected in corporate upskilling strategies. Companies rank AI 12 places higher in their skills strategies than in their evaluation of core skills and report that they will invest an estimated 9 percent of their reskilling efforts in it—a greater proportion indicating that although AI is part of fewer strategies, it tends to be a more important element when it is included.

The fear of job displacement by AI is a powerful force that cannot be underestimated. In a study published by Salesforce in 2023, for which they surveyed workers across industries, service professionals were the least likely to be using generative AI.[14] Just 24 percent of customer service said they were using generative AI for work, and only 15 percent said they plan to use generative AI in the future. Despite the hesitance to use generative AI, nearly half of the surveyed service professionals (48 percent) worry they will lose their jobs if they don't learn how to use the technology.

Remembering that this fear is not unique to the AI era is essential. As technology has advanced throughout history, individuals have faced the same apprehensions. From the Industrial Revolution to the rise of the Internet, the human spirit has prevailed, adapting and innovating.

This fear serves as a critical reminder of the challenges posed by cultural inertia in adopting AI in customer service and support. With the right strategies, transparency, and a commitment to nurturing employees' and customers' potential and skills growth, we can lead an era where AI and human expertise complement each other.

Resistance to Change

The nature of AI's disruptive potential drives individuals and organizations to often exhibit resistance to change. This resistance can be attributed to *cognitive dissonance*, a theory proposed by Leon Festinger.[15] Cognitive dissonance is a psychological phenomenon that occurs when an individual holds two or more contradictory beliefs, ideas, or values or participates in an action that goes against one of these three. In other words, when new information challenges existing beliefs or practices, individuals experience discomfort.

In the context of AI adoption, cognitive dissonance can occur when an individual has preconceived notions about AI and its capabilities, but the reality of AI's performance falls short of their expectations. Dissonance, induced by unconfirmed expectations, triggers the psychological state associated with negative emotions such as anger, guilt, regret, and discomfort, as concluded in this study of smart home users.[16]

For employees, this might manifest as resistance to learning new AI-driven systems and processes, while for customers, it could translate into skepticism about the effectiveness of AI-driven support.

Resistance to change is a natural response deeply ingrained in the human psyche. Understanding this resistance is vital for leaders and managers seeking to guide their organizations through the transformation, a required step toward developing strategies that minimize resistance and foster a culture that embraces innovation.

Overcoming Fear and Resistance

Let's now dive into the wisdom of psychological theories and models that explore human behaviors and cognitive patterns, which leaders and organizations can leverage to overcome these deeply rooted fears and resistance and move toward a successful cultural transformation. To facilitate a smoother transition and mitigate fear, consider these strategies:

- **Communication and transparency:** Inform employees and customers about the AI adoption process. Address their concerns openly and transparently. This aligns with the principles of the information-processing model in psychology, which suggests that information availability can reduce uncertainty.[17] See Chapter 9 for more on methods of communication.

- **Training and education:** Invest in training programs that empower employees to build their AI-related skills. The self-determination theory (SDT) indicates that intrinsic motivation, supported by training and development, can help individuals embrace change.[18]

- **Cultural transformation:** Foster a culture of innovation and learning. Use the social cognitive theory (SCT), which supports that portions of an individual's knowledge acquisition can be directly related to observing others within the context of social interactions and experiences, to encourage employees to learn by observing AI's positive impacts on their peers.[19]

- **Emphasize benefits:** Highlight the advantages of AI, such as efficiency and the reduction of repetitive tasks, to mitigate fear and uncertainty. In psychology, the prospect theory suggests that individuals are more sensitive to potential losses than gains, so emphasizing the gains can be persuasive.[20]

- **Support networks:** Create support networks where employees can share their experiences, challenges, and successes, fostering a sense of belonging and reducing resistance.

By understanding the psychology of fear, resistance, and change, companies can equip themselves to navigate the human element in AI adoption effectively. The journey is challenging, but it is through acknowledging these psychological nuances that we pave the way for a future where AI and humans work harmoniously to revolutionize customer service and support.

The Nature of Technological Change

In our journey to understand the complexities of AI adoption in customer service and support, it is crucial to unravel the essence of technological change itself. The story of humanity is, in many ways, a tale of innovation and adaptation, but it is also punctuated by moments of resistance, fear, and uncertainty. What lessons can we glean from history, and how can we apply them to navigate the uncharted territory of AI?

Throughout the ages, humanity has witnessed numerous technological revolutions that have reshaped our world. Consider the Industrial Revolution, a historical moment that marked the transition from agrarian economies to industrialized ones. The introduction of steam engines and mechanization prompted unprecedented progress but also generated fears of unemployment and obsolescence.

The Echoes of the Past: From Luddites to Lessons

Let us transport ourselves back to early 19th-century England, where the Industrial Revolution was in full swing. A group of textile workers, followers of a perhaps fictitious General Ned Ludd, became known as the Luddites and gained notoriety for their resistance to the mechanization of textile production.[21] These skilled artisans, fearing job displacement and a loss of their craft, resorted to smashing the newly introduced power looms. At first glance, their actions may seem futile, even misguided.

However, the Luddites' legacy is not one of simple obstinacy; it is a reminder of the human cost of technological change. The term Luddite is still used today to describe one who cannot or does not embrace technology.

While worker displacement is an integral aspect of the cultural transformation of AI in the workplace, it also deserves more attention, and you can dive into more in Chapters 15 and 18.

Consider, for a moment, the difficult situation of these workers. They weren't opposed to progress but were grappling with the profound impact of change on their livelihoods. The Luddite Rebellion illustrates the fear that can grip individuals when faced with the prospect of becoming irrelevant and no longer useful. Initially perceived as anti-technology, modern interpretations often view the Luddites as advocates for workers' rights and a more ethical approach to technological integration. While the Luddites were seen as resisting inevitable progress, their legacy prompts a reflection on how technological change can be managed and puts into perspective some lessons to consider for AI adoption:

- **Importance of transition support:** Supporting workers through retraining and education is crucial to ease the transition, as the lack of such support fueled the Luddites' resistance.

- **Balancing technology and humanity:** It's important to balance technological advancement with human-centric considerations, ensuring that technology enhances, not replaces, human capabilities.

- **Engaging all stakeholders:** Involving all stakeholders, including those most affected by AI, in discussions about its implementation can help mitigate resistance.

- **Proactive adaptation:** Rather than resisting change, by learning from the Luddites, society can focus on adapting to and shaping the changes brought by AI.

- **Ethical and moral considerations:** Ensuring ethical AI use and considering its societal impact is key to avoiding the pitfalls of uncontrolled technological advancement.

The story of the Luddites is more than a historical footnote. The Luddite movement serves as a historical mirror reflecting modern concerns about AI and technological advancement. While the contexts differ significantly, the underlying human reactions to rapid technological change—fear, resistance, and adaptation—are remarkably consistent. By examining their resistance, we gain insights into the human aspect of technological disruption, the fears it stirs, and the potential pathways to harmonizing technological advancement with societal well-being.

Understanding and learning from historical examples helps in appreciating the complexities of technological evolution and its impact on society. It can provide valuable insights into managing the transition toward an increasingly AI-integrated world. Humans were fearful of the control of fire and worried about the move from papyrus and turtle shells to newly invented paper as a writing surface. Fear of technical evolution is not a new thing.

Are these examples of resistance only a matter from the past? Fast forward to more recent history, and we encounter a different chapter in the story of technological change, this one much closer in time. In the 20th century, the proliferation of computers and automation technologies led the way to a new era of industry and commerce. The transition was not only challenging but also brought remarkable advancements. The lesson is clear: Innovation and adaptation are the hallmarks of human progress.

Yet, for every individual who embraced change and acquired new skills, there are some who clung to the past, resisting the tide of discovery. The struggles of these holdouts reveal that the road to transformation is seldom smooth. However, they also underscore the importance of resilience and an openness to new possibilities.

The Realization: "Aha" Moments from History

These historical anecdotes reveal a profound realization—technological change is not merely a linear march of progress but a complex interplay of human emotions, economic forces, and societal shifts. It reminds us that fear and resistance, though deeply rooted in our psyche, can be transcended.

The "Aha" moment lies in recognizing that history is not a mere chronicle of past events but a repository of invaluable lessons. By studying the struggles and triumphs of those who came before us, we gain a deeper understanding of today's challenges. We learn that fear and resistance are not impossible obstacles but part of the journey toward a brighter future.

Let us draw inspiration from the Luddites' plight and the triumphs of those who embraced change in the face of uncertainty. Armed with this historical wisdom, we are better equipped to pave the way for AI to coexist harmoniously with the human element in customer service and support. In these echoes of the past, we find the keys to unlocking a future where innovation predominates and the possibilities are limitless.

AI Adoption in the Multigenerational Workplace

In the dynamic landscape of AI adoption, organizations are not just navigating technological changes but also bridging generational gaps. In today's workplace, Baby Boomers, Gen X, Millennials (Gen Y), and Gen Z coexist, each with their unique characteristics, perspectives, and preferences. As companies strive to adopt and implement AI tools, they find themselves navigating a diverse workforce spanning multiple generations. Therefore, understanding the role of these generational differences is crucial for fostering a culture that embraces AI adoption seamlessly. What does success look like in this scenario? Successful AI adoption hinges on the technology and understanding and catering to these generational cohorts' diverse needs and attitudes.

According to a Salesforce's recent survey, there are significant generational distinctions among generative AI users.[22] Let's take a look at the numbers:

- 65 percent of generative AI users are Millennials or Gen Z, and 72 percent are employed.
- Nearly 6 in 10 users believe they are on their way to mastering the technology.
- 70 percent of Gen Z report using Gen AI, and 52 percent of them trust Gen AI to help them make informed decisions.
- 68 percent of non-users are Gen X or Baby Boomers.
- 70 percent of non-users would use generative AI more if they knew more about the technology.
- 64 percent would use generative AI more if it was more safe/secure.
- 45 percent would use generative AI more if it was integrated into the technology they already use.

These findings illustrate the disparities in attitudes toward AI, revealing a divide where younger generations are more engaged and older generations remain hesitant, primarily due to a lack of familiarity and perceived relevance. With Gen Z being the superuser group from these statistics, there is certainly a lot of work to be done within the older generations. Let's immerse ourselves in this generational landscape and explore ways to engage and drive adoption within each of these four cohorts based on their behaviors, adaptability to technology, and learning styles.

Baby Boomers

Baby Boomers (born 1946–1964) are often characterized by their strong work ethic, loyalty, and value for face-to-face communication. They tend to prioritize stability and are seen as less adaptable to new technologies compared to younger generations. They value structured environments and hierarchy and are known for their dedication and bringing a wealth of experience.

While not digital natives, many have adapted to technology out of necessity. They may be more cautious regarding technological change but can be won over with tangible benefits and clear communication. As for the learning style, Baby Boomers prefer traditional learning methods like seminars and face-to-face training over digital platforms.

When building the strategy to drive AI adoption within this generation, consider that Baby Boomers often value interpersonal relationships, and AI can enhance their ability to focus on personalized customer interactions by handling routine tasks. Although there might be a potential reluctance to embrace new technologies, implementing AI tools that streamline administrative tasks allowing Baby Boomers to spend more time on meaningful customer engagements, can be a value proposition for them. Training programs should emphasize user-friendly interfaces and highlight the positive impact on customer satisfaction.

Generation X

Generation X (born 1965-1980) is considered the "middle child" of generations because of its small size compared to the Baby Boomer and Millennial generations. Gen Xers are typically described as resourceful and independent and value work–life balance more than their predecessors. Gen Xers are known for their entrepreneurial mindset and adaptability. They often lead and bridge the gap between Baby Boomers and Millennials.

This generation witnessed the dawn of the digital age, as they were the first generation to grow up with personal computers. They are comfortable with technology and have integrated it into their lives. They value autonomy in learning and are receptive to a mix of traditional and digital learning tools.

In your AI adoption strategy, leverage the fact that Gen Xers are known for their adaptability and can serve as the bridge between older and younger generations, facilitating smoother AI integration. They may approach its adoption pragmatically, seeking efficiency and work–life balance. At the same time, balancing their skepticism with enthusiasm is crucial. In order to bring them on board, companies should communicate the long-term benefits of AI for job efficiency and satisfaction. One approach that will resonate with them is introducing AI-driven chatbots for routine inquiries, freeing them up to focus on complex problem-solving and strategic initiatives.

Gen Y/Millennials

Gen Y, also known as Millennials (born 1981-1996), are the first digital natives. They value flexibility, diversity, and purpose-driven work. They are collaborative and seek feedback and recognition. Millennials challenge traditional hierarchies and seek a more collaborative work environment. They are known for their enthusiasm for embracing new ideas and technologies.

Members of this generation were the first to grow up with the Internet and social media and are also known for their elevated usage of and familiarity with mobile devices. When it comes to learning, they show a preference for digital learning platforms, interactive training, and social learning. They thrive on feedback and continuous learning opportunities.

For your adoption strategy, Millennials will be among the first ones to readily embrace AI and can be a strong ally in championing AI initiatives within the organization. They are likely to view AI adoption as an opportunity for career advancement and may seek workplaces that leverage AI for productivity and innovation. Consider engaging millennials in designing and implementing AI solutions, leveraging their digital fluency for customer-centric innovations, as it can make a difference. Providing continuous learning opportunities can help them stay updated on evolving AI technologies.

Generation Z

Gen Z (born 1997-2012) is the most tech-savvy, having grown up in a fully digital environment. They value individuality and inclusiveness and are more pragmatic and financially minded than Millennials. They seek authenticity and transparency in the workplace. They are entrepreneurial and driven but also crave stability and security.

Extremely comfortable with technology, they tend to use fast, online, and decentralized technology, focusing on mobile-first platforms. Their learning style centers on on-demand learning, microlearning, and visual content. They value personalized and self-paced learning experiences.

As we have seen in the numbers outlined above, Gen Zers are your super-user population. Most of them use generative AI frequently and believe they are well on their way to mastering it. As the newest workforce entrants, they expect AI to be seamlessly integrated into their work environment, enhancing collaboration and efficiency. Think of them as digital natives with an innate understanding of technology who can contribute fresh perspectives and ideas for optimizing AI applications. Engaging this generation will require interactive and dynamic training methods, so consider developing gamified training modules that align with Gen Z's learning preferences to ensure an effective onboarding for AI tools.

In this multifaceted journey of AI adoption, generational diversity is not a challenge but an opportunity. Each generation brings unique perspectives, skills, and strengths. Organizations that harness this diversity and develop inclusive strategies spanning generations are better positioned to drive AI adoption successfully.

AI Adoption and Customer Expectations

Just as generational differences affect the workforce, they also influence customer expectations. Understanding these dynamics can be crucial for businesses striving to provide exceptional customer service.

According to a survey conducted by Salesforce in 2023, of more than 14,000 consumers and business buyers across 25 countries, consumers have become much less open to using AI over the last year. Currently, 73 percent of business buyers and 51 percent of consumers are open to using AI to improve their experiences.[23] Those figures have dropped significantly since the 2022 survey, from 82 percent and 65 percent, respectively, concerned about unethical use of the technology.[24] The same survey highlights how sentiments and motivations vary by age, impacting customer loyalty:

Millennials and Gen Z have a generally brighter view of generative AI than Baby Boomers and Gen X. This underscores that brands deploying generative AI for a broad customer base must tailor messaging for different demographics and prepare for varying degrees of uptake and reception.

Emerging technologies are far from the only influence on differing generational attitudes. Gen Z stands out for their willingness to take their dollars elsewhere in search of brands that better reflect their priorities. In 2022, 59 percent of Gen Z consumers switched brands, far exceeding older generations and introducing a new battleground for customer loyalty. In fact, Gen Z is nearly twice as likely as Baby Boomers to switch brands that better align with their values (21 percent versus 11 percent), showing the importance of brands tapping into what guides this group's beliefs.

These statistics put into perspective the key roles played by the ethical use of AI in the success of any AI strategy and a strong adherence to the principles of responsible AI in the design, development, and deployment of emerging technologies. No longer is AI a nice-to-have technology. Now, it's a business imperative for customer attraction and retention.

Knowing your customer base and understanding these generational nuances is crucial for companies aiming to drive AI adoption effectively, especially in an era where AI and technology are rapidly changing customer service and support industry dynamics.

Baby Boomer customers, who traditionally favor human interaction, show openness to AI assistance, especially when it enhances their experience. For them, the ideal model would blend AI-driven self-service with conventional support. Moving to Generation X, there's a shift toward valuing efficiency and convenience. AI solutions that expedite processes and offer tailored recommendations align with their expectations. Then, we see Gen Y/Millennials, who gravitate toward technology-driven solutions offering both convenience and personalization, making tools like chatbots and AI-powered recommendations particularly appealing. Finally, Generation Z customers, the digital natives, expect seamless AI integration in their customer interactions, demonstrating a greater propensity to embrace AI-driven support channels compared to previous generations.

In conclusion, the key to AI adoption success lies in recognizing the generational nuances and crafting a strategy that bridges the gaps while leveraging the strengths of each cohort. By doing so, organizations can ensure that AI enhances customer service and creates a harmonious workplace where every generation plays a vital role in shaping the future.

A New Era of Sustainability and Inclusion

Integrating AI in customer service and support is not just a technological upgrade; it's a cultural shift. Companies today are increasingly judged not only on their financial performance but also on their environmental and societal impact. In other words, in an era where profit is often king, a new narrative is emerging, one where sustainability and inclusiveness are not just moral choices but strategic business decisions.

In this context, AI emerges as a critical player. But how does digital technology influence such human-centric concerns? The marriage of AI with sustainable and inclusive practices is an investment with substantial returns. Companies adopting AI in these areas are witnessing a surge in customer loyalty, brand enhancement, and even operational efficiencies. AI-driven analytics help businesses optimize resources, reduce waste, and streamline processes, cutting costs and boosting the bottom line.

The journey toward AI-driven customer service is not without its challenges. Trust in AI, concerns about data privacy, and fear of the unknown are very present. Yet, when AI is applied with a focus on sustainability and inclusiveness, it does more than just solve problems. It builds bridges. It shows customers and employees alike that a company is committed to values that transcend profits. This commitment can transform skepticism into trust and reluctance into acceptance.

As we embark on this exploration, we're not just talking about technology; we're talking about a future in which businesses make the world a better place—a future where AI in customer service doesn't just mean smarter chatbots and quicker responses; it means a tangible contribution to a greener planet and a more inclusive society.

Sustainability in AI is more than a buzzword; it's a commitment to future generations. AI's ability to analyze complex environmental data revolutionizes how companies tackle climate change. From predicting energy needs to optimizing supply chains for minimal environmental impact, AI enables businesses to be planet-friendly while still serving and supporting their customers and being profit-oriented.

Inclusiveness—particularly for the more than 1 billion people with disabilities worldwide —represents an untapped market with enormous potential. AI-powered solutions in customer service, such as voice recognition, computer vision, and language translation tools, are not just about compliance with accessibility laws; they're about reaching wider audiences for both business and employment, understanding diverse needs, and fostering brand loyalty.

So, let us take you on the next leg of our journey, where AI is not just an algorithm or a tool, but a forerunner of a new era in business where technology, sustainability, and humanity converge.

The Role of Company Culture in Embracing AI

As we saw in Chapter 4, the journey toward an AI-driven future begins with visionary leadership. Leaders who champion AI as a tool for efficiency and a vehicle for corporate responsibility set the tone for their organizations. They inspire a culture where technology serves greater goals—environmental stewardship, social responsibility, and inclusiveness. Their vision transforms AI from a mere operational tool to a catalyst for positive change.

Employee engagement is critical in this AI Revolution. When employees understand and share the company's vision for AI, they become active participants. Training programs, workshops, and open discussions about AI's role and impact can demystify the technology and align it with the company's core values.

A culture that values innovation, responsibility, and inclusiveness will naturally gravitate toward AI solutions that reflect these principles. This alignment is crucial in ensuring that AI initiatives are technologically sound, ethically grounded, and socially responsible. Trust is the currency of the new AI era. Companies must build trust among their employees and customers by being transparent about their AI practices. This includes clear communication about how AI is used, how data is handled, and how these practices align with the company's commitment to sustainability and inclusion.

AI, Sustainability, and Climate Change

At the forefront of the AI Revolution transforming customer support, business leaders find themselves uniquely positioned to integrate their corporate strategies with the priorities of an evolving workforce. Millennials and Generation Z are not merely employees; they embody a shift toward prioritizing sustainability and climate change as central elements in their professional lives and brand loyalties. These younger generations, who will soon dominate the workplace, are drawn to companies that are committed to environmental responsibility.

AI, when leveraged thoughtfully, unlocks substantial opportunities to innovate sustainably, optimize efficiency, and minimize environmental impacts. By embedding AI within their sustainability strategies, leaders can motivate their teams and lead the charge toward a future where technology benefits humanity and the planet. This fusion of AI, sustainability, and climate consciousness promises to revolutionize customer support and cultivate a corporate culture that aligns perfectly with the next generation's values, making AI a valued ally that employees are eager to support and propel forward.

As we deal with the pressing challenges of climate change, AI emerges as a powerful opportunity with the potential to revolutionize our approach to environmental stewardship, propelling businesses toward a more sustainable future while ensuring their economic viability. Its ability to analyze vast data sets and predict trends enables businesses to make smarter, more sustainable decisions. From optimizing energy use in data centers to designing more efficient supply chains, AI is at the forefront of reducing carbon footprints and enhancing green practices.

The impact of AI on sustainability is not confined to a single industry; it spans across sectors. According to a study by Price Waterhouse Cooper, AI can enable future systems to be more productive related to sustainability, global climate change and the overall world economy:[25]

In waste management and recycling, AI-driven precision can assist with automatic sorting activities, helping to prevent contamination and predicting maintenance needs.[26]

In the IT industry, AI is optimizing datacenter operations, one of the largest energy consumers in the IT world, by intelligently managing power usage and cooling systems, leading to proactive management of these systems.[27]

The agriculture industry uses AI for precision agriculture, a practice that increases farmers' yields by using AI insights to better care for their crops by closely monitoring moisture, soil composition, and temperature.[28]

One of AI's most significant contributions to sustainability is its predictive capabilities. Businesses can make proactive changes to mitigate adverse effects by forecasting environmental impacts. This forward-looking approach is crucial in responsibly managing resources and reducing ecological footprints.

The role of AI in promoting sustainability also extends to consumer engagement. AI-powered platforms enable businesses to communicate their sustainability efforts effectively, fostering greater consumer awareness and participation. Companies are creating a more environmentally conscious customer base by aligning consumer behavior with sustainability goals through AI-driven recommendations and insights.

Looking back at our generational discussion, we see different generations' influence on a company's choices and direction. According to the World Economic Forum, Generation Z has the greatest influence and is most concerned about sustainability.[29] AI's positive impact in the area of sustainability and climate change can help reduce resistance to adoption and increase trust and usage, aligning closely with Gen Z's belief system, affecting their purchasing decisions and influencing their choices regarding the workplace. Gen Z's focus on aligning their jobs with their personal beliefs has a downstream effect on their desire to work for and ultimately stay with an organization.[30]

In all, integrating AI into sustainability efforts represents more than technological advancement. It's a call for innovation that respects and protects our planet. By harnessing the power of AI, businesses are not just committing to sustainability; they are leading the charge toward a more responsible, greener, and sustainable future.

AI and Inclusion of People with Disabilities

In a world striving for equality and accessibility, AI is a pivotal force in breaking down barriers for people with disabilities. AI's impact on inclusiveness is profound, especially in customer service. Voice recognition, chatbots equipped with natural language processing, and personalized AI assistants make services more accessible to people with various disabilities. These AI-driven tools are not just conveniences but essential bridges connecting individuals with disabilities to the world around them.

Personalization lies at the heart of inclusive AI. By tailoring interactions to individual needs and preferences, AI is creating customer service experiences that are more accessible and satisfying for everyone. This personalization extends beyond just language and speech recognition. It encompasses understanding and adapting to a wide range of physical and cognitive abilities.

AI technologies empower people with disabilities by providing them with tools that foster independence. From AI-powered apps that assist with navigation for people who are blind or have low vision, such as Volvo's Vision Mate app[31] or Microsoft's Seeing AI App,[32] to speech-to-text services that aid people with hearing impairments, such as the Ava app,[33] AI is significantly enhancing the quality of life and independence for many.

In the world of customer support, Be My Eyes has integrated Be My AI into its first contact center with stunning results.[34] Be Me Eyes is the first to globally deploy AI-powered visual customer service for individuals who are blind or have low vision through Microsoft's Disability Answer Desk.[35]

Be My AI is an AI tool that helps vividly describe images for sight-impaired people and helps companies provide state-of-the-art description services for customers who are blind or have low vision. Be My AI provides a 90+ percent successful call resolution with dramatically reduced call handle times. Calls can still be escalated to a human, but this is only required in 10 percent of use cases.

As you can see from these real-life applications, embracing inclusiveness through AI is not just a social responsibility; it's a business imperative. By making their services accessible to a broader range of customers, businesses are tapping into new markets and demonstrating a commitment to diversity and inclusion, which resonates strongly with modern consumers.

On the flip side, implementing AI solutions for inclusiveness comes with its unique challenges, such as ensuring privacy, understanding diverse needs, and maintaining the human touch in digital interactions.

Challenges and Considerations in AI for Sustainability and Inclusion

AI can potentially be our generation's most significant technological advancement. But with great power comes great responsibility. As the transformative benefits of AI become apparent, so do the risks and challenges. We need to be mindful that people will use this technology in bad and harmful ways. Algorithms can introduce bias, discrimination, errors, poor decision-making, and misinformation, causing mistrust among the people they intend to assist, including your customer base and workforce. Addressing these challenges effectively is crucial to ensuring that AI's impact is positive and aligned with the goals of creating a greener and more inclusive world, very often (if not always) linked to corporate social responsibility values and, therefore, with many company's cultural attributes.

The Sustainable Development Goals (SDGs), also known as the Global Goals, were adopted by the United Nations in 2015 as a universal call to action to end poverty, protect the planet, and ensure that all people enjoy peace and prosperity by 2030.[36] The 17 Sustainable Development Goals are the blueprint to achieve a better and more sustainable future for all. They are all interconnected and address the global challenges we face, including those related to poverty, inequality, climate change, environmental degradation, peace, and justice.[37] As per the World Economic Forum, artificial intelligence is vital in the race to meet the SDGs.[38] In the article "Why Artificial Intelligence is Vital in the Race to Meet the SDGs," the World Economic Forum (WEF) includes examples of AI technology driving improvements across several areas in the context of the SDGs.

According to an article published by *Nature*, AI has the potential to enable 134 targets across all 17 SDGs but may also inhibit 59 targets.[39] This duality underscores the need for careful consideration in the application of AI to ensure it supports rather than hinders sustainable developments. The fast development of AI needs to be supported by the necessary regulatory insight and oversight for AI-based technologies to enable sustainable development. Failure to do so could result in gaps in transparency, safety, and ethical standards.[40]

Inequality and Bias in AI Development

According to the same article published in *Nature*, another important drawback of AI-based developments is that they are traditionally based on the needs and values of the nations where AI is being developed.[41] Therefore, it is important to adopt decentralized AI approaches for the more equitable development of AI.[42] If AI technology and big data are used in regions where ethical scrutiny, transparency, and democratic control are lacking, AI might enable hate toward minorities and create biased election outcomes, among other risks. The term "nudging" represents using big data and AI to exploit psychological weaknesses to steer decisions.[43] Nudging creates problems such as damaging social cohesion, democratic principles, and even human rights.[44] This is especially relevant to the support industry, where leveraging a global workforce to deliver support 24/7 is often a best practice. Any mitigation of bias in AI models will best support the needs of the workforce and customers.

It is also important to note that AI technology is unevenly distributed worldwide, and there is another important shortcoming of AI in the context of our SDG discussion on gender equality. There is insufficient research assessing the potential impact of technologies such as smart algorithms, image recognition, or reinforced learning on discrimination against women and minorities. For instance, machine-learning algorithms uncritically trained on regular news articles will inadvertently learn and reproduce the societal biases against women and girls, which are embedded in current languages. Word embeddings, a popular technique in natural language processing, have been found to exacerbate existing gender stereotypes.[45] In addition to the lack of diversity in datasets, another main issue is the lack of gender, minorities, and people with disabilities in the AI workforce.[46] Diversity is one of the main principles supporting innovation and societal resilience, which will become essential in a society exposed to changes associated with AI development. But the reality of the numbers today does not present an encouraging scenario. In a 2023 report, the World Economic Forum found that women comprise only 30 percent of AI talent.[47]

Economic Impacts and Increased Inequalities

The technological advantages of AI have positive impacts on a number of economic SDGs, but they also contribute to increased inequalities. If AI-driven markets rely heavily on data analysis, the economic gap could widen, especially in low- and middle-income countries.

On the other hand, AI can help identify sources of inequality and conflict and potentially reduce inequalities—for instance, by using simulations to assess how virtual societies may respond to changes. However, there is an underlying risk when using AI to evaluate and predict human behavior: the inherent bias in the data. It has been reported that a number of discriminatory challenges, such as with people with disabilities[48] or Black individuals,[49] are faced in the automated targeting of online job advertising using AI or during recruiting activities, essentially related to the previous biases in selection processes conducted by human recruiters.[50] There is an imperative need to modify the data preparation process and explicitly adapt the AI-based algorithms used for selection processes to avoid such biases, because otherwise, AI will contribute to more inequalities rather than helping close the existing gaps.[51]

Addressing the Challenges

A multifaceted approach is necessary to address these challenges:

- **Regulatory insight and oversight:** Ensuring AI developments are supported by appropriate regulations to maintain transparency, safety, and ethical standards.
- **Sustainable and inclusive AI development:** Developing AI that respects environmental limitations and promotes inclusiveness.
- **Energy-efficient AI solutions:** Encouraging the development of energy-efficient AI technologies that rely on renewable energy sources.

Businesses and policymakers can harness AI's potential to drive sustainable and inclusive growth while mitigating its risks by understanding and proactively addressing these challenges. This approach will be crucial in realizing the full benefits of AI in a manner that aligns with global sustainability and inclusiveness goals and will also help to drive acceptance and trust in AI technology and, therefore, its adoption across the board.

Guiding the Change

To truly understand the transformative power of AI, it's essential to turn our attention to the real-world success examples that serve as beacons of inspiration. These companies have harnessed AI's capabilities to improve customer experiences and drive operational efficiency and corporate culture, resulting in remarkable outcomes. Let's dive into their journeys and discover what makes their AI adoption endeavors stand out.

These examples underscore the immense potential of AI and how AI adoption isn't just about technology; it's a cultural shift reshaping how businesses interact with their customers and employees. By learning from these trailblazers and applying the strategies and tools discussed in this book, your organization can also pave the way toward AI-driven customer service and support success.

- **Starbucks:** "AI for Humanity" at Starbucks is a concept focused on using AI to enhance human connections rather than replacing human workers with technology.[52] The vision, shared by CEO Kevin Johnson and Chief Technology Officer Gerri Martin-Flickinger, emphasizes the role of AI in improving every aspect of the business while maintaining Starbucks' commitment to human interaction. This approach involves using AI for tasks like inventory management, supply chain logistics, staffing predictions, and equipment maintenance, aiming to free up staff for more meaningful customer interactions. The Deep Brew initiative is a key part of developing a suite of AI tools tailored to individual store characteristics to create a better in-store and customer experience.[53] The goal is to use AI to amplify human connection, making it an invisible yet powerful aid in the daily operations of each Starbucks store. Deep Brew, launched in 2019, is an AI-driven platform that also enhances the brand's personalization engine.[54] Their mobile app, crucial to Starbucks' digital strategy, accounts for a quarter of the company's weekly transactions and nearly 50 percent of its revenue. The app's features, expanded through AI and marketing, include a rewards program, personalization, payment, and ordering, contributing to Starbucks' growth and expertise in cultivating customer loyalty through data.

- **NBA:** Since its creation on June 6, 1946, the National Basketball Association (NBA) has gone through many changes, including its very own digital transformation. Their vision was to transform the way fans engage with the league and its teams and players, offering a truly personalized experience where each fan's interests would drive the content they receive. This is core to the NBA's guiding principles and culture centered around the importance of engagement and the power of sports to create connections among people of different cultures and backgrounds.[55] According to NBA's SVP of digital and social content, Bob Carney, the league needed a way to scale up its content production and deliver personalized experiences to its fans, and the human staff could not handle the amount of content required for every game and every player.[56] The solution? With generative AI, the NBA is now analyzing and categorizing every play during games, generating individualized highlight packages for each player in every match, and creating social-style content that resonates with fans and drives them to the NBA app.[57] Carney added that generative AI did not result in any layoffs at the company. He also said that the league's app user base grew by 40 percent from 2022 to 2023, indicating the new strategy's success.[58]

- **Heineken:** As part of its ambition to become the best-connected brewer, Heineken constantly seeks ways technology can advance its mission.[59] This includes building connections between corporate executives and the information they need to make impactful, data-driven decisions; connections between employees and the resources they need to do their jobs effectively and efficiently; and, ultimately, connections between consumers and the beer they love. Heineken is using AI in a wide range of processes ranging from revenue management to predictive maintenance among others. For example, they have launched their own ChatGPT-based chatbot based on the Microsoft Azure OpenAI Service for their employees, and they are piloting an AI-enabled voice bot to help its on-site sales representatives log the status of each retail location, raise technical issues, and trigger any necessary processes on the Heineken side. This allows the company to update its business processes, creating efficiencies and saving time and energy on significant business challenges.

A Culture of Innovation for AI Future-Ready Growth

In this chapter centered around the important role that culture plays in the AI Revolution, innovation deserves its own callout, emphasizing its critical role in shaping and guiding the transformative impact of artificial intelligence. Embracing a culture of innovation is the cornerstone of thriving in the rapidly evolving landscape of AI. In a world where technology is advancing at an unprecedented pace, fostering an environment that not only accepts but actively seeks out innovation is crucial for any company aiming to leverage the full potential of AI. This pursuit of innovation isn't just about adopting new technologies; it's about cultivating a mindset that challenges the status quo, encourages creative problem-solving, and embraces the transformative power of AI.

When a company instills this culture among its teams, it unlocks a world of opportunities. Teams empowered to innovate become proficient at identifying and capitalizing on AI's potential to solve complex problems, streamline operations, and create new value for customers. This proactive approach to innovation ensures that the organization doesn't just keep up with technological change but stays ahead, turning disruptive trends into competitive advantages.

Moreover, an innovative culture is a magnet for talent. Top professionals are drawn to environments where their ideas can flourish and where they can be part of groundbreaking work. This creates a virtuous cycle—attracting the best minds leads to more innovation and attracts more talent.

For a company, the benefits are multiple. Innovation drives growth, enables better decision-making through data-driven insights, and opens new revenue streams.[60] It's not just about staying relevant in today's market but shaping tomorrow's markets. By embedding a culture of innovation, a company does more than adapt to the AI Revolution. It leads the revolution, crafting a future where technology amplifies human potential and drives progress.

In essence, embracing a culture of innovation is not just a strategy, it's a journey toward realizing the untapped potential of AI, harnessing its power to not only transform businesses but also to make a meaningful impact on society. The message is clear: to harness the full potential of AI, a company must first cultivate the seeds of innovation within.

As we conclude this chapter, it's essential to recognize that the success of AI within your organization hinges not only on the technology itself but also on the cultural alignment it fosters. Even if you hold reservations about climate change or the imperatives of accessibility, rest assured that your employees may not. Much of the younger generation in your work-force—educated, connected, and values-driven—expects and demands a commitment to these issues. Embracing AI means more than just adopting new technologies; it involves cultivating a culture of innovation that reso-nates with your employees' priorities and aligns with global challenges. By acknowledging and integrating their values into your strategic vision, you ensure that AI isn't just a tool for efficiency but a beacon of your company's adaptability and responsiveness.

This chapter isn't just a discussion—it's a roadmap for embedding these essential values deeply within your corporate ethos, ensuring that your journey with AI is as forward-thinking and impactful as the technology itself and your organization adapts and thrives in the new landscape of business and technology.

Endnotes

1   McKinsey & Company. 2020. "How COVID-19 has pushed companies over
     the technology tipping point—and transformed business forever." McKinsey
     & Company, October 5, 2020. [https://www.mckinsey.com/capabilities/
     mckinsey-digital/our-insights/how-covid-19-has-pushed-companies-over-the-
     technology-tipping-point-and-transformed-business-forever].

2   CX Today. 2020. "How AI Will Elevate Operational Efficiency by 25%." CX
     Today, December 15, 2020. [https://www.cxtoday.com/contact-centre/
     how-ai-will-elevate-operational-efficiency-by-25/#:~:text=According%20
     to%20leading%20analysts%2C%20Gartner,25%25%20boost%20in%20
     operational%20efficiency].

3   World Economic Forum. 2023. "The Future of Jobs Report 2023." World
     Economic Forum, May 2023. [https://www3.weforum.org/docs/WEF_Future_
     of_Jobs_2023.pdf].

4   World Economic Forum. 2020. "The Future of Jobs Report 2020." World
     Economic Forum, October 2020. [https://www3.weforum.org/docs/WEF_
     Future_of_Jobs_2020.pdf]

5   Rachels, Jason. 2018. "Culture Eats Strategy for Breakfast." American
     Customer Satisfaction Index, 2018. [https://www.acsi.org/docs/default-source/
     documents/cse/name/rachels_culture-eats-strategy-for-breakfast.pdf].

6   Practical Psychology. 2023. "Lewin's Change Theory: Definition +
     Examples." Practical Psychology, March 2, 2023. [https://practicalpie.com/
     lewins-change-theory/].

7   Practical Psychology. 2023. "Lewin's Change Theory: Definition +
     Examples." Practical Psychology, March 2, 2023. [https://practicalpie.com/
     lewins-change-theory/].

8   Brod, C. 1984. "Technostress: The Human Cost of the Computer Revolution."
     Addison-Wesley Publishing Company, 1984. [https://archive.org/details/
     technostresshuma0000brod].

9   Bhattacharyya, S., Krishnamoorthy, B., Kumar, A. 2023. "Machine learning
     and artificial intelligence-induced technostress in organizations: a study
     on automation-augmentation paradox with socio-technical systems as
     coping mechanisms." Emerald Publishing Limited, May 19, 2023. [https://
     www.emerald.com/insight/content/doi/10.1108/IJOA-01-2023-3581/full/
     html#:~:text=The%20phenomenon%20of%20technostress%20because%20
     of%20ML%20and,along%20with%20socio-technical%20measures%20to%20
     cope%20with%20technostress].

10   Vallance, Chris. 2023. "AI could replace equivalent of 300 million
     jobs—report" BBC News, March 28, 2023. [https://www.bbc.com/news/
     technology-65102150].

11   World Economic Forum. 2023. "The Future of Jobs Report 2023." World
     Economic Forum, May 2023. [https://www3.weforum.org/docs/WEF_Future_
     of_Jobs_2023.pdf].

12   World Economic Forum. 2020. "Don't Fear AI. It Will Lead to Long-Term Job
     Growth." World Economic Forum Agenda, October 26, 2020. [https://www.
     weforum.org/agenda/2020/10/dont-fear-ai-it-will-lead-to-long-term-job-growth/].

13 World Economic Forum. 2023. "The Future of Jobs Report 2023." World Economic Forum, May 2023. [https://www3.weforum.org/docs/WEF_Future_of_Jobs_2023.pdf].

14 Salesforce. 2023. "Top Generative AI Statistics for 2023." Salesforce News, 2023. [https://www.salesforce.com/news/stories/generative-ai-statistics/].

15 Festinger, Leon. 1957. *A Theory of Cognitive Dissonance.* Stanford University Press, 1957. [https://archive.org/details/FestingerLeonATheoryOfCognitiveDissonance1968StanfordUniversityPress].

16 Marikyan, D., Papagiannidis, S. & Alamanos, E. 2023. "Cognitive Dissonance in Technology Adoption: A Study of Smart Home Users." *Inf Syst Front*, 2023. [https://doi.org/10.1007/s10796-020-10042-3].

17 Mcleod, Saul, PhD. 2023. "Information Processing Theory In Psychology." *Simply Psychology*, updated February 1, 2024. [https://www.simplypsychology.org/information-processing.html].

18 Lopez-Garrido, Gabriel. 2023. "Self-Determination Theory: How It Explains Motivation." *Simply Psychology*, updated July 10, 2023. [https://www.simplypsychology.org/self-determination-theory.html].

19 Nickerson, Charlotte. 2023. "Albert Bandura's Social Cognitive Theory: Definition & Examples." *Simply Psychology*, updated February 2, 2024. [https://www.simplypsychology.org/social-cognitive-theory.html].

20 Nickerson, Charlotte. 2023. "Prospect Theory In Psychology: Loss Aversion Bias." *Simply Psychology*, October 10, 2023. [https://www.simplypsychology.org/prospect-theory.html].

21 Victorian Era. "Luddite Movement." Victorian Era. [https://victorian-era.org/luddite-movement.html?expand_article=1].

22 Salesforce. 2023. "Top Generative AI Statistics for 2023." Salesforce News, 2023. [https://www.salesforce.com/news/stories/generative-ai-statistics/].

23 Salesforce. 2023. "Businesses Adopting AI Risk a 'Trust Gap' with Customers—Salesforce Report." Salesforce News, August 28, 2023. [https://www.salesforce.com/news/stories/customer-engagement-research-2023/].

24 Salesforce. 2022. "Salesforce Report: Nearly 90% Of Buyers Say Experience a Company Provides Matters as Much as Products or Services." Salesforce News, May 10, 2022. [https://www.salesforce.com/news/stories/customer-engagement-research/].

25 Herweijer, C., Joppa, L. "How AI Can Enable a Sustainable Future." PwC UK. [https://www.pwc.co.uk/services/sustainability-climate-change/insights/how-ai-future-can-enable-sustainable-future.html].

26 Forbes Tech Council. 2023. "14 Ways AI Can Help Business and Industry Boost Sustainability." *Forbes*, November 22, 2023. [https://www.forbes.com/sites/forbestechcouncil/2023/11/22/14-ways-ai-can-help-business-and-industry-boost-sustainability/?sh=69770dc4ed04].

27 Forbes Tech Council. 2023. "14 Ways AI Can Help Business and Industry Boost Sustainability." *Forbes*, November 22, 2023. [https://www.forbes.com/sites/forbestechcouncil/2023/11/22/14-ways-ai-can-help-business-and-industry-boost-sustainability/?sh=69770dc4ed04].

28 Young, Sydney. 2020. "The Future of Farming: Artificial Intelligence and Agriculture." *Harvard International Review*, January 8, 2020. [https://hir. harvard.edu/the-future-of-farming-artificial-intelligence-and-agriculture/].

29 World Economic Forum. 2022. "Gen Z cares about sustainability more than anyone else-and is starting to make others feel the same." World Economic Forum, March 18, 2022. [https://www.weforum.org/agenda/2022/03/ generation-z-sustainability-lifestyle-buying-decisions/].

30 Ro, Christine. 2022. "How Climate Change Is Re-Shaping the Way Gen Z Works." BBC, March 1, 2022. [https://www.bbc.com/worklife/ article/20220225-how-climate-change-is-re-shaping-the-way-gen-z-works].

31 Campaigns of the World. 2023. "Vision Mate—Empowering the Visually Impaired with Volvo's LiDAR and AI Tech!" Campaigns of the World, December 2, 2023. [https://campaignsoftheworld.com/technology/vision- mate-by-volvo/#:~:text=Volvo%E2%80%99s%20Vision%20Mate%20App%20 Unleashes,individuals%2C%20both%20indoors%20and%20outdoors].

32 Al-Heeti, Abrar. 2023. "Microsoft's Seeing AI App Is Now Available on Android." CNET, December 4, 2023. [https://www.cnet.com/tech/mobile/ microsofts-seeing-ai-app-is-now-available-on-android/].

33 iAccessibility.com. "Ava: Transcribe Voice to Text." iAccessibility.com. [https://www.iaccessibility.com/apps/hard-of-hearing/index.cgi/ product?ID=276#:~:text=Ava%3A%20Transcribe%20Voice%20to%20Text%20 1%20%20Download,Deaf%20in%20more%20complex%20situations%3F%20 ...%20More%20items].

34 Be My Eyes. "Be My Eyes Integrates Me My AI™ into its First Contact Center with Stunning Results." Be My Eyes Blog. [https://www.bemyeyes.com/blog/ introducing-microsofts-ai-powered-disability-answer-desk-on-be-my-eyes].

35 Be My Eyes. "Microsoft joins Be My Eyes' Be My AI beta to take accessibility of its products to the next level." Be My Eyes Blog. [https://www.bemyeyes.com/ blog/microsoft].

36 United Nations Development Programme (UNDP). "The SDGS In Action." United Nations Development Programme. [https://www.undp.org/ sustainable-development-goals].

37 United Nations. "Take Action for the Sustainable Development Goals." United Nations. [https://www.un.org/sustainabledevelopment/ sustainable-development-goals/].

38 World Economic Forum. 2022. "Why Artificial Intelligence is vital in the race to meet the SDGs." World Economic Forum, May 11, 2022. [https://www.weforum. org/agenda/2022/05/artificial-intelligence-sustainable-development-goals/].

39 Azizpour, H., Balaam, M., Dignum, V., Domisch, S., Felländer, A., Fuso Nerini, F., Langhans, S., Leite, I., Tegmark, M., Vinuesa, R. 2020. "The role of artificial intelligence in achieving the sustainable development goals." *Nature Communications*, January 13, 2020. [https://www.nature.com/articles/ s41467-019-14108-y].

40 Azizpour, H., Balaam, M., Dignum, V., Domisch, S., Felländer, A., Fuso Nerini, F., Langhans, S., Leite, I., Tegmark, M., Vinuesa, R. 2020. "The role of artificial intelligence in achieving the sustainable development goals." *Nature Communications*, January 13, 2020. [https://www.nature.com/articles/ s41467-019-14108-y#Fig2].

41   Azizpour, H., Balaam, M., Dignum, V., Domisch, S., Felländer, A., Fuso
      Nerini, F., Langhans, S., Leite, I., Tegmark, M., Vinuesa, R. 2020. "The role
      of artificial intelligence in achieving the sustainable development goals."
      Nature Communications, January 13, 2020. [https://www.nature.com/articles/
      s41467-019-14108-y].

42   Goertzel, B., Montes., G. A. 2019. "Distributed, decentralized, and
      democratized artificial intelligence." Elsevier, April 2019. [https://www.
      sciencedirect.com/science/article/abs/pii/S0040162518302920?via%3Dihub].

43   Devillers, L., Sullins, J. 2018. "The Nature of Nudging." IEEE Learning
      Network, 2018. [https://iln.ieee.org/Public/ContentDetails.aspx?id=9E
      5F276557BD4F01A6C2A069C222A40E#:~:text=%E2%80%9CNudgin
      g%E2%80%9D%20refers%20to%20the%20ability%20of%20systems%20
      or,user%E2%80%99s%20lives%20for%20anything%20from%20dieting%20
      to%20depression].

44   Frey, B., Gigerenzer., G, Hafen, E., Hagner, M., Helbing, D., Hofstetter, Y.,
      van den Hoven., J., Zicari, R., Zwitter, A. 2018. *Will Democracy Survive Big
      Data and Artificial Intelligence?* Springer, Cham, August 28, 2018 [https://link.
      springer.com/chapter/10.1007/978-3-319-90869-4_7].

45   Chang, K., Kalai, A., Tolga, B., Saligrama, V., Zou, J. "Man is to Computer
      Programmer as Woman is to Homemaker? Debiasing Word Embeddings."
      NeurIPS Proceedings. 2016. [https://proceedings.neurips.cc/paper_files/
      paper/2016/hash/a486cd07e4ac3d270571622f4f316ec5-Abstract.html].

46   National Center for Science and Engineering Statistics. 2023. "Diversity
      and STEM: Women, Minorities, and Persons with Disabilities." National
      Science Foundation, January 30, 2023. [https://new.nsf.gov/news/
      diversity-and-stem-2023].

47   World Economic Forum. 2023. "Global Gender Gap Report 2023." World
      Economic Forum, June 20, 2023. [https://www.weforum.org/publications/
      global-gender-gap-report-2023/in-full/gender-gaps-in-the-workforce/].

48   Business Standard. 2022. "AI hiring tools discriminate against people with
      disabilities, warns US." Business Standard, May 15, 2022. [https://www.
      business-standard.com/article/international/ai-hiring-tools-discriminate-
      against-people-with-disabilities-warns-us-122051500167_1.html].

49   Zapata, Dawn. 2021. "New study finds AI-enabled anti-Black bias in
      recruiting." Thomson Reuters, June 18, 2021. [https://www.thomsonreuters.
      com/en-us/posts/legal/ai-enabled-anti-black-bias/].

50   Dalenberg, David Jacobus. 2017. "Preventing discrimination in the
      automated targeting of job advertisements." ScienceDirect, November,
      2017. [https://www.sciencedirect.com/science/article/abs/pii/
      S0267364917303758?via%3Dihub].

51   Maskey, Sameer. 2022. "How to Overcome AI-Led Biases in Recruiting and
      Hiring." BuiltIn, December 27, 2022. [https://builtin.com/artificial-intelligence/
      overcoming-AI-led-biases-in-HR].

52   Warnick, Jennifer. 2020. "AI for humanity: How Starbucks plans to
      use technology to nurture the human spirit." Starbucks Stories &
      News, January 10, 2020. [https://stories.starbucks.com/stories/2020/
      how-starbucks-plans-to-use-technology-to-nurture-the-human-spirit/].

53   Hyperight. 2021. "Deep Brew: Transforming Starbucks into an AI & data-driven company." Hyperight, June 30, 2021. [https://hyperight.com/deep-brew-transforming-starbucks-into-a-data-driven-company/].

54   Hyperight. 2021. "Deep Brew: Transforming Starbucks into an AI & data-driven company." Hyperight, June 30, 2021. [https://hyperight.com/deep-brew-transforming-starbucks-into-a-data-driven-company/].

55   NBA. "Our Guiding Principles." NBA. [https://careers.nba.com/nba-guiding-principles/].

56   Hyscaler. 2023. "How the NBA uses generative AI to create personalized content for fans." Hyscaler, October 25, 2023. [https://hyscaler.com/insights/nba-uses-generative-ai-for-content/].

57   Transform Staff. 2022. "The NBA launches a first-of-its-kind new app experience for fans, driven by the power of data." Microsoft Source. September 27, 2022. [https://news.microsoft.com/source/features/digital-transformation/the-nba-launches-a-first-of-its-kind-new-app-experience-for-fans-driven-by-the-power-of-data/].

58   Hyscaler. 2023. "How the NBA uses generative AI to create personalized content for fans." Hyscaler, October 25, 2023. [https://hyscaler.com/insights/nba-uses-generative-ai-for-content/].

59   Customer Stories. 2023. "Heineken connects employees with information across the company using Azure AI services." Microsoft, September 26, 2023. [https://customers.microsoft.com/en-GB/story/1685696409285197342-heineken-consumer-goods-azure-ai].

60   Banholzer, M., Fletcher, B., LaBerge, L., McClain., J. 2023. "Companies with innovative cultures have a big edge with generative AI." McKinsey & Company, August 31, 2023. [https://www.mckinsey.com/capabilities/strategy-and-corporate-finance/our-insights/companies-with-innovative-cultures-have-a-big-edge-with-generative-ai].

13

Defining the Metrics That Matter in This New Era of AI

Measure what is measurable and make measurable what is not so.

—Galileo Galilei

As we have journeyed through the deployment of AI around the world, we've been introduced to the transformative potential of artificial intelligence (AI) across various business scenarios in customer service and support. Our travels have taken us through the multiple ways in which AI promises to revolutionize service and support, from automating mundane tasks to facilitating data-driven decision-making. We've seen how AI stands as a beacon of innovation and efficiency in enhancing customer experiences and operational capabilities in the world of customer service and support. These innovations promise enhanced productivity, improved customer satisfaction, and significant cost reductions.

However, with great power comes great responsibility, or in this case, with great potential comes the great responsibility of accurately measuring its impact. While the preceding chapters laid out the potential and the mechanisms of AI deployment, here we address a crucial question: How do we measure the success of these AI implementations?

Integrating AI in customer service and support isn't just a technological evolution. It is a strategic business decision and represents a pivotal shift in how businesses engage with their most valuable asset: their customers. As with any substantial investment, stakeholders demand clarity on the return on investment (ROI) and the value added to the business. However, measuring the impact of AI in customer service extends beyond mere financial metrics. It encompasses much more, including technical performance metrics, business and operational impact metrics, user engagement and satisfaction, compliance and ethical metrics, innovation, and learning.

In today's data-rich environment, enhanced by advanced analytics and AI, companies must evaluate and update their success metrics and objectives and key results (OKRs) or key performance indicators (KPIs) to better align with current business needs and capabilities. It's all about redefining the metrics that matter in this new world powered by AI, what we measure, and how we can best measure our goal progress. It's not just about numbers; it's a story of innovation, adaptation, and the relentless pursuit of excellence in the AI-driven customer service landscape.

In this chapter, we will delve into three pivotal metric domains: the efficiency of AI models and systems, the performance of large language models (LLMs) in specialized tasks, and the nuanced metrics specific to customer service and support. These domains mirror the essence of input, output, and outcome metrics, offering a holistic view of AI's impact. These three categories cover a broad spectrum of considerations for AI systems. However, it is worth noting that this classification isn't exhaustive. Depending on how and where your organization deploys AI solutions, there might be other critical areas of metrics and/or different ways to categorize them.

This chapter serves as a blueprint for businesses looking to accurately assess the impact of their AI initiatives, ensuring that these technological advancements are not just innovations for their own sake but tools that genuinely enhance business performance and customer experience. As we venture into this exploration, we aim to complement the broader AI knowledge gained from the previous chapters and equip business leaders, managers, and decision-makers with the knowledge to make informed choices about AI in the customer service and support arena. Whether you're considering introducing AI into your customer service operations or looking to optimize existing AI functionalities, this chapter will guide you in navigating the complex landscape of AI integration, impact, and success measurement.

The Human Need for Measurement and the Pursuit of Success

In the grand scheme of things, the quest for success is an ever-present thread deeply integrated into our daily routine. We are constantly striving for progress, seeking tangible evidence of our accomplishments, and avoiding the sting of failure. But why? What drives us to measure success, and why is it vital to our sense of purpose and well-being?

Human beings are wired to progress. From the dawn of our species, survival depended on our ability to adapt and improve. According to Darwinian principles, survival and reproduction are the cornerstones of natural selection[1]. In ancestral times, early humans had to continuously seek ways to ensure their chances of survival. They had to compete with other species and even among themselves for limited resources such as food, water, and shelter. Success in obtaining these vital resources ensured the survival and growth of the tribe.[2] While the challenges contemporary humans face vastly differ from those of our prehistoric predecessors, the drive for progress remains deeply ingrained in our psyche.

Success in acquiring knowledge and adapting to changing environments was—and continues to be—paramount in the evolutionary timeline. Early humans who demonstrated innovative problem-solving skills and the ability to adapt to new challenges had a survival advantage.[3]

Our modern emphasis on education, research, and technological advancement reflects this drive for knowledge and adaptation. The pursuit of success in these areas is a direct descendant of our ancestors' quest for survival through adaptation and learning. Our desire to measure success is a way to track our progress on this timeless journey, providing us with motivation, satisfaction, and a sense of purpose.

OUR BIG BRAIN

Many characteristics are associated with human evolution, including the ability to walk on two feet, the use of tools, the ability to communicate using language, the development of culture, complex social interactions, and the ability to live longer than other primates.

Chief among the characteristics is the evolution of the brain, particularly the neocortex, which is associated with higher cognitive abilities. "It allowed early humans to develop problem-solving skills, plan complex strategies for survival, and engage in advanced communication, which laid the foundation for the development of culture and civilization."[4]

Our brain development enabled us to more easily acquire the knowledge and skills necessary to survive and adapt in a world of constant challenge and change.

Navigating the Metrics Mesh

Measuring the success of AI models and systems, particularly in contexts like customer support, involves a blend of traditional and new metrics, where industry-specific key performance indicators (KPIs) and modern AI-relevant metrics meet to help us achieve a more accurate and comprehensive understanding of the new business reality.

It is also a blend of traditional and modern measurement methods, combining the tried-and-true methods of the past with the innovative techniques of the present to gain a more complete picture of our surroundings. It's a reminder that while new technologies and approaches can be incredibly powerful, they should not be used at the expense of the knowledge and wisdom accumulated over time. It is a compromise, and there is space for both to co-exist and adapt to the new times we are experiencing.

Success can take different forms to manifest itself in this new era of AI, and while the list is certainly extensive, in the next sections we will break it down into three categories to help you navigate this new ecosystem. Two categories will center on AI itself, introducing you to a new set of metrics and terminology to consider including in your portfolio if you want to monitor the efficiency and performance of your AI deployment and their impact on a variety of areas of your business. The third one will focus on traditional business metrics and measures, many (if not all) present today in the scorecard of customer service and support organizations, and how these metrics are influenced by the integration of AI in existing business processes and the customer service lifecycle.

Technical Performance Metrics

In the Diagnose phase covered in Chapter 8, we introduced the importance of validating and tracking input and output metrics before deploying AI models, with the output becoming more important over time. Efficiency, effectiveness, accuracy, and reliability are key to establishing trust and credibility within your user base, so investing time in achieving optimal performance results will ensure that you deploy a high-quality AI model/system ready to accomplish your desired outcomes and business needs.

Measuring the efficiency of AI models introduces us to exciting concepts that might be unfamiliar but are crucial in unlocking the full potential of this innovative technology. We're not just adopting new technology; we're embracing a new language of innovation. Each new term and idea you encounter is a key to unlocking deeper insights and driving your enterprise toward unprecedented efficiency and success.

Quality Metrics

Quality metrics are essential in evaluating the effectiveness of AI models, particularly in how precisely these models perform their intended tasks. These metrics offer quantifiable insights into the model's performance, highlighting its strengths and areas needing improvement. By providing clear, numerical evaluations, quality metrics help fine-tune models, ensuring they meet the required standards of reliability and effectiveness for real-world application. This objective assessment is crucial for researchers, data scientists, and machine learning engineers, primarily during the development and diagnostic stages of AI models, so they can understand the model's performance before deployment. Once an AI model is deployed in a business context, these metrics can still be relevant in the detection phase, especially for ongoing monitoring and improvement.

Perplexity: Perplexity serves as a key indicator in assessing the performance of AI language models, offering insight into how well these models anticipate and understand the flow of language.[5] By measuring the model's predictive accuracy, perplexity highlights the model's proficiency in processing and generating coherent and contextually appropriate text.

- The basic idea reflected in the term's origin is that perplexity is a measure of how "surprised" or "confused" a language model is by a given sequence of words. Lower perplexity indicates that the model is more confident in its predictions.

- Mathematically, it is defined as the exponentiated average negative log-likelihood of a sequence of words. For a language model that assigns a probability P(w1, w2, ..., wN) to a sequence of N words, the perplexity is given by:

$$\text{Perplexity} = \exp\left(-\frac{1}{N}\sum_{i=1}^{N} \log P(w_i|w_1, w_2, ..., w_i-1)\right)$$

- The value of perplexity depends heavily on the dataset and the specific task. For instance, perplexity scores are typically higher for more complex texts. While useful, perplexity does not capture all aspects of language model quality, such as coherence, grammatical correctness, or factual accuracy. It should be used in conjunction with other metrics and qualitative assessments to get a comprehensive picture of a model's performance. Perplexity is a reference-free metric that doesn't require labeled data, which is an advantage and worth considering as a measure.

Recall: Also known as sensitivity or hit rate, recall is a critical metric in machine learning (ML) and statistics, primarily used in classification tasks.[6] It measures the model's ability to correctly identify all relevant instances within a dataset by assessing the proportion of actual positive cases that the model correctly identifies. It's particularly important in scenarios where missing a positive instance (for example, a disease in medical testing or a significant transaction in fraud detection) is more consequential than falsely identifying a negative instance as positive.

The formula for recall is:

$$Recall = \frac{True\ Positives\ (TP)}{True\ Positives\ (TP) + False\ Negatives\ (FN)}$$

In this formula, true positives (TP) are correctly identified positive cases, and false negatives (FN) are positive cases that the model incorrectly labeled as negative.

- A recall of 1 (or 100 percent) means that the model correctly identified all positive cases. High recall is particularly desirable when the cost of missing a positive is high, even if it means accepting more false positives (lower precision). Building on the applications mentioned earlier, think of medical diagnostics, where high recall is crucial to ensure diseases are detected, or fraud detection, where it is important to identify as many fraudulent activities as possible.

- It is often optimized in balance with precision, especially when missing a positive case has serious consequences.

Precision: Precision is a fundamental metric in the fields of ML and statistics, particularly in classification problems.[7] It measures the accuracy of a model in identifying only relevant instances from all the instances it predicts as relevant. In other words, it answers the question: "Of all instances the model classified as positive, how many are truly positive?"

$$Precision = \frac{True\ Positives\ (TP)}{True\ Positives\ (TP) + False\ Positives\ (FP)}$$

- Precision is calculated as a ratio; therefore, a lower precision indicates a higher number of false positives. High precision is desirable when false positives are more costly or undesirable than false negatives. Email spam filtering or manufacturing and quality control are two areas that require high precision to avoid marking legitimate emails as spam or ensure that defective products are correctly identified without discarding too many good ones.

- Precision is often evaluated alongside recall. Generally, there is an inverse relationship between precision and recall—improving one often degrades the other. This is known as the precision–recall tradeoff.[8] The appropriate balance between precision and recall depends on the specific context and the relative costs of false positives versus false negatives.

F1 score: Having explored precision and recall, two pivotal metrics in evaluating classification models, we now encounter a scenario where balancing these two becomes essential. This is where the F1 score comes into play.[9] It harmonizes precision and recall into a single metric, comprehensively measuring a model's accuracy. It's particularly useful when an equilibrium between precision (the model's correctness in positive predictions) and recall (its ability to find all positive instances) is critical.

$$F1 = 2x \frac{precision\ X\ recall}{precision + recall}$$

- An F1 score reaches its best value at 1 (perfect precision and recall) and its worst at 0. It's a good way to show that a model has a robust performance, especially in cases where you're dealing with imbalanced datasets that might render other metrics like accuracy less informative.

Text evaluation metrics (BLEU, ROUGE, METEOR): In the natural language processing (NLP) field, evaluating the quality of the text generated is key, and a variety of metrics have been developed to quantify this aspect. Compared to perplexity, these are reference-based metrics requiring labeled data—the ground truth.

BLEU (bilingual evaluation understudy), ROUGE (recall-oriented under-study for gisting evaluation), and METEOR (metric for evaluation of translation with explicit ordering) are metrics used to evaluate the quality of text generated by machine translation systems or other natural language processing tasks.[10] They compare the machine-generated text to reference texts created by humans.

- **BLEU** is primarily used in machine translation to evaluate the quality of translated text. Scores range from 0 to 1, with higher scores indicating better translation. It's best for aggregate evaluation (i.e., evaluating a large corpus) rather than individual sentences.

- **ROUGE** is used mainly in summarization tasks to evaluate the quality of automatic text summarizations. It primarily focuses on recall (i.e., how much of the reference content appears in the generated text). Higher scores indicate better summarization quality, focusing on content overlap.

- **METEOR** is also used in machine translation and is designed to address some of BLEU's shortcomings. It evaluates the alignment between the generated and reference texts, considering exact, stem, synonym, and paraphrase matches. Scores range from 0 to 1, with higher values indicating better translation. It tends to correlate better with human judgment on sentence-level evaluation than BLEU.

Likert scale assessments: Human evaluation plays a pivotal role in developing and diagnosing AI models. While quantitative metrics provide objective performance measures, human evaluation adds a subjective perspective crucial for understanding the real-world effectiveness of AI systems. This type of assessment captures nuances in language, emotion, and context that purely data-driven metrics might miss. As discussed in Chapter 8, in this approach, human evaluators rate the AI model's outputs on a Likert scale, typically ranging from 1 to 5.[11] The ratings address specific aspects like relevance, coherence, clarity, or fluency. This method provides a structured way for humans to assess qualitative aspects of the model's performance, giving insights into its practical effectiveness in real-world applications.

Efficiency Metrics

Evaluating the performance of Generative AI (GenAI) and LLMs goes beyond just accuracy and linguistic metrics. Operational metrics like processing cost, GPU/CPU usage, memory resources, latency, and multitasking ability are crucial for understanding the efficiency and scalability of these systems. These metrics are significant for various reasons.

GPU and CPU resources: Graphics processing unit (GPU) and central processing unit (CPU) resources are the backbone of AI processing power. CPUs are designed to handle a wide range of computing tasks but are limited in handling parallel processing tasks. Conversely, a GPU specializes in handling complex mathematical and geometric calculations, particularly those necessary for rendering images and graphics. GPUs are optimized for parallel processing, making them highly efficient for algorithms used in machine learning and deep learning tasks. This ability to process multiple computations simultaneously makes them ideal for the computationally intensive tasks required by AI models. The choice between GPU and CPU can significantly impact AI models' training time and efficiency.

However, this power comes with increased energy consumption and cost. High-end GPUs can be expensive, posing a financial barrier for smaller organizations or individual developers. Moreover, the energy requirements can be substantial, raising concerns about sustainability in large-scale AI operations.

Expanding on the importance of GPU and CPU resources in AI, it's noteworthy that the evolving landscape of AI is driving innovations in specialized hardware. For instance, Tensor processing units (TPUs)[12] developed by companies like Google are specifically designed for neural network machine learning. They offer significant advantages in terms of speed and efficiency compared to traditional CPUs and GPUs.

Another critical development is the rise of edge computing in AI, where computations are performed closer to data sources, reducing latency. This requires efficient CPU and GPU usage since the available resources at the edge are generally more constrained than in centralized data centers.

Regularly assessing these processors' utilization rates helps identify bottlenecks or inefficiencies. Metrics like throughput and task completion rates under different load conditions clearly show how well the resources are being used. The goal is to achieve high utilization of these resources without pushing them into states where performance is compromised, such as thermal throttling[13] or hitting memory limits. It's a delicate balance between pushing for maximum performance and ensuring the long-term reliability and stability of the hardware.

Regarding benchmarking, GPU and CPU performance in AI is often evaluated in terms of FLOPS (floating point operations per second, which measures computational speed, especially for parallel processing tasks.[14] Higher FLOPS indicate better performance but also correlate with higher energy consumption. Other benchmarks in this space often focus on throughput (for example, inferences per second) and energy efficiency (inferences per watt). Many AI projects' key targets are maximizing computational efficiency while minimizing costs and energy usage. This involves choosing the right balance of GPU and CPU based on specific model needs and available resources.

- Estimates suggest that in January 2023, ChatGPT used nearly 30,000 GPUs to handle hundreds of millions of daily user requests.[15] An assistant professor of electrical and computer engineering at the University of Washington interviewed for this article,[16] calculated that those queries may consume around 1 GWh daily, the equivalent of the daily energy consumption for about 33,000 US households.

- As AI advances, the trend is toward more energy-efficient and cost-effective computational solutions, balancing raw processing power with environmental and economic considerations. This includes optimizing existing hardware and developing new architectures to meet the growing demands of AI processing.

Cost of processing: The cost of processing in AI refers to the computational and financial resources required to train and run AI models. This metric is crucial because it directly impacts the scalability and accessibility of AI technology. Processing costs are measured in terms of computational time, energy consumption, and monetary expenses and vary based on model complexity, data size, and infrastructure efficiency.

- High costs can hinder innovation and deployment, especially for smaller organizations or applications requiring real-time processing. Therefore, optimizing AI models for lower processing costs without sacrificing performance is key. It's essential to balance the need for advanced AI capabilities with the practicalities of resource availability and economic constraints. This balance is vital for the sustainable and widespread adoption of AI technologies.

- In the practical landscape of AI, processing costs are often benchmarked using metrics like cost per training hour, energy consumption in kilowatt-hours, or cost per inference for deployed models.

For instance, according to a technical overview of OpenAI's GPT-3 language model, each training run required at least $5 million worth of GPUs.[17] However, the cost is far greater than that, as each model requires many training runs during the development and tuning phases. And the larger the model, the larger the cost. As seen in a 2023 *Forbes* article on the cost of AI, according to Sam Altman, OpenAI's cofounder, when asked at an MIT event in July 2023 about the cost of training foundation models, he said it was "more than" $50—$100 million, and getting more expensive.[18] "OpenAI itself says that the amount of compute used in the largest

AI training runs has been increasing exponentially, doubling every few months," Altman said.[19] From the same *Forbes* article: "Sam Mugel, Chief Technology Officer of Multiverse, which uses tensor networks and quantum computing to bring down costs, estimates that training the next generation of large language models will pass $1 billion within a few years."[20]

Memory resources: In AI systems, memory resources are crucial for both data storage and processing speed. The amount and efficiency of memory (RAM) dictate how much data the model can process at once and how quickly it can access this data.

- Measuring memory usage involves tracking metrics like total memory allocation, memory bandwidth usage, and cache misses. High memory utilization can improve performance but also risks causing bottlenecks if the system runs out of available memory.

- Efficient memory management is key to handling large-scale models and datasets, with metrics like latency being a critical performance indicator. AI models, especially deep learning models, require significant memory for weight storage and intermediate data during computations. High memory bandwidth ensures faster data transfer, which is vital for maintaining the speed of these computations.

- Memory usage optimization is essential, especially for large models or when processing large datasets. Efficient memory management can lead to faster training times and more responsive AI applications. However, it's a delicate balance; too little memory can throttle the performance or even halt AI processes, while too much can be costly and underutilized. Balancing memory requirements with computational efficiency is essential for AI deployments, especially in real-time or resource-constrained environments. This balance ensures the AI system is not only accurate but also responsive and cost-effective.

- In practical terms, benchmarks for memory performance in AI systems often include throughput under varying memory loads and memory utilization efficiency in complex tasks. The target is to maximize performance while minimizing latency and avoiding memory-related bottlenecks.

- Recent research in AI has been focusing on optimizing the memory usage of LLMs. An article published in *Ahead of AI* covers 10 noteworthy AI research papers from 2023 addressing various aspects of training LLMs, including the impact of data duplication, training order, and efficient fine-tuning of quantized LLMs that reduce the model's memory footprint.[21] This research indicates a continuous effort in the AI community to improve the performance of these models while managing their computational and memory demands.

Latency: Latency in AI models and systems refers to the time it takes for an input to be processed and the corresponding output to be generated. This metric is especially crucial in real-time applications where prompt responses are essential, such as in autonomous vehicles, interactive chatbots, or financial trading algorithms.

Latency is typically measured in milliseconds (ms) and can be monitored using profiling tools that track the time taken for each operation within the model's pipeline. High latency can severely impact user experience and the effectiveness of AI applications. Even a delay can lead to suboptimal decisions or user dissatisfaction in time-sensitive environments.

- Latency can be influenced by various factors, including the complexity of the AI model, the efficiency of the code, hardware capabilities (CPU/GPU speed), and network speed in cloud-based models.

- Reducing latency in AI systems is a complex task involving multiple layers of optimization, from the algorithmic level to the infrastructure and network level. It often involves model optimization techniques like simplifying the model architecture, using efficient algorithms, or upgrading hardware. Considering the entire data pipeline, including data preprocessing, model inference, and post-processing steps, is crucial. For cloud-based AI services, network latency plays a significant role, and strategies like caching, content delivery networks (CDNs), and optimized data protocols can be employed to reduce it.[22] Continuous monitoring and profiling help identify bottlenecks and areas for improvement.

- Edge computing is also a strategy used to reduce latency by processing data closer to where it's generated rather than relying on distant servers.[23]

- Benchmarking against industry standards or similar applications is important for setting realistic latency targets. The acceptable level of latency varies widely depending on the application. For instance, a few seconds might be tolerable in a recommendation system but unacceptable in high-frequency trading systems.

- Maintaining low latency is a balancing act—achieving it without compromising the accuracy or functionality of the AI system. It's a critical aspect of providing seamless and efficient AI-driven solutions.

Ability to multitask: The ability of an AI system to multitask effectively is vital for handling multiple tasks or applications concurrently. This capability is measured by assessing performance degradation when the system switches between tasks or processes simultaneous inputs.

Essential metrics include response time, accuracy retention across tasks, task-switching overhead, and resource allocation efficiency. Performance degradation, often quantified by a drop in accuracy or increased response time, is a key indicator of multitasking limits.

- Effective multitasking in AI relies on optimizing system architecture and algorithms, ensuring sufficient computational resources, and sometimes leveraging specialized techniques like parallel processing. Load-balancing algorithms and efficient resource management are vital for maximizing multitasking capabilities.

- In practice, the benchmark for effective multitasking varies depending on the specific application, the tasks' complexity, and the design of the AI system. There isn't a one-size-fits-all percentage; each AI application may set its own performance targets based on its unique requirements and constraints.

- Success in multitasking enhances AI systems' versatility and real-world applicability, making them more efficient and adaptable to complex environments.

Robustness and Reliability

Robustness and reliability in AI models and systems refer to their ability to consistently perform accurately across a wide range of conditions and inputs, including handling unexpected or "noisy" data. Handling noisy data often involves data preprocessing techniques, robust model design, and continuous training to improve the model's tolerance to such imperfections.

These metrics are critical for ensuring that AI systems are reliable and trustworthy, particularly in high-stakes applications like healthcare, finance, or autonomous vehicles. They help identify vulnerabilities and guide improvements to enhance the overall robustness of the system. Key metrics include:

Stress testing: Stress testing in AI involves putting the model through extreme or unusual conditions to evaluate its performance limits and resilience. This can include feeding it large volumes of data, data with high variability, or intentionally corrupted or "noisy" data. The goal is to identify when the model's performance degrades or fails. Key values to watch during stress testing are response times, error rates, and system resource usage. It's important to ensure the model remains stable and doesn't crash under high loads. Some risks to be mindful of include overfitting to stress test scenarios or ignoring real-world applicability.

Error rates: Error rates are key indicators of an AI model's accuracy and reliability, tracking the frequency and types of errors the model makes. They include the classification error rate, which is the ratio of incorrect predictions to total predictions, and specific rates for binary classification like the false positive rate (FPR), or how often the model incorrectly classifies a negative instance as positive, and false negative rate (FNR), or how frequently the model misses positive cases, labeling them as negative instead.

These metrics are crucial for fine-tuning AI models, providing insights into the model's performance and areas needing improvement. The acceptable benchmarks for these rates vary by application, emphasizing the need for context-specific evaluation and continuous monitoring.

Consistency: Consistency in AI models refers to their ability to deliver stable and reliable outputs for similar or repeated inputs. It's a measure of the model's dependability and predictability. Consistency is particularly vital in applications where users expect uniform responses to similar queries.

- It's often assessed by comparing the variation in the model's responses to identical or nearly identical inputs over multiple instances. Ensuring consistency involves rigorous testing and fine-tuning of the model to handle variations in input data without significant fluctuations in output.

- To further detail consistency in AI models, it's important to understand that it goes beyond mere repetition of responses. A consistent AI model should produce similar outcomes for similar input scenarios, demonstrating a deep and reliable understanding of the input data. This consistency is especially crucial in applications like customer service, where varying responses to the same query can lead to confusion and mistrust.

- Methods to ensure consistency include robust training with diverse datasets and implementing checks within the model to identify and correct inconsistencies. Regularly evaluating the model's performance on a set of standard queries can also help maintain and improve its consistency over time. This practice ensures the model remains aligned with its intended function and provides dependable outputs regardless of slight input variations.

- High consistency is a sign of a mature, well-trained AI model, indicative of its readiness for real-world applications.

Adversarial robustness: Adversarial robustness in AI is a complex area involving investigating and mitigating adversarial attack vulnerabilities. In other words, it refers to the model's ability to withstand attacks designed to confuse or deceive it. These attacks exploit model weaknesses using subtly altered input data, misleading or challenging, known as adversarial examples, crafted to cause the model to produce errors and incorrect outputs.

- Assessing adversarial robustness is crucial for applications where security and reliability are paramount. Testing involves exposing the model to various adversarial examples and measuring its response accuracy.

- The field includes developing and evaluating adversarial attack strategies to understand model weaknesses and devise defense mechanisms. Methods to enhance adversarial robustness include adversarial training, regularization techniques, and employing more complex or diverse model architectures.

- For instance, slight, often imperceptible alterations in image data can lead image recognition systems astray. To counter this, researchers often use adversarial training, where models are exposed to these tricky inputs during training to improve their resilience.

- The challenge lies in improving robustness without significantly compromising the model's performance on regular inputs. Enhancing robustness often requires balancing the increased computational demands and potential tradeoffs in model simplicity and general performance. As AI systems are increasingly deployed in sensitive areas, addressing adversarial threats is vital for safeguarding their reliability and trustworthiness.

Generalizability: In simple terms, generalizability refers to a model's ability to perform well on new, unseen data that was not part of its training set. It indicates how well the model has learned the underlying patterns rather than just memorizing the training data.

- Generalizability is crucial for the model's applicability in real-world scenarios, as it ensures reliability across diverse data inputs. Models are tested on separate validation and test datasets.

- It is typically measured using cross-validation techniques and performance metrics on unseen datasets. Cross-validation involves dividing the data into subsets, training the model on some subsets, and testing it on others. This helps assess the model's performance on data it hasn't encountered during training. Common metrics used include accuracy, precision, recall, and F1-score, evaluated on a validation or test set distinct from the training set. A model that maintains high performance on these metrics with new data is considered to have good generalizability.

- Techniques to enhance generalizability involve techniques beyond basic training. One approach is feature engineering, where input data is processed and optimized to make it more representative of real-world scenarios. Another key method is transfer learning, where a model trained on one task is adapted to perform different but related tasks, leveraging its learned features. Regular updates and retraining with new data help the model stay relevant in evolving environments. Ultimately, the goal is to create AI models that excel in training data and adapt flexibly and accurately to varied, real-world situations, making them valuable in dynamic environments where data characteristics can change.

Scalability

Scalability metrics assess the model's ability to handle increasing workloads, amounts of data, or more complex tasks without a loss in performance. Key scalability metrics include:

Throughput: This metric gauges the processing volume the system can handle efficiently, typically measured in tasks or transactions per second. It's a key indicator of the system's ability to manage growing workloads. Higher throughput under increased load indicates better scalability.

Latency under load: Measures how the system's response time changes as the workload increases. Stable latency, despite increased load, suggests strong scalability.

Resource utilization efficiency: Assesses how effectively the system uses its computational resources (CPU, GPU, and memory) as demands grow. Efficient utilization under scaling conditions is indicative of a scalable system.

Cost-effectiveness at scale: Evaluates the financial and computational costs relative to the scale of operation. A scalable AI system remains cost-effective even when handling larger or more complex tasks.

These operational metrics are essential for assessing AI models' practical deployment and scalability. They provide insights into the cost-effectiveness, efficiency, and user experience. Continuous monitoring and optimization of these metrics are key to maintaining a competitive and sustainable AI system. For benchmarking, it's vital to establish clear targets and thresholds that align with the specific requirements and constraints of the deployment environment and application domain.

Business and Operational Excellence Metrics

In the pursuit of success, metrics serve as the compass by which we navigate our journey, provided that measurement is a fundamental aspect of human cognition and problem-solving.[24] Metrics enable us to convert abstract concepts like success into concrete, measurable terms. This transformation facilitates clarity and precision in setting goals, tracking progress, and assessing outcomes.

In addition to motivation, metrics play a crucial role in decision-making and evaluation. They provide us with the data needed to make informed decisions, optimize strategies, and hold people accountable for achieving goals and objectives.

To comprehensively evaluate AI's impact on the customer service and support ecosystem, it's essential to consider a broad spectrum of metrics. Let's explore the key categories into which these metrics can be bucketized, each offering unique insights into customer service operations. If you enjoyed the 6Ds Framework, get ready to discover another group of magical 6s. This time around, we're looking at the six categories of diverse metrics that provide a holistic view of AI's impact on customer service and support.

They reveal the direct effects of AI and shed light on indirect impacts like enhanced customer experience and employee satisfaction. Let's explore each category and understand why each metric type is crucial in painting a complete picture of AI's effectiveness.

Efficiency and effectiveness metrics in customer service: In general terms, these metrics indicate how AI streamlines operations and reduces time consumption.

Among the many flavors that the metrics under this category might take, they mostly gravitate around calculating the average time it takes to resolve the query or issue the customer reported: average handling time (AHT), mean time to resolution (MTTR), first contact resolution (FCR), customer pain time (CPT), first day/week resolution (FDR/FWR), and so on. They all aim to show how quickly issues are being resolved. Generally, customers are more satisfied and have better experiences when their issues are resolved quickly.

However, it is not only about speed. For example, with the FCR metric, we can also extrapolate views on the ease of access to "help" resources that customers have and if service agents have the tools and information required to solve the issues independently in one go.

The most immediate advantage of using AI to positively influence these metrics is the discoverability of content that allows customers and service agents to gain faster access to a wider range of information and resources. Whether AI assists directly in resolving standard queries submitted by customers or feeds this information to service and support agents, this translates into a reduction of the time invested in troubleshooting and the subsequent back-and-forth communications and allows for a much faster resolution and ticket closure.

- AI's promises to improve the metrics in this category are starting to take shape. For example, Microsoft's Office of the Chief Economist partnered with the Dynamics 365 product group to conduct a study of early Copilot in Dynamics 365 Customer Service results. After six months post-deployment at Microsoft, one of the largest customer service teams in the world, Copilot in Dynamics 365 Customer Service saw a 12 percent reduction in AHT for low-severity chat cases in one area of their commercial support business. It was also found that in one Microsoft support business, 10 percent of cases that usually require colleague collaboration were independently resolved with the help of the virtual assistant.[25]

Service quality metrics: These metrics are important for assessing the effectiveness and reliability of the service provided to customers. They go beyond just efficiency and cost to measuring the quality of interactions and the accuracy of information provided.

- Do you recall being welcomed with this automatic message when calling a customer service desk? "Your call may be monitored for training and quality purposes." This is one way to measure these quality metrics, encompassing various aspects like the clarity of information provided, adherence to company protocols, and the professionalism of the interaction.

- Quality of support (QoS) can be measured for AI systems by analyzing customer feedback on their interactions with AI tools like chatbots. For instance, after interacting with a chatbot, customers might be asked to rate the clarity and helpfulness of the information provided. This is an additional quality check, on top of the existing thumbs up and thumbs down mechanisms that are often made available after every interaction, and constitutes another way to rate the quality of the responses provided.

- Compliance rates fall under this category too. For example, you could measure how well customer service adheres to internal policies and external regulations. This is crucial in industries where compliance is tightly regulated. Compliance can be assessed for AI systems by reviewing how AI tools follow regulatory guidelines, like privacy laws, during customer interactions. Regular audits can be conducted to ensure compliance.

- Quality metrics provide a benchmark for evaluating the performance of human agents and are instrumental in maintaining high service standards. As AI technologies are integrated into customer service, these same metrics need to be adapted and used to assess the performance of AI systems, ensuring they meet or exceed the quality standards set by human agents.

Customer experience metrics: These metrics play a pivotal role because their core purpose remains to gauge customer satisfaction, effort, and loyalty. They provide valuable insights into the customer's perception of the service. Every interaction matters.

As mentioned, one of the most immediate impacts of AI in customer service is on response time. AI-driven systems, like chatbots and automated responses, can significantly reduce the time it takes to address customer queries. Measuring the change in response times pre and post-AI implementation offers a clear efficiency metric.

However, it's not just about how quickly queries are addressed but also how effectively. The resolution rate measures the percentage of customer issues resolved on the first interaction. A higher rate indicates that AI tools are both responding and resolving, which is key to customer satisfaction.

Two metrics stand out at the heart of the customer experience: customer satisfaction score (CSAT) and net promoter score (NPS). They are more than just metrics. They are the essence of customer-centric AI systems. CSAT is derived directly from customer feedback and measures immediate customer satisfaction through post-interaction surveys that provide insights into how well AI tools meet customer needs. NPS goes a step further by measuring long-term loyalty and the likelihood of customers recommending your service.

Beyond CSAT and NPS, metrics like the customer effort score (CES) and customer retention rate add depth to understanding customer service quality. CES assesses the ease with which customers can resolve their issues, a factor where AI can play a transformative role by streamlining processes and interactions. Meanwhile, customer retention rate tracks the company's success in keeping its customers over time and offers insight into long-term satisfaction and loyalty.

Understanding these metrics is not just about gathering data; it's about comprehending what it tells us about the AI's performance and alignment with business objectives. For instance, a reduction in response time due to AI may lead to increased customer satisfaction, as reflected in CSAT and NPS scores. Similarly, improving the resolution rate can translate into tangible cost savings, as it may reduce the need for follow-up interactions or involvement of higher-cost human support.

Employee engagement metrics: British business magnate Richard Branson once famously said, "If you take care of your employees, they will take care of the clients."[26] Simply put, the key to engaging your customers is to engage your workforce.

Employee engagement metrics are crucial as they reflect the level of commitment and satisfaction employees feel toward their job and the organization. When AI is integrated effectively into the workplace, it can significantly enhance job satisfaction by automating mundane tasks, reducing workload, providing insightful data for decision-making, and facilitating a more engaging work environment.

In a business ecosystem where employees and customers are invaluable, boosting employee engagement through AI has a ripple effect. Enhanced job satisfaction from AI's support in the workplace benefits the employees and positively impacts customer interactions. This improvement in service quality, driven by engaged employees, can significantly elevate the customer experience.

Furthermore, fostering a work environment where employees feel valued and engaged is key to retaining talent and decreasing agent turnover rates, thus maintaining a skilled and motivated workforce that is essential for a company's success and growth. Quoting Richard Branson once again, "Train people well enough so they can leave, treat them well enough so they don't want to."[27]

Financial metrics: Financial metrics provide a clear picture of the economic benefits and feasibility of AI implementations in customer service. These metrics collectively offer a comprehensive view of AI's financial efficacy in enhancing customer service operations, underscoring its role as a strategic tool for economic optimization and competitive advantage.

- The cost-per-contact metric evaluates the total expense incurred for each customer interaction. AI can significantly reduce these costs by automating responses and streamlining processes, leading to more efficient service delivery.

- Return on investment (ROI) goes a step further, measuring the financial gains from AI investments against the costs involved in creating, deploying and maintaining this solution. This includes both direct expenditures, like technology acquisition, and indirect benefits, such as improved customer satisfaction and retention.

- Beyond the qualitative benefits, AI's integration can lead to quantifiable financial advantages, including reduced labor costs due to automation, decreased response times yielding efficiency improvements, and overall operational cost reductions. These savings are pivotal in justifying AI investments and in understanding their long-term financial impact on the organization.

These metrics collectively articulate the economic rationale behind AI integration, underlining its value as a strategic investment in enhancing service quality and business growth.

Operational metrics: These metrics offer insights into the overall operational health and responsiveness of the customer service and support teams.

Measuring the percentage of calls or interactions answered within the contractual service level agreement (SLA) directly measures how swiftly and effectively the team/organization responds to customer needs.

SLAs are critical in customer service as they define the standard of service customers expect. Meeting SLAs is essential not only for customer satisfaction but also for maintaining a brand's reputation. Consistently fulfilling SLA terms reassures customers of a company's reliability and commitment to quality service, which can significantly enhance customer trust and loyalty. Failure to meet SLAs can also lead to contractual penalties and damage the company's market standing. Thus, adhering to SLAs is both about avoiding negatives and reinforcing a positive, customer-centric brand image.

- Backlog size is a critical operational metric in customer service, representing the number of unresolved customer queries at any given time. A smaller backlog size generally suggests quicker query resolution and a more responsive service team. Efficient management of backlog size is essential for maintaining high levels of customer satisfaction and ensuring timely support. It's particularly important in high-volume service environments, where managing the backlog can effectively prevent service delays and enhance the overall customer experience.

- When analyzed over time, the backlog size can uncover trends and peak periods, guiding resource allocation. Effective management of these metrics, particularly through AI integration, can lead to a more agile and customer-centric operation, enhancing both immediate customer satisfaction and long-term loyalty, which are vital for a business's success and reputation.

This expanded view of business and operational excellence metrics offers a comprehensive understanding of AI's role in customer service and support. Considering how these metrics interact and influence each other is important, providing a multi-dimensional assessment of AI's effectiveness.

Also, it's important to note that not all metrics will be equally relevant for every business. The nature of your customer interactions, the type of AI tools implemented, and your specific business goals will dictate which metrics are most pertinent. The key is selecting and tailoring these metrics to provide a comprehensive, clear, and accurate picture of AI's impact on customer service operations.

Ethical and Compliance Metrics

Measuring ethics and compliance in AI systems is a complex and evolving area. Unlike metrics for efficiency or accuracy, which are often quantifiable, metrics for ethics and compliance are more nuanced and can vary depending on the context and regulatory environment. Here's a breakdown of how these aspects can be measured:

Metrics for Ethics in AI

These metrics are critical in assessing and mitigating bias in AI systems. They help ensure that AI algorithms do not perpetuate existing societal biases or create new forms of discrimination.

It's important to note that these metrics are not one-size-fits-all solutions. The choice of metric depends on the specific context and the ethical considerations relevant to the application.

Bias and fairness metrics: Measures like disparate impact, equality of opportunity, and statistical parity help assess whether an AI system is biased against certain groups.[28]

Disparate impact: Disparate impact refers to a situation where a policy or practice, even if neutral on its face, disproportionately affects a specific group or class of individuals, typically negatively. In the context of AI, it measures whether the outcomes of an algorithm unintentionally harm certain groups (for example, based on race or gender). It is often calculated by comparing outcome ratios between different groups. A common benchmark is the "80 percent rule," where the selection rate for any race, sex, or ethnic group should be at least 80 percent of the rate for the group with the highest rate.

Equality of opportunity: Equality of parity ensures that individuals have an equal chance of receiving positive outcomes, regardless of their membership in certain groups. In AI, equality of parity typically means ensuring that the likelihood of a positive outcome (like being hired for a job or granted a loan) is the same for all groups when considering relevant qualifications. Its calculation involves measuring and comparing true positive rates among different groups.

Statistical parity: Statistical parity, also known as demographic parity, occurs when the decision probability is independent of a specified sensitive attribute (like race or gender). In AI, this metric assesses whether each group ihas an equal probability to be assigned to the positive outcome. It's calculated by comparing the rate of positive outcomes across different groups and looking for disparities. Sometimes, improving one type of fairness metric can lead to decreases in another, reflecting the complex nature of fairness in AI. It's worth noting that these metrics alone can't ensure the fairness of AI systems. They should be part of a broader strategy that includes human oversight, ethical guidelines, and ongoing monitoring.

Transparency and explainability indexes: Transparency and explainability indexes in AI are qualitative assessments focusing on the clarity and understandability of a model's decision-making processes.[29] These indexes evaluate how well the reasons behind AI decisions can be comprehended and articulated technically and in lay terms. This aspect is crucial in building trust in AI systems, especially in critical areas like healthcare or finance, where understanding AI decisions can impact outcomes significantly.

Transparency and explainability indexes are typically measured through a combination of methods. They include expert reviews where specialists analyze the model's decision logic, user studies where non-expert users assess how understandable the model's outputs are, and algorithm-based evaluations that quantify aspects like feature importance. These metrics often involve scoring systems based on how clearly the model's reasoning can be articulated and understood. The challenge lies in balancing technical accuracy with understandability, ensuring that explanations are both accurate and accessible to non-specialist audiences.

A model scoring high in these indexes indicates its decisions are both accurate and interpretable, enhancing user trust and accountability in AI deployments. Transparent and explainable AI models facilitate better user acceptance, regulatory compliance, and ethical AI practices.

Auditability and accountability checks: Auditability and accountability checks in AI involve processes and mechanisms that ensure AI systems comply with ethical standards and regulatory requirements and align with societal values.[30]

- Auditability refers to the ability to inspect and review AI systems to verify their compliance and performance.

- On the other hand, accountability checks ensure clear lines of responsibility for AI decisions and outcomes.

- Auditability and accountability in AI are measured through structured audits, compliance checks, and ethical assessments. These evaluations often involve both internal and external reviews, where experts analyze the AI systems against established ethical guidelines, legal standards, and regulatory requirements. These checks are vital for maintaining public trust in AI systems, particularly in sectors where AI decisions have significant consequences.

- Interesting in this context is the emerging field of AI ethics audits, akin to financial audits, which are becoming more prevalent as AI systems increasingly influence various aspects of society and industry. These audits assess compliance and promote transparency, ensuring that AI systems are responsibly developed and deployed.

Metrics for Compliance in AI

Compliance metrics in AI are crucial for ensuring that AI systems adhere to legal standards, ethical norms, and industry-specific regulations. These metrics help assess whether AI deployments align with data protection laws like general data protection regulation (GDPR), industry guidelines, and ethical principles. They play an important role in building trust and credibility in AI applications, ensuring that AI benefits are realized without compromising legal and ethical boundaries. Compliance metrics are integral for the responsible development and use of AI, safeguarding against misuse and promoting positive societal impacts.

Regulatory adherence scores: Regulatory adherence scores are a set of metrics used to evaluate how well AI systems comply with relevant legal and regulatory frameworks. These scores are critical in industries requiring strict regulatory compliance, such as finance, healthcare, and data privacy. They assess the extent to which AI applications meet standards set by laws like GDPR or the Health Insurance Portability and Accountability Act of 1996 (HIPAA), ensuring that they operate within legal boundaries.

- Regulatory adherence scores are typically measured through comprehensive audits and reviews, which compare the practices and outputs of AI systems against established legal and regulatory standards. This process often involves detailed assessments conducted by legal and technical experts who scrutinize the AI system's data handling, decision-making processes, and overall operational compliance.

- High scores indicate strong compliance, reflecting the AI's alignment with legal requirements and ethical standards. These scores are instrumental in maintaining user trust and avoiding legal penalties, underscoring their importance in responsible AI deployment.

Privacy protection metrics: Privacy protection metrics in AI focus on evaluating how well AI systems manage and safeguard personal and sensitive data. These metrics assess the effectiveness of data encryption, anonymization processes, and adherence to data minimization principles. They measure compliance with data privacy laws such as GDPR, indicating how robustly an AI system protects user data from unauthorized access and breaches.

Privacy protection metrics in AI are evaluated through a combination of data audits, security assessments, and breach incident reports. High scores in privacy protection metrics are crucial for maintaining user trust, especially in sectors handling sensitive information. Ensuring strong privacy protection is both a legal requirement and a key aspect of ethical AI development.

Security compliance metrics: Security compliance metrics involve assessing the robustness of AI systems against cyberthreats and vulnerabilities. These metrics measure the system's adherence to cybersecurity standards and practices. This includes evaluating the strength of encryption protocols, the effectiveness of firewalls and intrusion detection systems, and the frequency and handling of security breaches.

Regular security audits and penetration testing are key methods for measuring these metrics. High compliance scores indicate robust security measures, which are essential for protecting sensitive data and maintaining the integrity of AI systems in the face of increasing cyber threats.

Ethics and compliance in AI are largely governed by a combination of quantitative metrics (like bias measurements) and qualitative assessments (like transparency and regulatory adherence). What is considered a "good" or "bad" score can vary greatly depending on the specific application, industry standards, and societal norms; however, legal requirements often set the minimum compliance score standards.

An open-source toolkit, originally designed by Microsoft, called Fairlearn, makes available both an interactive visualization dashboard and mitigation algorithms to help designers and developers of AI systems assess the fairness of their AI model and make informed decisions to mitigate unfairness.[31] Recognizing that AI models create a sociotechnical challenge in that it is very difficult to create and ensure a fully unbiased model, organizations will need to make tradeoffs based on competing priorities and goals. This reinforces the need to set strong goals and OKRs up front as you begin your model design so that you can more easily align priorities and make necessary tradeoffs to help you reach your desired end state.

The field is rapidly evolving, with new standards and regulations being proposed and implemented regularly. See *https://airevolutionbook.com* for updates.

User Engagement and Satisfaction

In this new era of AI-driven solutions, user engagement and satisfaction metrics offer a window into how effectively AI systems meet user needs and expectations. They are vital chapters in the story of AI's impact on consumer experiences. The interaction between users and AI systems reveals much about the technology's value, appeal, and relevance. As AI continues to integrate into various aspects of our lives, gauging how users interact with, perceive, and value these systems becomes essential.

This focus on user-centric metrics is not just about improving technology. It's about ensuring AI solutions are aligned with human experiences and expectations, fostering a harmonious and beneficial relationship between AI and its users.

Together, these metrics paint a comprehensive picture of how well an AI system resonates with its users, guiding ongoing enhancements to enrich user experience and satisfaction.

High user retention rates, particularly in consumer-facing applications, indicate the system's success in delivering value and maintaining user interest. User engagement metrics reveal the depth of user interaction with the system, shedding light on its usability and appeal. Feedback analysis provides qualitative insights, capturing user sentiment and perspectives. Together, these metrics are essential for continually refining AI solutions, ensuring they resonate with users and foster positive experiences. This focus on user engagement and satisfaction is key to building AI systems that are both technologically advanced and deeply attuned to user needs.

User retention rates: User retention rates are especially important in consumer-facing applications. It measures the proportion of users who continue to use the AI system over a period, reflecting its ability to meet user needs and preferences.

User engagement metrics: User engagement metrics track how users interact with the AI system, including frequency, duration, and depth of interaction. They provide insights into the system's appeal and usability.

- **Feedback analysis:** Feedback analysis helps in understanding user perceptions, preferences, and areas for improvement through the gathering and analyzing of user feedback which offers qualitative insights into the user experience.

Together, these metrics paint a comprehensive picture of how well an AI system resonates with its users, guiding ongoing enhancements to enrich user experience and satisfaction.

Innovation and Learning

In the dynamic field of AI, innovation and learning focus on the system's capacity to assimilate and meaningfully evolve. This section dives into the core of what makes AI revolutionary—its ability to adapt, innovate, and intelligently apply accumulated knowledge. In these aspects, AI transcends from being a mere tool to a transformative agent with a unique ability to develop.

AI's adaptability, innovation, and knowledge application echo the evolutionary strides of life itself, where learning leads to profound changes. As AI systems assimilate and evolve, they transform from tools into agents of change, embodying the essence of human creativity and problem-solving. This ability to continuously learn and adapt makes AI a participant in our world and a creator of new realities and solutions, redefining the boundaries of technology and imagination.

Let's delve into how these technologies evolve and contribute creatively to various domains:

Adaptability: This aspect examines the AI system's capacity to learn from new data and experiences over time, adjusting its algorithms and outputs accordingly. It's a measure of the system's flexibility and its ability to stay relevant despite changing environments.

It can be assessed by testing the AI on datasets it was not trained on and observing its performance. Changes in accuracy, error rates, and the ability to maintain consistency in outputs under varying conditions are key indicators. Additionally, the AI's learning curve over time, reflecting how it incorporates new information and improves its outputs, is a crucial measure of adaptability. This assessment helps determine the AI's ability to evolve and remain effective as it encounters new challenges and information.

Innovation metrics: These metrics assess the AI's contribution toward novel solutions or significant improvements in existing processes. It reflects the system's capability to automate, innovate, and enhance tasks. These metrics can include the number of new processes or products developed using AI, improvements in efficiency or productivity attributed to AI integration, and advancements in solving complex problems. They also consider the impact of AI in driving research and development in new directions.

Innovation metrics help quantify AI's role in fostering progress and its effectiveness in pushing the boundaries of current technology and knowledge.

Knowledge retention and transfer: This metric evaluates the AI system's ability to retain and apply learned information to different yet related tasks. It's crucial for systems that are expected to build upon their experiences and knowledge over time to enhance their effectiveness and efficiency.

- Retention is about how well the AI remembers and utilizes its past experiences, while transfer involves leveraging that knowledge in different yet related contexts. Effective knowledge retention and transfer enable AI systems to become more proficient over time, adapting their responses based on accumulated knowledge and experiences, enhancing their utility and efficiency in diverse applications.

- Measuring knowledge retention and transfer in AI involves evaluating how effectively the AI applies previously learned information to new situations. This can be quantified by testing the AI on tasks that are similar but not identical to those it was trained on and measuring its performance. Metrics such as accuracy, error rate, and time taken to adapt to new tasks are considered. Additionally, tracking improvements in the AI's performance over time as it is exposed to new data can indicate effective knowledge retention and transfer capabilities.

Each component plays a vital role in determining AI systems' long-term value and impact, ensuring they are not just functional but also progressively intelligent and contributory to innovation. Together, these facets underscore AI's profound impact on reshaping and advancing various fields and industries.

As we close this chapter, let's reflect on a few pivotal considerations:

Spend time developing an evaluation framework that aligns with the specific goals and requirements of the task at hand. This framework should be flexible to adapt as the model evolves or as the task requirements change.

Regularly monitor these metrics and adjust strategies based on the feedback and performance data.

It's important to strike a balance between the different metrics. Improving one metric (like reducing the average handling time) shouldn't negatively impact another (like customer satisfaction).

A comprehensive approach to measuring and improving AI performance in customer support or other industries involves a combination of technical AI efficiency metrics, industry-specific KPIs, and task-specific performance measures. The key is establishing benchmarks and then continuously adapting and refining the evaluation criteria to meet the evolving needs and goals of the business and users.

Endnotes

1   van Wyhe, John. 2002. "The Complete Work of Charles Darwin Online." Darwin online. ed. 2002. [http://darwin-online.org.uk/].

2   Hill, K., Kaplan, H., et al. (2000). "Food sharing among Ache foragers: Tests of explanatory hypotheses." *Current Anthropology* (2000): 41(1), 39-71.

3   Barkow, J.H., Cosmides, L., & Tooby, J. (Eds.). *The Adapted Mind: Evolutionary Psychology and the Generation of Culture.* Oxford University Press (1992): 19-136.

4   Gover, Jasmine. 2023. "Stages of Evolution in Humans." Collegdunia. com. September 5, 2023. [https://collegedunia.com/exams/ stages-of-evolution-in-humans-biology-articleid-8289].

5   Rasowsky, Yishai. 2023. "Perplexity in NLP: A Comprehensive Guide to Evaluating Language Models." Medium. February 27, 2023. [https:// yishairasowsky.medium.com/perplexity-in-nlp-a-comprehensive-guide-to- evaluating-language-models-f87cb45ee429].

6   Evidently editors. "Accuracy vs. precision vs. recall in machine learning: what's the difference?" EvidentlyAI. Accessed January 31, 2024. [https://www.evidentlyai.com/classification-metrics/ accuracy-precision-recall#what-is-recall].

7   Evidently editors. "Accuracy vs. precision vs. recall in machine learning: what's the difference?" EvidentlyAI. Accessed January 31, 2024. [https://www. evidentlyai.com/classification-metrics/accuracy-precision-recall#what-is-recall].

8   Bennett, George. 2020. "The Precision-Recall Trade-Off." Medium. June 21, 2020. [https://datascience-george.medium.com/the-precision-recall-trade-off- aa295faba140].

9   Wood, Thomas. "What is the F-score?" Deepai. Accessed January 31, 2024. [https://deepai.org/machine-learning-glossary-and-terms/f-score].

10   Dhungana, Kamal. 2023. "NLP Model Evaluation: Understanding BLEU, ROUGE, METEOR, and BERTScore." Medium. December 5, 2023. [https:// medium.com/@kbdhunga/nlp-model-evaluation-understanding-bleu-rouge- meteor-and-bertscore-9bad7db71170].

11   Bhandari, P., Nikolopoulou, K. 2020. "What is a Likert Scale? | Guide & Examples." Scribbr. June 22, 2023. [https://www.scribbr.com/methodology/ likert-scale/].

12   Semiconductor Engineering editors. "Tensor Processing Unit (TPU)." Semiconductor Engineering. Accessed February 1, 2024. [https:// semiengineering.com/knowledge_centers/integrated-circuit/ic-types/ processors/tensor-processing-unit-tpu/].

13   Harper, Christopher. 2022. "Thermal Throttling Guide (Prevent your GPU & CPU from Thermal throttling)." CGDirector. April 27, 2022. [https://www. cgdirector.com/thermal-throttling-guide/].

14   Wikipedia contributors. "FLOPS." Wikipedia, The Free Encyclopedia. January 29, 2024. [https://en.wikipedia.org/wiki/FLOPS].

15   Ludvigsen, Kasper Groes Albin. 2022. "The Carbon Footprint of ChatGPT." Medium. December 21, 2022. [https://towardsdatascience.com/ the-carbon-footprint-of-chatgpt-66932314627d].

16   McQuate, Sarah. 2023. "Q&A: UW researcher discusses just how much energy ChatGPT uses." University of Washington. July 27, 2023. [https://www.washington.edu/news/2023/07/27/how-much-energy-does-chatgpt-use/].

17   Li, Chuan. 2020. "OpenAI's GPT-3 Language Model: A Technical Overview." Lambda. June 3, 2020. [https://lambdalabs.com/blog/demystifying-gpt-3].

18   Smith, Craig S. 2023. "What Large Models Cost You—There Is No Free AI Lunch." *Forbes*. Updated January 1, 2024. [https://www.forbes.com/sites/craigsmith/2023/09/08/what-large-models-cost-you--there-is-no-free-ai-lunch/?sh=34b274d24af7].

19   Smith, Craig S. 2023. "What Large Models Cost You—There Is No Free AI Lunch." *Forbes*. Updated January 1, 2024. [https://www.forbes.com/sites/craigsmith/2023/09/08/what-large-models-cost-you--there-is-no-free-ai-lunch/?sh=34b274d24af7].

20   Smith, Craig S. 2023. "What Large Models Cost You—There Is No Free AI Lunch." *Forbes*. Updated January 1, 2024. [https://www.forbes.com/sites/craigsmith/2023/09/08/what-large-models-cost-you--there-is-no-free-ai-lunch/?sh=34b274d24af7].

21   Raschka, Sebastian PhD. 2023. "Ten Noteworthy AI Research Papers of 2023." Ahead of AI. December 30, 2023. [https://magazine.sebastianraschka.com/p/10-ai-research-papers-2023].

22   CacheFly team. 2023. "Supercharging Content Delivery Networks with Machine Learning." CacheFly. December 9, 2023. [https://www.cachefly.com/news/supercharging-content-delivery-networks-with-machine-learning/].

23   Wikipedia contributors. "Edge computing." Wikipedia, The Free Encyclopedia. February 1, 2024. [https://en.wikipedia.org/wiki/Edge_computing].

24   Gallistel, C. R., & Gelman, R. (2000). "Non-verbal numerical cognition: From reals to integers." *Trends in Cognitive Sciences* (2000): 4(2), 59-65.

25   He, Emily. 2023. "From Microsoft to global brands, Dynamics 365 Copilot is helping transform customer experiences across service, sales, and marketing." Microsoft Blog. September 7, 2023. [https://cloudblogs.microsoft.com/dynamics365/bdm/2023/09/07/from-microsoft-to-global-brands-dynamics-365-copilot-is-helping-transform-customer-experiences-across-service-sales-and-marketing/].

26   GoodReads contributors. "Richard Branson > Quotes." GoodReads. Accessed February 1, 2024. [https://www.goodreads.com/author/quotes/115943.Richard_Branson].

27   GoodReads contributors. "Richard Branson > Quotes." GoodReads. Accessed February 1, 2024. [https://www.goodreads.com/author/quotes/115943.Richard_Branson].

28   Saplicki, Carolyn., Bante, Mitali. 2022. "Fairness Explained: Definitions and Metrics." Medium. November 11, 2022. [https://medium.com/ibm-data-ai/fairness-explained-definitions-and-metrics-9690f8e0a4ea].

29   Balasubramaniam, Nagadivya., et al. 2023. "Transparency and explainability of AI systems: From ethical guidelines to requirements." *ScienceDirect*. July 2023. [https://www.sciencedirect.com/science/article/pii/S0950584923000514].

30   Burciaga, Aaron. 2021. "How to Build Responsible AI, Step 1: Accountability."
      Forbes. Updated April 21, 2022. [https://www.forbes.com/sites/
      forbestechcouncil/2021/10/04/how-to-build-responsible-ai-step-1-
      accountability/?sh=6de1baefb492].

31   Bird, S., et al. 2020. "Fairlearn: A toolkit for assessing and improving fairness
      in AI." Microsoft. September 22, 2020. [https://www.microsoft.com/en-us/
      research/uploads/prod/2020/05/Fairlearn_WhitePaper-2020-09-22.pdf].

14

Utilization of AI for Operational Success

Whatever you do, do it well. Do it so well that when people see you do it, they will want to come back and see you do it again, and they will want to bring others and show them how well you do what you do.

—Walt Disney

Customer service and support is one of the top enterprise scenarios for applying AI technology. The ability to forecast customer case arrival volume directly impacts resourcing, budget, customer satisfaction, and, at a high level, operational excellence. This forecasting is not merely a predictive tool but a strategic asset that ensures organizations can deliver timely, effective customer service, thereby maintaining high levels of customer satisfaction and loyalty. Accurate forecasting enables optimal staffing, resource allocation, budget adherence, and strategic planning, allowing organizations to be proactive rather than reactive. By leveraging advanced methodologies, including AI and the Erlang distribution, businesses can refine their forecasting accuracy, thereby enhancing customer experience and supporting sustainable business growth.

In today's competitive landscape, the financial implications of integrating AI into customer service are important to consider. AI can be a pivotal tool for optimizing resource allocation and reducing operational costs, yet it comes with risks. Accurate forecasting of customer case volumes, powered by AI, enables businesses to build a strategic plan for staffing and resource allocation, minimizing the financial strain of over or understaffing in customer service.

The financial risks associated with the initial investment in AI technology and the potential for unforeseen costs in implementation and integration cannot be overlooked. It necessitates a rigorous analysis of cost versus benefits, ensuring that the long-term financial advantages justify the upfront expenditures and ongoing operational costs, paving the way for a strategically sound and financially sustainable AI integration in customer service.

The future of AI is promising, and rigorous financial analysis across a wide range of customer service and support opportunities for deployment areas will be required.

Case Volume Forecasting

Forecasting customer case volume is crucial in a service and support organization as it directly impacts the ability to deliver timely and effective customer service. Accurate predictions enable optimal staffing, ensuring that the team is neither overwhelmed by unexpected surges nor underutilized during periods of low volume. This balance is essential for maintaining high levels of customer satisfaction and loyalty, as well as for controlling operational costs and keeping employee morale high. By anticipating case volumes, organizations can allocate resources more efficiently, invest in necessary training, manage budgets, and implement strategic improvements. Ultimately, forecasting empowers support organizations to be proactive rather than reactive, enhancing the overall customer experience and supporting business growth.

Importance of Forecasting in Customer Service

Forecasting in customer support is critical to help maintain service quality and operational efficiency. It allows organizations to plan for demand, ensuring the right number of agents or support engineers can handle customer inquiries without excessive wait times or backlogs. This foresight helps manage resources effectively, reducing costs by avoiding overstaffing while preventing burnout in understaffed scenarios.

The abstract of the article "Modeling and Forecasting Call Center Arrivals: A Literature Survey and a Case Study" published in the *International Journal of Forecasting* synthesizes very well the challenge at hand:

The effective management of call centers is a challenging task, mainly because managers consistently face considerable uncertainty. One important source of this uncertainty is the call arrival rate, which is typically time-varying, stochastic, dependent across periods and call types, and often affected by external events. The accurate modeling and forecasting of future call arrival volumes is a complicated issue critical for making important operational decisions in the call center, such as staffing and scheduling.[1]

Accurate forecasting supports strategic planning, from scheduling and training to tooling and implementing technological enhancements. Careful planning helps improve customer satisfaction by providing timely, efficient service and supports business scalability by adapting to trends and demand patterns. Forecasting can help with:

- **Staffing and resource optimization:** Leveraging AI to help improve forecasting accuracy can help with staffing and a cost-effective way to optimize resources. Improved forecasting accuracy ensures staffing levels are aligned with expected case volumes, optimizing resource allocation and minimizing overstaffing costs and the risk of underperformance due to understaffing.

- **Customer satisfaction:** Organizations can maintain quick response times and high-quality support by accurately predicting case volumes and planning accordingly, directly contributing to improved response times, customer satisfaction, and loyalty.

- **Strategic planning:** Using AI to improve forecasting accuracy helps to enable proactive decision-making for training, technological investments, self-help and diagnostic content and workload distribution, facilitating continuous improvement in service delivery and the ability to scale operations efficiently to meet case demand.

Erlang Distribution

The Erlang distribution is a statistical model often used for support forecasting, helping predict customer case arrival rates and durations.[2] In modern support organizations, it's used to calculate staffing requirements, ensuring enough agents are available to handle incoming cases efficiently, thus optimizing wait times and service quality in line with customer demand.

ERLANG DISTRIBUTION

A.K. Agner Krarup Erlang (January 1, 1878—February 3, 1929) was a Danish mathematician, statistician, and engineer who invented the fields of traffic engineering and queueing theory.[3] The Erlang distribution, which measures the time between incoming calls, can be used with the expected duration of incoming calls to produce information about the traffic load measured in Erlang. This can determine the probability of packet loss or delay according to various assumptions about whether blocked calls are aborted (Erlang B formula) or queued until served (Erlang C formula). The Erlang B and C formulas are still in everyday use for traffic modeling for applications such as the design of call centers.[4] One Erlang equals 60 minutes per hour in call minutes; an Erlang represents 1 hour of total traffic volume.

The Erlang B formula calculates the blocking probability in a system without a queue. In other words, if all service elements are already in use, a newly arriving call will be blocked and subsequently lost. It's particularly useful for scenarios with no waiting room for calls; additional calls are rejected if all servers are busy. It's essential for capacity planning and ensuring the system can handle the expected traffic without excessive call losses.

Erlang C is a traffic modeling formula primarily used in call center scheduling to calculate delays and predict call wait times. This mathematical equation enables call centers to predict their load and calculate the number of service/support agents required to service the desired number of calls to achieve a targeted service level.[5]

How AI Improves Volume Forecasting Accuracy

AI can help enhance call center volume forecasting by integrating the Erlang distribution, Erlang B and C formulas, and several other data types into its predictive analytics. Many examples show how AI and neural networks can be applied to call center forecasting.[6] AI algorithms can process vast amounts of historical case data, including case durations and inter-arrival times, to accurately model case traffic using the Erlang distribution—and then use this historical data to make predictions of future volume. This forecasting helps estimate with more precision the required staffing levels to meet service level agreements (SLAs) established with customers and maintain high levels of customer satisfaction based on other metrics like response rate and time to resolution. Furthermore, the Erlang C formula, which calculates the probability of a caller needing to wait and the expected wait time, can be optimized by AI algorithms to account for complex variables such as call abandonment rates, peak hours variability, and agent efficiency. By leveraging AI, support organizations can dynamically adjust their forecasts in near real-time and quickly adjust available staffing, significantly improving operational efficiency and customer satisfaction and reducing costs associated with over or understaffing.

These formulas, fundamental tools in queueing theory and telecommunications for predicting wait times and service capacity, have broad applications. Combined with AI, they can significantly advance research and practical applications in several areas.

Predictive Analytics for Demand Forecasting

There are several factors to consider when using predictive analytics in forecasting. Earlier in this chapter, we learned about case arrival rates—or hourly, daily, weekly, and monthly case volume. While there is a relationship between staffing and initial response time, resolution time, time to close, escalation rate, and the case complexity are other factors to consider. It's also important to consider customer satisfaction (CSAT), agent satisfaction (ASAT) and morale, and the tool's response time and complexity. These factors make for an intricate set of contributing factors that influence support organizations' resourcing and staffing requirements.

CASE STUDY OF SUCCESSFUL AI IMPLEMENTATION IN FORECASTING

Thornhill, Ontario–based CAA Club Group (CCG) wanted to save time and labor creating forecasts while generating predictions—such as roadside assistance call volumes—that covered the auto club's full scope.

CCG's data science team sought to "optimize resource allocation" for its membership through automated forecasts on member assistance and CCG staffing, working with "hundreds of millions of rows" of data from multiple sources.[7]

The short-term forecasts predicted call volume and service type for every hour in the following week. Forecasts were specific to each of the nearly 600 microregions within the club's coverage area and were also consolidated by broader regions.

This highly granular forecast is critical for staffing and staging vehicles where they're most likely to be needed 24/7—reducing response times for stranded members. Their lead data scientist can easily run the models daily during intense winter weather to factor the changing road and weather conditions into their forecasts.[8]

Challenges and Considerations in AI-Based Forecasting

AI-based forecasting presents numerous challenges and considerations that organizations must navigate to harness its full potential effectively. One primary challenge is the quality and quantity of data required. AI models thrive on large, diverse datasets for training. However, collecting, cleaning, eliminating bias, and ensuring the relevance of this data can be costly and resource-intensive. Data privacy and security also become paramount, as sensitive information is often involved in forecasting models.

Another significant challenge is the complexity of AI models. While they offer nuanced insights, their "black box" nature can make it difficult for stakeholders to validate the accuracy and understand how decisions are made, potentially leading to trust issues. Ensuring transparency and explainability in AI operations is crucial for adoption and confidence in AI-based decisions.

Model accuracy and overfitting represent additional concerns. AI models, especially those based on historical data, may not always accurately predict future events, particularly in the face of rapid and unprecedented change or unique anomalies. Overfitting is an issue within machine learning and statistics where a model learns the patterns of a training dataset too well, perfectly explaining the training dataset but failing to generalize its predictive power to other datasets. Overfitting to past data can make models less adaptable to new patterns or trends. Continuous monitoring, updating, and validation of AI models is necessary to maintain their accuracy over time. It's important to leverage subject matter expertise to help ensure ongoing accuracy.

Also, forecasting algorithms need to consider ethical use and bias mitigation. AI models can inadvertently perpetuate or amplify biases present in the training data, leading to unfair or discriminatory outcomes. Organizations must be vigilant in identifying and correcting biases within their models, ensuring that AI-based forecasting is both fair and equitable.

Addressing these challenges requires a pragmatic and rigorous approach, combining technological innovation with ethical considerations, transparency, and ongoing evaluation to ensure AI-based forecasting tools are both powerful and responsible.

Case Analysis and Troubleshooting

Using AI in customer support case analysis and troubleshooting has the potential to revolutionize the way businesses interact with their customers. By leveraging machine learning algorithms, natural language processing, generative AI, and predictive analytics, AI-based systems can quickly understand and categorize customer inquiries, identify common issues, and suggest solutions based on previous cases, speeding up response times and ensuring accuracy and consistency in the support provided. AI-driven tools can analyze trends in customer issues, helping companies provide self-help and proactively address problems before they escalate. Furthermore, AI can assist human support engineers by providing them with real-time information and recommendations, enhancing their ability to solve complex cases. This synergy between AI and human intelligence leads to faster response times, improved customer satisfaction, reduced support costs, and provides valuable insights into product and service improvements.

Application of AI to Automated Case Analysis

AI can be applied to case analysis in several innovative ways to improve service and support agent efficiency and accuracy.

- AI algorithms can be utilized for intelligent categorization of cases, where they automatically sort incoming issues based on their nature, urgency, and topic, ensuring that they are addressed by the appropriate service and support personnel.

- As we learned, AI-driven predictive analytics can forecast case volumes and complexities, enabling organizations to allocate resources more effectively.

- Through natural language processing (NLP), AI can understand and interpret the nuances of customer issue descriptions and communication, extracting relevant information to provide troubleshooting steps, case routing, and helping to offer faster resolutions.

- AI can automate the generation of responses for common queries, significantly reducing response times and freeing up human agents to tackle more complex issues. Machine learning models can continuously learn from past cases, improving their ability to suggest solutions and identify underlying patterns, thereby preventing future occurrences of similar issues.

Together, these AI applications transform case analysis into a more streamlined, accurate, and proactive process.

Benefits of AI Case Analysis and Troubleshooting

Integrating AI and automated case analysis and troubleshooting offers a variety of benefits that significantly enhance the efficiency and effectiveness of customer support operations. AI can ingest case data into generative AI models and return troubleshooting suggestions, case summaries, and sentiment analysis, among other things. One of the primary advantages of leveraging AI is improved response times. AI algorithms can process and analyze cases much faster than human agents and provide suggestions to a "human in the loop," enabling support agents to promptly address customer inquiries and issues. This rapid response capability helps maintain high levels of customer satisfaction and loyalty.

AI can also bring a level of consistency and accuracy to case resolution that is hard to achieve with human agents alone. By leveraging vast amounts of historical case data, AI systems can identify the most effective solutions to specific problems, reducing the likelihood of errors and ensuring that customers receive reliable support. This consistency is particularly valuable in complex cases where human agents might have varying levels of expertise.

AI also enhances the scalability of customer support operations. As businesses grow and the volume of customer issues and support cases increases, AI systems can easily adjust to handle the higher workload without requiring proportional increases in human staff. This scalability ensures that customer support quality remains high, even during peak periods. AI-powered case analysis can uncover additional insights into common customer issues and trends, providing businesses with valuable data that can inform product improvements and strategic decisions. By identifying and addressing the root causes of frequent problems, companies can leverage AI capabilities to reduce the overall volume of support cases and improve the overall customer experience.

AI technologies can also help free human agents to focus on more complex, sensitive, and nuanced cases requiring a personal human touch. By automating routine inquiries and solutions, AI allows human agents to dedicate more time and resources to providing empathetic and detailed support where it is most needed, enhancing the overall effectiveness of customer support teams.

Routing

Support case routing is an important component of a successful customer service operation by ensuring that inquiries are directed to the most appropriate agents or departments for efficient and effective resolution. This process is vital for optimizing response times and improving customer satisfaction.

As Bo Anne Marij de Vries stated in her case study and insights into AI case routing:

AI-based case sorting techniques use AI algorithms and technologies to automate and optimize the process of categorizing and sorting various types of cases or tasks. These techniques leverage machine learning and natural language processing capabilities to analyze and classify incoming cases or tasks based on their characteristics, content, or other relevant factors. Case-based reasoning offers a framework for creating systems and a cognitive model of individuals. By offering cases for a person to employ in solving an issue, the case-based decision-aiding method improves a person's memory.[9]

For example, an agent may have solved a similar problem for a different customer a year ago, or they might have a colleague who's taken a similar case, and by seeing case histories of similar cases, they can solve their current case more efficiently and effectively.

AI can significantly enhance case assignment by analyzing incoming cases in real-time, summarizing and identifying their nature, complexity, and urgency through natural language processing and machine learning algorithms. By automatically categorizing and prioritizing cases based on these and several other factors, AI ensures they are assigned to the best-qualified agents to handle them based on expertise, availability, and current workload. This intelligent routing streamlines the resolution process and balances the workload among support staff, leading to faster resolutions and a better overall customer experience. Many factors, such as response time, customer satisfaction, real-time learning, and complexity, can all play a role in intelligent routing.

Definition and Importance of Efficient Routing

Effective and efficient support case routing is pivotal in the landscape of customer service and support, as it is the backbone for delivering timely and accurate support. Routing cases to a qualified agent ensures that customer inquiries and issues are promptly addressed by people equipped with the right expertise and resources to address them. This targeted approach significantly reduces resolution times as well as the need for unnecessary handovers between agents or transfers between teams that add delays, directly contributing to customer satisfaction and loyalty. In addition, effective and efficient routing optimizes the distribution of work across support staff, helping to prevent burnout and ensuring a high level of service quality. Ultimately, the impact of efficient case routing extends beyond immediate customer interactions, contributing to a positive brand reputation and fostering trust and reliability in the company's support services.

Overview of AI Technologies in Routing

AI is revolutionizing support case routing by introducing sophisticated capabilities such as intent determination, intelligent call routing, and automated chat summarization and triage. By leveraging natural language processing and machine learning algorithms, AI can accurately understand and interpret the intent behind customer inquiries, whether communicated through voice, email, or chat. This precise determination of customer intent allows for categorizing cases based on their nature, urgency, and complexity, facilitating the automatic routing of cases to the most appropriate support channel or agent specialized in that particular area.

There is a lot of great research on network routing optimization, node optimization, and neural networks that can contribute to how best to assign cases to the right agent. Intelligent call routing utilizes AI to analyze incoming calls in real-time, assessing the customer's needs and history to route the call to the agent best equipped to provide a resolution efficiently. This improves the customer's experience by reducing wait times, increasing first-call resolution rates, and enhancing agent satisfaction by aligning cases with their expertise.

Automated chat triage employs AI to manage initial customer interactions through chat platforms, identifying the issue and either resolving simple queries directly or escalating more complex cases to human agents. This tiered approach to case handling streamlines the support process, ensuring that customers receive quick, accurate, and personalized assistance, thereby significantly improving the efficiency and effectiveness of customer support operations.

In addition, AI can summarize case descriptions and provide recommendations for troubleshooting before the agent is even assigned the case.

Benefits of AI-Driven Routing for Operational Efficiency

AI-driven routing significantly enhances operational efficiency within customer support and service delivery environments. By automating the intelligent distribution and assignment of cases, inquiries, and calls, organizations can achieve a higher level of service quality and operational agility by increasing response time and reducing case handoff or escalation. This technology streamlines processes and ensures that resources are utilized most effectively, leading to improved agent satisfaction, customer satisfaction, and reduced operational costs.

There are several operational and financial benefits to AI-driven routing:

- **Improved response times:** AI-driven routing systems quickly analyze incoming cases and direct them to the appropriate support engineers, significantly reducing wait times and streamlining the initial contact process.

- **Enhanced accuracy in case assignment:** By leveraging historical data and pattern recognition, AI algorithms can more accurately match cases to the engineers best equipped to resolve them. This precision reduces the likelihood of misassignments and the need for re-routing, ensuring that each case is handled by the right expert from the start.

- **Increased first-contact resolution rates:** Intelligent AI routing increases the chances that customers will have their issues resolved in the first interaction. This is achieved by predicting the complexity of cases and aligning them with engineers with the specific skills and available resources to handle them effectively.

- **Optimized agent workload:** AI systems can distribute cases evenly among support engineers, considering the current workload and expertise. This balanced distribution helps prevent burnout and ensures that no single engineer is overwhelmed, maintaining high productivity and morale.

- **Scalability:** AI-driven routing systems can adjust to fluctuating case volumes and complexity without requiring proportional staff increases. This adaptability makes scaling customer support operations more feasible as business demands grow.

- **Improved customer satisfaction:** Quick, accurate case resolution directly increases customer satisfaction. Customers appreciate rapid service and correct handling of their issues on the first try, leading to a better overall service experience.

- **Agent satisfaction:** When cases are appropriately matched to their skills, support engineers feel more competent and engaged. This satisfaction comes from handling cases within their expertise, leading to less frustration and a more rewarding work experience.

- **Data-driven insights:** AI routing provides valuable data on case handling, outcomes, and customer feedback. These insights can be used to refine processes, identify training needs, and improve overall service strategy, creating a feedback loop that continuously enhances performance.

- **Cost reduction:** Efficient routing reduces the time and resources spent on each case, lowering operational costs. Additionally, increased first-contact resolution rates and optimized workloads decrease the need for follow-ups and excess personnel, further cutting expenses.

AI-driven routing technology enables AI (and organizations) to analyze, categorize intelligently, and route inquiries to the most appropriate resources—human or diagnostic tools—ensuring that customers receive timely and accurate responses. The benefits of implementing AI-driven routing include improving customer satisfaction through faster resolution times and increasing operational efficiency by optimizing agent workloads and reducing costs, all while increasing agent satisfaction by delivering cases that match the expertise of the agent that receives it. Furthermore, the ability of AI to adapt and learn from interactions allows for continuous improvement in routing accuracy and efficiency, making it an invaluable tool for businesses looking to streamline their customer support processes and improve service quality.

Examples of AI-Driven Routing Improving Customer Service

Tracking the first company to launch AI-driven case routing is challenging due to the rapid and concurrent development of AI technologies across various sectors. Many players, including startups, tech giants, and specialized software providers, are contributing to its development, with one of the main ones being Salesforce.[10] Salesforce's evolution of case classification and case routing has been marked by integrating its Einstein AI technology, enhancing the CRM platform's ability to automate and optimize customer service processes.[11] Since 2016, Salesforce Einstein AI has progressively introduced capabilities for analyzing customer inquiries, predicting the best course of action, and routing cases to the most appropriate agents based on multiple variables such as expertise and availability.

Another example in this area is SearchUnify's Intelligent Case Routing (ICR) system.[12] Rather than adhering to traditional, rigid case routing protocols, SearchUnify's ICR system is designed to intelligently assess, prioritize, and assign customer inquiries in real time. A notable feature of this system is the Escalation Predictor, which can predict escalations before they happen using a sophisticated algorithm that analyzes sentiment, priority levels, and other critical factors. This proactive approach not only streamlines the support process but also significantly reduces the likelihood of customer dissatisfaction escalating into more severe issues. By identifying potential red flags early, the system ensures that high-priority cases are escalated to the top of the queue, allowing agents to address them with the urgency they require. The system incorporates sentiment analysis and customer profiling into its routing decisions. By understanding the customer's mood and the context of their inquiry, the ICR system can tailor the support experience through advanced NLP techniques, ensuring that customers feel understood and valued. Incorporating the K-nearest neighbor (KNN) algorithm further refines the routing process by classifying cases based on their similarity to previously resolved issues.[13] This approach ensures that agents are matched with inquiries suited to their skill set and those they are most likely to resolve efficiently based on historical data.

A notable case study showcasing the innovative application of AI in intelligent case routing and support, albeit in a different context, involves the global healthcare research giant IQVIA. IQVIA leveraged AI-driven analytics and technology to significantly enhance patient identification processes. By utilizing AI-powered modeling, IQVIA increased the precision of patient identification by an impressive 15 times and improved healthcare professional (HCP) linkage precision by 10 times.[14] This advancement demonstrates the power of AI in healthcare data analytics and its potential to streamline operations and improve outcomes in various sectors.

This example complements the previously discussed SearchUnify case by illustrating AI's broad applicability and transformative potential across different domains. While SearchUnify focuses on customer support and case routing within a business context, IQVIA's application of AI showcases how intelligent technologies can revolutionize data processing and analysis in healthcare, leading to more accurate and efficient patient care.

These case studies collectively highlight the versatility of AI in enhancing decision-making, reducing operational costs, and improving service delivery across industries. The AI advancements in these examples are not just about automation but also about making more informed, data-driven decisions that can lead to better outcomes for customers in a support scenario and patients in a healthcare setting.

Financial Considerations

As we've seen throughout this book, the speed of AI advances continues to increase. This section will look at the financial considerations that service and support leaders must consider before deploying AI in their organizations. There is a temptation to assume that deployment of AI will lead to immediate cost savings, perhaps achieved by getting rid of human agents and replacing them with AI-based chatbots. This is not achievable today, and perhaps not ever. However, that does not dismiss AI as a cost-saving opportunity.

The true value of AI in customer service lies not just in cost-cutting but in enhancing the quality of service, leading to greater customer satisfaction and retention. By automating routine inquiries, AI allows human agents to focus on more complex and emotionally nuanced interactions, thereby increasing the overall efficiency of the service team. AI-driven analytics can provide deeper insights into customer behavior and preferences, enabling companies to tailor their services more effectively and identify new revenue opportunities. It's also important to consider the long-term scalability benefits of AI, as these systems can handle a growing volume of queries without the need for proportional increases in staff, thus offering significant financial advantages as the business expands.

Initial Investment Costs

It's important to consider the investment costs of deploying AI models. Do the benefits of AI models outweigh the costs, both holistically and financially? To answer this question, it's important to understand the costs and get an accurate estimate of the benefits. This involves a detailed analysis of upfront costs, such as purchasing or developing AI software, setting up the necessary infrastructure, and training employees to work with the new technology. Additionally, businesses must account for ongoing operational expenses, including maintenance, updates, and licensing fees, to ensure a comprehensive understanding of the total financial commitment required for AI deployment.

Development or Purchase of AI Software

The first consideration is "buy or build" or some combination of the two. Likely, organizations will want AI models trained on their proprietary content. It's also likely that customer service and support organizations may not have existing software engineers or data science capabilities. So, one of the early decisions is whether to hire these skill sets into the organization or rely on partners or vendors. This decision needs careful consideration, as it will significantly impact the organization's long-term capabilities and financials. The temptation might be to hire a vendor or purchase off-the-shelf software. The speed of software advances in the AI world is incredibly rapid, and the organization that outsources this work may find themselves out of date—and/or rehiring the vendor—as the technology will likely change and improve in a few months.

Careful consideration should be given to evolving the skills within the organization, including software engineers, data scientists, content creators, and overall knowledge management, to focus on AI model building to support the existing agents. Investing in internal capabilities allows for greater customization and adaptability of AI solutions to meet specific organizational needs and challenges. This approach fosters innovation and ensures that the organization remains at the forefront of AI advancements, enabling it to quickly adapt to new technologies and maintain a competitive edge in the market. Developing in-house AI expertise can significantly reduce dependency on external vendors, leading to cost savings in the long run and more control over intellectual property and data security. It also encourages a culture of continuous learning and improvement, empowering employees with future-ready skills that are invaluable in the rapidly evolving digital landscape.

Infrastructure Requirements (Hardware, Software, Cloud Services)

Likely, the organization will require infrastructure improvements and upgrades to support running these AI models. AI vendors can help take some of the hardware burden, but thinking long-term is important. Outsourcing to cloud service providers may allow for an easier transition as hardware technology advances, but upgrading network infrastructure and agent hardware may be required.

In addition to considering the immediate infrastructure needs, organizations must also plan for scalability. As AI applications grow and data volumes increase, the demand on the infrastructure will also rise. This means investing in scalable cloud services and flexible hardware solutions that can grow with the organization's needs. Furthermore, ensuring that the software stack is up to date and compatible with AI technologies is crucial for maintaining operational efficiency and maximizing the benefits of AI investments. Lastly, cybersecurity measures must be integrated into the infrastructure planning to protect sensitive data and AI models from potential threats. Consider the security, privacy, and safety considerations from the previous discussion of Responsible AI.

Integration with Existing Customer Service Platforms

It will be important to integrate with existing support tools such as case management, support diagnostics, analyzers, and others, depending on the organization. This integration might be costly or may drive changes in tools and tool vendors. The financial impact could be non-trivial.

Training Costs for Staff to Manage and Operate AI Systems

Training costs for existing staff can be a significant amount. Support organizations are typically staffed to handle existing demand, so pulling staff out for training will require careful planning. The complexity of AI systems means that training is not a one-time event but an ongoing process to keep pace with technological advancements. This necessitates a continuous education and professional development budget to ensure staff remains proficient in the latest AI technologies. Organizations may need to consider the costs associated with hiring new talent or specialists with expertise in AI to fill any gaps in their current team's capabilities. Investing in partnerships with educational institutions or online learning platforms can also be a strategic way to mitigate training costs while ensuring access to high-quality AI education and resources. It's critical to create a culture that values and rewards learning and innovation to help motivate staff to engage in training and adapt to new technologies more quickly, accelerating the potential financial gains that AI can deliver.

Operational Costs

Before deploying AI, estimating and understanding ongoing operational costs is important. Estimating the operational costs of AI systems is an important part of long-term financial planning and sustainability. The maintenance and updates of AI systems are technical necessities and financial commitments, as they ensure the systems remain effective and secure against evolving technological advances, security threats, content curation and creation costs, and model improvements. The costs associated with data storage and security can be significant, given the vast amounts of data AI systems process and the critical importance of protecting this data from breaches. If done in-house, energy consumption is another important factor, as AI systems, especially those requiring intensive computational power, can substantially increase power usage. Licensing fees for third-party AI solutions also add to the operational costs, which can vary widely depending on the AI's complexity and capabilities. The hope is that AI technology productivity gains will offset these costs, but it's important to go into this with eyes wide open. Organizations must also consider the potential costs of compliance with data protection regulations, which can involve both financial and operational adjustments to ensure that AI systems are used ethically and legally.

As AI technology evolves, these costs may become immaterial compared to the efficiency gains, but it is important to understand both sides of the equation to effectively decide the right course of action.

Cost Savings and Efficiency Gains

Within the sphere of organizational optimization, achieving cost savings and efficiency gains stands as a paramount objective. Let's explore how advancements in artificial intelligence and automation strategies drive productivity and pave the way for substantial reductions in labor costs.

Improved Agent Productivity and Efficiency

One of the most important and biggest early impacts of AI models is to make humans significantly more productive and efficient—not to replace them. As of this writing, and probably for a long time to come, a human armed with the proper tools will dramatically outperform an AI—or a human—working independently. The first goal shouldn't be to reduce salary costs but to optimize the efficient delivery of the highest quality output with the lowest possible cost input. Focusing AI investments on "human-in-the-loop" productivity is the best way to get started.

This approach leverages the unique strengths of both humans and AI, combining human creativity, empathy, and strategic thinking with AI's speed, accuracy, and data processing capabilities. By doing so, organizations can tackle complex problems more effectively and make more informed decisions. Integrating AI into workflows can automate routine tasks, freeing employees to focus on higher-value activities requiring human insight. This not only boosts morale by reducing monotonous work but also accelerates innovation and growth within the organization. As discussed in Chapter 13, keeping a close eye on metrics, KPIs, and OKRs will help determine how and where to focus your human agents. By continuously analyzing usage and performance data, AI systems can identify inefficiencies and suggest improvements, ensuring that the productivity gains from AI integration are sustained over time.

Reduction in Labor Costs Through AI and Automation

There will likely be a wide range of adoption of the new AI world. Some agents will dive in and see productivity gains, while others may stay away. Encouraging everyone to try things out and learn what works for them is important. The reduction in labor will come first through efficiency gains and being able to automate repetitive tasks.

It's critical not to move too fast here. Productivity gains will only come when models are proven accurate and responsive, which may not be the case on day one. There will also be new roles that will evolve and need to be funded.

The transition to AI and automation offers a promising future for reducing customer service labor costs, but it requires a nuanced approach to ensure that productivity gains are realized without sacrificing quality or employee morale. New jobs will be created and will be critical to training AI models. Encouraging a culture of experimentation and adaptation among employees can help identify the most beneficial uses of AI, allowing for a smoother integration of these technologies into daily operations while empowering individuals to embark on new learning paths. As repetitive tasks are automated, employees can be redeployed to more important strategic roles, necessitating an investment in training and development to equip customer service agents with the necessary skills to make this transition. Moreover, the creation of new roles, such as software engineers and data scientists, underscores the evolving nature of the workforce and the importance of strategic planning in workforce development to harness the full potential of AI and automation.

An important recommendation is that all initial productivity gains achieved by deploying AI technology accrue to the individual first. If a support engineer/agent is closing five cases per week without AI and improves to closing five cases in three days with AI, the extra two days should accrue back to the support engineer/agent, with a strong emphasis on skills growth. In the long term, that allows the company to benefit from redeploying agents to other parts of the business that may be short-handed and in need of qualified staff. This approach not only incentivizes employees to embrace AI technologies but also fosters a culture of continuous learning and improvement within the organization. Employees can explore new roles and challenges by prioritizing developing their skills and capacities, further driving innovation and adaptability in a rapidly changing business landscape. This also has a huge positive impact on morale. Instead of having more cases piled upon them, the most productive employees can develop, grow, and advance their careers.

Customer-Facing AI: Risk and Reward

While the benefits of AI in customer-facing roles are significant, the risks must be carefully managed to maintain trust and satisfaction. Implementing robust testing and feedback mechanisms can help mitigate the risk of providing incorrect information, ensuring that AI systems learn and improve over time. Integrating AI with "human-in-the-loop" oversight offers a safety net where complex or sensitive issues are automatically escalated to human agents, combining the efficiency of AI with the nuanced understanding of humans. It's important to be transparent with customers about using AI in their service experience, which can also grow customer trust, especially when they are informed about how their data is used to personalize services. Continuous investment in AI technology and training for both AI systems and human staff is essential to adapt to evolving customer expectations and maintain a competitive edge in customer service. It's hard to predict our AI future, but ensuring that customer focus is job one is important.

Integrating AI with customer-facing operations introduces a significant competitive advantage by offering personalized experiences that can meet each customer's unique needs and preferences. That said, a level of risk accompanies putting this technology directly in customers' hands. If done correctly, the level of service personalization, powered by advanced data analysis, enhances customer satisfaction, fosters loyalty, and encourages repeat business. Moreover, the scalability benefits of AI ensure that businesses can efficiently manage fluctuations in customer demand without the need for substantial increases in staffing or resources. However, balancing this automation with a personal experience—human oversight—is crucial to maintaining a personal touch and managing complex customer issues effectively. AI can help provide the ability to offer 24/7 support through AI-driven solutions like chatbots or virtual assistants to ensure that customers have access to assistance at any time, significantly improving the overall customer experience and satisfaction while at the same time offering better work–life balance to employees.

Integrating AI into customer service enhances existing operations and opens up avenues for revenue generation that might have been previously untapped. By leveraging AI to help analyze customer interactions and feedback, it's easy to identify patterns and preferences, enabling organizations to tailor their offerings more effectively to individual customer needs, thereby increasing the likelihood of upselling and cross-selling.

AI-driven insights can help customer service and support organizations better anticipate and address customer needs proactively, aiming to improve customer satisfaction and loyalty—key drivers of long-term revenue growth. This ability to provide personalized experiences at scale can significantly differentiate a brand, product, or service in a crowded market, making it a more attractive choice for potential customers. This application of AI in customer service helps service organizations contribute more directly to product strategy by using AI to aggregate customer listening channels to provide strategic feedback. The efficiencies and cost savings realized through AI can be reinvested into innovation and customer experience enhancements, creating a virtuous cycle that further drives revenue and growth.

The deployment of AI technologies, while offering significant advantages, also introduces risks. There could be unexpected costs from development overruns or additional staff training requirements. There may be strategic changes in the skills makeup of a service organization. There could be a tangible risk of customer dissatisfaction, which can stem from impersonal service experiences or errors in the AI's output. One illustrative case involved Air Canada, where their website's chatbot, tasked with providing real-time customer support, incorrectly communicated about reduced rates and refund policies. Misled by this information, a passenger pursued a claim when the airline did not honor the stated policies. Air Canada's defense that the chatbot was a separate legal entity and independently responsible did not hold in court. The Canadian tribunal ruled in favor of the passenger, affirming the airline's accountability for all content delivered through its platforms, interactive or otherwise. This ruling serves as a pivotal learning opportunity. It highlights the critical importance of accuracy and reliability in automated customer service tools. In response, Air Canada undertook a thorough review of its AI systems, enhancing their chatbot's algorithm to better align with their policy frameworks and refining its response accuracy. This proactive approach improved their customer service capabilities and reinforced the importance of oversight in AI implementations. By embracing this challenge as a catalyst for improvement, Air Canada set a precedent for digital responsibility, turning a moment of fault into a step forward in their commitment to customer satisfaction and trust.

Adopting a phased deployment strategy will be the most effective approach to mitigate these risks, allowing the gradual integration of AI systems, enabling organizations to manage costs more predictively and adjust training programs as needed. It's important to pick carefully among a variety of customer service and support metrics to monitor on a regular, probably weekly, basis to track how the deployment is progressing. Continuous monitoring is critical, ensuring that any issues with customer service quality or system errors are identified and addressed promptly. By implementing these mitigation strategies, organizations can navigate the challenges associated with AI adoption, ensuring that the benefits far outweigh the risks.

The deployment of AI technologies in customer service and support organizations introduces a complex landscape of financial planning and strategic decision-making for these organizations. A clear understanding of the trade-offs involved is crucial for successful deployment, which, over time, can lead to significant efficiency gains and long-term financial savings. All while maintaining a healthy organizational culture and, if done well, enabling customer service to contribute to company strategy on a much larger scale than in the past. However, this does not come for free. The process of validating and tuning AI models introduces new costs, including the need for significant human input to achieve optimal outcomes. These evolving roles highlight the necessity of human involvement in managing AI systems, which incurs additional costs. Service and support leaders need to consider changes in organizational skills, including software engineering, data science, content creation, and knowledge management, to remain competitive and current. Leaders are thus faced with critical decisions based on a set of trade-offs, where cost-efficiency opportunities might compete with alternative growth opportunities. The choice between deploying AI models to reduce costs or to improve quality and increase revenue represents a real dilemma for financial leaders, who must consider the return on investment and the time value of money in their project funding decisions. All this must be done in an environment of rapid technological change. Not an easy task.

An organization's strategic priorities play a pivotal role in determining which projects receive the necessary funding and resources to succeed. Finding the right balance between growth and optimization remains a challenge, exacerbated by the expanding role of AI models in business operations. Support leaders must understand the trade-offs and evaluate the return on investment for AI-based pilots and experiments. The value of a project is assessed not just by its costs and benefits but also by the time horizon over which these factors play out, alongside the comparative metrics of alternative projects. It's also critical to consider the human element. Domain experts on the front line are incredibly valuable to the business. AI does not know everything. It needs to be trained, and front-line agents are the ones who have the training data in their heads. This complexity requires finance leaders to help provide clarity and direction in decision-making, cutting through the complexity to guide the organization toward its strategic goals.

The risks and mitigation strategies associated with AI deployment will require careful planning and strategic foresight. The potential for unexpected costs and customer dissatisfaction underscores the need for a methodical approach to AI integration. Phased deployment and continuous monitoring emerge as essential strategies, allowing organizations to A/B test and manage risk. By understanding these dynamics, watching key metrics, and implementing robust mitigation strategies, customer service and support organizations can take control of this AI Revolution and ensure that their journey toward AI adoption is marked by informed decision-making and strategic resilience, ultimately leading to successful outcomes and the realization of AI's full potential.

In conclusion, the strategic importance of financial planning in AI deployment cannot be overstated. As organizations navigate the intricate balance between costs and benefits, the insights and clarity provided by finance leaders by leveraging traditional metrics become invaluable. To ensure operational success, leaders must understand the immediate operational and financial opportunities and the implications of AI projects. The long-term impact on the organization's strategic direction by applying AI to areas of forecasting, routing, and troubleshooting can be game-changing. By effectively partnering with finance leaders, service and support organization leaders can make informed decisions that align with their overall strategic priorities, ensuring the successful deployment of AI technologies that drive growth and optimization for years to come.

Endnotes

1   Ibrahim, R., L'Ecuyer, P., Shen, H., Ye, H. 2016. "Modeling and forecasting call center arrivals: A literature survey and a case study." ResearchGate. March 2016. [https://www.researchgate.net/publication/298428256_Modeling_and_forecasting_call_center_arrivals_A_literature_survey_and_a_case_study].

2   Australian Customer Experience Professionals Association Website. "Erlang Calculator for Call Centers." Australian Customer Experience Professionals Association. Accessed February 27, 2024. [https://acxpa.com.au/glossary/call-centre-erlang-calculator/].

3   Wikipedia contributors. "Agner Krarup Erlang." Wikipedia, The Free Encyclopedia. February 24, 2024. [https://en.wikipedia.org/wiki/Agner_Krarup_Erlang].

4   Wikipedia contributors. "Erlang distribution." Wikipedia, The Free Encyclopedia. January 2, 2024. [https://en.wikipedia.org/wiki/Erlang_distribution].

5   Awati, Rahul. 2022. "Erlang C." TechTarget. March 2022. [https://www.techtarget.com/searchunifiedcommunications/definition/Erlang-C].

6   Chanpanit, T., Udomsakdigool, A. 2020. "Big Data Framework for Incoming Calls Forecasting in a Call Center." ResearchGate. June 2020. [https://www.researchgate.net/publication/343953202_Big_Data_Framework_for_Incoming_Calls_Forecasting_in_a_Call_Center].

7   Ehrlich, Chris. 2023. "AI in Customer Experience: 5 Companies' Tangible Results." CMSWire. August 14, 2023. [https://www.cmswire.com/customer-experience/ai-in-customer-experience-5-companies-tangible-results/].

8   Pecan website. "CAA Club Group optimizes roadside assistance for members." Pecan. Accessed February 27, 2024. [https://www.pecan.ai/customer/caa-demand-forecast/].

9   Marij de Vries, Bo Anne. "Techno-Optimism and Its Impact on Repetitive Civil Servant Decision Making." Delft University of Technology. January 19, 2024. [file:///C:/Users/emilym/Downloads/Master_Thesis_Bo_de_Vries_4728823_update.pdf].

10 Cyntexa Blog editors. "Evolution of Artificial Intelligenece in the Salesforce Ecosystem." Cyntexa. November 1, 2023. [https://cyntexa.com/blog/evolution-of-ai-in-salesforce/].

11 Salesforce Product Support editors. "Route Work with Einstein Case Routing." Salesforce. Accessed February 29, 2024. [https://help.salesforce.com/s/articleView?id=sf.omnichannel_einstein_case_routing.htm&type=5].

12 Vijan, Anish. 2023. "Intelligent Case Routing: Your AI-Powered Wingman For Support Teams." SearchUnify. March 27, 2023. [https://www.searchunify.com/sudo-technical-blogs/intelligent-case-routing-your-ai-powered-wingman-for-support-teams/].

13 Geeks for Geeks contributors. "K-Nearest Neighbor (KNN) Algorithm."
    Geeks for Geeks. Accessed February 29, 2024. [https://www.geeksforgeeks.
    org/k-nearest-neighbours/].

14 IQVIA editors. "AI Case Study—How IQVIA Increased Target Patient
    Identification 15x." IQVIA. April 25, 2023. [https://www.iqvia.com/library/
    case-studies/ai-case-study-how-iqvia-increased-target-patient-identification-15x].

15

Evolution of Support Roles with AI

The future belongs to those who prepare for it today.

—Malcolm X

As we enter this new era of AI, there will be inevitable changes in how we work.

Throughout history, we've seen continuous transformations in technology, nature, the arts, and nearly every sector or industry. For example, technology has impacted the way humans accomplish tasks since the invention of writing by the ancient Sumerians, the Mesopotamian wheel, and the printing press in the early 13th century. Cloth is not made the same way it was in the 17th century. Books are not printed the same way they were before Gutenberg in 1450 Europe. However, AI is a little different and perhaps more intimidating as the speed of innovation and the reality of AI's potential sets in. In this chapter, we'll explore what it means for the evolution of roles in customer support and how you can help mitigate the fear associated with change—helping to retain a skilled workforce best suited to meet the needs of the AI Revolution for many years to come.

A Journey Through History

The journey of technological evolution and its impact on work can be traced back thousands of years. The Egyptians were pioneers in using simple machines like levers and ramps for construction, dramatically changing the scale and speed of building the pyramids, for example. Their advancements in agriculture and irrigation influenced food production for thousands of years, supporting larger populations and increasingly complex societies.

The Greeks made notable contributions to mathematics, physics, and engineering and laid foundational principles that would influence centuries of technological development. The Antikythera—a hand-powered mechanism to simulate the solar system—is often regarded as the first known analog computer and exemplifies the sophistication of Greek technology.

The vast Roman Empire brought about large-scale engineering feats. The Romans introduced road systems, aqueducts, and advanced building techniques, significantly enhancing trade, communication, and urban living. Roman innovations were in physical technology and organizational systems, with examples such as their legal and governance structures, which have long-lasting influences even today.

The Industrial Revolution represented a major seismic shift in human history and the way we work. The introduction of steam power, mechanized manufacturing, and the factory system reshaped the global economy, urban landscapes, and social classes. It was a time of powerful social change, when manual labor transitioned to machine-based production, creating new job types and demanding new skills. It was a great metaphor for today's AI revolution.

In the late 20th century, the advent of digital technology and the Internet sparked another revolution. This era transformed how we access information and communicate with one another and changed the commercial economy. The rise of this digital economy has reshaped industries and spurred the creation of entirely new ones.

Each of these historical phases demonstrates how technology acts as a catalyst for change, continuously evolving the nature of work and society. As we now embrace AI, we are part of this ongoing narrative of advancement, facing challenges but also unlocking unprecedented possibilities for the future.

Evolving Needs of the Business

As we've discussed throughout this book, AI will introduce change at a speed and scale that is unfathomable for many. We have never experienced such a step change in technology that has quickly disrupted workflow and jobs—simultaneously introducing fear, anxiety, and excitement. With the advent of anything that creates some level of change, businesses must evolve to remain competitive, especially where customer loyalty is scarce.

We've seen dramatic changes in the technology industry, even in relatively recent years. A college student in the 1980s with a computer science degree specializing in Fortran or COBOL programming would likely be unemployable today, as the standard for programming language skills has shifted. Similarly, a dBase III expert in the 1990s or a C programmer who did not evolve could not make the leap. With hardware knowledge, a great shift has occurred in recent decades—from mainframe computers to personal computers to mobile and wearable devices. And now with the introduction of AI, it's incumbent on all workers to fully embrace this new innovative technology and evolve.

Imagining a Customer Service and Support Organization of the Future

We've explored in depth many of the integration points within a customer service and support organization that will benefit from AI incorporation. To help make this a reality, you'll need to think through your current customer support journey, organization structure, and people resource needs.

Customer Support Journey and Evolving Roles

Envisioning the current customer support journey is a good place to start as you design, develop, and implement your AI support strategy. The customer support journey likely doesn't start at the earliest stages of engaging with customers. There is work done to attract and encourage customer purchases before they ask for help and support. However, once a purchase has been made, they may look to you for help at some point in the lifetime of the product or service acquired.

Every single entry point through which a customer might contact support should be evaluated for areas of AI integration and how they might inform the evolution of and/or the need for new roles. This will ensure adopting and retaining your new AI strategy designed to best serve customers and meet your business goals.

Touchpoints Along the Customer Support Journey and Support Role Requirements

Role requirements will differ depending on factors such as the industry, company size, customer audience, support structure (insource/outsource), and AI strategy for customer service and support. Understanding customer and business goals at each touchpoint will help you best identify how your AI and human support align to deliver your desired results. From a customer perspective, they are typically looking to solve any issues as quickly as possible so they can get on with their business. From a business perspective, anything an organization can do to help deflect expensive support engagement is celebrated. Here is a good sampling of the types of role responsibilities required for different touchpoints of AI integration in a large support function.

Preventive and Preemptive Support

The ideal scenario for most customers is preventing an issue before it happens. Issues are fixed without them knowing they had an issue in the first place. This type of support often resides with the product design and development teams. Checking telemetry for quality of products and usage. However, support, particularly AI, can play a vital role by monitoring current support interactions for trending issues and quickly raising these for resolution before more customers experience the problem.

AI can also assist in monitoring customer's technical environments, such as checking for security gaps, the success of past issue resolution and configuration optimization, and automatically correcting anything out of place.

Roles needed to optimize preventive support opportunities include the need for strong data scientists and AI specialists in support functions to create, evaluate, and tune the AI model recommendations. The organization can benefit from people with deep machine learning expertise who can create AI models that align directly with the unique business needs of support and help build solutions to automatically solve customer issues.

Proactive Support

In the technology industry, onboarding new software or hardware and integrating existing technology architecture is often an important touchpoint for customers. Many purchasers of technology don't have the in-house technical expertise to solve a myriad of potential issues. Acquiring onboarding assistance ensures your entire technology stack works as expected without creating additional problems.

AI can play a role in quickly assessing the potential nuances of introducing specific technology into existing architecture, alerting any onboarding specialists to potential problems that they can proactively help mitigate. Also, AI could assist with configuring the new (and existing) technology settings to optimize for the company's needs to ensure that the system is as secure as possible from outside threats.

When a customer or support agent encounters a problem, diagnostic tools can help diagnose that issue quickly by checking known incorrect configurations, analyzing log files for errors, and suggesting ways to get things back into working order. Diagnostics enhance the efficiency of resolving customer problems and collect valuable data on common issues and their resolutions. This data forms the basis for training more sophisticated AI models, leading to smarter, more intuitive support tools.

These tools are pivotal in making support more efficient by providing actionable insights into why software applications behave in certain ways. These diagnostics can provide insights into system performance, health, and other potential issues. They can also make certain updates to configurations or settings, helping to resolve detected issues. AI can significantly enhance the development of support diagnostics by automating and optimizing various aspects of the process.

Direct in-product support is where customers can search for answers to questions about product usage or connect to targeted web results, getting help quickly and easily. With AI, the answer is often displayed or offered to the user without them making a specific request, assisting with the continued workflow of the user.

Previously, curated self-help assets with human intelligence were more controlled, leaving less room for dynamic answers. When you remove the human layer, you rely on AI to make those decisions for you, and currently, AI doesn't always get it right. A key area to consider when deploying AI into a self-help context is to ensure you ground your index in your company data. Doing this lets you control the knowledge corpus AI uses to generate its answers. You can even take it a step further and create targeted AI assets to deploy against certain scenarios.

Initially, the integration of AI in onboarding, in product, diagnostics, and self-help will provide immediate solutions for common problems, reducing the workload on human support staff and improving customer satisfaction through rapid problem-solving. Over time, as AI continues to evolve and improve, it will become more adept at handling a wider range of issues, including more complex and nuanced problems. AI can automate more solutions to check or change settings, validate account information, and determine or signify customer intent, resulting in decreased human engagement with proactive customer interactions and helping with actioning solutions. Employing subject matter experts in support to write articles, curate content, and build automated diagnostics to help customers solve their own issues will be an increased need in the proactive support space.

Reactive Support

Traditionally, reactive support is considered the bread and butter of support organizations. It's where the largest human engagement takes place now and likely in the future, even with increased AI integration. This integration will be prevalent throughout reactive support engagements, assisting human support agents at each step.

For example, AI chatbots can handle customer inquiries around the clock, providing immediate support and reducing customer wait times for human agents. This 24/7 capability is especially beneficial for multinational companies with international customers or those seeking assistance outside regular business hours.

AI-based routing of support tickets directly to human agents who are skilled and available to assist without an extended wait time or bouncing around from agent to agent will be particularly helpful to customers.

AI models can quickly analyze customer data and tailor responses accordingly, offering personalized recommendations and solutions. For support organizations who may use traditional templates for consistency when communicating with customers, this AI integration creates a more engaging experience for customers, making them feel valued and understood.

The ability of AI to understand complex questions and requests, even if they're phrased in informal or ambiguous language, eliminates the need for customers to repeat themselves or struggle to articulate their issues. AI can suggest real-time responses and solutions to customer service agents, helping them handle complex inquiries more effectively. Real-time responses can be especially helpful for new agents or those dealing with unfamiliar issues.

AI can be used to automatically generate and update knowledge base articles based on similar past successful solutions offered to customers and new product features, ensuring that customer service agents can access the latest information about products, services, and troubleshooting steps. This access to past successful solutions reduces the time and effort required for humans to keep knowledge bases current at all times.

AI can translate customer inquiries and responses in real time, providing support in multiple languages. This expands the reach of customer service teams and caters to a global audience.

Through sentiment analysis, AI can analyze customer interactions in real time and identify areas where agents can improve. This feedback can be used to provide in-the-moment, targeted coaching and additional development opportunities. AI can detect when a customer is getting frustrated during a conversation, as well as monitor longitudinal sentiment trends for the organization.

AI can automate repetitive tasks, such as data entry and scheduling appointments, freeing up agents' time to focus on providing personalized support to customers.

Requiring all human support agents to learn how AI can help them throughout their customer engagement is key to the role evolution in the reactive support engagement area, where AI is the prime assistant. AI can help you learn how to prompt the AI model to return the best results, rely on AI for help completing mundane or repetitive tasks, and help you communicate with clarity, empathy, and intent.

Retention Support

As we touched on previously, a company's brand image is critical for its success and is highly influenced by the quality and consistency of customer service. A positive brand image contributes to a growing customer base, customers' purchasing decisions, and, ultimately, their loyalty to the brand itself.

Great support agents not only solve the issue the customer is concerned with but also take it a step further and provide additional information to ensure the customer is set up for success. Support agents can help their customers via knowledge article sharing, suggesting additional helpful solutions and products, and/or empowering the customer with information to help themselves if the issue arises again. AI could be greatly utilized in customizing, compiling, and sharing this information with customers, reducing the support agent's time spent on these activities.

By deeply understanding your customer's desires and future goals, AI can assist in helping support agents up-sell or cross-sell products and solutions by offering suggestions in line with a customer's needs. AI integration at this stage can also help identify these sales opportunities and flag customers for potential ad campaigns and sales force engagement.

Depending on the retention strategy and level of AI integration, AI will likely assist support agents in this area by taking on many time-consuming and mundane tasks. Associated tasks could include helping identify and hand off sales leads to sales teams and compiling resources designed to empower customers in the future, freeing up support agents to focus on other critical customer engagement activities requiring a human touch.

This era promises a future where AI-driven customer support is more proactive, personalized, and effective, continuously learning and adapting to meet customers' ever-changing needs. While many fear job displacement as a result of AI integration, there are immense possibilities that AI can bring to make support roles more fulfilling and challenging. American community organizer and author Saul Alinsky underscores this point: "Evolution is inevitable, and it's time to ride the wave of change. The threat is usually more terrifying than the thing itself."

New Support Roles with the Advent of AI

With all these different customer touchpoints and opportunities to integrate AI, we discussed many existing support roles that will need to evolve to work in concert with AI innovation. In addition, new roles will need to be defined and funded to ensure successful AI adoption in customer service organizations. New roles will continually be added to this list as the technology advances.

Exciting new roles include:

- **AI strategist for support:** This role involves understanding the unique business needs of support and potential AI integration points to best define the AI strategy. They identify the areas where AI can be implemented throughout the customer support journey.
- **Support data scientists:** This role is responsible for developing and training AI models. They use their expertise in deep machine learning to create AI systems to meet the business's needs aligned with the AI strategy.
- **AI ethics officer:** While this role might live in the support organization, it's important to have someone dedicated to ensuring that the AI systems in support are designed and used ethically, respecting customer privacy and data security. They should be fully connected to the broader company's responsible AI strategy.

- **Support content strategist:** This role involves planning, developing, and managing the structure of support content, including knowledge base articles, troubleshooting steps, and product feature information. The goal is to create a system that is intuitive to navigate, easy to access and update, and can scale with the business.

- **Support content curators:** Content curators find and organize support content and ensure it is formatted and ready for AI model ingestion. Typically, they source content from multiple sources, which is then mapped to the appropriate AI content strategy for easy use.

- **Support content creators:** These roles are responsible for producing content that is easily ingested and used by the AI model in a way that ensures reliable and accurate output. This content is normally support-based content used by customers, AI bots, or support agents to answer customer queries and provide detailed issue resolution. They also ensure the support content is consistent, accurate, and up to date.

- **Content program/project manager:** The content PM is a project or program manager dedicated to overseeing content curation and creation and the content library. Depending on the content library's size, this role could be large or small. If there are many content resources to be indexed, this role can be big and time-consuming. Also, tasks may be required to convert content to a different format more easily ingested into the model, depending on how content is formatted. It's helpful for the content project manager to be steeped in the subject to better understand the inventory and address any content gaps. The content PM will be responsible for the content creation timeline, project management for content creators, coverage and gap analysis, recruiting authors or SMEs, and working with model builders on content formatting. This role could also play a part in responsible AI reviews, especially early in the project, by understanding how to scan content for bias and recruit diverse reviewers and SMEs for content validation. The content PM can also help keep content creators on task and motivated. Rewards, praise, formal remits, and other techniques may be required to keep the content creators involved in a constant effort to improve content.

- **Prompt engineer:** This role is responsible for designing and testing the prompts that guide the AI model for use in customer interactions aligned with the organization's goals. They also monitor the AI model's performance and feedback and adjust prompts as needed.

- **AI trainer:** This role is responsible for training and improving the AI model for accurate outputs. This role is less technical than a data scientist. They aggregate feedback and work with content creators to help improve the quality of the source content. They also help troubleshoot and fix any issues or errors arising in the AI systems.

- **AI analyst:** An AI analyst's role is to measure and evaluate the success of AI models. They analyze data to track and evaluate the AI tools' effectiveness and efficiency metrics. They also identify and recommend opportunities for additional innovation and improvement.

As customer service organizations implement AI, new skill sets, roles, and career paths will emerge as current roles evolve and adapt to the new technology. Roles will require technical, creative, and interpersonal skills to succeed in support organizations.

Adapting roles will be important, though not all roles will be brand new. For example, many existing roles will retain their core function, but their focus and daily tasks will change. Current roles with a new focus could include:

- Program management roles to manage AI projects, including content creation and schedules
- Data science/data analysis roles to understand subject matter expert feedback from initial deployments
- Support engineer roles to greatly empathize with customers and solve their deep technical problems

There are many opportunities to get people involved in this new era while maintaining some semblance of stability. Remember, AI is an enhancer, not a substitute for human intelligence and empathy.

Preparing Your Workforce for the Future

Now that you have your AI strategy defined and are beginning to communicate, you'll want to approach the topic of role evolution with sensitivity, honesty, and a forward-looking perspective.

Here are nine key points to consider as part of this communication— and it should be a discussion, with feedback welcome, not just one-way communication.

- **Acknowledgment of change and impact:** It's really important to be honest and direct. Even if timelines and degree of impact are unknown, you must acknowledge that change is coming. If you try to sugarcoat it, you are doing your people a disservice. They see what's coming, and as a leader, you will look out of touch if you try to be overly positive with only great things to say. Start with openly acknowledging the reality of the situation and the impact of implementing AI and automation, which will absolutely change the current job landscape. It's important to recognize employees' concerns and anxieties regarding their jobs. Show empathy toward anyone whose role may be affected in some way by AI implementation. This sets a tone of understanding and respect for the challenges ahead and opens the door for healthy discussion and a trusting relationship.

- **Commitment to transparency:** Again, people can see AI is coming, and it will become increasingly visible as AI models improve. You must commit publicly to transparency. You will strengthen your role as a leader by sharing more, even if the news isn't what employees want to hear. You must commit to maintaining transparency throughout the transition process. This involves sharing what you and the leadership team know about upcoming changes as soon as possible, including which roles will have changes, the expected change timeline, and how decisions are being made. You need to balance your message with the hard truth combined with an expression of optimism, reskilling opportunities, transition timelines, etc. Transparency helps build trust and allows employees to feel more secure, knowing they will have time to prepare for what's coming. Employ open communication practices discussed in earlier chapters.

- **Emphasis on reskilling and upskilling opportunities:** You want to highlight your personal commitment and the organization's commitment to supporting employees through reskilling and upskilling programs. Even if informal, it is important to be open and honest about what it takes to gain the skills necessary for any role shifts. Training opportunities could range from formal training to time off for learning to creating knowledge-sharing forums. There are many ways to do this, and it's critical to explain early how the organization plans to support and invest in training and development programs to help employees adapt to new roles or enhance their skills to work alongside AI technologies. Doing so demonstrates a commitment to the workforce's future and the value placed on employees' growth and adaptability. Transparency makes a big difference. If employees expect company-provided training, which is not part of the plan, inform them early so they are not surprised. One idea would be to give your professionals something in return as you see productivity gains from AI in customer service and support. For example, if a support engineer can do their current work in 35 hours instead of 40, they control what they do with those extra 5 hours, provided learning and reskilling are emphasized. You don't have to offer this forever, but this is a great way to foster goodwill, at least initially.

- **Vision for the future and new opportunities:** This is deliberately not the first item on this list. Vision won't make a difference without transparency or acknowledgment of change. However, people want to know that you have a clear vision of how AI integration will benefit the organization and its customers, including creating new job opportunities, improving job quality, and enhancing products and services. Emphasize how these changes will position the company—and your organization—for long-term success and sustainability and how your employees are vital to achieving this future. See also Chapter 4, "Vision of Success."

- **Support systems and resources:** Walk through the support systems and resources available to employees. You need to engage your leadership, HR, and finance teams early, probably well ahead of any deployments, to develop guidelines/policies and investment plans for the resources you will need to help employees through this massive change. These could include career counseling, job placement services, mental health resources, financial planning assistance, work visa support, and many others. Making sure employees know there is a support network in place can help alleviate some of the stress and uncertainty associated with change.

- **Engagement and dialogue:** It's critical to encourage and maintain an open dialogue and engagement with employees. Invite them to share their thoughts, concerns, and ideas about the transition to AI. This can be through forums, surveys, or town hall meetings. There should *always* be an anonymous option. Consider bringing in outsiders to help facilitate. Listening to employees helps you understand their concerns and can yield valuable insights into how the transition can be managed more effectively. It also helps you understand where people feel most at risk and the topics they are most passionate about. It fosters a culture of inclusion, where employees feel their voices are heard and valued. It's important because in the future, even if they are displaced, depending on your business, these people could be your customers or working for competitors, so having an open dialog and willingness to listen and engage will be critical to future success.

- **Flexible transition plans:** As part of your leadership planning, consider that employee needs and situations will differ. An early-in-career new hire may have different requirements and be impacted differently than a caregiver, pregnant mother, or new dad. It's important to emphasize your organization's commitment to flexible transition plans considering individual employee needs. Recognize each employee's unique situation and offer personalized support wherever possible,

such as providing different timelines for transition, part-time training options, or remote work opportunities to accommodate a variety
of personal circumstances. This once-in-a-generation transition to AI
might require some adjustments. You can show a strong commitment
to supporting employees as workers and individuals with diverse needs
during this time of change.

- **Reassurance on ethical considerations:** This is an important area to
  consider. It's likely a discussion regarding ethical AI is already happening, and removing bias, offensive content, and so on is critical.
  You should address how AI will be implemented in a way that respects
  privacy, ensures fairness, and promotes inclusivity. By openly discussing the ethical framework guiding AI deployment, leaders can alleviate
  concerns about the misuse of technology and reinforce the organization's values. Again, no clear guidance on what this messaging should
  be, but you need to consider what it means to you and your organization so as not to come across as inauthentic. See also Chapter 11,
  "Responsible AI and Ethical Considerations in Customer Support."

- **Community engagement and economic contributions:** It's important
  in your messaging to highlight the organization's role in contributing to
  the broader community and economy through the transition to AI. This
  might involve initiatives to partner with non-profit organizations, support
  local job creation, partnerships with educational institutions to prepare the future workforce, or investments in technologies that address
  societal challenges. You need to be aware of what's happening across
  all industries, and if you are not involved in partnerships or supportive
  of broader community efforts, then start those collaborations sooner
  rather than later. It will help people engage if you can showcase how the
  organization intends to use AI for the greater good, even if indirectly.
  It can also help frame the transition in a positive light, demonstrating a
  commitment to not just corporate success but also societal progress.

By focusing on these important points—and there are likely many others
specific to your business—you can address the challenges of AI and role
evolution in a way that is constructive, supportive, and geared toward the
future. It's about balancing the need for organizational progress with the
well-being and development of your workforce.

Real-World AI Adaptation

In this part of the chapter, we provide some examples of AI adaptation across a wide variety of domains that you can tailor to help craft your messaging for your organization. By leading with an angle designed to inspire people to dive in headfirst and embrace the new technology in a way that mirrors some great examples in history, you'll be able to allay fears of displacement with a vision that not only acknowledges that change is coming but also celebrates the potential for growth and evolution.

These examples are not all applicable in every circumstance, and we won't go into a lot of detail here, but hopefully this can spark your imagination to underscore that this transition, which holds a little apprehension for all of us, is not a new thing. Whether it's human or natural science, the "adapt or die" precipice has a long history we can draw from to help people find their own paths forward.

Nature offers some of the most profound and compelling lessons in adaptation. The Darwinian concept of evolution, where species evolve to survive in ever-changing environments, serves as a powerful metaphor for today's workplace. Just as animals and single-cell organisms develop new traits to thrive in their habitats, customer service and support professionals can acquire new skills and adapt to technological advancements surrounding them, turning potential displacement or existential threats into opportunities for growth and innovation.

The art world provides equally stirring narratives. Countless artists, musicians, and actors have faced the quandary of how to adapt and set new trends to incorporate new technologies to stave off what would be certain obsolescence. Yet history is filled with incredible stories about those who embraced change and thrived, reinventing their craft and, in the process, discovering new forms of expression and reaching wider audiences with unparalleled success. These stories exemplify resilience and the ability to evolve without losing one's essence but rather enriching it.

The "adapt or die" principle is evident in business. This concept is not only the expertise of single-celled organisms—companies that have navigated the tumultuous waters of technological disruption often emerge stronger, embracing innovation, retraining their workforce, and often completely reinventing their business models. These are not mere random tales of survival but stories of transformation and triumph, where embracing change has opened new avenues for success. The examples are many and offer the opportunity to draw great parallels to the challenges we face in integrating AI into customer service and support.

These narratives—whether from nature, the arts, or the business world— all serve as a beacon of inspiration. They demonstrate that adaptation is not about the loss but more optimistically about transformation and growth. In 2000, Netflix tried to sell its business to Blockbuster for $50 million. Blockbuster declined and laughed them out of the office. Today, Netflix is worth almost $250 billion—with a B—and Blockbuster barely exists.[1] Adapt or die is nothing new. Stories can be a source of strength and a reminder that with the right mindset and skills, they can ride the wave of technological change, not as passive bystanders but as active participants shaping their own futures.

The AI world is very new, and we don't know what the future holds. However, we *do* know that we'll get there sooner if we have engagement, curiosity, and participation across the organization. In doing so, we can transform apprehension into aspiration, fostering a workplace environment where continuous learning, adaptability, and innovation are encouraged and celebrated. This approach alleviates fears and positions both individuals and organizations to thrive in an AI-augmented future.

We need to collectively tackle it as a team, get excited about the future, not live in fear, and leave our future to be decided for us.

As the following examples show, life, work, and creative pursuit have always been about learning and adaptation. Darwin's Survival of the Fittest theory illustrates this in nature, but there are hundreds of examples beyond nature. As we embark on the journey of our coexistence with machines in this new world, it's important that you, as a leader, use historical examples to show that what we are going through now is not unique to this generation—or even to the human race. The need to learn and adapt has been important for millions—probably hundreds of millions—of years. We offer this list of examples across domains to spur your imagination to find the best story for you and your organization to illustrate that we are not the first to "adapt" or face obsolescence (or worse). We will leave it to you to research and choose the stories that resonate most with you.

The idea of adapting to a changing world is visible in almost all experiences. We urge you to explore the following examples as thought-provoking, creative inspiration as you think through how you want to convey the tidal change of AI to your organization and workforce.

Nature

There is no more fundamental example of adaptation than what we see in nature. Going back to single-celled organisms evolving over time toward the first tadpole to grow legs and walk out of the water to find food. There are many scientific terms to describe adaption and hundreds of scientific studies of the beauty of nature's ability to evolve with the times. Some nature-related examples to get your creative juices flowing include:

- Darwin's survival of the fittest
- Symbiosis
- Homoplasy
- Competitive exclusion principle
- Red Queen effect and Red King hypothesis
- Natural selection and algorithmic optimization
- Ecosystem dynamics and AI systems
- Biomimicry
- Predator–Prey dynamics
- Resource allocation and foraging theory

Technology and Labor

The influence of invention and "technological" advancement in adaptation are also long established. It's estimated that about 800,000 years ago, humans discovered the ability to control fire. This changed everything in many ways. Can we say this is equivalent to the change we'll see with AI in customer support? Dramatic, perhaps, but it's a good story to illustrate that change is not new. Below are several great examples of technological shifts that changed the way we live and work:

- Controlled use of fire
- Agricultural tools
- The wheel
- Paper
- Printing press
- Steam engine
- Assembly line
- Programmable logic controllers
- Automated teller machines (ATMs)
- Internet
- Mobile phones

Artists and Musicians

Artists and musicians are probably the most famous domains where we see bold adaptations. Envision Impressionist painters free from constraints and how they moved into the art of nature in ways the Realists never did. There are likely hundreds of examples in this realm; this list is meant to spark your imagination:

- Cave painters
- Greek vase painters
- Leonardo da Vinci
- Pablo Picasso
- Vincent Van Gogh
- Claude Monet
- Georgia O'Keefe
- Henri Matisse
- Alphonse Mucha
- Salvador Dali

- Johann Sebastian Bach
- Wolfgang Amadeus Mozart
- David Bowie
- The Beatles
- Bob Dylan
- Madonna
- Elton John
- U2
- Prince

Authors and Writing Styles

There is a long list of authors who broke new ground in the technology they developed, the way in which they wrote, or the genre or style they used. The idea of adapting to a changing world is visible in almost every great literary piece. Some examples for you to explore and take inspiration from include:

- Egyptian cuneiform
- Early religious texts
- Charles Dickens
- George R.R. Martin
- F. Scott Fitzgerald
- Jane Austen

- Emily Dickinson
- Henry David Thoreau
- Agatha Christie
- Ian Fleming
- Stephen King
- J.K. Rowling

Actors

The journey of actors over time clearly marks signs of adaptation. Not only do they alter their self to fit the needs of the character they play, they also adapt to different types of roles over their career. Not to mention adapting to the media style of the time, such as stage performance, silent film, animation, live action, etc. Their willingness to reinvent themselves and embrace change can be an inspiration for all:

- Edwin Booth
- Eleanora Duse
- Sarah Bernhardt (1844)
- Charlie Chaplin
- Mickey Mouse
- Marlon Brando
- James Dean
- Marilyn Monroe
- Charlize Theron
- Leonardo DiCaprio
- Nicole Kidman

Companies

Companies often have to reinvent themselves as they face disruptive environmental forces in which they operate, such as economic upturns or downturns, technological shifts, or changing customer needs or preferences. Those companies that survive adapt to the change instead of resisting it. Following are some companies that have adapted rather than resisted change:

- Kodak
- Nokia
- Ford Motor Company
- General Electric
- Apple
- Netflix
- Microsoft
- Nintendo
- LEGO
- IBM
- Harley-Davidson
- The Coca-Cola Company
- Harrods
- Unilever
- Federal Express
- Tata

Inventors

In their quest for innovation, inventors face countless obstacles. Their unrelenting persistence despite failure—experimenting with different materials, tweaking designs, adjusting models—ultimately leads to transformative breakthroughs. These breakthroughs often change our world and propel innovation further—adding to the never-ending cycle of adaptation. Examples of inventors that have changed our world include:

- Leonardo da Vinci
- Galileo Galilei
- Johannes Gutenberg
- Ada Lovelace
- Charles Babbage
- Thomas Edison
- Nikola Tesla
- Douglas Turing
- Grace Hopper
- James Dyson

- Alexander Graham Bell
- Alfred Nobel
- George Washington Carver
- Benjamin Franklin
- Rudolf Diesel
- Ching Shih
- Hassan Kamel Al-Sabbah
- Rafa'a al-Tahtawi
- Sakichi Toyoda

We are entering a new era of generational change. Rest assured that AI will change everything. People's work will change. As an organizational leader, people will look to you for reassurance. Reassurance that their jobs are safe, that life will go on. But there are no guarantees. Your response should draw upon lessons from history. Organisms and world leaders have taught us that progress sometimes requires change.

We have seen throughout history that humans have always adapted to new technology in the workforce. The printing press, initially a threat to the manuscript illuminators, opened the doors for widespread distribution of the Lutheran Bible. The power loom disrupted spinners but changed the economics of clothing manufacturing. The steam engine changed the distribution of beef from the Chicago stockyards. What will AI do? Will people adapt and new types of jobs be created, or will humans stand on the sideline, watching the machines take over our lives?

These examples illustrate how dynamic growth, creativity, and progress come from change and the ability to adapt. Whether in nature, particular industries or careers or the business world, those who can adapt will thrive. In this way, the changes being introduced through the advent of AI are no different than what we've experienced throughout history.

Policy Perspectives

As we enter this new era when AI and humans working together, it's important to consider a variety of policy perspectives to help ensure a strong partnership between humans and machines. The world of AI is absolutely upon us. AI technology will continue to improve at such a rapid pace that we will continue to witness AI taking over tasks that humans have historically performed. We need to be deliberate about how and where we draw the line and what safeguards we need to put in place to ensure that society benefits from a healthy balance between humans and machines. To achieve this balance, fostering an environment where continuous learning and adaptation are encouraged is crucial, enabling humans to work alongside AI effectively.

As we've discussed often, ethical considerations must be at the forefront of AI development to protect against misuse and ensure equitable access to technology for all parts of society. Finally, public and private sector collaboration is essential to establish standards and regulations that guide the responsible development, deployment, and use of AI, ensuring it serves everyone equally.

As we enter an era when machines may displace human workers, how should we think about changes such as a universal basic income (UBI) for all? And perhaps the idea of implementing a robot tax could be considered to mitigate the economic impact of automation on the workforce, providing funds to support social welfare and job transition programs. Additionally, investing in reskilling initiatives is vital to prepare the current workforce for the shift toward more technologically advanced job roles, ensuring that no one is left behind in the transition.

Increased Investment in STEAM Education and Training

In this era of rapid technological advancement, when AI and machines are becoming integral to our daily lives and work, the importance of increased investment in STEAM[2] (science, technology, engineering, arts, and mathematics) education cannot be overstated. As AI systems and automation take on more tasks traditionally performed by humans, the demand for a workforce proficient in STEAM fields is growing exponentially. We need students who are keeping pace with AI by staying current in the science, technology, engineering, arts, and math fields. This investment is crucial for fostering innovation, maintaining a competitive edge in a global economy, and ensuring societal resilience against the challenges posed by AI and automation.

STEAM education can help equip students with critical thinking, problem-solving, and technical skills necessary to understand and interact with AI and machine technologies. By investing in STEAM, we are preparing future generations for careers that do not yet exist, ensuring they are adaptable and capable of driving forward the innovations that will shape our future. Moreover, a strong foundation in STEAM disciplines is essential for developing responsible and ethical AI and ensuring that technologies are designed to benefit humanity as a whole.

Universal Basic Income

Universal basic income (UBI) is a social welfare proposal in which all citizens of a given population regularly receive a minimum income through an unconditional transfer payment (without a means test or needing to work). In contrast, a guaranteed minimum income is paid only to those who do not already receive enough income to live on. A UBI would be received independently of any other income. It is sometimes called a full basic income if the level is sufficient to meet a person's basic needs (at or above the poverty line). If one's earnings are less than that amount, it may be called a "partial basic income." No country has yet introduced either, although there have been numerous pilot projects, and the idea is discussed in many countries. Some have labeled UBI as *utopian* because of its historical origin.[3]

As we enter the age of an AI Revolution, with its significant influence on the workforce, the role of universal basic income becomes increasingly important. We really don't know how to predict the days ahead. Will AI create new types of jobs like the Industrial Revolution or Internet-era technologies did? Or will humans find themselves on the outside looking in?

The automation of jobs traditionally performed by humans could lead to widespread displacement, exacerbating unemployment and economic inequality. In this context, UBI offers a potential solution to cushion the economic impact on individuals, providing a safety net that allows people to navigate the transition more smoothly. It could foster an environment where individuals are encouraged to pursue education, retraining, and personal development without the immediate pressure of job loss. Moreover, UBI could stimulate innovation and entrepreneurship by providing individuals with the financial stability to take calculated risks. As the economy transforms with AI, UBI could play a critical role in ensuring that the benefits of technological advancements are broadly shared, helping to mitigate social tensions and promote a more inclusive society. The introduction of UBI, in tandem with other supportive policies, could help create a workforce that is resilient, adaptable, and prepared for the challenges and opportunities of an AI-driven future.

Robot Tax

A robot tax is a legislative strategy to balance the replacement of workers by machines and bolster the social safety net for displaced people. While the automation of manual labor has been contemplated since before the Industrial Revolution, the issue has received increased discussion in the 21st century due to newer developments such as machine learning.[4] The aim is to mitigate the economic impact of job displacement and fund social welfare programs.

As we navigate the age of AI and its profound influence on the workforce, the concept of a robot tax emerges as a critical tool for addressing the challenges posed by the automation of human work. By taxing employers for using robots and AI that substitute for human employees, governments can generate revenue to support social initiatives, including retraining programs for workers displaced by technology. This approach seeks to counterbalance the loss of income tax revenue due to reduced employment and encourages companies to consider the social implications of rapidly adopting automation.

In addition, the funds accumulated through a robot tax could be instrumental in investing in education, particularly in STEAM (STEM + Arts) fields, preparing future generations for a job market intertwined with AI and technology. Implementing a robot tax could serve as a strategic measure to ensure that the economic benefits of automation are more evenly distributed across society, helping to alleviate inequality and fostering an adaptable and resilient workforce in the face of technological progress.

As we start to see AI, robots, and automation deployed in more workforce scenarios, it's important to think about how, or if, governments will shift some of the burden of worker re-education to employers versus the government or society.

Worker Protection in Technologically Advanced Workplaces

Data protection and privacy laws, such as the General Data Protection Regulation (GDPR) in the European Union, set strict guidelines for how personal data should be collected, processed, and stored by organizations, including those in technologically advanced workplaces. These laws ensure that employees' and customers' privacy rights are respected and protected in the age of big data and AI.

There are a number of fast-moving regulatory efforts to help protect workers in the world of AI. The salient point is that as we move to an AI-driven world, we need society and government to protect users and data, workers, and employers as AI gets smarter and smarter.

Regulatory Frameworks for Ethical AI Deployment in the Workforce

The deployment of AI brings with it transformative potential across various sectors, from healthcare and education to finance and transportation. However, this rapid technological advancement also raises significant ethical concerns, including privacy violations, algorithmic bias, job displacement, and security risks. Regulatory frameworks for ethical AI deployment are crucial to navigate these challenges, ensuring that AI technologies are developed and used in ways that are beneficial to society without infringing on individual rights or exacerbating inequalities.

Workforce Reskilling and Upskilling Initiatives

The organization must recognize the importance of allowing time for upskilling or reskilling of employees. For leaders of customer support and service organizations, AI can bring huge competitive advantages beyond any cost savings they can get from role elimination. As mentioned previously, it will not be long before the combination of humans plus machines will be significantly better than either on their own, so building a culture where humans feel they can reskill and find new ways to contribute will make your organization better. Following are some reasons why it's important to value human contributions in this era of AI:

- **Maintaining a competitive edge:** Organizations that invest in reskilling and upskilling their workforce can stay ahead in rapidly changing industries by harnessing new technologies efficiently.

- **Employee retention:** Supporting continuous learning and development helps retain top talent by demonstrating an organizational commitment to employee career growth and satisfaction.

- **Adaptability to technological changes:** Training programs can help prepare employees to adapt to technological advancements, ensuring the organization remains agile and responsive to market demands.

- **Fostering innovation:** Upskilled employees bring fresh perspectives and innovative solutions, driving creativity and improvement in products and services.

- **Closing skill gaps:** By identifying and addressing skill shortages within their workforce, organizations can avoid the productivity pitfalls of rapid technological change.

- **Enhancing company reputation:** Organizations that invest in their employees' growth are more attractive to prospective talent and are often seen as industry leaders. AI will change the employment landscape and organizations on the cutting edge will be the ones who flourish.

- **Boosting employee morale and engagement:** Employees who feel supported in their professional development are more engaged, motivated, and committed to their organization's goals.

- **Reducing turnover costs:** Investing in current employees' development is often more cost-effective than recruiting new talent, reducing turnover and associated costs.

- **Building a versatile workforce:** A workforce with diverse skills is better equipped to take on varied roles and responsibilities, enhancing operational flexibility.

- **Corporate social responsibility:** Supporting employees through transitions reflects positively on a company's ethical stance, contributing to a positive social impact by mitigating the adverse effects of automation on the workforce.

Preparing for the Future: Individual and Collective Actions

Where AI and automation, robotics, the Internet of Things (IoT), and machine learning transform the job market, individuals can be proactive and take positive steps to ensure their skills remain in demand and machines do not easily replace them. First and foremost, focusing on cultivating soft skills such as critical thinking, creativity, empathy, fun, play, sarcasm, and complex problem-solving is crucial. These human-centric skills are difficult for AI to replicate and are highly valued across all domains and industries.

Engaging in continuous learning and professional development is another key strategy. This involves staying updated with industry trends and technological advancements and acquiring new skills and certifications, particularly in areas where human oversight is required, like ethical decision-making, strategic planning, and leadership.

In addition, individuals should consider diversifying their skill set to include digital literacy and understanding basic principles of AI and machine learning, which can enhance their ability to work alongside advanced technologies rather than be replaced by them. Employees must understand the state of AI, and organizations must encourage and facilitate employee education in the age of AI.

Networking and building professional relationships can also provide insights into emerging skills and job opportunities. Lastly, adopting a flexible and adaptable mindset toward career progression can open up new pathways that may be less susceptible to automation, ensuring long-term employability in an AI-driven future. The world is changing quickly, and we all need to stay up to date.

Organizations will play a pivotal role in supplementing the efforts of individuals to remain indispensable in an AI-driven world. To support their workforce effectively, companies should foster a culture of lifelong learning by providing access to training and development programs tailored to the evolving needs of the industry. This could include workshops, online courses, and seminars focused on emerging technologies, digital literacy, and soft skills enhancement.

Another strategic approach is investing in helping employees develop a personalized career development plan. By understanding each employee's unique aspirations and potential, organizations can offer targeted upskilling opportunities that align with the individual's career goals and the company's strategic direction.

Organization leaders must create an environment that encourages innovation and experimentation. Employees should feel empowered to propose new ideas, explore interdisciplinary projects, and apply their new skills in practical settings. This leverages human creativity and fosters a sense of ownership and value in their contributions beyond what AI can achieve.

Moreover, implementing mentorship and coaching programs can facilitate knowledge sharing and reinforce a supportive community within the workplace. Experienced professionals can guide less experienced colleagues through the complexities of adapting to technological advancements and enhancing collective intelligence—especially those who have lived through previous eras of technological change.

Organizations can anticipate future skill requirements and identify potential gaps early by engaging in strategic workforce planning. In actively preparing their employees for future roles and responsibilities, companies can ensure a smooth transition to increasingly automated environments, maintaining a competitive edge while demonstrating a commitment to their workforce's well-being and professional growth.

Given the transformative potential of AI and the historical context of human adaptation to technological change, it's clear that we stand on the cusp of a new era where the symbiosis between humans and AI can lead to unprecedented opportunities. As we embark on this new journey with AI, let us remember that every technological leap has been a canvas for human creativity, resilience, and growth, paving the way for us to rise to new heights of innovation and collaboration.

Embracing AI with foresight and wisdom, we cannot stand on the sidelines but must put ourselves at the forefront of this new frontier, where our partnership with technology nurtures the seeds of future jobs, industries, and ways of life that are as of yet unimagined, ensuring that the narrative of human progress is one of shared success and enduring legacy.

Endnotes

1   Cagnassola, Mary Ellen, Giella, Lauren. 2021. "Fact Check: Did Blockbuster Turn Down Chance to Buy Netflix for $50 Million." *Newsweek*. March 11, 2021. [https://www.newsweek.com/fact-check-did-blockbuster-turn-down-chance-buy-netflix-50-million-1575557].

2   Wikipedia contributors. "STEAM fields." Wikipedia, The Free Encyclopedia. February 25, 2024. [https://en.wikipedia.org/wiki/STEAM_fields].

3   Wikipedia contributors. "Universal basic income." Wikipedia, The Free Encyclopedia. February 20, 2024. [https://en.wikipedia.org/wiki/Universal_basic_income].

4   Wikipedia contributors. "Robot tax." Wikipedia, The Free Encyclopedia. February 5, 2024. [https://en.wikipedia.org/wiki/Robot_tax].

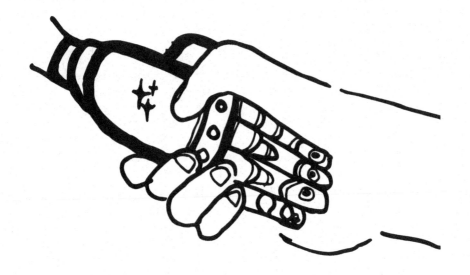

PART IV

Gamified Learning and the Future of Work in Support

Integrating artificial intelligence (AI) into customer service and support organizations is nothing less than transformative. It has the potential to generate unprecedented innovation and improvements with the seamless integration of technology and human expertise, which will open up new possibilities in the industry.

Gameplay is steeped in history to teach valuable lessons and foster collaboration. Humans and animals both use play as a way to teach and learn. We explore the idea of gamification to enhance learning and increase the adoption of AI. It is a fun strategy that also catalyzes innovation. In addition, it can potentially drive additional engagement and foster a work culture of continuous improvement and creativity.

As you settle into your vision of what AI will deliver for your business, understand that leading in the era of AI will require a multifaceted approach. It will require you to comprehend and embrace the complexities, harness the potential AI can deliver, and drive unprecedented value for your organization. Your employees will look to you to set an example in embracing the changes that AI integration will surely introduce.

In looking forward to what's possible, the future of work within customer service is ready to be redefined by AI's capabilities and unlock untapped potential. The integration of AI in customer service and support organizations further paves the way for a future of work that is more productive and efficient and more enjoyable and fulfilling.

As we close out our discussion on the AI Revolution in customer service and support, the next steps for the practical application of AI in your business are not just about technological adoption but also about strategic integration, cultural adaptation, and ensuring that AI tools augment the human element rather than replace it. The ultimate goal we are all trying to accomplish is to enhance the overall customer experience, and by integrating AI into your organization, you will be able to set new standards in customer service excellence. The practical application of AI in customer service is not a distant dream. The journey toward AI integration is one of discovery, innovation, and excellence that we're all in together. Welcome to the revolution!

16

Games, Play, and Novelty in the Age of AI

The creation of something new is not accomplished by the intellect but by the play instinct acting from inner necessity. The creative mind plays with the objects it loves.

—Carl Jung

AI promises to transform customer service, boosting efficiency, enabling personalized engagements, and extracting actionable customer insights from extensive datasets. This innovation equips service agents to offer faster responses and deliver the friendly and warm personal experience that customers truly value —a hallmark of customer care where services are customized to each customer's unique preferences, needs, and history. Imagine entering your local cafe where the barista knows your usual order. AI in customer service aspires to replicate this level of personal attention and familiarity, anticipating customer needs, providing tailored recommendations, and remembering previous interactions.

Such personalization makes customers feel recognized and valued and significantly boosts their satisfaction and loyalty toward a brand.

However, transitioning fully to AI-enhanced customer service is not straightforward and involves navigating a series of challenges. Effectively addressing these is key to ensuring AI's integration into customer service is as smooth and impactful as possible, unlocking its full potential to transform the customer experience.

Integrating AI into customer service is comparable to transplanting a new, more powerful engine into a classic car. The car is familiar and reliable; its controls are second nature to its driver. But the new engine, while promising a faster, smoother ride, is complex and unfamiliar. It requires new knowledge to operate and may not fit seamlessly into the well-worn grooves of the old machine. The driver, accustomed to the old ways, must now learn to navigate the enhanced power and responsiveness without stalling or crashing—translating into an organizational context. This means adapting to the enhanced capabilities of AI without disrupting the flow of daily operations.

Historically, implementing new technologies in the workplace has always been met with a blend of anticipation and apprehension. A historical parallel can be drawn from the introduction of personal computers in the workplace during the 1980s.[1] Initially met with skepticism, the potential of PCs was not immediately recognized, and employees were hesitant to abandon their trusted typewriters and paper files. However, as software programs became more user friendly and relevant, training programs were implemented and the personal computer became an indispensable tool in offices worldwide. The transition was facilitated by a gradual approach—starting with basic tasks like word processing and data entry—allowing employees to build confidence and proficiency.

Fast-forward to today: The introduction of AI presents a unique set of technical and cultural challenges. Technically, AI systems require the integration of sophisticated algorithms and data processing capabilities into existing IT infrastructures, which can be daunting for organizations without the required expertise. Culturally, employees fear that AI might usurp their roles—leading to job displacement—or alter their work so dramatically that it might render their current skills obsolete.

Moreover, AI is not a plug-and-play solution. It necessitates a foundational change in business processes and workflows. It requires employees to learn new tools and adapt to the dynamic nature of machine learning outputs. This evolving landscape can unsettle even the most adaptable employees, creating resistance deeply rooted in uncertainty and the discomfort of relinquishing established routines.

In this light, gamification can be seen as the oil that ensures the new engine runs smoothly within the old chassis. By turning the process of AI adoption into a game—with levels to achieve, points to earn, and rewards to unlock—employees are encouraged to engage with the technology, overcome challenges, and eventually master the new system in a way that feels natural and enjoyable. Just as games provide tutorials in the early stages to help players adjust, gamification in the workplace can guide employees through the AI learning curve, ensuring that by the end, they are not just passengers but skilled drivers of change.

Blogger Eric Zimmerman discusses gameplay as an artificial shared space for play within the broader context of real-life experiences. It's like an alternate world where you enter, engage in social interactions, and derive different understandings and meanings from your engagement and play.

In the following pages, we will explore the concept of gamification as an adoption strategy. By engaging with the challenges AI poses—such as the need for continuous learning and adaptation, the disruption of familiar processes, and the fear of redundancy—we set the stage for understanding how gamification can catalyze change. With its ability to make learning interactive and rewarding, gamification presents a compelling method to convert these challenges into opportunities for growth and engagement. It is a strategy that promises not just to transform resistance into enthusiasm, paving the way for a seamless fusion of AI into the daily rhythm of customer service and support.

Humans and Play: A Deeper Dive with Historical Context

Throughout history, humans and other animals have also used play as a learning method. Whether it's kittens, mock fighting to learn survival skills, or human children playing make-believe cooking or shopping to mimic adult behaviors, play has always been a strategy for learning.

As we enter into the world of AI, there's a lot of apprehension. Author Scott Eberle discussed play: "Scholars conventionally find play difficult to define because the concept is complex and ambiguous. The author proffers a definition of play that takes into consideration its dynamic character, posits six basic elements of play (anticipation, surprise, pleasure, understanding, strength, and poise), and explores some of their emotional, physical, and intellectual dimensions. He argues for a play ethos that recognizes play as evolution-based and developmentally beneficial. He insists, however, that, at its most elemental, play always promises fun. In this context, any activity that lacks these six elements, he contends, will not fully qualify as play."[2]

While play is not uniquely human, it offers an interesting intersection between the worlds of humans and machines. We read earlier about DeepMind's ability to "play" the game of Go better than the best human. But if we look at these six basic elements of play, where are the elements of anticipation, surprise, or pleasure? A large-scale, heavily-trained AI model executing machine learning algorithms doesn't promise fun, does it? Yes, it might "win" the game, but doesn't the game just become a math exercise at that point?

The idea of novelty and play have been an integral part of human experience since our very beginnings. As we move to a world where we coexist with machines and AI, play will become an even more important part of our symbiotic relationship. A computer vision application will never play peek-a-boo to learn trust like a young child would. Similarly, a human may never be able to learn the probability of an asteroid's impact by scanning the night sky the way AI might.

Play, at least at this stage of AI development, remains solely in the human domain—and while AI can learn rules and become skilled at following the roles to outperform humans at "games," the idea of using play to learn will continue to be an important component of the living animal kingdom.

Games with rules like chess and Go have been learned by machines, but hide and seek, charades, kids playing make-believe, and Ring Around the Rosie are still human-only domains.

We can use the idea of games and play—and the success of these techniques to teach—to help customer service and support professionals to better learn how to apply AI to their work. Through play, not only can these professionals enhance their skills, but they can also actively contribute to the improvement of AI systems. At the current stage, AI still requires human involvement; gamification facilitates interactions between AI-based systems and humans, leading to the collection of more labeled or feedback data. This iterative process, reinforced by human feedback through playful engagement, facilitates the enhancement and refinement of AI algorithms, thereby improving their effectiveness and accuracy.

At its core, gamification is the application of game design elements and principles in non-game contexts. It's about making activities that are not traditionally game-like more engaging, interactive, and fun by incorporating elements such as points, levels, challenges, and rewards. The concept aims to leverage the motivational power of games—the thrill of achievement, the excitement of competition, and the satisfaction of growth—to encourage desired behaviors in various settings like education, business, and more.

Historical Origins and Evolution

Games and play have been integral to human existence for thousands of years. The term *gamification* is relatively new, but the concept has roots that go far back in history:

Historical records indicate that elements akin to applying game mechanics have been used for centuries in work, education, and military training.

BUILDING OF MENKAURE

According to Egyptologists, the third pyramid of Giza—the pyramid of Menkaure—was built by large "gangs" of laborers. They were separated into two "teams," the "Friends of Menkaure" and the "Drunkards of Menkaure." The two teams would "tag" the stones with their team symbol to identify their team's contribution of work to the whole. We can imagine this as a form of early gamification.[3]

In education, the application of game-like elements can be traced back to initiatives like the Boy Scout movement, founded in 1908.[4] The Boy Scouts used a system of awarding badges to recognize and motivate members' achievements, a principle similar to modern gamification practices. This approach capitalizes on the intrinsic motivation of achieving status and recognition through badges.

Using game-like elements in military training, which can be seen as an early form of gamification, has a long and rich history. Historically, militaries have utilized various forms of simulations and strategy games to enhance training and strategic planning. This approach dates back centuries and has evolved significantly over time.

The ancient game of Petteia, originating in Greece around the 5th century BCE, stands out as a significant historical board game due to its strategic and complex nature.[5] Its roots reflect the strategic military nature of society at the time. The game, which involves a battle of wits between two players played on a grid board (similar to a modern chess or checkers board), was often used by military leaders to train in strategic thinking and decision-making. The game held high societal value and its importance often transcended recreational entertainment, as it was often used in education to teach tactics and strategy to young boys. Additionally, historical references in Greek literature suggest the game's widespread popularity.

With the advent of computer technology, military simulations took a significant leap forward. The first truly computerized war games were developed in the late 1940s and early 1950s, such as the *Air Defense Simulation*[6] and the *Carmonette*[7] series. These systems greatly reduced the manual work involved in traditional board games and allowed for more complex mathematical models and larger-scale simulations. This period marked the beginning of the transition to the sophisticated computer-simulated training environments used in the military today.

Along with the introduction of computers to the workplace in the 1980s, a technological revolution also took gamification to a new level. Frequent flyer programs, introduced during this era, brought forth the concept of gamified customer loyalty rewards. Airlines, like American Airlines, launched its AAdvantage program in 1981, beginning a new approach to customer engagement and retention.[8] Frequent-flyer programs are not just about accumulating and redeeming points. They also offer different tiers or levels of status, which can provide additional benefits and privileges. This tiered system adds another layer of gamification, creating a sense of progression and achievement for the participants.

The influence and success of these loyalty programs in the airline industry have been substantial. They have helped retain customers by rewarding their experience and inspired similar loyalty strategies in various other industries. The gamified elements of these programs, such as earning points, achieving status, and unlocking rewards, tap into the human psychological desire for achievement and recognition, making them an effective tool for customer engagement.

In the mid-2000s, badges as a form of virtual achievement gained prominence with platforms like Foursquare. Users were awarded badges for specific activities, such as checking in at different locations. This gamified aspect of Foursquare enhanced user engagement and encouraged repetitive use, turning the act of visiting and exploring new places into a game-like experience. This marked a shift toward social gamification, where individuals could showcase their achievements to their social networks. The success of badge systems contributed to the development of broader gamification strategies that focused on building communities and fostering social interactions.

Coining of the Term

British computer programmer Nick Pelling first introduced the term *gamification* in 2002.[9] Pelling conceptualized gamification while developing user interfaces for electronic devices and ATMs to make their usage more engaging and enjoyable. Despite coining the term in the early 2000s, it wasn't until around 2010 that the concept of gamification started gaining widespread recognition as well as significant attention in academic circles. Universities and researchers began to study its effects more rigorously, contributing to a deeper and more robust understanding of how and why gamification can be effective. This academic interest led to numerous studies and papers exploring gamification's psychological and sociological aspects and its impact on human behavior. The academic exploration of gamification has contributed to its validation as a legitimate field of study. This academic attention also played a role in refining the application of gamification, ensuring that it is used ethically and effectively to enhance user experiences without exploiting them.

Taiwanese-American businessman and one of the earliest pioneers in the industry of gamification, Yu-kai Chou, described it as follows: "Effective gamification is a combination of game design, game dynamics, behavioral economics, motivational psychology, UX/UI (user experience and user interface), neurobiology, technology platforms, as well as ROI-driving business implementations."[10]

Current State of Gamification and AI

The integration of gamification and AI has reached a pivotal stage, marking a significant evolution in how both technologies are applied to engage, educate, and motivate users across various sectors. This fusion has created highly sophisticated, adaptive, and personalized experiences, transforming the landscape of user engagement and interaction. Let's explore the current state of gamification and AI, highlighting key developments, applications, and the impact of their convergence.

Gamification Today: Diverse Applications Across Sectors

Gamification has transcended its initial applications in marketing and consumer engagement, becoming a vital tool in education, healthcare, corporate training, and behavior modification. Its principles are now used to:

- **Enhance learning:** Educational platforms incorporate game mechanics to motivate students, making learning more interactive and enjoyable. Gamification in education has improved retention rates, fostered engagement, and facilitated personalized learning paths.

- **Promote health and wellness:** Gamified health apps encourage healthy lifestyle choices, using rewards and challenges to motivate physical activity, diet tracking, and mental health exercises.

- **Drive employee engagement:** In the corporate world, gamification strategies are employed in training and development and onboarding processes and to boost productivity and employee satisfaction.

AI's Role in Enhancing Gamification

AI has significantly enhanced the capabilities of gamified systems through:

- **Personalization:** AI algorithms analyze user data to tailor experiences, challenges, and rewards to individual preferences and performance, making gamification more effective.

- **Adaptive learning systems:** In educational applications, AI enables the creation of adaptive learning environments that adjust in real-time to the learner's progress, providing personalized pathways that improve learning outcomes.

- **Behavior prediction:** AI's predictive analytics forecast user behaviors and preferences, allowing for the proactive customization of gamified experiences to keep users engaged and motivated.

- **Dynamic content generation:** AI facilitates the generation of new content, scenarios, and challenges, keeping the gamified experience fresh and ensuring long-term engagement.

Key Elements of Gamification

Gamification employs various components to create engaging and motivating experiences, both in digital environments and real-life contexts. Here's a detailed look at these key components:

- **Points:** Points are a fundamental element in gamification, serving as a quantifiable measure of progress or achievement. They provide immediate feedback and a sense of accomplishment, encouraging continued participation.

- **Badges:** Badges are visual symbols of accomplishments, skills, or milestones achieved by the user.[11] Research published in *Computers in Human Behavior* found that badges positively affect motivation, particularly when symbolizing personal achievement or status. They also add a collectible element that can be highly motivating.

- **Leaderboards:** Leaderboards rank users based on their performance or achievements, fostering a sense of competition. Leaderboards can increase motivation and performance, especially in competitive individuals. However, they must be designed carefully to avoid discouraging those lower on the leaderboard.

- **Levels:** Levels indicate a user's progression and are often linked to increasing difficulty or unlocking new content. Levels help maintain a sense of ongoing progress and challenge, essential for sustained engagement.

- **Challenges and quests:** These are specific tasks or objectives that users must complete, often within a set timeframe. Challenges and quests tap into the human desire for accomplishment and problem-solving, giving users a clear sense of purpose.

- **Feedback and rewards:** Immediate feedback and rewards for completing tasks or achieving goals. Feedback mechanisms are crucial for learning and motivation. Immediate rewards after task completion can enhance motivation and satisfaction.

- **Storytelling and narrative:** Incorporating a narrative or storyline into the gamification experience can greatly enhance engagement and emotional investment.

- **Social connectivity:** Social elements in gamification can foster a sense of community, allowing users to connect, collaborate, or compete with others. Social features can lead to higher user retention and engagement.

- **Customization and personalization:** Personalization allows users to customize aspects of their gamification experience and can increase the relevance and engagement of gamified systems and user satisfaction.

These components can create powerful and compelling experiences when strategically integrated into gamified systems. Gamification taps into various aspects of human psychology, including the need for achievement, social interaction, and personal growth. By leveraging these elements, gamification can effectively motivate, engage, and educate users in diverse contexts.

The Intersection of Gamification and Psychology

The intersection of gamification and psychology is a fascinating and multifaceted domain deeply rooted in understanding human behavior and motivation. This field explores how game mechanics can influence our actions, encourage learning, and drive engagement, leveraging psychological principles to create meaningful and compelling experiences.

Intrinsic versus Extrinsic Human Motivation

In gamification, understanding the dynamics of intrinsic and extrinsic motivation is key. These forms of motivation explain why people engage in certain behaviors and how they can be encouraged to continue those behaviors.

The self-determination theory (SDT) emphasizes three fundamental human needs: competence (feeling skilled and effective), autonomy (feeling in control of one's actions), and relatedness (feeling connected to others).[12] SDT plays a crucial role in understanding intrinsic and extrinsic motivation in gamification. Their work has been instrumental in exploring how these forms of motivation influence human behavior.

Intrinsic motivation is driven by personal satisfaction, curiosity, mastery, autonomy, and relatedness. For instance, a game that challenges players' skills or offers a captivating story can intrinsically motivate them to continue playing. In gaming, this could be the joy of solving a puzzle or the thrill of completing a challenging level.

In contrast, extrinsic motivation involves external rewards like points, badges, or leaderboards. While effective in the short term, extrinsic motivators might not sustain engagement over time without intrinsic elements.

According to the self-determination theory, intrinsic motivation is linked to higher-quality learning and well-being.[13] The theory also highlights the risks associated with extrinsic motivation, given that while extrinsic rewards can initially increase motivation, they may decrease intrinsic motivation over time, especially when the rewards are perceived as controlling or undermining autonomy. This phenomenon, known as the "over-justification effect," suggests that external rewards can diminish a person's inherent interest in an activity.[14]

The Role of Dopamine

Dopamine, often called the feel-good neurotransmitter (a chemical that ferries information between neurons in the brain), plays a crucial role in how we experience pleasure and reward. When a person achieves a goal or receives a reward, dopamine is released, creating a sense of pleasure and satisfaction. This positive sensation encourages the individual to repeat the behavior that led to the reward, forming associations between certain behaviors and the consequences. In gamification, dopamine is released when a player achieves a goal or receives a reward (like points, badges, or level-ups). This release reinforces the behavior that led to the reward, making the player more likely to repeat it, a cycle that is known as the "dopamine loop." This is why well-designed gamified systems are so engaging and can motivate continued participation.

Dopamine is not just about pleasure; it's also linked to motivation. The anticipation of a reward can result in a dopamine surge, which influences the willingness to work and strive toward goals. This anticipation can be as motivating as the reward itself due to the dopamine release. Gamification leverages this by setting up challenges and milestones players are eager to achieve.

Dopamine initiates and helps sustain a behavior, which is crucial in long-term engagement in gamified systems. These systems exploit the "dopamine loop" by offering rewards or achievements at regular intervals, keeping users engaged and motivated to continue participating in the activity.[15] This loop is important to understanding why gamified elements can be so compelling and addictive.

The Flow Theory

Another psychological theory applied in gamification is the Flow Theory, developed by psychologist Mihaly Csikszentmihalyi, which describes a state of deep immersion and engagement in an activity, characterized by a loss of self-consciousness and a sense of time.[16] This state, often referred to as being "in the flow," occurs when there's a balance between the perceived challenges of the task and the individual's skills. In this state, people experience heightened focus, control, and enjoyment. Flow is more likely to occur when the activity is intrinsically rewarding, and it's considered vital for achieving high levels of personal satisfaction and growth. Games are designed to achieve this state by balancing challenge and skill level, ensuring that the player is neither bored (too easy) nor overwhelmed (too hard). Elements like progressive difficulty, immediate feedback, and clear game goals are designed to facilitate flow, enhancing user experience and motivation. By aligning challenges with individual abilities, gamification harnesses the power of flow to create immersive and satisfying experiences.

Cognitive Psychology in Game Design

Cognitive psychology, a subfield of psychology focused on understanding mental processes, delves into areas like attention, memory, language processing, problem-solving, decision-making, perception, and learning.[17] It explores how we concentrate on certain aspects of our environment while ignoring others, how we store and recall information, understand and use language, and make choices. It also examines how we interpret sensory inputs to make sense of the world around us and how we acquire new knowledge and skills. These principles are vital for creating effective learning and training methodologies, including gamified approaches for skill enhancement.

Cognitive psychology in AI adoption is about designing interfaces and interactions that naturally align with how the human mind processes information. For example, using AI to provide personalized learning experiences that adapt to individual cognitive styles and capacities enhances user engagement and efficiency. This approach makes AI more user-friendly and leverages our cognitive strengths, such as pattern recognition and strategic thinking, making the experience with AI both intuitive and intellectually rewarding. Games often require players to use critical thinking, planning, and strategy, engaging cognitive functions and providing a mental workout that can be both rewarding and challenging. Games can also enhance cognitive skills like attention, memory, and spatial reasoning. Puzzle games, for instance, often require players to remember patterns or solve complex problems.

A thoughtful integration of cognitive psychology principles in gamification design ensures that users are not just using a tool but engaging in a mentally stimulating interaction that sharpens their cognitive abilities while achieving their goals.

Social Psychology in Gamification

Social psychology in gamification explores how social interactions and human behavior influence and are influenced by gamified experiences.[18] It considers group dynamics, social influence, and community building within gamified systems. This perspective helps adopt AI technologies, as it emphasizes the importance of collaborative learning, competition, and social rewards through engaging users. By fostering a more collaborative and socially enriched learning environment, this approach promotes individual learning and facilitates the development of a supportive community around AI technologies.

For instance, AI learning platforms incorporating social forums or group challenges promote shared learning and problem-solving. A research article published in the *Plos One* journal explored the effectiveness of gamification in enhancing engagement in online programs.[19]

The review included various studies, revealing that gamification features like leaderboards, badges, points, and rewards can significantly increase user engagement. Importantly, the review found that while gamification positively impacts engagement, especially in the short term, its effects may diminish over time.

This finding emphasizes the need for ongoing innovation and adaptation in gamification strategies to maintain long-term user engagement and interest. The study also suggested that leaderboards could be particularly effective in increasing engagement due to their emphasis on social comparison and motivation through competition.

These insights are crucial for developing effective gamification strategies in AI technology adoption, underlining the importance of incorporating social psychology principles to foster community, collaboration, and sustained user involvement.

Where Games Work and Where They Don't: The Skills–Behaviors Matrix

Game mechanics may increase short-term performance but damage employee satisfaction and motivation if deployed incorrectly. The idea of a "Do More Work" badge is how many companies use gamification techniques. The assumption that adding a game on top of regular work will motivate employees to work harder and longer is not as true as it may seem. This will result in a situation where the employee is confused between the extrinsic rewards of the game, the organization's extrinsic rewards, and the intrinsic rewards that bring them to work. Consider this: An employee who does poorly in a game designed around the skills in their job can be humiliated by "losing" to others or can be confused about whether winning means a promotion or salary increase. For instance, if Dan was playing the "Do Dan's Job" game, it would be strange for

Dan to place fifth on the leaderboard or be unable to move past a basic level. Many companies will deploy off-the-shelf game mechanics such as badges, points, and leaderboards and then be surprised at either the employee pushback or the short-term increase in productivity followed by a large drop in satisfaction and motivation.

Skills and Behaviors

One of the challenges in deploying games in the workplace is competition between the game's rewards and the organization's inherent rewards. In other words, will employees play the game to earn points, or will they just spend time doing their job to earn a paycheck? The exchange rate between points and pay, game levels, and promotion is hard for anyone to determine. This coexistence can lead to strange reactions to games deployed in the wrong areas of the organization.

The Skills–Behaviors Matrix shown in **Figure 16.1** is a comprehensive view that covers the scenarios where games in the workplace work and where they don't. Microsoft first published this matrix in a research paper in 2015 after many years of learning from successful and unsuccessful game deployments focused on crowdsourcing employee effort.[20]

Skills-Behavior Matrix	Core work skills	Unique work skills	Expanding work skills
In-role behaviors	✕	✕	✓
Organizational citizenship behaviors	✓	✕	✕

FIGURE 16.1 Skills and behaviors matrix

Skill Types

Following are the three types of skills:

- **Core work skills:** Core skills are skills that everyone uses regularly as part of their day-to-day tasks. Examples might include the ability to type or speak a language or industry-specific skills such as programming a computer or driving a truck.

- **Unique work skills:** Unique skills are skills that are specific to an individual or set of individuals and are generally the reason employees are paid. Examples of unique skills include deep technical knowledge of an area, the relationship with a given customer or client, the ability to drive a certain type of vehicle or achieve a specific trade license or certification. These unique skills differentiate employees and are often the basis for rewards from the organization.

- **Expanding work skills:** Expanding skills are skills that an employee can learn to differentiate themselves, improve their performance, and take on new tasks.

Behavior Types

The following are the behavior types:

- **In-role behaviors:** In-role behaviors are things that an employee does every day as part of their job. Examples include showing up for work, logging into a computer, performing a certain test, and checking on the status of a machine. The organization rewards the completion of these tasks or behaviors with a paycheck, bonus, or promotion.

- **Organizational citizenship behaviors (OCBs):** Organizational citizenship behaviors (OCBs) are individual discretionary behaviors, not directly or explicitly recognized by the formal reward system, that, in the aggregate, promote the effective functioning of the organization.[21] Several models identify different types of citizenship behaviors, but generally, they cover behaviors such as altruism, conscientiousness, doing the right thing, good sportsmanship, and civic duty. Research shows that citizenship behaviors have a direct relationship to the health of the organization, as well as its productivity and profitability.[22] Also, while these behaviors are not specifically rewarded by an organization, employees who exhibit citizenship behaviors generally fare better in their careers over the long run.

The checkmarks in Figure 16.1 represent the intersection of desired skills and behaviors and show where workplace games can succeed. Where there are Xs, this combination of skills and behaviors could be unsuccessful or damaging.

The two areas where games are successful in the workplace are to help expand the skills used in everyday in-role behaviors and to apply core skills to citizenship behaviors. Helping employees grow their skills through learning is an easy place to apply games in the workplace. Language learning software such as Rosetta Stone or Duolingo are great examples of the application of game mechanics and learning. The rewards in these games do not conflict with the organization's rewards, but the skills are immediately applicable.

Another interesting area in which to deploy games in the workplace is the application of core skills for improving organizational citizenship behavior. This is perhaps best explained through an example. In 2007, the Microsoft Windows team deployed an internal game to encourage employees around the world to help validate the linguistic quality of Windows. At that time, Windows supported over 100 languages and contained thousands of text strings that needed to be quickly and accurately translated. The Windows Language Quality Game was deployed for one month, attracting 4,000 players who reviewed 500,000 screens through gameplay. The core skills in this game were the ability to natively speak a language and the citizenship behavior to help the Windows team ship an important product for Microsoft. In many foreign subsidiaries, management supported this effort by allowing their employees to "play" as part of their work to increase the quality of the Windows 7 product.

Games and Big Data: Crowdsourcing Data Generation

In the world of online services, there is tremendous value in using "big data" to help improve the customer experience. User feedback and telemetry data generated from service usage can be applied to identify problems, improve existing experiences, and build better features to improve future experiences. However, to gather comprehensive user feedback and telemetry data, users sometimes need encouragement to try new features, especially in areas of the service they may not be familiar with. This is where gamification comes in: game mechanics can motivate users to use all the services available to generate comprehensive telemetry data. This data can then be used to train or enhance AI models.

There is a strong relationship between the use of games, game theory, and gamification in the data collection, creation, and application of machine learning models. In Chapter 2, we introduced some machine learning techniques that warrant revisiting specifically in relation to gamification. These include supervised learning, unsupervised learning and reinforcement learning.

Supervised Learning

Supervised learning is a type of machine learning where a computer is trained to make predictions or decisions using examples that are already labeled with correct answers or descriptions. This machine learning approach is similar to learning with a teacher who provides clear examples and expected or desired outcomes. This is easily seen in **Figure 16.2**.[23] However, acquiring vast amounts of accurately labeled data can be both costly and labor-intensive introducing a challenge in levering this technique. This is where gaming can intersect with supervised learning, offering a unique solution to this challenge.

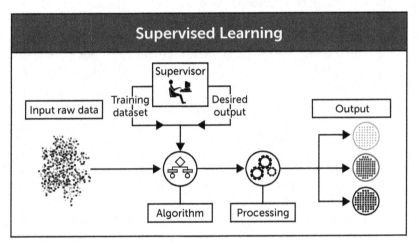

FIGURE 16.2 Supervised learning

Most games are controlled environments with well-defined rules and objectives, making them ideal for generating high-quality, labeled datasets. Players' interactions within a game generate predictable and measurable outputs based on their inputs and actions within the game's structured framework or set of rules. For example, in a game designed to simulate driving, every decision the player makes—speed, route, or lane changes, and responses to traffic signals—is a potential data point that can be used to train AI models in tasks such as autonomous vehicle navigation.

Games can also be specifically designed to enhance the effectiveness of supervised learning models by systematically or deliberately varying the conditions under which data is generated. This controlled variability directs game players to produce a wide range of scenarios and outcomes, enriching the training dataset and allowing the supervised model to learn more robustly from more accurately labeled data. This approach supports the model's ability to generalize across different real-world situations and enhances its accuracy and reliability by using data labeled by humans while playing the game.

A perfect example of this is the ESP game, developed by Luis Von Ahn.[24] In this game, two players who do not know each other's identity are shown the same image. They each type a one-word description of the image until their descriptions "match." This act of typing and submitting multiple one-word descriptions essentially created text metadata for each image. This became the Google Image Labeler game.[25]

The connection between supervised learning and gaming can be a productive one. Games provide a scalable and engaging way to generate the diverse and extensive labeled datasets required for training advanced supervised learning models. This makes the data collection process more cost-effective—even fun—and leverages games' inherently interactive and rule-based nature to improve the quality and applicability of AI solutions across various domains. Games and play can strengthen the data-driven backbone of supervised learning, promising more nuanced and adaptable AI models for real-world applications.

To provide a simple example, imagine a follow-up action at the closing of a customer support case that requests additional data ("labeling") to be entered by a subject matter expert (SME) who was not involved in the case (the "supervisor"). This is a volunteer activity for the SME; it's an organizational citizenship behavior that improves the organization. Introducing game mechanics to engage and reward SMEs for taking action is a great way to improve data quality. Games have rules, and by design, supervised learning can be done best with vast sets of labeled data, which can be gathered in all areas by designing the game rules to reward the SMEs for labeling the data through their gameplay.

Unsupervised Learning

Unlike its supervised sibling, unsupervised learning operates without labeled data or outcomes. Unsupervised learning identifies hidden patterns and structures within data, as seen in **Figure 16.3**.[26] This type of machine learning excels in scenarios where the data lacks explicit tags or predefined categories. In the gaming context, unsupervised learning finds a fertile ground for application due to the complex and rich datasets that games naturally generate. These environments, filled with player choices, interactions, insights, and outcomes, provide a dynamic setting from which unsupervised algorithms can extract valuable insights.

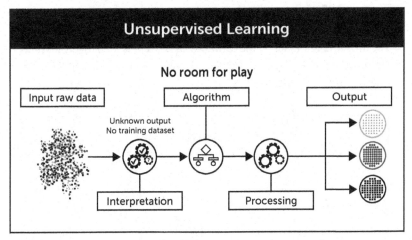

FIGURE 16.3 Unsupervised learning

Game mechanics can be added to optional actions or behaviors within a game to gather data. A good example of this is the Windows Language Quality Game. In this "game," the players reviewed the quality of localized versions of Windows screens and user experience (UX) design, and game mechanics rewarded them for identifying problems or validating accuracy.[27]

The "work" performed in the game is optional and not part of any incentive or reward system. Giving feedback can be gamified to help use game mechanics to encourage the player to take the extra time to give feedback, thereby generating additional data.

Reinforcement Learning

Reinforcement learning is another form of machine learning where models are trained to make a series of decisions by learning to maximize the rewards they receive for their actions. Unlike supervised learning, which relies on labeled data, reinforcement learning operates through trial and error, with the system gradually discovering which actions yield the most reward in a given environment. See **Figure 16.4**, where this technique is depicted.[28] This method simulates the process of a human learning how to play a game, where players adjust their strategies based on the outcomes of their moves.

A great example of reinforcement learning's application in gaming is Google DeepMind's AlphaGo.[29] AlphaGo was developed to apply machine learning to play the board game Go, known for its strategic complexity. The AI system learned to play Go at a superhuman level by playing millions of games against itself, gradually improving its strategies through a reinforcement learning framework known as Monte Carlo Tree Search (MCTS).[30] In this framework, AlphaGo made decisions in simulated games and received rewards and feedback in the form of wins or losses, effectively learning from every game played without any human intervention. In 2015, AlphaGo was the first machine to defeat a champion human Go player.

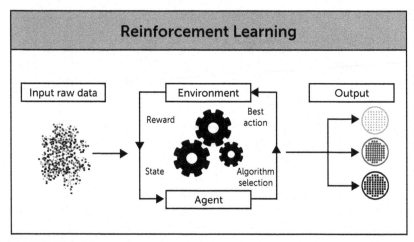

FIGURE 16.4 Reinforcement learning

The interaction between reinforcement learning and games is particularly compelling because games provide structured yet complex environments that challenge AI systems to learn from dynamic content. The learning process in AlphaGo, for example, involved understanding the intricacies of Go strategies from scratch, making decisions that no human player who knew the rules would ever attempt, and developing novel strategies that have since influenced how humans play the game at the highest levels.

The principles of reinforcement learning, as we saw with AlphaGo, apply to a wide range of real-world applications beyond games. From learning from simulating customer support interactions to optimizing logistics and manufacturing processes to developing more sophisticated navigation systems for autonomous vehicles, the ability of reinforcement learning systems to adapt to complex environments and learn optimal strategies through self-play and minimal intervention is proving invaluable. This capability reflects a significant shift in how AI systems are developed, moving from being solely dependent on human-generated data to an era when AI can independently generate its own learning and improvements.

We see gamification helping with unsupervised or reinforcement learning systems by gathering input raw data. Again, since games have rules that players follow, these rules can direct players to do things that generate data in areas of need. For example, in software development, product telemetry generated by users performing a certain action is useful in understanding how a feature is used. Before a product is released, users may be motivated and engaged through game mechanics to try a certain scenario to generate telemetry data to tune the product features.

Data Quality of Game Mechanics

There are two attributes of data that can successfully impact the quality of the user experience: precision and authenticity (as shown in **Figure 16.5**). The precision attribute impacts whether there is a sufficient volume of representative data to draw statistically significant conclusions. The authenticity attribute impacts how representative the collected data is of real user actions. The challenge is that many traditional big data techniques—A/B testing and synthetic transactions—do not necessarily provide the authenticity of real user data, and real user data does not provide the precision necessary to draw insightful conclusions. The concept of a "gamified transaction" enables the best of both worlds—high precision and authenticity.

Data authenticity

Data precision High	Synthetic transactions	Gamified transactions
Low	A/B test transactions	Authentic transactions
	Low	High

FIGURE 16.5 User transaction types

Examples of Data Crowdsourcing

Waze, the popular navigation app, stands out as a prime example of how gamification and crowdsourced data can be harnessed to improve user experience and service efficiency. By incentivizing users to report real-time traffic conditions, road hazards, and police sightings, Waze integrates gamification elements into its platform, transforming the solitary act of navigation into a collaborative, engaging community effort. Users earn points, badges, and other rewards for their contributions, which can lead to higher status levels within the app's community.

This system motivates users to participate actively and enhances the accuracy and timeliness of the app's traffic data. The clever use of gamification and the power of crowdsourcing allows Waze to offer a dynamic, user-driven navigation service that adapts to real-world conditions more effectively than traditional GPS systems. Through this approach, Waze exemplifies how gamification can foster a sense of community and purpose, collectively achieving a more informed and smoother driving experience for all its users.

Wikipedia epitomizes the transformative potential of crowdsourcing in data generation, standing as a testament to its global user community's collective intelligence and collaborative spirit. By empowering individuals from diverse backgrounds to contribute, edit, and refine content, Wikipedia harnesses its contributors' vast and varied expertise to assemble an expansive repository of knowledge.

This model of participatory content creation allows Wikipedia to cover an astonishing range of topics, from the unconventional to the mainstream, ensuring that the information is both comprehensive and up to date. Contributors, motivated by a shared commitment to knowledge dissemination, engage in continuous content verification and improvement, leveraging crowdsourcing to generate data, review, and maintain its accuracy and reliability. Through this approach, Wikipedia demonstrates how collaborative efforts can create a valuable and dynamic information resource accessible to anyone with Internet access, thereby democratizing knowledge in the digital age.

Crowdsourcing models, as exemplified by Waze and Wikipedia, offer innovative approaches to data generation and knowledge sharing, leveraging the collective input of users worldwide. However, these models face inherent challenges, including quality control issues, vulnerability to vandalism and misinformation, biases due to uneven contributor diversity, and privacy concerns. Waze contends with the specific difficulties of ensuring real-time data accuracy and minimizing driver distraction, while Wikipedia grapples with maintaining the reliability of its open-edit content and managing conflicts over controversial topics. Despite these obstacles, both platforms employ strategies like algorithmic data processing, community moderation, and strict guidelines to uphold the integrity and utility of their services, showcasing the potential benefits of crowdsourcing when effectively managed.

The intersection of games and play is naturally connected with AI and machine learning. At a high level, this is maybe not as surprising as one would think. We know all animals use games and play to learn, so why wouldn't a machine benefit from similar techniques? What's exciting about this future is directing human behavior through gameplay to help machine learning be more effective.

Elements of Enterprise Game Design

Elements that influence the successful endeavor of gamifying an activity consider the persona or style of play, the mechanics of how the game is designed, and the game's ultimate deployment and success metrics.

Badges, points, leaderboards and levels are quite popular in gamification platforms. However, it's not enough to simply add a badge to a website and call it a success. Ian Bogost, professor at the Georgia Institute of Technology, captures this well: "The rhetorical power of the word 'gamification' is enormous… Gamification is reassuring. It gives vice presidents and brand managers comfort: they're doing everything right, and they can do even better by adding 'a games strategy' to their existing products, slathering on 'gaminess' like aioli on ciabatta at the consultant's indulgent sales lunch…. Gamification is easy. It offers simple, repeatable approaches in which benefit, honor, and aesthetics are less important than facility."[31]

People must understand that game mechanics are not a panacea. Gamifying someone's job won't deceive them into working harder or trick them into working weekends. When applied thoughtfully, purposefully, and selectively, game mechanics can help improve business processes, but misuse can also be detrimental.

Player Personas

All good game design considers player types. Players can be motivated by different elements of play and different game mechanics or elements. It's important to consider the type of player and design games that appeal to one or more of the following player personas.

- **Player versus player:** This is a game mechanic widely popular in competitive sports where the result is the glory and shame of the scoreboard. While many players can be motivated by competition, it is not for everyone. In fact, in the workplace, there are some cultures where competitive game mechanics will backfire. For example, in some Eastern cultures, if an employee shows up on a leaderboard ahead of their boss, they will stop playing until the boss can return to their rightful position at the top. This could undermine the intent of competitive game mechanics to drive productivity, so it's important to understand the audience and use appropriate motivational techniques.

- **Player versus self:** This game mechanic can be represented simply by "Can I beat my own score?" Many people are not motivated by external competition or extrinsic rewards but are highly motivated to compete with themselves to raise their level of personal best.

- **Player versus environment:** This game mechanic embraces external challenges such as puzzles, scavenger hunts, hidden mysteries, and exploration.

Game Mechanics and Deployment Tips

The following are some useful game mechanics and deployment tips:

- **Duration:** Minimizing the duration of crowdsourcing games to a set number of weeks tends to work best for maintaining player interest. This approach often provides flexibility to adjust rules or scoring or even redesign the game to enhance results or foster greater motivation to play, although there are always exceptions to this guideline.

- **Playtest:** Playtesting is a game design practice that has players playing iterative early versions of the game—even as a paper mockup—to allow game designers the chance to iterate and make the game engaging, fair, and fun for all.

- **Voluntary participation:** The most important thing about a game is to ensure that play is voluntary and players feel like they are helping others. Players will play for different reasons, and that's okay; the important aspect is to employ different techniques designed to entice play.

- **Game master role:** Players who have questions or complaints about the game should have a human game master available to help. The game master usually sends an introductory email announcing the game, its rules, and how to sign up. They also dispense game advice and take feedback from players. Generally, a single person is sufficient, but for large-scale games with lots of players, it's possible that a game master team may be needed.

- **Prizes and rewards:** In general, the recommendation within the workplace is not to use prizes and rewards—extrinsic motivators—and to rely instead on the intrinsic motivation of altruism and citizenship. Unfortunately, prizes can skew behavior, particularly when the prize is large.

- **Measures of success:** Just as we measure the success of our business, it's important also to determine appropriate measures of success for gamification deployment. Consider the end goal of why you are deploying gamification techniques in the first place and determine the metrics that align best with your goals that you can measure. Take a baseline measurement before deploying gamification to help determine areas of improvement and the success/failure of the experience.

Gamification Strategy for AI Adoption

Now that we have an idea of the elements that influence the successful endeavor of gamifying an activity, let's dive deep into the steps to develop your own gamification strategy while also looking into the nuances and considerations that make it effective.

Understanding the AI Landscape in Your Organization

Before embarking on the journey of gamification, it is essential to understand the current state of AI adoption in your team/organization/company. This understanding involves assessing how AI tools are being used, identifying departments or processes where AI could bring significant improvements, and recognizing the barriers to its adoption. For instance, if employees find AI tools intimidating or complex, a gamification strategy could be tailored to simplify and demystify these technologies.

Setting Clear Objectives

The objectives for gamifying AI adoption should align with your organization's broader goals. These goals must be clearly defined, whether it's enhancing productivity, improving data accuracy, or fostering a culture of innovation. This clarity will guide the design of your gamification strategy, ensuring that every element serves a specific purpose. Your objectives should align with your vision, which we visited in Chapter 4.

Identifying and Understanding Your Audience

The success of a gamification strategy largely depends on how well it resonates with its audience. Understanding your employees' demographics, motivations, and learning styles is crucial. As outlined in Chapter 12, "Cultural Considerations," several generations coexist in today's workforce and customer base (Baby Boomers, Generation X, Generation Y/ Millennials, or Generation Z), each with unique motivations, preferences, and backgrounds. For example, a younger workforce might appreciate a more competitive, leaderboard-driven approach for individuals, while a team that values collaboration might engage better with group challenges and collective rewards.

Creating the Gamification Framework

Designing the gamification framework is a creative process that involves selecting the right mix of game elements. This selection is not random but should be based on your objectives and audience analysis. The framework should balance being challenging enough to engage but not so difficult that it becomes frustrating. The design must also ensure that the gamification seamlessly integrates with the AI tools in use, providing a unified user experience.

Pilot Testing and Gathering Feedback with Diverse Participant Profiles

Before full-scale implementation, conducting a pilot test is important. This smaller-scale deployment provides valuable insights into how players receive the gamification strategy and allows for adjustments before a wider rollout. Feedback during this phase is crucial and should be actively sought and carefully considered.

When setting up the pilot test for your gamification strategy, it's imperative to be intentional about the composition of the participant group. This group should reflect your broader organization, encompassing a range of profiles or personas—from those resistant to change to enthusiastic AI adopters. Including individuals who are skeptical or hesitant about AI technology is particularly beneficial. Their early involvement can provide invaluable insights into potential barriers and challenges, and their evolving experience throughout the pilot can guide adjustments that make the final rollout more inclusive and effective.

Similarly, engaging with "super users" or early adopters of AI technology can offer a different perspective. They can help identify advanced features or deeper engagement strategies that less experienced users might miss. Their enthusiasm can also be contagious, helping to build momentum, interest, and interaction among other employees.

Balancing these profiles with a group of average users—those who are neither strongly resistant nor avid proponents of AI—is also key. This middle group often represents most of your workforce and provides a realistic gauge of how the gamification strategy will be received on a larger scale.

This approach ensures that the gamification strategy is tested and refined to address the concerns and leverage the enthusiasm of all user types. It also leads to a more well-rounded and effective strategy, ultimately fostering greater buy-in and reducing resistance when the program is launched broadly. Engaging a wide spectrum of user-profiles early in the development process makes the strategy more robust, inclusive, and capable of driving toward your AI goals.

Effective implementation and communication: When rolling out the gamification strategy, clear and motivating communication is key. Employees should understand the purpose of this initiative and how it benefits them and the organization. Do not underestimate the power of asking, "What's in it for them?" versus feeling this is just another initiative at a corporate level. This understanding fosters buy-in and enthusiasm. The rollout should be monitored closely, with an eye on engagement levels and user feedback.

Following are some additional considerations:

- **Cultural alignment:** The gamification strategy must reflect and respect the company's culture. For instance, gamification should emphasize collaborative challenges and collective achievements in a company where teamwork is highly valued. Misalignment with company culture can lead to reduced participation or even resistance.

- **Ethical considerations and data privacy:** Given the data-driven nature of AI and gamification, ethical considerations and data privacy cannot be overlooked. The strategy must comply with all relevant data protection and security laws, regulations, and ethical guidelines. Transparency about collecting, using, and protecting data is crucial in building trust.

- **Adaptability and continuous improvement:** The landscape of AI and employee engagement is constantly evolving. Therefore, the gamification strategy should not be static. It needs regular reviews and adaptations, incorporating user feedback and changing needs. This flexibility ensures the strategy remains effective and relevant over time.

- **Defining and tracking success:** Success in gamification can be measured through various key performance indicators (KPIs), such as engagement rates, proficiency improvements, and frequency of AI tool usage. Regularly tracking these indicators helps in understanding the gamification strategy's impact and identifying areas for improvement.

- **Feedback loops and iterative development:** Establishing channels for ongoing feedback is essential for the iterative development of the gamification strategy. Employees should have easy ways to provide feedback on their experiences. This input is invaluable for making informed adjustments and ensuring the strategy aligns with users' needs and preferences.

Implementing a gamification strategy for driving AI adoption and regular usage is not a one-time project but an ongoing journey. It requires commitment, flexibility, and a willingness to learn and adapt. You can maintain engagement and foster a culture that embraces innovation and continuous learning by continuously refining the strategy and staying attuned to your employees' evolving needs and AI advancements. Play, a uniquely human trait, is critical in engaging people with AI-driven technologies, as game mechanics tap into our innate behaviors and motivations.

Measuring the Impact of Gamification

Assessing the effectiveness of a gamification strategy in driving AI adoption should be considered. The success of gamification initiatives is not just about the immediate engagement they generate by players but also about their long-term impact on users' behavior and proficiency with AI technologies. A mix of key performance indicators (KPIs) and qualitative measures is essential to comprehensively evaluate this impact.

Identifying Relevant KPIs

The selection of KPIs should directly align with your initial objectives. For instance, if the aim is to increase the usage of AI tools, relevant KPIs might include:

- **Engagement metrics:** This includes data like log-in frequency, session duration, and user participation rates in gamified activities.
- **Learning progression:** This includes metrics such as the completion rates of AI learning modules, quiz scores, or the rate of progression through different levels of the gamification system.
- **Behavioral changes:** Measuring the frequency and depth of AI tool usage post-gamification compared to before.
- **Performance improvements:** Evaluating improvements in job performance or task efficiency due to increased AI adoption and proficiency.
- **User feedback scores:** Ratings or scores provided by users regarding their experience with the gamified AI tools.

Gathering and analyzing data related to these KPIs requires a systematic approach. This might involve leveraging analytics tools integrated into your AI and gamification platforms. Regularly reviewing these metrics provides insights into the effectiveness of your gamification strategy and guides necessary adjustments.

Qualitative Measures

Though more subjective, qualitative data offers invaluable insights into the user experience and satisfaction levels. This data can be gathered through:

- **User surveys and interviews:** Conducting regular surveys or interviews to gather users' opinions, suggestions, and feelings about the gamified AI tools.

- **Focus groups:** Engaging small groups of diverse users in discussions to gain deeper insights into their experiences and perceptions.

- **Anecdotal evidence:** Observations and informal feedback from users can often reveal unforeseen effects of the gamification strategy, both positive and negative.

Integrating feedback loops into the gamification system can provide real-time data and insights. These loops enable immediate adjustments and foster a culture of continuous improvement, ensuring the gamification strategy remains relevant and effective in promoting AI adoption.

A balanced approach, employing quantitative and qualitative measures, provides a comprehensive picture of the impact of the gamification strategy. While quantitative data can validate the effectiveness with hard numbers, qualitative insights can guide improvements in user experience and engagement strategies. This combination helps fine-tune the gamification approach and ensures its success in fostering AI adoption.

Continuous monitoring of evaluation methods helps quickly identify improvement areas and adapt the strategy in response to changing user needs and organizational goals. It is not a one-time event but an ongoing process, and it needs to be embedded in the gamification design phase to ensure it is part of the plan.

Learning from Successes and Failures

In the rapidly evolving landscape of AI and gamification, the journey to integrate these technologies is marked by a spectrum of experiences ranging from groundbreaking successes to instructive failures. These triumphant and challenging stories provide invaluable insights into the complexities and potential of using AI and gamification in various domains. This section explores and analyzes these diverse experiences, shedding light on what propels certain initiatives to succeed while others encounter obstacles.

Success stories serve as powerful testimonies to the potential in front of us. They exemplify how integrating AI with the engaging elements of gamification can lead to innovative solutions, enhanced user experiences, and significant advancements in fields ranging from education to entertainment and beyond. These successes are not just about the triumph of technology but also about human ingenuity in harnessing it for creative, effective, and impactful applications. By examining these stories, we can distill key strategies, approaches, and practices that contribute to the successful deployment of AI and gamification.

On the flip side, stories of failure are equally important. They offer critical lessons and cautionary tales about the challenges and pitfalls of integrating AI and gamification. Failures often reveal underlying complexities, unanticipated variables, and the importance of aligning technological capabilities with user needs and expectations. By analyzing these less successful endeavors, we can gain insights into the importance of adaptability, user-centric design, and the need for rigorous testing and iteration. These stories highlight that failure is not a setback but an opportunity to learn, refine, and innovate.

Together, the success and failure stories form a comprehensive narrative that underscores the dynamic nature of AI and gamification integration. They provide a holistic understanding of what works, what doesn't, and why. This balanced perspective is important for anyone looking to venture into this space, offering a roadmap informed by both the achievements and the challenges encountered by pioneers in the field.

Let's delve into specific case studies of both success and failure, aiming to extract valuable lessons and insights that can guide future endeavors in the fascinating intersection of AI, gaming, and gamification.

Duolingo and AI-Driven Language Learning

Integrating gamification and AI has led to numerous success stories across different domains. One is corporate training, where companies have implemented gamified training modules with AI-driven analytics to provide employees with customized learning experiences, improving knowledge retention and job performance. Health and fitness apps, like Fitbit and MyFitnessPal, also use gamification and AI to personalize health challenges and track progress, significantly improving user engagement and health outcomes.

Another prime example of gamification seamlessly integrated with AI to create an effective and engaging language learning platform for over

19 million daily users is Duolingo.[32] As a free mobile app, Duolingo offers language learning in a game-like format, where users earn points, level up, and receive immediate feedback—key gamification elements.

What's the secret of Duolingo's AI integration? Duolingo employs AI algorithms to personalize learning experiences.[33] The AI assesses a user's learning pace, strengths, and weaknesses to adapt lessons accordingly,[34] ensuring a tailored learning journey for each user and maximizing efficiency and retention.

As for user engagement, the gamified elements of Duolingo, such as earning virtual coins, unlocking new levels, and competing in leagues, keep users motivated and engaged. This approach has proven effective in maintaining consistent user participation, a common challenge in online learning platforms.

Is this gamified approach bringing results? It certainly has. In 2022, the app saw a significant increase in "power users," defined as those who open it more than 15 days a month. This surge coincided with the introduction of gamification features, which included revamping the app's interface and the overall structure of the learning tracks.[35] Adding and adjusting gamification features has been crucial to this success. According to Sensor Tower's August 2023 report, Duolingo gathered about 19 million users daily, solidifying its position as a significant player in language learning apps.[36]

Classroom Gamification and Frequent Flyer Programs

The article "10 Bad Gamification Examples: Learning from Failed Projects"[37] discusses various unsuccessful gamification initiatives, highlighting the importance of strategic planning and understanding user engagement.[38] It points out common mistakes such as misaligned rewards, neglecting user motivation, and failing to maintain long-term engagement.

One of the projects this article shares showcases a teacher's attempt to gamify the classroom by replacing grades with experience points (XP) for tasks like homework completion and class attendance to motivate students. This approach primarily utilized a points, leaderboards, and badges (PLBs) reward system, assuming these elements alone would enhance the learning experience. In the skills and behaviors matrix shown earlier in Figure 16.1, these would be in-role behaviors already required/expected to be accomplished by the students. However, the lack of deeper, intrinsic motivation behind these rewards led to the initiative's eventual discontinuation.

Ultimately, the points only led to gaining a badge. The case underscores the challenge of relying on extrinsic rewards without fostering genuine engagement or addressing the underlying motivational needs of students. We can extrapolate this example into the corporate world, as it is valuable for organizations contemplating the use of gamification to enhance their employees' AI literacy, where their employees become students and the managers/supervisors become the teachers who must motivate them to consume and complete the training and learning resources. Such programs should be thoughtfully tailored to spark genuine interest and provide meaningful rewards, ensuring that employees gain AI knowledge and are motivated to apply it, fostering a culture of continuous learning and innovation.

Another case study discussed in this article centers around the limitations of frequent flyer programs in effectively using gamification elements. While these programs aim to encourage loyalty through rewards such as status miles and award miles, they often fail to make the experience genuinely engaging or fun for most participants.

The high thresholds for earning meaningful rewards can demotivate infrequent flyers, illustrating the challenge of applying gamification in a way that genuinely enhances user engagement and loyalty. Drawing from the example of frequent flyer programs, corporations aiming to boost AI adoption among their customers can learn the importance of integrating meaningful gamification elements that offer real value and engagement. Just as high thresholds in frequent flyer programs can demotivate participants, overly complex or unrewarding AI adoption initiatives may fail to engage users. Companies should design their AI gamification strategies to provide clear, attainable benefits, ensuring that participating in AI-driven services feels rewarding and accessible to all, thus fostering wider adoption and enthusiasm for AI technologies.

These case studies serve as a cautionary tale for organizations aiming to implement gamification, emphasizing the need for meaningful integration of game elements into the user experience to avoid disenchantment and project failure.

Beyond Points and Leaderboards: The Future of Gamification Strategies

The evolution of gamification strategies over the years showcases a transformative journey from basic game mechanics to sophisticated, narrative-driven experiences. This evolution reflects broader technological advancements and a deepening understanding of human psychology and motivation. As we dig into this progression, we also glimpse the future, where emerging technologies and AI promise to redefine what's possible in gamifying experiences across various domains.

From Points and Badges to Complex Narratives

As discussed, in the early days, gamification strategies largely revolved around simple reward systems, such as points, badges, and leaderboards. These elements tapped into basic human desires for achievement and recognition, making routine tasks more engaging.

Over time, the importance of context and storytelling emerged. Gamified applications began incorporating narratives and themes, transforming mundane activities into parts of a larger story. This shift highlighted the power of context, making gamification more immersive and emotionally engaging.

The evolution further embraced sophisticated UX designs that are intuitive and user-friendly, ensuring that gamified systems are accessible and enjoyable for a broader audience.

Quoting again Taiwanese-American businessman and one of the earliest pioneers in the industry of gamification, Yu-kai Chou: "If something is engaging because it lets you express your creativity, makes you feel successful through skill mastery, and gives you a higher sense of meaning, it makes you feel very good and powerful."[39]

Hyper-Personalization Through AI

The future of gamification lies in hyper-personalization, where AI algorithms will tailor every aspect of the gamified experience to individual users' preferences, behaviors, and learning styles. AI will enable the dynamic adjustment of challenges, rewards, and narratives, ensuring that each user's journey is uniquely engaging and optimally challenging. This personalization level will enhance user engagement and significantly improve outcomes, whether in learning or workplace productivity.

Motivation, Immersive Learning, and Training

The proliferation of smartphones and social media has integrated gamification into daily life, enabling real-time social experiences—allowing users to compare achievements, compete, and collaborate—and enhancing engagement.

Internet of Things (IoT) technology integrates physical objects into gamified systems, making everyday activities and environments part of the game. This opens up new avenues for behavior change, such as fitness challenges linked to wearable devices.

Augmented reality (AR) and virtual reality (VR) technologies have begun to transform gamification by creating more immersive experiences. For instance, gamified learning environments using VR can simulate real-life scenarios for training purposes, offering hands-on experience without the associated risks or costs.

AR and VR technologies are set to revolutionize gamified learning and training environments by providing highly immersive experiences. Imagine medical students performing complex surgeries in a risk-free, gamified VR environment or history students exploring ancient civilizations through AR simulations. These immersive experiences will make learning more effective and memorable, offering hands-on practice and exploration that traditional methods cannot match.

Blockchain-Powered Gamification

Integrating blockchain technology with gamification introduces new transparency, security, and user empowerment levels. Blockchain could enable secure, tamper-proof systems for tracking achievements and managing digital rewards, potentially even allowing users to transfer rewards across different gamified platforms. Moreover, blockchain could facilitate the creation of decentralized gamification ecosystems where users have more control over their data and contributions.

AI-Powered Personalization

Integrating AI and machine learning algorithms into gamified systems promises a new era of adaptive learning, predictive analytics, and dynamic content generation, collectively enhancing the user experience to unprecedented levels. These advanced technologies empower gamified platforms to finely tune user interactions, adapting to individual learning styles, paces, and preferences in real time. This personalization ensures that each user's engagement is maximized for effectiveness, creating a highly tailored educational journey.

Furthermore, AI's capability to analyze vast datasets on user behavior and preferences enables the predictive modeling of future interactions, allowing for the customization of challenges and rewards that keep users consistently motivated and engaged.

Beyond personalization and predictive analytics, AI excels in generating dynamic content, creating a limitless variety of challenges and narratives that evolve in response to user actions. This keeps the gamified experience perpetually fresh and captivating, ensuring that users remain engaged over the long term by continuously presenting them with novel and relevant content.

Together, these capabilities signify a transformative shift in how gamified systems interact with users, offering a deeply personalized, engaging, and ever-evolving learning environment.

Additional Considerations

While the fusion of gamification and AI offers promising avenues for enhancing engagement and personalization, addressing these challenges is essential for its sustainable and ethical development. By prioritizing ethical and practical considerations, data privacy and security, carefully balancing the use of external motivators, and committing to accessibility and inclusivity, developers and practitioners can develop the full potential of this powerful synergy.

Ethical and Practical Considerations

As AI becomes more integral to gamification, ethical considerations, and user-centric design principles are becoming increasingly important. Ethical AI practices will be crucial in maintaining trust and ensuring that gamification remains a positive force in users' lives.

Moreover, the effectiveness of gamification in influencing user behavior brings to light an ethical imperative: the need to meticulously balance motivational design with respect for user autonomy. This involves crafting gamification strategies that motivate and engage without resorting to manipulative practices, thereby preserving the integrity of the user's decision-making process.

Data Privacy and Security

The personalized experiences that make gamified AI systems so engaging rely heavily on collecting and analyzing extensive user data. This raises significant concerns regarding data privacy and security. Users entrust these systems with sensitive information, from personal preferences to behavioral patterns, assuming their data is protected. However, the risk of data breaches or unauthorized use remains a pressing issue. Ensuring robust data protection measures and transparent data handling practices is crucial to maintaining user trust and complying with increasingly stringent data protection regulations.

Overdependence on Technology

Another challenge is the potential for overdependence on technology, which could paradoxically undermine the very motivation gamification seeks to enhance. While gamified and AI-driven systems are designed to motivate users by making tasks more engaging, there's a risk that users may become reliant on external rewards and feedback, diminishing their intrinsic motivation. This overreliance could lead to a scenario where the absence of gamified elements or rewards results in reduced interest and engagement in the task itself. Balancing motivational design to ensure it complements rather than replaces intrinsic motivation is essential for the long-term success of gamification strategies.

Accessibility and Inclusivity

Furthermore, ensuring that gamified AI systems are accessible and inclusive presents a significant challenge. These systems must cater to a diverse user base with varying levels of technological proficiency, physical and cognitive abilities, and access to technology. This requires thoughtful design that considers a wide range of needs and preferences, from user interfaces that accommodate users with disabilities to ensuring that gamified applications are usable on low-end devices and in areas with limited Internet connectivity. Achieving this level of accessibility and inclusivity is paramount to prevent the exacerbation of existing digital divides and to ensure that the benefits of gamification and AI can be universally realized.

Together, these considerations form the foundation of a responsible and impactful gamification approach—one that prioritizes user welfare while harnessing the power of personalized engagement.

In the age of AI, games, play, and fun embody the human element and celebrate the human spirit in our AI partnership. Machines and algorithms cannot replicate our inherent human creativity and personality. The playgrounds of our human minds represent all that makes us human and relevant in this new AI world. Games can challenge us, while play frees our spirit to experiment without risk, and fun keeps us vibrant and engaged, ensuring that even as we move forward with this new and intimidating AI technology, we humans remain grounded in the joyous and boundless curiosity that defines us as a race.

These elements remind us that at the very heart of every human advancement lies the curious and playful human spirit, eager to explore the unknown. Through play, we learn creativity, industriousness, resilience, adaptability, and the value of the human race, ensuring that our journey alongside AI is not just one of efficiency and logic but also of imagination, creativity, and endless wonder. Human and machine—better together in partnership than they would be alone.

The future of gamification is bright. The continued integration of AI promises a new era of gamification that is as exciting as it is innovative.

Endnotes

1 Mayor, Dana. 2023. "Computers in the 1980s." History Computer. March 12, 2023. [https://history-computer.com/computers-in-the-1980s/].

2 Eberle, Scott G. "The Elements of Play Toward a Philosophy and a Definition of Play." Journal of Play. 2022. [https://www.museumofplay.org/app/uploads/2022/01/6-2-article-elements-of-play.pdf].

3 Tyldesley, Joyce Dr. 2011. "The Private Lives of the Pyramid-builders." BBC. February 17, 2011. [https://www.bbc.co.uk/history/ancient/egyptians/pyramid_builders_01.shtml].

4 TeachThought Staff. 2023. "A Brief History of Gamification In Education." TeachThought. September 27, 2023. [https://www.teachthought.com/education/a-brief-history-of-gamification-in-education/].

5 Round, Paul. 2023. "Mastering the Ancient Board Game: Rules of Petteia." Cards and Boards. August 3, 2023. [https://cardsandboards.net/mastering-the-ancient-board-game-rules-of-petteia/].

6 McLeroy, Carrie. 2008. "History of Military gaming." Soldiers magazine. August 27, 2008. [https://www.army.mil/article/11936/history_of_military_gaming].

7 Wikipedia contributors. "Carmonette." Wikipedia, The Free Encyclopedia. December 14, 2022. [https://en.wikipedia.org/wiki/Carmonette].

8 Wikipedia contributors. "AAdvantage." Wikipedia, The Free Encyclopedia. December 25, 2023. [https://en.wikipedia.org/wiki/AAdvantage].

9 Spinify blog. "Who started gamification?" Spinify. Accessed February 29, 2024. [https://spinify.com/blog/gamification-history/].

10 The Octalysis Group. "Yu-Kai Chou." Accessed April 29, 2024. [https://octalysisgroup.com/experts/yu-kai-chou/].

11 Hamari, Juho. 2017. "Do badges increase user activity? A field experiment on the effects of gamification." *Science Direct*. June 2017. [https://www.sciencedirect.com/science/article/abs/pii/S0747563215002265].

12 Center for Self-Determination Theory contributors. "The Theory." Center for Self-Determination Theory. Accessed February 29, 2024. [https://selfdeterminationtheory.org/the-theory/].

13 Center for Self-Determination Theory contributors. "The Theory." Center for Self-Determination Theory. Accessed February 29, 2024. [https://selfdeterminationtheory.org/the-theory/].

14 The Decision Lab contributors. "Why do we lose interest in an activity after we are rewarded for it?" The Decision Lab. Accessed February 29, 2024. [https://thedecisionlab.com/biases/overjustification-effect].

15 Cutillo, Matthew. 2021. "Dopamine-Driven Feedback Loops: What Are They?" Monmouth University. March 24, 2021. [https://outlook.monmouth.edu/2021/03/dopamine-driven-feedback-loops-what-are-they/].

16 TheoryHub contributors. "Flow Theory." TheoryHub. Accessed February 29, 2024. [https://open.ncl.ac.uk/academic-theories/8/flow-theory/].

17 Mcleod, Saul PhD. 2024. "Cognitive Approach in Psychology." SimplyPsychology. Updated May 27, 2024. [https://www.simplypsychology.org/cognitive.html].

18 Cherry, Kendra MSEd. 2023. "5 Important Social Psychology Concepts." Very Well Mind. November 3, 2023. [https://www.verywellmind.com/things-you-should-know-about-social-psychology-2795903].

19 Looyestyn, J., Kemot, J., Boshoff, K., Ryan, J., Edney, S., Maher, C. "Does gamification increase engegement with online programs? A systematic review." Plos One. March 31, 2017. [https://journals.plos.org/plosone/article?id=10.1371/journal.pone.0173403].

20 Smith, Ross., Popa, Dana. "Why Play Matters at Work: Gamification is more than just a passing fad." ResearchGate. July 2015. [https://www.researchgate.net/publication/280222776_Why_Play_Matters_at_Work_Gamification_is_more_than_just_a_passing_fad].

21 Organ, D. W. (1988). *Organizational Citizenship Behavior: The Good Soldier Syndrome.* Lexington, MA: Lexington Books. p.4

22 Murambinda, Brandon. "Organizational Citizenship Behavior: Benefits and Best Practices." The Human Capital Hub. Accessed February 29, 2024. [https://www.thehumancapitalhub.com/articles/organizational-citizenship-behavior-benefits-and-best-practices].

23 van Loon, Ronald. 2018. "Machine Learning Explained: Understanding Supervised, Unsupervised, and Reinforcement Learning." DataFloq. January 23, 2018. [https://datafloq.com/read/machine-learning-explained-understanding-learning/].

24 Wikipedia contributors. "ESP game." Wikipedia, The Free Encyclopedia. June 23, 2023. [https://en.wikipedia.org/wiki/ESP_game].

25 Wikipedia contributors. "Google Image Labeler." Wikipedia, The Free Encyclopedia. August 14, 2023. [https://en.wikipedia.org/wiki/Google_Image_Labeler].

26 van Loon, Ronald. 2018. "Machine Learning Explained: Understanding Supervised, Unsupervised, and Reinforcement Learning." DataFloq. January 23, 2018. [https://datafloq.com/read/machine-learning-explained-understanding-learning/].

27 Chiang, Oliver. 2010. "When Playing Videogames At Work Makes Dollars And Sense." *Forbes.* August 9, 2010. [https://www.forbes.com/2010/08/09/microsoft-workplace-training-technology-videogames.html?sh=6572d9156b85].

28 van Loon, Ronald. 2018. "Machine Learning Explained: Understanding Supervised, Unsupervised, and Reinforcement Learning." DataFloq. January 23, 2018. [https://datafloq.com/read/machine-learning-explained-understanding-learning/].

29 Wikipedia contributors. "AlphaGo." Wikipedia, The Free Encyclopedia. March 5, 2024. [https://en.wikipedia.org/wiki/AlphaGo].

30 Wikipedia contributors. "Monte Carlo tree search." Wikipedia, The Free Encyclopedia. April 15, 2024. [https://en.wikipedia.org/wiki/Monte_Carlo_tree_search].

31 Bogost, Ian. 2011. "Gamification Is Bullshit." *The Atlantic.* August 9, 2011. [https://www.theatlantic.com/technology/archive/2011/08/gamification-is-bullshit/243338/].

32 Duolingo Team. "Introducing Duolingo Max, a learning experience powered by GPT-4." Duolingo blog. March 14, 2023. [https://blog.duolingo.com/duolingo-max/].

33   Marr, Bernard. "The Amazing Ways Duolingo Is Using AI and GPT-4." *Forbes.* April 28, 2023. [https://www.forbes.com/sites/bernardmarr/2023/04/28/the-amazing-ways-duolingo-is-using-ai-and-gpt-4/?sh=220b9d861346].

34   Henry, Parker. "How Duolingo uses AI to create lessons faster." Duolingo blog. June 22, 2023. [https://blog.duolingo.com/large-language-model-duolingo-lessons/].

35   Mercado, Andrea. "10 Duolingo Statistics to Start Learning a New Language in 2024." Skillademia. November 27, 2023. [https://www.skillademia.com/statistics/duolingo-statistics/].

36   Scacchi, Marco. "Duolingo's gamified success: A language learning triumph." Sensor Tower. August 2023. [https://sensortower.com/blog/duolingos-gamified-success-a-language-learning-triumph].

37   Russ, Ricardo. "10 Bad Gamification Examples: Learning from Failed Projects." Keep them Engaged. Accessed February 29, 2024. [https://keepthemengaged.com/10-bad-gamification-examples-learning-from-failed-projects/].

38   Russ, Ricardo. "10 Bad Gamification Examples: Learning from Failed Projects." Keep them Engaged. Accessed February 29, 2024. [https://keepthemengaged.com/10-bad-gamification-examples-learning-from-failed-projects/].

39   Chou, Yu-kai. (2017). Actionable Gamification - Beyond Points, Badges, and Leaderboards. Milpitas, CA: Octalysis Media. p.31

17

Leadership Excellence in the Era of AI

The ultimate measure of a man is not where he stands in moments of comfort and convenience, but where he stands at times of challenge and controversy.

—Dr. Martin Luther King, Jr.

Today's customer service and support leaders are at the forefront of their own revolution, steering their organizations into the uncharted territory of AI. This transition parallels other historical and technological transformations, such as the Industrial Revolution's shift from manual to mechanized production or the digital revolution's move from analog to digital technologies. Each of these pivotal moments required visionary leadership, a willingness to embrace the unknown, care and empathy for their constituents, and a steadfast commitment to navigating the challenges of radical change. Similarly, the AI Revolution in customer service and support presents a unique opportunity for today's leaders to author the next chapter in their organization's history, leveraging AI to redefine service excellence, enhance operational efficiency, and create unprecedented value for customers. Just as the pioneers of the past have shown, successfully navigating this transformation will require a blend of vision, courage, and innovation.

However, unlike previous revolutions, the AI Revolution is characterized by an unprecedented speed of advancement and widespread impact. The rate at which AI technologies evolve and integrate into various aspects of our business and life is nothing short of exponential. What was cutting-edge yesterday may become obsolete tomorrow, and staying ahead of the curve requires learning, adaptation, and proactive anticipation of what lies ahead.

This rapid metamorphosis demands agility, foresight, and a willingness to continuously learn and adapt for customer service and support leaders. In essence, the AI Revolution is not just about adopting new technologies—it's about embracing a mindset of perpetual evolution and transformation.

In this chapter, we embark on a deeply personal journey—one that illuminates the pivotal role of leaders in shaping the future of their organizations through the integration of AI. After navigating through fundamentals such as vision and strategy in previous chapters, it's time to explore the profound shifts in leadership paradigms demanded by this new era. Leaders must be willing to challenge the status quo, push boundaries, and empower their teams to think creatively and adaptively in the face of uncertainty, and this chapter is here to equip you to thrive in that journey.

Leadership in the Age of AI

In the age of artificial intelligence, leadership takes on significant new dimensions and challenges. The rapid evolution of AI technologies demands leaders who are not only business and technologically savvy but also visionary, ethical, and adaptable. These leaders must balance leveraging AI for competitive advantage and ensuring its use aligns with societal values and organizational ethics. Let's dive into the essential leadership traits and considerations in the age of AI, offering a thought-provoking exploration of what it means to lead in this transformative era.

Visionary Leadership

In the context of AI, visionary leaders can foresee the potential impacts and opportunities of AI technologies for their organizations and society at large. They are experts at imagining future scenarios where AI enhances human capabilities, transforms industries, and solves complex societal problems. Visionary leaders inspire their teams and stakeholders by painting a compelling picture of a future in which AI and human intelligence amplify each other, leading to unprecedented levels of innovation and progress.

Consider a leader who envisions an AI-driven customer service system that anticipates and responds to customer needs in real-time, offering solutions before the customer even identifies a problem. This leader is not just reacting to technological trends but is actively shaping a future where technology creates deeper, more meaningful connections with customers.

The role of leaders in driving successful AI adoption is crucial. As visionaries, leaders must articulate a clear and compelling vision for how AI can enhance service delivery, streamline operations, and create customer value. They must champion the adoption of AI technologies, secure the necessary resources, and foster an organizational culture that embraces innovation and change.

Let's delve into this need to foster a culture of innovation and cultivate an environment where innovation will thrive, and continuous learning is valued. Innovation is at the heart of AI integration but comes with inherent risks. You must foster an environment encouraging innovation, risk-taking, and failure to navigate these challenges. For some, this will immediately translate into the concept known as the "fail fast and move on" culture, particularly prevalent in innovative and agile organizations, mainly in the tech industry and startups. This culture encourages risk-taking and innovation by removing the stigma associated with failure. Instead of viewing failure as a setback, it is seen as a valuable learning opportunity that can lead to improved strategies and outcomes in the long run.

It's important to note that while the "fail fast and move on" approach can be highly effective in certain contexts, in fields where safety, regulatory compliance, or ethical considerations are paramount, a more cautious and deliberate approach may be necessary. Implementing robust risk management practices, such as introducing sandbox environments where AI technologies can be tested and refined in a controlled setting before deployment, is a great option in these scenarios, allowing for risks to be identified and mitigated safely.

Additionally, for individuals and teams, it's essential to provide psychological safety and support mechanisms to ensure they feel empowered to take risks and learn from failures without fear of repercussions. Encouraging experimentation and allowing for failure are essential to this culture, as they lead to discovery and improvement. Quoting James Joyce, "Mistakes are the portals of discovery."

Ethical Stewardship

Ethical stewardship is paramount in the age of AI. Leaders must ensure that deploying AI technologies adheres to the highest ethical standards, protecting privacy, ensuring transparency, and avoiding bias. This requires a deep understanding of the ethical implications of AI and a commitment to developing AI in a way that benefits all members of society equitably.

Imagine an AI system designed to optimize customer service routes inadvertently biases against a certain demographic due to historical data patterns. An ethical leader would correct this bias and implement systemic changes to prevent similar issues, demonstrating a commitment to fairness and equality.

Ethical considerations must be at the forefront of AI integration. Leaders must champion ethical AI development as it becomes more integrated into customer service and organizational operations. Ethical AI development involves establishing clear guidelines that govern the use of AI, including principles of fairness, transparency, accountability, and privacy. Implementing checks and balances to prevent bias, safeguarding customer data privacy, and ensuring AI decisions are explainable and justifiable are also in scope.

One of the best practices to consider is developing an AI ethics board within the organization that reviews and approves AI projects, ensuring they meet established ethical standards and societal expectations. Leaders should also advocate for including ethicists and social scientists in AI development teams to ensure diverse perspectives are considered.

Building trust with customers and the broader community is essential for successfully implementing AI. Organizations should engage in open dialogue about their use of AI, including the benefits and the measures taken to mitigate risks. Transparency about AI decisions and processes helps build confidence and trust among stakeholders.

Adaptability and Continuous Learning

The only constant in the AI landscape is change. This is when leaders must embody adaptability and be willing to pivot strategies in response to new technological advancements and societal shifts. Continuous learning is a part of this adaptability, as leaders must stay informed of AI developments and their implications for business and society. This continuous learning involves a commitment to understanding the fundamentals of AI and its potential impacts. Key activities include engaging with AI experts, participating in forums and think tanks, and immersing themselves in continuous learning to stay ahead of technological trends.

Leaders like Microsoft's Satya Nadella exemplify this trait by advocating for a "learn-it-all" culture over a "know-it-all" culture, emphasizing the importance of growth and adaptability in the face of technological evolution. A "learn-it-all" culture champions continuous learning, collaboration, and humility, fostering a growth mindset where individuals and teams are encouraged to seek new knowledge, admit ignorance, and embrace feedback.[1] Mistakes are viewed as valuable learning opportunities, and there's an emphasis on collective success over individual expertise. In contrast, a "know-it-all" culture prioritizes individual expertise, stifles collaboration, and fosters arrogance and resistance to change. This closed-mindedness can lead to stagnation and internal conflict, hindering innovation and adaptation.

An approach to consider is implementing regular AI literacy programs for executives and decision-makers, ensuring that the leadership team can make informed decisions about AI investments and initiatives.

Collaborative Mindset

AI's complexity and broad impact require leaders to foster collaboration across disciplines, industries, and borders. It's critical to break down silos within organizations and seek partnerships and alliances that accelerate innovation and ethical AI development. This collaborative mindset extends to involving diverse voices in AI development, ensuring that the technology reflects a wide range of perspectives and needs.

Creating cross-functional teams that include AI experts, ethicists, customer service professionals, and customers can lead to more holistic and innovative approaches to integrating AI into customer service. Leaders should promote cross-functional collaboration to integrate diverse perspectives and expertise in AI initiatives, ensuring well-rounded and impactful solutions.

Courage to Lead Change

Implementing AI in customer service is not without its challenges, including resistance from within the organization and concerns from customers accustomed to traditional service models. Leaders must have the courage to drive change, making tough decisions that balance technological advancement with human considerations.

Embracing the courage to lead change, especially in the dynamic landscape of today's world, requires a deep understanding of what truly drives survival and success. This insight is beautifully encapsulated in a quote often attributed to Charles Darwin, reflecting the essence of adaptability and responsiveness. Darwin stated, "It is not the strongest of the species that survive, nor the most intelligent, but the one most responsive to change." This perspective underscores the significance of adaptability over mere strength or intelligence. In the context of leadership, it serves as a powerful reminder that the ability to navigate and respond to change is paramount. Leaders who embody this adaptability can steer their organizations through the uncharted territories of innovation and transformation, ensuring survival and thriving success in an ever-evolving world.

This courage includes being transparent about the potential impacts of AI, such as role evolution and taking proactive steps to mitigate these challenges through retraining and redeployment. The successful integration of AI into customer service requires buy-in from all levels of the organization. It becomes imperative for leaders to build an inclusive culture that values the contributions of both AI technologies and human employees. This involves clear communication about the role of AI in the organization, training programs to help employees adapt to new technologies and initiatives that celebrate the successes of AI integration.

A cultural initiative that can positively impact organizations is launching a mentorship program where AI-savvy employees can share their knowledge and skills with others, fostering a sense of community and shared purpose in the AI transformation journey.

Leading with Emotional Intelligence

As AI takes on more cognitive tasks, the value of emotional intelligence (EQ) in leadership becomes increasingly important. Leaders must demonstrate empathy, understanding, and adaptability in managing the human aspects of AI integration. This includes addressing fears and concerns about AI, leading with compassion during transitions, and recognizing the unique contributions of human employees in an increasingly automated world.

Why the Q?

Emotional quotient, more commonly known as emotional intelligence, refers to the ability to perceive, understand, and manage emotions in oneself and others and use that awareness to guide thoughts and behaviors.[2] You can think of the Q as the emotional intelligence quotient, essentially stating its practical and measurable nature. The five common components of EQ include self-awareness, self-regulation, motivation, empathy, and social skills. A high EQ enables one to effectively deal with stressful situations, such as change. EQ is also a critical component of leadership, allowing leaders to effectively communicate, set the right tone for the organization, and understand how their decisions affect others.

AN INSPIRATIONAL LEADERSHIP STORY

One compelling story that showcases exemplary leadership during a technological transition is the story of Katharine Graham and *The Washington Post* in the late 20th century.[3] This period marked a significant shift for the newspaper industry, transitioning from traditional typesetting and manual layout processes to digital publishing systems. Katharine Graham's leadership through this transformative era changed the newspaper and set a precedent for the industry.

In the early 1980s, *The Washington Post*—under the leadership of Katharine Graham—faced the immense challenge of transitioning to digital production processes. This move was spurred by the need for greater efficiency and the potential to improve the quality of the newspaper's journalism. The transition involved significant financial investment, retraining employees, and overhauling the entire production process—risks that were met with skepticism from within the organization and the industry at large.

Graham's leadership during this period was visionary. She recognized early on that integrating computer technology was a matter of operational efficiency and a strategic imperative to ensure the newspaper's future relevance and competitiveness. Several key leadership qualities marked her approach to the transition: a clear vision of the transformative potential of digital technology for *The Washington Post* and the newspaper industry, embracing change for growth and sustainability, demonstrating remarkable courage in making difficult decisions, including significant financial investments in new technologies and an outstanding ability to adapt to new technologies. She understood that leadership in the digital age required openness to innovation and change.

The successful digital transition of *The Washington Post* under Katharine Graham's leadership secured its position as a leading national newspaper and demonstrated the power of visionary leadership in navigating technological change. This case study is an inspiring example for leaders facing the AI Revolution in customer service, highlighting the importance of vision, courage, adaptability, inclusivity, and ethical leadership in steering organizations through transformative periods.

Hosting regular open forums where employees can express their thoughts and concerns about AI, providing a platform for empathetic dialogue and collaborative problem solving, can showcase EQ in action.

The AI Revolution in customer service and support calls for leaders who are not only forward-thinking and technologically and business savvy but also deeply committed to ethical principles, inclusivity, and the well-being of their employees and society. These leaders will navigate the complexities of AI integration with a clear vision, ethical compass, and an unwavering focus on the human element. By embodying these traits, leaders can harness AI's transformative power to drive organizational success and contribute to a future where technology and humanity converge for the greater good. The journey is complex and fraught with challenges, but the personal and professional rewards are boundless for leaders who navigate it successfully.

The Transformational Journey

Integrating AI into your business requires a deeper dive into each aspect of the transformative process, so let's unfold the layers of this narrative to provide a more comprehensive blueprint for leaders embarking on this pioneering voyage.

As a leader, recognizing the transformative potential of AI is just the beginning. The real challenge lies in envisioning how these capabilities can be harnessed to drive business growth and contribute to societal well-being. This involves asking probing questions about your organization's role in leveraging AI, and you need to get yourself equipped and ready to answer them.

The Compass: Defining Your Vision in Greater Detail

Your vision for integrating AI should be both aspirational and actionable. It should outline the desired outcomes, values, and principles guiding your AI initiatives. This means considering the ethical implications of AI technologies, such as bias, privacy, and job displacement, and committing to transparency, accountability, and inclusivity in your AI practices.

To craft a compelling vision, engage with stakeholders across your organization and beyond, including employees, customers, community leaders, and even critics. These dialogues can provide valuable insights into the hopes, fears, and expectations surrounding AI, which can inform a more nuanced and inclusive vision.

These are some strategies and approaches for engaging stakeholders you may consider for fostering participation and the collection of diverse and meaningful insights:

- **Roundtable discussions and workshops:** Organize interactive sessions where stakeholders from different areas of your organization and customers and community leaders can share their perspectives on AI. Use these forums to explore concerns, opportunities, and ethical considerations. Facilitate workshops with creative methodologies like design thinking to co-create solutions and identify potential AI applications that align with your organization's values and stakeholders' needs.

- **Surveys and feedback mechanisms:** Deploy targeted surveys to gather quantitative and qualitative data on stakeholders' views regarding AI in customer service. These surveys can be customized for different groups (e.g., employees, customers, industry experts) to capture a wide range of insights. Additionally, implement ongoing feedback mechanisms, such as digital suggestion boxes or dedicated AI innovation forums, to continually collect and incorporate stakeholder input into your AI strategy.

- **Stakeholder advisory boards:** Establish an advisory board that embodies a broad spectrum of perspectives, including ethicists, technologists, customer representatives, and employees from various departments. This advisory board is pivotal in overseeing the ethical deployment of AI technologies, evaluating AI initiatives for potential biases or ethical dilemmas, and laying the cornerstone of your company's AI vision. Their guidance is integral in shaping a vision aligned with the company's values and anticipates and addresses the complexities of AI integration, ensuring that the roadmap is aspirational and deeply rooted in ethical practice.

By employing these strategies, you can engage stakeholders meaningfully, ensuring that your vision for AI in customer service and support is aspirational and grounded in the practical insights and collective wisdom of your entire stakeholder community. This collaborative approach enriches your AI vision and builds a solid foundation for its successful implementation, ensuring that it is responsive to the needs, values, and ethical considerations of all involved.

The Map: Charting Your Course with Precision

Charting your course in the AI landscape involves a strategic blend of short-term wins and long-term goals. Begin by identifying areas where AI can have an immediate impact, such as automating routine tasks to improve efficiency or using AI-powered analytics to gain deeper insights into customer behavior. These quick wins can demonstrate the value of AI to your organization and build momentum for more ambitious projects. Simultaneously, work on laying the groundwork for long-term transformation:

- Invest in the infrastructure needed to support AI initiatives, such as data storage and computing resources.
- Establish governance frameworks to ensure ethical AI use.
- Foster a culture of innovation where experimentation is encouraged, and failures are viewed as learning opportunities.

The Crew: Assembling Your Team with Care

Building a team for the AI era goes beyond hiring technical talent. It's about creating a multidisciplinary group that reflects a wide range of perspectives and skills. This includes individuals who can bridge the gap between technology and business, such as product managers and business analysts, as well as experts in ethics, law, and social sciences who can navigate the broader implications of AI. The future of support includes multiple disciplines, including traditional support engineers, software engineers, ethicists, data scientists, content creators, and others. We need to move AI learning upstream to provide these models directly to customers.

This list of roles for executing an AI vision in customer service is meant to serve as a foundation for consideration. It is not exhaustive and may not encompass all the roles required for every organization. Depending on your AI initiatives' specific needs, scale, and scope, additional roles may be necessary; also, some of the listed roles might not apply. It's important to tailor the team composition to align with your company's unique objectives and the specific challenges you aim to address with AI in customer service. This framework is designed to be a starting point, inviting you to think critically about the range of expertise and perspectives needed to bring your AI vision to life effectively, with a multidisciplinary team where each member contributes unique skills and insights to drive success.

- **AI strategist:** Leads the vision for AI integration, ensuring alignment with business objectives and stakeholder values. They identify opportunities where AI can enhance customer service and outline strategic approaches for implementation.

- **Data scientist:** Analyzes and interprets complex data to develop AI models tailored to customer service needs. Their expertise in machine learning algorithms and predictive modeling is crucial for creating intelligent systems that improve customer interactions.

- **AI ethics officer:** Guides the team on ethical considerations, ensuring AI applications respect privacy, fairness, and inclusivity. They play a vital role in developing guidelines and practices that prevent bias and safeguard customer rights.

- **Software developer:** Builds and integrates AI technologies into existing customer service platforms. They are responsible for the technical development, ensuring AI solutions are scalable, secure, and efficient.

- **User interface (UI)/user experience (UX) designer:** Designs intuitive interfaces and experiences for AI-driven customer service tools. They ensure that interactions with AI are user-friendly, accessible, and engaging for customers.

- **Quality assurance (QA) analyst:** Tests AI applications to ensure they meet quality standards and functional requirements. Their work is crucial for identifying and fixing issues before deployment, ensuring reliability and performance.

- **Legal and compliance officer:** Ensures AI implementations comply with regulations and legal standards, particularly concerning data protection and consumer rights. They help navigate the complex legal landscape surrounding AI technologies.

- **Change manager:** Facilitates the adoption of AI technologies within the organization and by customers. They develop training programs and support structures to ease transitions, address resistance, and foster a culture open to innovation.

- **Communication specialist:** Manages internal and external communications about AI initiatives, ensuring transparent and consistent messaging. They are key in building trust and engagement among employees, customers, and stakeholders.

Each of these roles contributes to a cohesive effort to implement AI in an ethical, customer-focused way, and aligned with the company's strategic vision, ensuring the successful transformation of customer service through technology.

Investing in education and training is crucial to empowering your team to thrive in the era of AI, including partnerships with universities, online courses, and internal workshops to ensure your team stays abreast of the latest developments in AI and related fields.

The Voyage: Navigating the Journey with Resilience

Integrating AI is fraught with challenges, from technical hurdles to ethical quandaries. Leading through these challenges requires a balance of determination, flexibility, and empathy. Be prepared to pivot your strategies as you learn from experience and the AI landscape evolves. Foster an environment where feedback is valued, and resilience is built through collective learning and adaptation.

Remember, the success of your AI initiatives is not just measured by the technological advancements you achieve but by the positive impact you create for your employees, customers, and society at large.

The Legacy: Creating a Lasting Impact

As you navigate this journey, remember the legacy you want to build. This legacy should reflect a commitment to using AI as a force for good, enhancing human capabilities (rather than replacing them), addressing societal challenges, and promoting sustainability and equity.

Your legacy will also be defined by the culture you cultivate—one that embraces change, values ethical considerations, and champions innovation for the betterment of society. This is the legacy that will endure long after the technologies have evolved.

Integrating AI in customer service and support is transforming our organizations and reshaping the essence of how we interact and excel in service delivery. This chapter underscores a truth as enduring as leadership itself—that at the heart of technological advancement lies the spirit of visionary leadership. It's an invitation to all who dare to lead, to embrace AI's boundless possibilities and seize the vast opportunities ahead of us.

We'd like to invite you to embrace this moment as your own call to greatness, to redefine the parameters of what is possible in customer service and support. As you embark on this exciting journey, remember that the essence of true leadership lies in the ability to inspire, empower, and lead with passion and authenticity. Treat this opportunity as more than a transition—it's an opportunity to redefine excellence, build deeper connections, and lead with courage that inspires those around you. Step forward with confidence, knowing that the path you carve today will shape the landscape of customer service and support for years to come.

Embarking on the AI journey is not just a business transformation; it's a call to leadership in the highest sense. It's an opportunity to shape the future and steer the course of technology toward a horizon reflecting our highest aspirations for humanity and the planet. Let this expanded narrative be a beacon for your journey, illuminating the path toward a future where AI and human potential converge to create a world of endless possibilities.

Endnotes

1   Downs, G. 2019. "Satya Nadella: 'The Learn-It-All Does Better Than the Know-It-All'." *The Wall Street Journal*. January 23, 2019. [https://www.wsj.com/video/satya-nadella-the-learn-it-all-does-better-than-the-know-it-all/D8BC205C-D7F5-423E-8A41-0E921E86597C].

2   Frothingham, Mia Belle. 2024. "Emotional Intelligence (EQ)." *SimplyPsychology*. January 29, 2024. [https://www.simplypsychology.org/emotional-intelligence.html].

3   Washington Post staff. 2021. "Washington Post company history." *The Washington Post*. January 1, 2021. [https://www.washingtonpost.com/company-history/].

18

Future of Work: Navigating the AI Revolution

The best way to predict the future is to create it.

—Peter Drucker

As we stand on the threshold of a new era, the AI Revolution is set to redefine customer service and support as we know it today. This rapidly approaching reality holds great promise but also presents the challenge of balancing human intuition with machine precision. Will AI enhance our connections with customers or make interactions impersonal? The outcome is uncertain.

Join us as we explore the future of work through seven possible scenarios, where AI and human ingenuity converge to shape a brighter, more efficient, and deeply connected world... or maybe not. We don't know the answer, but in this chapter, we want to give you some tools to help you find the answer for yourself and your team. The future is now, and how we navigate the AI Revolution will shape customer service for generations to come.

Navigating the AI Revolution

The future of work will see dramatic changes across all industries with the advent of AI. Customer service and support could see a wide range of potential changes. On one hand, we may see AI-based chatbots take over 100 percent of human interaction. We might also see the most successful companies retain human support, perhaps even charging extra to talk to a human. We may see legislation like the forecasted "right to talk to a human" law in the European Union, as predicted by Gartner, anticipating that the EU could make it a part of its consumer protection laws in customer service by 2028.[1] For all we know, AI might get so good that AI customer service is reserved for premium customers. Or we may see some type of hybrid of all these. We know that human empathy and creativity will always have value in conversing with other humans. We also know that AI will create new jobs that don't exist today, just as other technologies throughout history have done.

THE LOOM OF PROGRESS, PART TWO

Let's continue the fictitious story we started in Chapter 1.

As Mary and Elizabeth contemplated their future and the disruption to their livelihood, the power loom grew in importance. This new technology introduced changes to life that were unimaginable before. Production of textiles became more efficient, and manufacturers soon realized the tremendous cost savings with increased production. Consumers were thrilled with the abundant choices available at a fraction of the cost, allowing full wardrobes to be purchased, whereas before, the price of a single outfit was prohibitive to most. New textile uses were developed as consumers realized the versatility of cloth patterns and colors could be used in decorative and practical functions.

The spinners and weavers' fear of the new machines wasn't unfounded. Clearly, their jobs were no longer needed in the same way as before. Being one of the first to recognize this, Elizabeth felt sure she could adapt to the increased speed. However, Mary contemplated what her life would be like now that her job was almost obsolete. She resolved not to let this get her down and committed to overcoming her fear by learning all she could about the operation of the machine and the value her bosses and consumers saw in its output.

Each night, after work, Mary and Elizabeth discussed and debated at length what actions they should take to maintain their livelihood. Elizabeth felt that as a weaver, she at least had a chance to remain employed as long as she could adapt to the quicker speeds required. However, Mary had more pressing concerns because her job would soon be eliminated, and she knew decisions had to be made quickly.

As Simon Winchester stated:

If all knowledge, if the sum of all thought, is to be made available at the touch on a plate of glass, then what does that portend? If the electronic computer is swiftly becoming so much more powerful and more able than even the most prodigiously able of all human brains—then what is the likely outcome for that very human society that has been the principal beneficiary of human intelligence for all of the world's inhabited existence? If our brains—if we, that is, for our brains are the permanent essence of us—no longer need knowledge, and if we do not need it because the computers do it all for us, then what is human intelligence good for? An existential intellectual crisis looms: If machines will acquire all our knowledge for us and do our thinking for us, then what, pray, is the need for us to be?[2]

This chapter is a thought experiment to help you prepare for the unknown future ahead.

The next few months saw additional power looms being introduced to the factory floor. Fear grew, and rumors of spinner job eliminations proliferated throughout the ranks. Mary remained calm as she had a plan. With Elizabeth at her side, she began to learn all she could about how these new machines worked, becoming an invaluable resource to management because the new loom machines weren't perfect and experienced some challenges over time. Mary became a catalyst of innovation as she experimented with introducing multiple colors of yarn into the machines, pushing the weavers to create new, interesting patterns and textures.

After a time, Mary realized she was no longer fearful of the future but excited about the possibilities. This new loom technology was helping the textile industry evolve and was introducing new jobs and ways to work. Once this realization happened, Mary became confident in her newfound knowledge and the value she brought to her work every day. Elizabeth also noticed a shift in her ability to be more creative with her weaving, given the many colors, patterns, and textures made possible through the power loom's quicker output.

While the power loom helped transform the cottage industry into large-scale manufacturing, bringing more efficiency and productivity to the textile industry, Mary and Elizabeth thrived in their knowledge and ability to transform and adapt. In the end, those who could learn and grow alongside the evolution of machines helped change the world.

THE ORACLE AT DELPHI

In ancient Greece, Persia, Egypt, and Rome, citizens unsure of the future would visit oracles to get predictions. Probably the most famous was the Greek oracle of Delphi—Pythia, a high priestess and messenger for Apollo.[3] People would travel to Delphi to get her guidance, where she held court at Pytho, channeling the Greek god Apollo. Pythia was known to pronounce judgment to all those in attendance when she fell into a trance-like state and channeled the god. The sanctuary at Delphi was closed around 393 CE after the Roman emperor Theodosius directed all pagan sanctuaries to be closed.[4]

Today, we don't have the same access to the Oracle at Delphi, although we imagine that someone in ancient Greece or Rome watching us interact with ChatGPT would not believe that statement. This invites some entertaining thinking about prompt engineering preparation on the road to Delphi!

What we do have is the ability to do thought experiments—alone or with others—to consider which of the possible futures mentioned in this chapter (or others not mentioned) will play out for our organizations and how, as leaders, we can best prepare ourselves and our organizations for all possible outcomes.

Drawing inspiration from the ancient practice of seeking guidance from the Oracle of Delphi, we find ourselves at a crossroads of uncertainty and possibility in our modern era. Just as the ancients turned to Pythia for insights into their future, we too can harness the power of foresight, albeit through a different medium. By engaging in these thought experiments, we can embark on a journey to explore the multitude of potential futures that lie before our organizations, equipping ourselves with the wisdom to navigate the challenges and opportunities that await us.

Just as the Oracle of Delphi served as a conduit between the divine and the mortal, offering insights that shaped the futures of empires and individuals alike, artificial intelligence stands today as our own modern oracle, harnessing the vast expanse of human knowledge and human-built computational power to illuminate our path forward, guiding us through the complexities of the new age of AI with predictions and insights once thought beyond human reach. It's fun to imagine a pilgrim en route to Delphi encountering a cellphone with a ChatGPT app and how they might compare the two experiences.

It's been a few thousand years, but we think we can score a win for humanity; consulting Pythia is accessible on our phones now—no travel required.

Thought Experiment Considerations

When organizational leaders evaluate potential futures, there are several things to consider in the thought experiment. As described by James Robert Brown and Fehige Yiftach: "Thought experiments are basically devices of the imagination. They are employed for various purposes such an entertainment, education, conceptual analysis, exploration, hypothesizing, theory selection, theory implementation, etc. Some applications are more controversial than others. Few would object to thought experiments that serve to illustrate complex states of affairs, or those that are used in educational contexts."[5]

Thought experiments are an important tool in philosophy, physics, and other disciplines, allowing individuals and organizations to explore hypotheses, theories, and principles through imaginative reasoning rather than empirical methods. When conducting a thought experiment, there are several important considerations to ensure its effectiveness and relevance. Here are four of the most important considerations:

- **Clearly defined starting assumptions:** The starting assumptions or premises of a thought experiment must be clearly defined. Ambiguity in the premises can lead to unclear or misleading conclusions. The initial premises must be clear and plausible within the context of the experiment, even if they are hypothetical.

- **Internal consistency:** The scenario and logic within the thought experiment must be internally consistent with itself. This means that the conclusions drawn should logically follow from the premises without contradicting them or introducing external factors not accounted for in the initial setup and premises. Consistency is crucial for a thought experiment to be considered valid and for its conclusions to be taken seriously.

  The trolley problem is a good example.[6] A trolley (or autonomous vehicle) is hurtling toward five people who will be killed. You are standing next to a lever that controls the trolley's direction. If you pull the lever, the trolley will be redirected to an area where there is just one person. You have two options:

  - Do nothing, and the trolley kills the five people.

  - Pull the lever, redirecting the trolley where it will kill one person.

  The thought experiment maintains internal consistency by ensuring that the consequences of each action logically follow from the premises without introducing contradictions or external factors not accounted for in the initial setup. The dilemma is constructed to explore ethical principles, specifically the moral implications of actively causing harm to save more lives versus passively allowing more harm to occur.

- If you choose to do nothing, it is consistent with the premise that inaction will result in the trolley continuing on its current path, leading to the death of five people.

- If you choose to pull the lever, it is consistent with the premise that your action directly causes the trolley to switch tracks, resulting in the death of one person instead of five.

The thought experiment does not introduce any external factors that could undermine the internal logic, such as proposing that the trolley could perhaps stop on its own or the people being able to get out of the way. The scenario is deliberately constructed to force a choice within a closed logic system, ensuring that each choice's conclusions (the ethical implications) directly follow from the premises.

Internal consistency is crucial in any thought experiment because it allows for a focused exploration of ethical decision-making and the moral weight of action versus inaction. By ensuring that the scenario is logically coherent and self-contained, the thought experiment facilitates clear, meaningful insights into the principles of utilitarianism and ethics without being muddled by irrelevant considerations, alternatives, or contradictions. This clarity and consistency make the thought experiment valuable for philosophical inquiry and discussion.

- **Relevance to the question at hand:** A thought experiment should be directly relevant to the question or problem it aims to explore. It should be designed to shed light on the specific issue—in our case, the future of AI in customer service and support—providing insights or challenging assumptions in a meaningful way. Irrelevant or tangentially related thought experiments may be interesting as side projects but fail to advance understanding of the core issue.

- **Simplicity and economy:** While thought experiments can be complex, they should be as simple as possible to effectively convey the idea or test the hypothesis without unnecessary complications. This principle, often related to Occam's Razor—the problem-solving principle that recommends searching for explanations constructed with the smallest possible set of elements—suggests that among competing hypotheses that predict equally well, the one with the fewest assumptions should be selected.[7] Simplicity ensures that the thought experiment remains focused, and irrelevant details do not obscure its conclusions.

How Will AI Reshape Customer Service and Support?

In the rapidly evolving landscape of customer service and support, the integration of AI puts us at a crossroads. AI can potentially redefine our traditional notions of support and customer interaction. It can do things humans cannot, including instant answers, 24/7 availability, and instant sentiment analysis. On the other hand, humans are good at thinking on their feet, responding immediately to disruption, and providing empathy and genuine human-to-human caregiving. As we venture into the future of customer service, we provide seven potential scenarios for consideration, each offering a unique blend of technology and human touch designed to elevate the customer experience to unprecedented levels. From AI-driven models capable of handling 100 percent of customer interactions to hybrid approaches that balance technological efficiency with the irreplaceable value of human empathy, these futures envision a world where customer service is not just a function but a personalized journey.

Whether through the creation of AI-based customer advocates, the rise of specialized AI coaches, or the advent of premium AI-driven experiences complemented by human support, these scenarios invite us to imagine a not-so-distant future where technology and humanity coalesce to create more meaningful, efficient, and personalized customer engagements. As we stand on the brink of these transformative possibilities, we are witnessing a shift in customer service dynamics and a complete reimagining of the essence of customer connection and satisfaction. The unknown future is simultaneously debilitating and liberating!

Navigating the AI Revolution in customer service and support is akin to charting a course through uncharted waters, where technological advancement, human capability, emotion, and creativity intersect. As we contemplate our collective future, it's clear that the integration of AI into customer service is not a question of if or when, but how—how to do this the right way. At this stage of the game, we don't know the answer. The six potential futures outlined in the following sections (and probably others we haven't considered) offer a glimpse into a world where AI and human capabilities do not compete with one another. Still, in collaboration and partnership, each enhances the other to create a customer service experience that is both efficient and empathetic. Humans plus machines will always be better than either one on their own.

Moreover, the thought experiment inspired by the Oracle of Delphi reminds us of the importance of foresight and preparation. By considering these potential futures, we can develop flexible and resilient strategies, ensuring that our organizations are not just reactive but proactive in the face of the change that the new world of AI will bestow upon us. This approach will enable us to survive and thrive in the AI Revolution, creating a future where technology and humanity work in harmony to elevate the customer service experience to new heights.

Thought experiments like the trolley problem are thought-provoking, imaginative devices that can help us approach complex ethical dilemmas, demonstrating their utility in educational and conceptual analysis contexts. The trolley problem, in particular, challenges us to weigh the consequences of our actions versus inactions within a strictly defined scenario, fostering deep ethical contemplation and debate. When applying Occam's Razor (the simplest solution is better than the more complex solution) to the trolley problem, one might argue for the solution that assumes the least—in this case, choosing the action that results in the fewest deaths, although the ethical simplicity of this solution is subject to philosophical debate. However, this application of Occam's Razor does not diminish the complexity of the moral and ethical considerations in play, as it merely guides the decision toward the option with fewer immediate consequences, not necessarily the morally correct one. Thus, the trolley problem serves as a tool for exploring theoretical ethical frameworks and highlights the limitations of applying principles like Occam's Razor to nuanced human values and moral judgments.

Considering these historical, philosophical examples is important as you contemplate the future of customer service and support. Our goal in this chapter is to jumpstart your thinking and have you consider your own organization's potential future and how you want to approach it.

The key to successfully navigating this AI Revolution lies in our ability to adapt and innovate. While recognizing its potential to transform their industry and finding new ways to apply their skills, we also must embrace AI as a tool that can transform our customer service and support world. By focusing on the unique strengths of both AI and human agents, we can create a hybrid model that leverages the efficiency and scalability of AI while retaining the irreplaceable human touch that fosters genuine connections and trust. We are just beginning our amazing journey where humans and machines can partner to serve other humans—our customers—in ways we cannot do alone. It's a thrilling and apprehensive time of change, but as a leader in customer service and support, you are right at the forefront of this change and can direct it in service to your constituents.

This is the dawning of this new era where AI and human ingenuity converge; we stand on the precipice of redefining customer service and support and the essence of human-machine partnership and collaboration. This journey, though fraught with risk and uncertainties, holds the promise of a future where technology amplifies our human strengths, enabling us to deliver customer experiences that are more personalized and efficient and deeply empathetic, compassionate, and understanding. As we navigate these uncharted waters, let us embrace the spirit of innovation and the boundless potential of AI as our partner in our quest to enrich human connections. Together, we can forge a path that leads to a brighter, more inclusive future where every interaction is a testament to the synergy between human warmth and technological prowess. In this future, AI does not replace the human touch but elevates and amplifies it, creating a world where every customer feels seen, heard, and valued. This is not just the future of customer service; it is the future of how we connect, understand, and care for each other in an increasingly digital world.

"It is possible to believe that all the past is but the beginning of a beginning, and that all that is and has been is but the twilight of the dawn. It is possible to believe that all the human mind has ever accomplished is but the dream before the awakening." –H. G. Wells

Future 1: The AI-Only Customer Service Model

In potential future number one, we move to a world where AI chatbots and virtual assistants have become sophisticated enough to handle 100 percent of customer service interactions across all industries. These AI systems are powered by advanced machine learning algorithms, enabling them to understand and respond highly accurately to a wide range of customer emotions and queries using voice, text, and video. Companies have embraced this model for its cost-effectiveness and the ability to provide 24/7 support without the limitations of human work hours, HR issues, scheduling, and human paychecks. However, this shift has led to significant worker displacement in the customer service sector, with former employees needing to find new roles in an increasingly automated economy. While customers enjoy instant responses and resolutions, some express nostalgia for the personal touch and nuanced understanding that only human interactions can provide. The introduction of the ATM to the world of banking is a good metaphor.

Future 2: Premium Human Support in a Hybrid Service Model

In scenario number two, most customer service interactions are managed by AI, but companies offer the option of speaking to a human agent for a premium. This model caters to customers who value human empathy and personal connection, particularly for complex issues requiring deep understanding and emotional intelligence. If we extend our ATM metaphor, this is where banks open small "boutique" branches staffed with one teller. In Future 2, human agents are highly skilled and trained in specific areas, making them experts in providing solutions and advice, elevating the status and perception of customer service professionals. This approach not only retains jobs but also enhances the perceived quality of customer service, creating a new market for premium support services. The hybrid model successfully balances technological efficiency and the irreplaceable value of human interaction.

Future 3: The Co-Evolution of AI and Human Roles

In the third potential future, AI and human customer service agents work as collaborative partners, with AI handling routine inquiries and human agents taking on complex or sensitive issues. This co-evolution leads to the creation of new roles focused on AI supervision, training, and sentiment/ emotional intelligence analysis, ensuring that AI systems continue to learn and improve from human interactions. Education and training programs evolve to prepare workers for these new roles, emphasizing critical thinking, empathy, and technical skills. Content creation roles to enhance AI and machine learning start to develop. Companies that adopt this model are praised for their commitment to maintaining a human touch in an increasingly digital world, fostering customer loyalty. This future represents an optimistic scenario where technology and humanity enhance each other, creating more meaningful jobs and improving the overall customer experience. The idea is that a human plus a machine is better than either one individually.

Future 4: The Rise of Personalized AI Customer Advocates

In future number four, AI technology has advanced to the point where each customer is assigned a personalized AI advocate. This could be the "digital twin" of a human support engineer who has previously helped them. It could also be a small language model that's trained specifically on their configurations, usage patterns, and support patterns. These AI advocates can understand individual customer preferences, history, and behaviors to an unprecedented degree, offering highly personalized support, upselling opportunities, and product recommendations. These models integrate seamlessly with various services and platforms, acting as a central hub for all customer service needs and improving customer interactions by making them more efficient and tailored to individual preferences. This approach significantly enhances customer satisfaction by providing a level of personalization that goes beyond what human agents are capable of based on their limited memory and lifespan. However, this deep personalization raises concerns about privacy and data security, prompting stricter regulations and new standards for AI transparency and customer data protection.

Future 5: The Rise of Specialized AI Coaches and Consultants

In this future, number five, the customer service landscape has evolved to include AI-based coaches and consultants who work alongside human agents. These AI systems are designed not to interact directly with customers, but only work to support and enhance the capabilities of human agents by providing real-time data analysis, recommendations, and even sentiment analysis and emotional intelligence coaching. This setup keeps humans in the loop and enables human agents to handle a wider range of inquiries more efficiently and effectively, including complex and sensitive issues, by leveraging AI-driven insights and suggestions. The role of customer service professionals expands to include AI management and interpretation, requiring a new skill set that blends technical proficiency with traditional customer service skills. A lot of the heavy lifting of support interactions is done by AI coaches, with humans providing the "last mile" service. This future sees a symbiotic relationship between humans and AI, each playing to their strengths to deliver an unparalleled customer service experience.

Future 6: AI-Driven Premium Experiences with Human Support for Routine Inquiries

For future number six, in an unexpected twist on the future of customer service, AI has advanced to the point where it can provide premium, highly personalized experiences that were once the domain of top-tier human agents. In this scenario, AI systems can handle complex, nuanced interactions, including managing high-value customer accounts and delivering important, even mission-critical, solutions tailored to individual customer needs. These AI agents use vast machine learning capabilities to understand preferences and history and even predict future needs, offering a level of service that goes well beyond human capabilities. Meanwhile, human agents are tasked with handling mundane routine inquiries and issues that require less personalization. This reversal of roles challenges traditional notions of premium service, with companies leveraging cutting-edge AI to offer customers a luxury experience while ensuring that human agents can provide a warm, empathetic touch for those who prefer it.

Future 7: AI Fizzles Out, and Nothing Changes

This seventh future feels highly unlikely, but the experiment would not be complete without it. In this scenario, a front-line service agent continues to perform tasks similar to what they have always done. The grand AI Revolution has had no impact on the daily lives of customers and support engineers.

Exploring the Seven Futures

As we conclude this exploration of the seven potential futures of AI in customer service and support, we find ourselves on the brink of a revolutionary new era. Each scenario offers a unique view into how AI might reshape our approach to customer interaction, from complete automation to intricate human-AI partnerships. These visions, ranging from the total displacement of human customer support roles to their evolution and coexistence with AI, underscore a pivotal moment in our journey with technology. These futures are not merely hypothetical—they are blueprints that invite us to envision and actively shape how AI integrates into the fabric of our customer interactions.

As we stand at this crossroads, the paths laid out before us are not just hypothetical routes but potential realities that could dictate how we interact, serve, and support our customers in the not-too-distant future. The choices we make today—from the technology we embrace to the values we uphold—will define the landscape of customer service for years to come.

Let this be a call to action for all leaders and innovators in the field to prepare for change and actively shape it. Embrace the potential of AI with foresight and responsibility, ensuring that as we advance technologically, we do not lose sight of the human element that remains at the heart of customer service. Whether AI becomes a tool that complements our human workforce or one that redefines the very essence of the role depends on the wisdom with which we steer this ship.

With the conclusion of this chapter, we invite you to reflect on these futures, not as distant realities but as imminent possibilities that require your engagement and decisions. The future is not just something that happens to us; it is something we create.

This is the dawn of a new era in customer service—an era where we hold the keys to a kingdom of possibilities. It's time to step forward with courage and creativity to shape this future. Let us embark on this journey with a clear vision and a firm resolve to use AI not just as a tool for innovation but as a sign of progress in the truest sense. Together, we can forge a future where technology and humanity converge to create unprecedented value for all our stakeholders. Embrace this challenge, and let us redefine what it means to serve in an increasingly connected world.

Endnotes

1   Fisher, Rhys. 2024. "By 2028, the EU Will Mandate 'the Right to Talk to a Human' In Customer Service, Predicts Gartner" CXToday. February 19, 2024. [https://www.cxtoday.com/contact-centre/by-2028-the-eu-will-mandate-the-right-to-talk-to-a-human-in-customer-service-predicts-gartner/].

2   Winchester, Simon. *Knowing What We Know*. Barnhill Press Ltd, Sandisfield, MA, 2023. p 7.

3   Wikipedia contributors. "Pythia." Wikipedia, The Free Encyclopedia. February 17, 2024. [https://en.wikipedia.org/wiki/Pythia].

4   Jones, Gabriel. 2013. "Pythia." World History Encyclopedia. August 30, 2013. [https://www.worldhistory.org/Pythia/].

5   Brown, James Robert., Fehige, Yiftach. "Thought Experiments." Stanford Encyclopedia of Philosophy. November 28, 2023. [https://plato.stanford.edu/cgi-bin/encyclopedia/archinfo.cgi?entry=thought-experiment].

6   Wikipedia contributors. "Trolley problem." Wikipedia, The Free Encyclopedia. February 8, 2024. [https://en.wikipedia.org/wiki/Trolley_problem].

7   Wikipedia contributors. "Occam's razor." Wikipedia, The Free Encyclopedia. February 23, 2024. [https://en.wikipedia.org/wiki/Occam%27s_razor].

19

Next Steps and Conclusion

*Study hard what interests you the
most in the most undisciplined,
irreverent and original manner possible.*

—Richard Feynman

We have covered a lot of ground, and this book has been quite the
journey. The AI Revolution is certainly upon us, and we thank you,
dear reader, for sticking with us this far. This journey is just beginning for all of us. It's been interesting to work through the writing
process, knowing that it's very possible that what we write today
will be obsolete and out of date tomorrow. We've tried to make
this book as evergreen as possible.

There are a few lessons learned that are important to keep in mind:

- It's not the AI that will take an agent's job; the agent's job will
be taken by someone really good at using AI. So, it's incumbent
upon everyone to learn. We all have an equal opportunity.

- The world of work is ever-changing. How many full-time spinners and weavers do you know today? If you've been in the workforce for 10 years or more, does your first job still exist today? The skills required are always changing.

- The world of AI is moving faster than ever. The best approach you can take—for yourself and for your organization is to learn, learn, learn. Stay up to date with what's happening. Start an AI study group, watch online videos on AI, read academic papers, experiment, and play.

- As we navigate the AI Revolution, it's crucial to recognize that adaptability and continuous learning are both beneficial and essential. The landscape of technology and work is transforming at an unprecedented pace, making it imperative for individuals and organizations alike to remain agile. Embracing a mindset of lifelong learning and curiosity can open doors to new opportunities and ensure resilience in the face of change. It's about harnessing the power of AI to augment our capabilities rather than viewing it as a threat to our livelihoods.

- The democratization of AI technology means that access to powerful technology and resources is more widespread than ever. This accessibility encourages a culture of innovation and creativity, allowing people from diverse backgrounds to contribute to using, developing, and applying AI in service to customers. It's an invitation to everyone, regardless of their current skill level or profession, to shape the future. By engaging with AI, we can all steer its evolution in a direction that benefits our customers—and perhaps even humanity as a whole.

- Organizations that share knowledge, best practices, and lessons learned will be the ones who succeed in leveraging AI to serve customers responsibly.

- You are responsible for leading through change. Create a powerful vision to give your organization a strong roadmap to the future of customer service and support.

We are biased, but the fact that you are reading this book means you are ahead of the game. Many times, we've felt like we are living next door to Johannes Gutenberg, the inventor of the printing press, and while we take out the garbage, he summons us over, opens his garage, and says, "Hey, check this out. I'm working on this new thing called the printing press." It feels like that's where we are today—and given that you have read this far, you have seen Gutenberg's garage! And you can act on that.

Next Steps

This is an exciting time in the world of customer service. We are surfing the wave of huge change. AI technology is advancing at the speed of light. Hundreds of millions worldwide are contributing training data to make new models better than ever. New modalities—images, sound, video—are unlocked every day. In this era of rapid change and transformation, those of us in the service industry are pioneering a customer service revolution fueled by AI's rapid evolution and global collaboration. With new AI channels like images, sound, and video, we're breaking barriers, enhancing customer empathy, and shaping a future where technology elevates every interaction, making the world more connected and understanding than ever before.

Dream Big About How and Where You Can Apply AI Technology in Your Organization

You are a leader. You are reading this book for a reason—maybe you are curious, maybe you're panicked. But you are here, and in this fast-paced world, we want to inspire you to think big.

"Every great dream begins with a dreamer. Always remember, you have within you the strength, the patience, and the passion to reach for the stars to change the world."—falsely attributed to Harriet Tubman.[1]

We included this falsely attributed quote for a number of reasons. First, it conveys a "dream big" message that's important to help motivate you. Second, it warns us that we must be careful of what we read and what AI proposes to be real. Most importantly, we want you to know that this journey requires you to be a dreamer with strength, patience, and passion to reach for the stars. It's a great quote, no matter who said it.

AI technology is moving incredibly fast; even if something is impossible today, it won't be soon. As a leader, you must embrace the idea that AI in customer support and service requires visionary thinking and an openness to innovation. The pace at which AI technology evolves means that today's limitations will vanish tomorrow. As a leader, don't just consider the immediate applications of AI, such as chatbots and automated responses; consider the potential to transform your customers' experience through insights, predictive analytics, and personalized service offerings. By staying informed about AI advancements and fostering a culture of experimentation in your organization, you can position your organization at the forefront of customer service innovation. Do some big-picture thinking about integrating AI across various touchpoints to enhance agent efficiency and effectiveness, customer satisfaction, and ultimately, drive business growth in ways previously unimagined, including insights, upselling, and customer engagement.

The following quote by Naba Banerjee of AirBnB, from a *Me, Myself, and AI* podcast interview, speaks to embracing AI for good and overcoming the fear of potential harm:

My greatest wish for the world, actually, is to not be so afraid; to give it a chance. Because I think sometimes our fear of the bad holds us from embracing the good. There is so much wasted effort that goes into activities that should be automated through AI—so many patients who are not getting treatment; so many companies that probably need help and need so much funding to stand up basic things that can be done by AI; so many countries, probably, who are underdeveloped [but could] get so much advantage. I know that when it falls into the wrong hands, it can be used for bad, but the world has more good people than bad people, and I believe in the power of us using AI for good—using our collective goodness.[2]

Learning is the Best Way You Can Prepare

The advancements in AI are moving quickly. As a leader, you must carve out time to learn. The most important thing for service and support leaders in the AI era is adopting a continuous learning mindset. Knowledge is power, especially in a rapidly changing field. Embrace every opportunity to learn because staying informed is the key to leveraging AI effectively and confidently leading your team.

Mahatma Gandhi said, "Live as if you were to die tomorrow. Learn as if you were to live forever."

In the rapidly evolving landscape of AI technology and customer expectations, the guidance for leaders is clear: learn, learn, learn, and keep on learning. Being a leader requires a relentless commitment to education and self-improvement. Leaders must immerse themselves in the latest industry trends, technological advancements, and best practices. This continuous learning journey enables you to anticipate changes, build innovative solutions, and adapt cutting-edge strategies that keep pace with technological change. Customer service and support leaders can inspire adaptability and agility in their teams by fostering a culture of curiosity and resilience. In a world that moves at breakneck speed, the ability to learn and adapt is not just an advantage; it's a necessity for staying relevant and leading with confidence and foresight.

Be Responsible for Your Organization's Use and Deployment of AI

At the forefront of integrating artificial intelligence within your organization, it's imperative to approach its use and deployment with a sense of responsibility and ethical consideration. As John Quincy Adams famously said, "If your actions inspire others to dream more, learn more, do more, and become more, you are a leader."

This guidance is particularly pertinent when navigating AI technologies' complex and evolving landscape. Customer service and support leaders are responsible for ensuring AI's ethical use and deployment within their organizations, including establishing clear guidelines prioritizing data privacy, security, and fairness in AI applications. Leaders must advocate for transparency in AI operations, enabling stakeholders to clearly understand how AI decisions are made.

It's essential to implement robust governance frameworks that monitor AI's impact on customers and society as a whole, addressing potential biases and ensuring that AI solutions do not perpetuate inequality or injustice. By fostering a culture of the ethical use of AI, leaders can build trust among customers and employees alike, ensuring that the organization's AI initiatives contribute positively to society and uphold the highest standards of responsibility and integrity to help us all build a better future with a human and AI partnership.

Hire Technical Talent into Your Support Organization

For customer service and support leaders to stay abreast of rapidly advancing AI technologies, it's imperative to integrate a diverse and new array of deep technical talent into their teams. Hiring software engineers and data scientists brings in the expertise needed to develop, deploy, and refine AI models that can transform customer interactions. Content creators and knowledge management experts will be crucial in curating data and insights that fuel AI systems, ensuring they deliver relevant and accurate support.

This multidisciplinary approach not only enhances the organization's capability to innovate and stay current, but by putting these folks in the same teams as support domain experts, you can ensure that AI implementations are grounded in a deep understanding of customer needs, technological possibilities, and the latest advancements in AI, keeping the organization at the cutting edge of customer service excellence.

Building the AI Team: the Hub and Spoke Model

As you deploy AI research and development investments across any organization, it's important to recognize domain expertise. There will be a temptation to create a central "AI Team," but that is a limiting idea for this fast-moving tech. Yes, a central team to act as a hub, but you need to empower satellite teams to experiment within their domains without the restrictive oversight of a central team that can't possibly keep up with the pace of innovation. Poet Stanley Victor Paskavich put it nicely: "The wheel of life has many spokes, yet so few people ever leave the hub."

Spread New Tech Capabilities across Your Organization

In the rapidly changing landscape of AI integration into customer service, adopting a hub-and-spoke organizational model that offers a strategic approach to embedding technical capabilities throughout an organization is important. Chinese politician and founder of the People's Republic of China (PRC) Mao Zedong said, "Let many flowers bloom,"[3] encouraging many ideas from many sources. The idea is to let people innovate at the edges in their own domains. Don't try to control things in a central team, particularly with a fast-moving technology like AI.

Rather than concentrating expertise within a large, centralized "AI Team," consider distributing AI investments, skills, and knowledge across various customer teams, with a small central group of architects and planners acting as the hub. This central hub focuses on overarching strategy, governance, and ensuring consistency in AI initiatives, while the spokes—individual teams within different business units—apply AI technologies to specific challenges and opportunities in their areas.

This decentralized approach encourages innovation and agility, allowing for tailored AI solutions that are closely aligned with each team's unique needs and objectives. It also fosters a culture of continuous learning and collaboration, as knowledge and best practices are shared between the hub and the spokes, with employees interacting directly with domain experts. By sprinkling technical capabilities throughout the organization, businesses can more effectively leverage AI to drive efficiency, enhance customer experiences, and create competitive advantages.

Moreover, the hub-and-spoke model ensures that AI adoption is aligned with the organization's strategic vision while allowing for the flexibility and specialization needed to respond to rapidly changing technologies, customer and product changes, and market demands. This balance between centralized oversight and decentralized execution is key to successfully navigating the complexities of AI integration in today's fast-paced business environment.

Understand the Financial Impact of Deploying AI

You will hear a wide variety of views on the financial impact of AI in customer service, from those who believe that AI will save millions to those who are complete naysayers and don't expect it to save a dime. Your job is to be realistic and understand how you plan to measure the financial impact of AI integration. In many customer service and support organizations, your people or headcount cost is the highest percentage of your budget. However, people also play the largest role in ensuring customer satisfaction. Modeling and thinking through your strategic approach when forecasting financial impact is important.

Irish poet and playwright Oscar Wilde said, "When I was young, I thought that money was the most important thing in life; now that I am old, I know that it is."

Organizational leaders must prioritize and understand the financial impact of deploying AI in customer service. This process thoroughly analyzes initial investments and up-front costs against long-term benefits, including cost savings from automation and efficiencies and potential revenue growth from an improved customer experience. Leaders must consider not only the direct costs associated with AI technology, such as development, integration, and maintenance, but also the indirect costs, like staff training, change management, and content development. Equally important is evaluating ROI through key performance indicators such as customer satisfaction scores, resolution times, and service scalability. By carefully assessing these financial implications, leaders can make informed decisions that align AI deployments with strategic business objectives, ensuring a balance between innovation and fiscal responsibility.

Consider the Risks and Rewards of Putting AI Directly in the Hands of Your Customers

Putting AI directly in customers' hands presents a delicate balance of risks and rewards. On the one hand, AI can significantly enhance the customer experience by providing personalized services, instantaneous self-help support, and innovative interaction models, leading to increased satisfaction and loyalty. On the other hand, significant risks are associated with wrong answers, data privacy concerns, potential biases in AI decision-making, and the impersonality of interactions that could detract from the customer experience. Leaders must navigate these challenges carefully, ensuring robust data protection measures and continuous monitoring for bias, hallucinations, and model drift while balancing the importance of maintaining a human touch in customer interactions. By thoughtfully managing these aspects of customer interactions, organizations can harness the full potential of AI to revolutionize customer engagement while safeguarding customer trust and satisfaction.

Pay Attention to Your AI Training Content

We are entering a new world where customer support knowledge, often expressed in wikis and support articles, is no longer considered content. Content itself has always taken a back seat in the world of support. Now, as we enter the world of AI, this content represents the teacher for our machine assistants.

Renowned computer scientist Fei-Fei Li said, "If our era is the next Industrial Revolution, as many claim, AI is surely one of its driving forces."

In the era of AI-driven customer service, the competitive importance of content has escalated dramatically. As AI systems rely heavily on machine learning based on the quality and comprehensiveness of the data they are trained on, meticulously curated training content becomes crucial for ensuring these systems operate accurately, effectively, and ethically. Leaders must invest in organizational skills to develop rich, diverse, and accurate training datasets that reflect the real-world scenarios that AI will rely on. This includes not only technical accuracy but also cultural sensitivity and bias mitigation. By prioritizing high-quality machine learning content, organizations can enhance AI's human support and decision-making capabilities, ensuring it aligns with organizational values and customer expectations and elevates customer service experience.

Build a Culture That Rewards Learning

In this time marked by ever-increasingly rapid technological change, building a culture that rewards learning is more than a strategic advantage—it's an absolute requirement for survival and growth. A learning culture empowers organizations to hang on for the ride through the relentless pace of innovation, particularly in AI and digital transformation, by developing a workplace culture that is continuously evolving, adaptable, and ready to embrace new challenges.

Blues musician B.B. King said, "The beautiful thing about learning is nobody can take it away from you."

Encouraging and rewarding ongoing education ensures that agents are forward thinking and proficient in current technologies, preparing for future shifts in the industry. Such an environment promotes a proactive rather than reactive approach to technological advancements, enabling organizations to lead and innovate rather than follow market trends. Moreover, a learning-centric culture attracts and retains top talent, individuals who seek environments where growth is supported, encouraged, and celebrated. In today's fast-moving trends, investing in a culture that values and rewards learning is essential for driving innovation, maintaining a competitive edge, and achieving long-term organizational resilience.

Pay Attention to the Latest Developments

As we venture deeper into an era when machines increasingly surpass human capabilities in intelligence and efficiency, you and your teams must stay abreast of the latest technological developments. The rapid advancement in AI and machine learning means that machines are no longer just tools, but they become partners in shaping the future of business and society.

Apple co-founder Steve Wozniak said, "Wherever smart people work, doors are unlocked.

For leaders and organizations, this underscores the need to maintain a keen focus on industry trends and an openness to experimenting and adapting these innovations. If it means hiring a technical assistant to help you bridge the gap between current capabilities and future needs, then it's a strategic investment worth making. Such a role can provide invaluable insights into emerging technologies, ensuring that your organization remains competitive, innovative, and ready to leverage the full potential of AI technology.

Help Your Team Prepare for a New AI Future

As a leader, you stand front and center at this time of change. The future is filled with unknowns and opportunities. It beckons us to embrace an AI transformation. It's your duty and privilege to prepare your team for this journey, providing time to equip themselves with the skills, knowledge, and mindset they will need to thrive.

Poet and civil rights activist Maya Angelou said, "If you find it in your heart to care for somebody else, you will have succeeded."

By fostering an environment of continuous learning, innovation, and resilience, you can empower your team to navigate challenges and seize the opportunities that lie ahead. Remember, the greatest legacy you can leave is a team well-prepared for a future they can shape with confidence and optimism.

Closely Monitor Government Policy, Legislation, and AI Regulations

It's important to follow current events in AI-related government policy, legislation, and regulations. These frameworks are not just bureaucratic hurdles; they will become the guiding principles that ensure AI is developed and deployed in a manner that is ethical, responsible, and in alignment with societal values. As AI technologies become more integrated into every aspect of our lives, from healthcare to finance, the legal landscape will continue to shift. Paying close attention to these changes is essential for organizations to navigate potential risks, capitalize on opportunities, and lead the way in ethical AI innovation. Being proactive in understanding and adapting to these regulations will safeguard your operations and position your organization as a leader in deploying AI responsibly.

Conclusion

As we stand in the early days of the AI Revolution in customer service and support, the call for visionary leaders willing to work hard to learn about technology has never been more urgent. Customer-focused leaders are being pulled on stage by their CEOs and CTOs and asked to deliver unprecedented change to their businesses by deploying AI solutions. This transformative era presents to us in the 21st century what our ancestors in the generations past faced with the advent of any new technology—the opportunity for those at the helm to redefine the essence of how we engage with new change. For those of us in customer service, this means new and exciting ways to engage with customers, leveraging AI to create experiences that are not only more efficient but profoundly personalized and empathetic—a new way of working.

The leaders of today and tomorrow are challenged with navigating this complex and rapidly changing environment, where the integration of AI into customer interactions demands not just technological acumen but a deep understanding of human needs and expectations. We live in a time that simultaneously challenges us to be innovative, experimental, deliberate, and thoughtful. As we advance, we must balance our customer-focused past while engaging with new AI technology with a deep sense of responsibility and a commitment to enhancing the customer experience. The AI Revolution is not just about technology; it's about the people it serves—our employees, customers, partners, and the leaders who guide its path. By embracing this moment with courage, creativity, and a relentless pursuit of learning, we can forge a future where AI transforms customer service and elevates it to new heights of excellence and connection.

It begins with you!

> *It had long since come to my attention that people of accomplishment rarely sat back and let things happen to them. They went out and happened to things.*
>
> —Leonardo da Vinci

Endnotes

1   Larson, Kate Clifford Ph.D. "Bound For the Promised Land: Harriet Tubman, Portrait of an American Hero." Harriett Tubman Biography, accessed April 1, 2024. [http://www.harriettubmanbiography.com/harriet-tubman-myths-and-facts.html].

2   Banerjee, Naba, Khodabandeh, Shervin, Ransbotham, Sam. 2023. "Me, Myself, and AI Episode 704 Detecting the Good and the Bad with AI: Airbnb's Naba Banerjee." MIT Sloan Management Review, July 18, 2023. [https://sloanreview.mit.edu/audio/detecting-the-good-and-the-bad-with-ai-airbnbs-naba-banerjee/].

3   Martin, Gary. "Let a thousand flowers bloom." The Phrase Finder, accessed April 1, 2024. [https://www.phrases.org.uk/meanings/226950.html].

Glossary

For more terms and updates, see *https://airevolutionbook.com.*

A

A/B test transactions A/B test transactions expose two different iterations of a feature or product to a subset of users in a controlled experiment to determine the preferred feature or product.

Accuracy metrics Accuracy metrics in machine learning refer to measures used to evaluate the performance of a model by comparing its predictions to the actual outcomes or labels in the dataset.

Action plan generation The process of creating a structured set of steps or strategies designed to achieve specific objectives or goals within a given timeframe or context.

Adaptability The capacity to learn from new data and experiences over time.

Adversarial debiasing A machine learning technique aimed at mitigating bias in models by simultaneously training a classifier to make accurate predictions while also training an adversary to identify and mitigate biases in the classifier's decisions, thus promoting fairness and reducing discrimination.

Adversarial robustness An AI model's capability to preserve its performance and accuracy when faced with adversarial inputs specifically designed to mislead or manipulate its predictions.

Agent satisfaction (ASAT) Measures the contentment and well-being of customer service agents with their job environment, tools, and overall work conditions.

Agglomerative clustering A hierarchical, bottom-up clustering technique that begins with each data point as its own cluster. Clusters are then progressively merged based on similarity, continuing iteratively until the desired number of clusters is achieved.

AI model A computer program trained on a dataset to recognize specific patterns or make decisions autonomously without requiring ongoing human intervention.

Algorithmic impact assessment Refers to evaluating the potential effects and consequences of deploying algorithms or machine learning models on stakeholders, including individuals, communities, and society. This process assesses factors such as fairness, transparency, privacy, and potential biases to mitigate harmful impacts and promote ethical algorithm use.

Anglophone data Consists of datasets primarily in English, commonly used in linguistic analysis, natural language processing, and other language-related tasks.

Anonymization The process of removing or altering personally identifiable information from data to protect individuals' privacy and confidentiality while maintaining the usefulness and integrity of the data for analysis or other purposes.

Application programming interface (API) A set of rules and protocols for building and interacting with software applications, facilitating communication between different software components.

Artificial intelligence (AI) Refers to machines designed to perform tasks that typically require human intelligence, such as understanding language, recognizing patterns, solving problems, and making decisions.

Auditability and accountability checks Processes and mechanisms that ensure AI systems adhere to ethical standards, regulatory requirements, and societal values.

Augmented reality (AR) The simulation of real-life scenarios enhanced by technology.

Authentic transactions Real actions done by real users in real environments.

Average handling time A metric used in customer service operations that measures the time taken to resolve a support case—the average of which becomes the benchmark.

B

Backlog size Represents the total number of unresolved customer queries at a given moment.

Base prompt The starting point of interaction with an AI model, typically embedded in the user interface to uniformly affect all users.

Bilingual evaluation understudy (BLEU) A metric used to evaluate the quality of machine-generated text by comparing it to one or more reference texts.

Blockchain A secure digital ledger where information is stored in blocks that are linked across the Internet, making it nearly impossible to alter once it's recorded, ensuring transparency and trust.

C

Caching The process of storing copies of frequently accessed data in a temporary storage location, such as a cache, to reduce access times and improve system performance.

Centers of Excellence Specialized units within organizations that focus on developing and sharing expertise, best practices, and innovative solutions in a particular area or domain. They serve as hubs of knowledge and excellence, driving continuous organizational improvement and innovation.

Central processing unit (CPU) The primary component of a computer that handles most processing tasks and executes instructions. It is often called the "brain" of the computer.

Centroid-based clustering Involves grouping data points around central points, or centroids, by assigning each point to the nearest centroid.

Chain-of-thought A sequence of connected ideas or thoughts that flow naturally from one to another, often forming the basis of reasoning or decision-making. Chain-of-thought prompting involves providing sequential cues or prompts to guide an AI model's responses, encouraging it to generate coherent and logical outputs that follow a consistent line of thinking.

ChatGPT An AI chatbot developed by OpenAI powered by a large language model (LLM).

Chunking In AI model development, dividing large datasets or complex inputs into smaller, more manageable segments or "chunks."

Classification error rate The proportion of incorrectly classified instances or observations by a classification model, typically calculated as the ratio of misclassified instances to the total number of instances in the dataset.

Claude An AI chatbot developed by Anthropic and the name for the underlying LLM that powers it.

Client relations associate Interacts with clients daily, building relationships and providing services that help to build trust between the client and the company.

Clustering A machine learning technique used to group similar data points or objects into clusters, where objects within the same cluster are more similar to each other than those in other clusters, without predefined labels or categories.

Code coverage Measures the extent of a software application's source code executed by automated tests. It quantifies the percentage of lines, statements, branches, or conditions tested, indicating the thoroughness of the testing process. Higher code coverage suggests a reduced likelihood of undetected bugs or issues in the software.

Commingling Occurs when a generative AI model combines two or more documents with similar content, potentially leading to hallucinations in the output.

Compliance metrics Metrics measure the extent to which AI systems adhere to legal standards, ethical norms and industry-specific regulations.

Compliance rates Measure how well customer service adheres to internal policies and external regulations.

Concept drift Occurs in machine learning when the statistical properties of the target variable or the relationships between variables change over time, necessitating model adaptation or retraining to sustain performance.

Consistency Consistency in a learning algorithm ensures that it converges to the true underlying pattern or relationship in the data as the amount of training data increases, resulting in more accurate and reliable predictions.

Constitutional AI process A framework that governs the design, deployment, and operation of artificial intelligence systems to ensure they adhere to predefined ethical standards and legal principles.

Content delivery network (CDN) A distributed network of servers strategically located across various geographic regions, designed to deliver web content, such as images, videos, and web pages, to users with high performance and reliability.

Content moderation classifiers Machine learning models trained to analyze and categorize user-generated content, such as text, images, or videos, to determine its appropriateness, legality, or adherence to community guidelines, enabling platforms to enforce content moderation policies effectively.

Content The digital information in a document, on a website, podcast, video, or other media.

Contextual understanding In machine learning, the ability of a model to interpret and comprehend data within the broader context of the problem domain, incorporating relevant information to make accurate predictions or decisions.

Continuous bag of words (CBOW) The CBOW model predicts a target word based on the context around it. In this model, AI functions like a guessing game, deducing a missing word from the surrounding words in a sentence to enhance its language understanding.

Continuous monitoring Involves the ongoing observation and assessment of systems, processes, or data in real-time or at regular intervals to detect, analyze, and promptly respond to changes, anomalies, or events.

Corrective feedback Information provided to an individual or system that aims to correct errors, misunderstandings, or deviations from desired performance.

Cost per contact A metric that evaluates the total expense incurred for each customer interaction.

Cost-effectiveness at scale Evaluates the financial and computational costs in relation to the scale of operation.

Counting In the context of natural language processing (NLP), calculating the frequency of an n-gram in a corpus. This is done by dividing the number of occurrences of the specific n-gram by the total number of n-grams in the corpus. This metric helps in understanding the commonality of certain word combinations in texts and is used in tasks such as language modeling and statistical machine translation.

Cross-validation method A statistical technique used to assess the performance of a machine learning model by splitting the dataset into multiple subsets, training the model on a subset of the data, and evaluating it on the remaining data. This process is repeated multiple times, with different subsets used for training and evaluation, to obtain more reliable estimates of the model's performance.

Curation Involves the systematic process of selecting, organizing, and enhancing data to improve its quality, relevance, and usability for specific purposes.

Customer care How an individual, group, or business treats their customers.

Customer effort score (CES) Measures the ease with which customers can resolve their issues.

Customer pain time (CPT) Quantifies customer pain by measuring the delay from incident or ticket creation to the status change, indicating waiting on customer input.

Customer retention rate (CRR) Measures a company's success in retaining customers over a specific period.

Customer satisfaction (CSAT) A metric used to measure the level of satisfaction customers experience with a product, service, or interaction with a company. It is typically assessed through surveys or feedback forms, where customers rate their satisfaction on a scale or provide qualitative feedback about their experience.

Customer sentiment analysis A process of analyzing text data, such as customer reviews, comments, or social media posts, to determine the sentiment expressed toward a product, service, or brand. It typically involves classifying the text as positive, negative, or neutral to understand customer opinions and attitudes.

Customer service Encompasses the company's assistance and guidance to individuals who purchase or utilize its products or services.

Customer service agent A person who interacts with customers to provide assistance, address inquiries, resolve issues, or facilitate transactions.

Customer service representative (CSR) Employees tasked with interacting directly with customers to handle and resolve complaints, facilitate process orders, and offer information regarding an organization's products and services.

Customer support Encompasses the range of services a company provides to assist customers with inquiries, issues, or concerns related to the company's products or services. This assistance can include troubleshooting technical problems, answering questions about product features, providing guidance on product use, and resolving customer complaints or issues.

D

Data augmentation The practice of adding additional training data by altering existing samples to improve model robustness and performance.

Data fidelity Data's accuracy, reliability, and completeness, reflecting its alignment with the true or intended information without errors, omissions, or distortions. High data fidelity indicates close alignment with real-world phenomena, while low data fidelity suggests inaccuracies or discrepancies.

Days to close (DTC) Measures the average time, in days, to complete the support cycle and close the customer case.

Days to resolve (DTR) Also known as Time to Resolution (TTR), a metric that quantifies the average duration, in days, taken to deliver the final solution to the customer.

Deep learning A subset of machine learning that involves the use of artificial neural networks with multiple layers (hence the term "deep"). These neural networks can learn hierarchical representations of data, automatically discovering patterns and features from raw input.

Demonstrations Examples or instances provided by humans or other sources to illustrate desired behavior or outcomes. They serve as training data for learning algorithms, enabling them to learn patterns, strategies, or policies by observing and imitating the demonstrated behavior. Demonstrations are often used in techniques like imitation learning, which aims to replicate human or expert actions.

Density-based clustering A method that groups data points into clusters based on the density of their distribuion, where regions of lower density separate dense regions of data points.

Direct message (DM) Often abbreviated as DM, private communication sent between individuals on a messaging platform or social media network, typically not visible to other users.

Disparate impact Occurs when an algorithm or model systematically produces unequal outcomes for different groups based on protected characteristics like race or gender, even if those characteristics are not explicitly considered as input features. This bias can adversely affect certain groups, potentially resulting in discrimination or unfair treatment.

Distance-based clustering A method of grouping data points into clusters based on their distances from one another, typically using metrics like Euclidean distance.

Divisive clustering A top-down hierarchical clustering technique where all data points initially belong to a single cluster. Then, clusters are recursively divided into smaller clusters based on dissimilarity until each data point forms its own cluster or until a stopping criterion is met.

E

Embeddings from language models (ELMo) A form of deep contextualized word representation constructed from a long short-term memory (LSTM) language model. ELMo captures complex aspects of word usage, including syntax and semantics, and how these aspects vary across diverse linguistic contexts. This capability is particularly beneficial for comprehending words with multiple meanings (polysemy).

Employee engagement metrics Reflect the level of commitment and satisfaction employees feel towards their job and the organization.

Equality of opportunity Ensuring that all the groups have the same likelihood of achieving a positive outcome when relevant qualifications are considered. Its calculation involves measuring and comparing true positive rates among different groups.

Erlang A unit of measurement used in telecommunications to quantify the total traffic load on a system. One Erlang represents the continuous use of one voice path for an hour and can be used to assess the capacity needed to handle call volumes effectively.

Ethical principles In AI development, ethical principles such as privacy, security, transparency, inclusiveness, and accountability, guide the responsible creation and implementation of AI models.

Euclidean distance The length of the straight line between two points in the Euclidean space, often used to assess similarity between data points.

EU AI Act The European Union Artificial Intelligence Act (EU AI Act) is a regulation passed in March 2024 by the European Commission aimed at establishing a common regulatory and legal framework for the development, deployment, and use of artificial intelligence systems within the European Union to ensure their safety, fairness, and compliance with ethical standards, while also promoting innovation and protecting fundamental rights.

Extrinsic motivation Refers to the drive to perform an activity or engage in a behavior based on external rewards or pressures, rather than for the intrinsic enjoyment or satisfaction of the activity itself. These external factors can include money, grades, praise, or avoiding negative consequences.

F

F1 score A metric for binary classification that combines precision and recall into a single measure, offering a balanced assessment of a model's accuracy.

False negative rate The false negative rate in binary classification is the proportion of positive instances that are incorrectly classified as negative by a model. It is calculated by dividing the number of false negatives by the sum of true positives and false negatives.

False positive rate The false positive rate in binary classification is the proportion of negative instances that are incorrectly classified as positive by a model. It is calculated by dividing the number of false positives by the sum of true negatives and false positives.

Feedback analysis A qualitative assessment that provides insights into the user experience by evaluating subjective feedback and observations.

Few-shot prompting Involves providing instructions to an AI model along with a limited number of examples—typically between two and ten—showcasing the desired response.

Fine-tuning Fine-tuning an AI model involves adjusting pre-trained parameters on new data to improve specific task performance.

First Contact Resolution (FCR) A metric used in customer service that indicates whether a customer's issue was resolved during their initial contact.

First-day/week resolution (FDR/FWR) Metrics used in customer service to measure the speed at which a support case is resolved within the first day or first week, respectively.

Floating point operations per second (FLOPS) A measure of a computer's performance, specifically its capability to perform floating-point arithmetic operations within a given time frame. FLOPS is typically used to quantify the computational power of processors, GPUs, and other hardware components.

Flow theory The flow theory, developed by psychologist Mihaly Robert Csikszentmihalyi in 1970, describes a state of deep immersion and engagement in an activity characterized by a loss of self-consciousness and sense of time.

Formatting content Involves the arrangement and structuring of data, which includes elements such as layout, styling, and organization to enhance clarity and presentation.

Fréchet inception distance (FID) A metric used to assess the quality of images generated by AI models. It compares the feature distributions of generated images to real images using a feature space derived from a pre-trained neural network. A lower FID score indicates closer similarity to real images, indicating higher quality and greater realism and diversity in the generated images.

Front line service delivery Professionals who directly interact with customers or clients in the workplace. These individuals are typically the primary point of contact between the organization and the customer or the public, playing a crucial role in representing the company and addressing customer needs.

G

Gamification The use of game design elements, such as point scoring, leaderboards, and challenges, in non-game contexts to engage and motivate people to achieve their goals.

Gamified transactions Activities conducted by users who are influenced by game mechanics, encouraging engagement through elements typical of game playing, such as scoring points, competing, or completing challenges.

General Data Protection Regulation (GDPR) A comprehensive legal framework established by the European Union to safeguard the personal data and privacy of individuals within the European Union (EU) and the European Economic Area (EEA). It sets strict guidelines for collecting, using, and sharing personal information.

Generalizability The ability of a model or theory to apply its learned knowledge or principles to new, unseen data or situations beyond the initial training or validation set. High generalizability in a model or theory indicates its effectiveness in making accurate predictions or decisions across diverse contexts or scenarios, demonstrating robustness and reliability in its application. Generalizability is key for evaluating the performance and applicability of machine learning models and scientific theories.

Generative adversarial network (GAN) A type of artificial intelligence model consisting of two neural networks: a generator and a discriminator. The generator creates new data samples, such as images, while the discriminator evaluates these samples to distinguish between real and fake data. GANs learn to generate realistic data that closely resembles the original training data through competition and collaboration between the two networks.

Generative AI (GenAI) A subfield of artificial intelligence that employs computer algorithms to produce outputs resembling human-created content, including text, images, code, and more. Generative AI models learn patterns and structures from input training data, enabling them to generate new data with similar characteristics.

Global Vectors for Word Representation (GloVe) A model used in machine learning to obtain vector representations of words. While similar to Word2vec, GloVe enhances its embeddings by incorporating both global word usage statistics and local contextual information, providing a more comprehensive understanding of word relationships.

Graphics processing unit (GPU) A specialized electronic circuit designed to rapidly manipulate and alter memory to accelerate the creation of images in a frame buffer intended for output to a display device. Widely used in computers and gaming consoles, GPUs excel at rendering graphics-intensive applications like video games, multimedia content, and computer-aided design (CAD) software. Moreover, due to their parallel processing capabilities,

GPUs have become essential for accelerating computations in scientific simulations, machine learning, and artificial intelligence.

Grounding The process of ensuring that an AI system's decisions or outputs are rooted in and supported by relevant and accurate data, providing a solid foundation for its functionality and reliability.

Guest Relations Managing interactions with guests to provide them with information and assistance, ensuring a positive experience.

H

Hallucination The generation of incorrect or fabricated answers by an AI model, often producing outputs that do not align with reality or the context of the given task.

Health Insurance Portability and Accountability Act (HIPAA) A U.S. law enacted to establish privacy standards aimed at protecting patients' medical records and other health information shared with health plans, doctors, hospitals, and other healthcare providers.

Help desk The frontline support system for users encountering technical issues or seeking assistance with software, hardware, or system-related queries. It acts as a central point of contact where users can report problems, ask questions, and receive guidance to resolve issues efficiently. Whether staffed by human agents or supported by automated systems, help desks provide real-time customer assistance and support.

Hierarchical clustering A cluster analysis method that builds a hierarchy of clusters by recursively merging or dividing data points based on their similarity, resulting in a tree-like structure known as a dendrogram.

Hierarchical Dirichlet Process (HDP) A nonparametric Bayesian approach to clustering that enables the creation of an infinite number of clusters, which can be shared across related groups.

HotpotQA A benchmark dataset tailored for question-answering (QA) tasks in machine learning. This curated collection includes multi-hop questions and their corresponding answers with strong supervision of supporting facts aimed at improving the system's performance by enabling more explainable predictions. The dataset is collected by a team of NLP researchers at Carnegie Mellon University, Stanford University, and Université de Montréal.

Hub-and-spoke model A hub-and-spoke model in organizational structure is characterized by a central entity (the "hub") that acts as the main point of coordination or control, while subsidiary entities (the "spokes") primarily interact with the central hub rather than directly with each other. This model is commonly used to streamline organizational communication, decision-making, and resource allocation.

Human-in-the-loop (HITL) A hybrid engagement model that combines the efficiency of AI with the nuanced understanding of human operators, integrating human expertise to enhance AI-driven processes.

Hyper-personalization The use of AI and real-time data to deliver tailored content, products, and services to individual users and customers. In gaming, it represents the future of personalized experiences, where AI algorithms customize every aspect of the gaming journey to align with individual preferences, behaviors, and learning styles, enhancing user engagement and satisfaction.

I

Inception score A metric used to evaluate the quality and diversity of images generated by generative adversarial networks (GANs). It measures the network's ability to produce realistic images by analyzing both the quality of individual images and the diversity across the generated samples.

Incremental learning A machine learning paradigm where models are continuously updated and refined over time as new data becomes available without retraining the entire model from scratch.

Index Typically, a data structure used to efficiently retrieve and store information, especially in databases and search engines.

Industry A group of interconnected or related companies based on their primary business activities, often sharing similar products, services, or market segments.

Information security management system (ISMS) An information security management system (ISMS), or information security management standard, is a structured framework comprising policies and procedures aimed at systematically managing an organization's sensitive data. Its primary objectives are to uphold data security standards and minimize the risk of unauthorized access or breaches.

Ingestion Data ingestion in the context of AI involves the process of collecting vast quantities of data, importing, preparing, and loading data from various sources into an AI model for analysis, training, or inference.

Innovation metrics Innovation metrics assess the extent to which an AI model contributes to developing novel solutions or significant enhancements in existing processes.

Input metrics Input metrics measure the elements or resources provided at the beginning of a process. Similar to measuring ingredients when baking a cake, they assess the quantities or characteristics of what is being introduced into the effort.

Intent determination The process by which artificial intelligence identifies and interprets the underlying purpose or reason behind a user's inquiry or interaction.

Internet of Things (IoT) The network of interconnected devices embedded with sensors, software, and other technologies, enabling them to collect and exchange data with each other and with external systems over the Internet.

Interpolation A statistical method that combines the probabilities of different n-grams, such as unigrams, bigrams, and trigrams, to strike a balance between specificity and generality in language modeling.

Intrinsic motivation The drive to engage in an activity for the inherent enjoyment, interest, or satisfaction it provides, rather than for external rewards or pressures. People motivated intrinsically find the activity itself rewarding and fulfilling.

K

Key performance indicator (KPI) A measurable target used to assess how effectively individuals or businesses are progressing toward business goals. KPIs are metrics tied to specific goals during a certain period of time.

K-means clustering An unsupervised machine learning algorithm that groups the unlabeled dataset into different clusters. It assigns data points to one of the K clusters depending on their distance from the center of the clusters (centroid). It iteratively optimizes the positions of the centroids to minimize the distance between points and their assigned centroids, effectively grouping similar data points together.

Knowledge retention An AI model's capacity to retain and apply previously learned information over time.

Knowledge Transfer The process by which an AI model applies previously acquired information or expertise from one task to another, even if the tasks are different but related.

L

Large language models (LLMs) Artificial intelligence models trained on extensive collections of text data, enabling them to understand and generate human-like language. ChatGPT, for example, is an instance of an LLM that utilizes this vast corpus of text to engage in natural language conversations.

Large-scale AI models Sophisticated neural networks trained on vast datasets, enabling them to perform complex, multifaceted tasks efficiently. These models are characterized by their capacity to process and analyze large volumes of data, allowing them to tackle multifaceted challenges with high accuracy and efficiency.

Latency In computing and networking, the time data travels from its source to its destination on a network. Latency under load refers to the delay experienced when a system, service, or network is operating at full capacity or facing high requests or traffic.

Latent Dirichlet Allocation (LDA) A probabilistic topic model that assigns topics to documents based on distributions of words. It is one of the most popular methods for uncovering themes or topics within large collections of text data.

Likert Scale A psychometric tool commonly used for assessing attitudes, opinions, or perceptions. It involves presenting respondents with a series of statements or items and asking them to indicate their level of agreement or disagreement, typically on a scale ranging from "strongly agree" to "strongly disagree" or through numerical ratings.

Long short-term memory (LSTM) A type of recurrent neural network (RNN) architecture used in artificial intelligence and machine learning. It's designed to process and remember sequential data over long periods, addressing the challenge of retaining important information while filtering out irrelevant details. LSTMs are widely employed in tasks such as natural language processing, speech recognition, and time series prediction, where understanding context and capturing long-term dependencies are crucial.

M

Mean time to resolution (MTTR)
A metric used in customer service to measure the average time it takes support agents to resolve customer issues for a case to be considered resolved/solved.

Meta-learning A machine learning subfield where algorithms are trained to optimize their own learning process based on past experiences.

METEOR (metric for evaluation of translation with explicit ordering)
A metric used to evaluate machine translation quality by comparing the similarity between the machine-generated translation and a reference translation, considering both lexical and syntactic factors.

Mixture Of Experts (MOE) A machine learning technique that involves training multiple sub-models, each specializing on different subsets of data and becoming an "expert." These experts' outputs are then combined using a gating mechanism that dynamically determines the relevance of each expert's output for a given input.

Model drift Also known as model decay, the degradation of model performance over time due to changes in the underlying data distribution, obsolescence of features, or the model becoming less representative of the problem it was designed to solve.

Model tuning Adjusting an AI model's parameters to optimize its performance on specific tasks. This can involve modifying various aspects of the model, such as learning rates, model architecture, or input features, to better align with the desired outputs.

Monte Carlo tree search (MCTS)
A search algorithm used by AI to make decisions in complex situations, such as games. It works by simulating many possible moves from a current position and seeing which ones lead to winning outcomes. The AI uses these simulations to build a tree of decisions, continuously updating and improving its choices based on the results of these simulated games. This allows the AI to make better decisions without needing help from humans.

N

Net promoter score (NPS) A metric that assesses the willingness of customers to recommend a company's products or services to others. It can be viewed as an indicator of customer loyalty and satisfaction. It is based on a single survey question asking customers to rate the likelihood of recommending the company, service, or product to a friend or colleague. Customers respond on a scale from 0 to 10, where scores of 9-10 are considered "promoters," scores of 7-8 are "passives," and scores of 0-6 are "detractors."

Neural language models (NLM)
Advanced computational models that utilize neural networks to learn and understand the semantic and syntactic relationships within language. These models are trained to capture distributed representations of words and their sequential contexts in large datasets of text.

Noise level The amount of unwanted or random disturbances in data or signals that can make it hard to see or understand the important information they contain. Reducing this noise helps in getting clearer and more accurate results.

Non-negative matrix factorization (NMF)
A method used to break down a large matrix into two smaller ones, with the rule that none of the values in these matrices can be negative. This technique is especially useful when the data does not naturally have negative values, like in image processing (where the brightness of pixels is always positive) or in text analysis (where counts of words or

features are also always positive). NMF helps to uncover patterns and components in such data.

O

Objectives and Key Results (OKR) A goal-setting framework used by teams and individuals to set clearly defined goals with measurable results.

One-shot prompting The model is given a single example or instruction to guide its task execution or learning process. This technique is used to see how well a model can perform a task or generate appropriate responses based on limited input.

Optimized data protocols Communication protocols engineered to enhance the efficiency and effectiveness of data transmission across networks by minimizing overhead and maximizing throughput.

Organization An entity composed of individuals working collectively toward a shared objective, such as a company, institution, or association.

Output metrics Quantifiable indicators used to measure the results or outcomes of a process, project or activity. If input metrics measure ingredients, output metrics measure the size of the cake, the calories, the score in a baking contest.

Overfitting An issue in machine learning where a model is trained to fit perfectly to its training data, including the noise and random details. As a result, it performs poorly on new, unseen data because it has learned to recognize the specific patterns and anomalies of the training set rather than the underlying trends. This makes it less effective at making predictions or decisions based on new information.

Overjustification effect A psychological phenomenon observed when external rewards are introduced to motivate an activity that an individual is already inherently interested in. This effect occurs when these rewards, especially if perceived as overly controlling or undermining one's autonomy, decrease

intrinsic motivation. As a result, the person may become less interested in the activity for its own sake, relying instead on external incentives.

P

Partitioning clustering A technique used in data analysis that divides a dataset into distinct, non-overlapping clusters, where each data point is assigned to exactly one cluster based on predefined criteria such as the distance or similarity between data points.

Perplexity Measures the performance of a language model by quantifying how well the model predicts a sample of text. It is commonly used in natural language processing tasks such as language modeling and machine translation. A lower perplexity indicates that the model is better at predicting the sample text, with lower uncertainty or confusion in its predictions. Perplexity is calculated as the exponentiation of the cross-entropy loss, normalized by the number of words in the sample text.

Personally identifiable information (PII) A broad range of information or data that can be used to identify, contact, or locate a specific individual. This includes, but is not limited to, personal identifiers such as name, Social Security number, address, email address, or biometric records.

Playtest A game design practice where early versions of a game are tested by players, providing valuable feedback to game designers. Through iterative play sessions, designers observe how players interact with the game, identify potential issues, and gather insights into what aspects of the game are engaging, fair, and enjoyable. This process allows designers to refine and improve the game mechanics, balance, and overall experience to ensure the final product is engaging and enjoyable for all players.

Proximal policy optimization (PPO) A reinforcement learning algorithm used in machine learning to train agents in decision-making tasks. It operates by iteratively adjusting the agent's policy in small increments, based on trial-and-error experiences, and observing the resulting outcomes, allowing the agent to learn from its actions and improve over time.

Precision   A metric used to evaluate the performance of an AI model in classification tasks. It measures the model's accuracy in correctly identifying the relevant instances from all predicted ones. It is also defined as the accuracy of positive predictions.

Precision-recall trade-off   Describes the inverse relationship between precision and recall, whereby improving one degrades the other. You can't have both precision and recall high[md]if you increase precision, it will reduce recall, and vice versa.

Preference-based feedback   Input provided by users indicating their preferences, likes, or dislikes regarding certain items, actions, or choices. This feedback is often used to personalize recommendations and improve user experiences in recommendation systems and interactive applications.

Preprocessing   The initial phase of data preparation in which raw data is transformed, cleaned, and organized to make it suitable for analysis and model training.

Pre-trained language model   An AI system that has undergone initial training on a vast text dataset to comprehend and generate human-like language. This comprehensive pre-training equips the model to perform a range of language-related tasks, such as translation, summarization, and conversation, without requiring fine-tuning for specific applications.

Preemptive support   Anticipating and fixing issues without the customer knowing they had an issue in the first place.

Privacy protection metrics   Measures designed to evaluate the effectiveness of AI systems in managing and safeguarding personal and sensitive data.

Proactive support   A customer service approach where companies take steps to assist customers before they reach out for help. This could be offering new products or services that customers might find useful, promptly addressing any problems or errors as they occur, and going the extra mile to ensure a positive customer experience. Preemptive actions are taken to prevent anticipated threats, while proactive actions are broader initiatives to prevent potential future issues.

Prompt chaining   A technique used in natural language processing to guide the generation process of a language model. It involves sequentially applying a series of prompts, allowing the model to generate more complex and coherent outputs, improving quality. The model can build upon previous inputs by chaining prompts together, resulting in more contextually relevant and structured responses.

Prompt design   The thoughtful creation of input prompts and conversational stimuli to guide the responses of an AI model toward desired outcomes. Effective prompt design ensures clarity and provides contextual cues.

Prompt engineering   Crafting precise instructions to maximize an AI model's performance. It optimizes AI models for specific tasks through rule-based prompts, data augmentation, and prompt tuning. Prompt engineering goes beyond prompt design by fine-tuning the model's parameters, augmenting training data, and refining prompt strategies to achieve optimal performance across various tasks and domains.

Prompt library   A collection of predefined and carefully curated prompts or input templates designed to interact with language models, eliciting specific responses and actions from an AI system.

Prompt tuning   A specific component of prompt engineering that refers to the process of iteratively adjusting and refining the input prompts used to guide the responses of an AI model. This technique involves experimenting with different prompt formulations, structures, or parameters to optimize the model's performance for a specific task or objective.

Prompt An input provided to a language model or other AI system to initiate a specific task or interaction. It can take various forms, such as a question, a statement, or a command, and is typically designed to guide the AI system's response generation.

Q

Quality assurance (QA) A systematic process implemented to ensure that products or services meet specified requirements and standards. QA aims to prevent defects, errors, and issues and enhance customer satisfaction.

Quality of service (QoS) The overall performance of a network or service, particularly the performance seen by the users. To quantitatively measure the quality of service, several aspects are considered, such as resource availability, bandwidth, and latency, to meet specific user requirements.

R

ReAct A framework that blends reasoning and action with language models (LLMs) to generate spoken and text-based actions for tasks. These actions alternate, and external observations provide feedback. This method helps LLMs synchronize reasoning and action, allowing them to think and then act.

Reactive support Assistance provided to customers after they initiate contact with the organization for help. This support can be delivered through various channels such as chat, phone, and email engagement.

Real-world knowledge Encompasses information, insights, or principles about the external world that are not explicitly present in the training data but are leveraged by models to make predictions or decisions that resonate with human intuition or understanding.

Recall A metric used to evaluate the performance of a classification model, particularly in tasks where the goal is to identify all relevant instances within a dataset. It measures the proportion of positive instances the model correctly identifies as positive. In other words, recall indicates the model's ability to capture all relevant instances of a particular class. A high recall value suggests that the model effectively identifies most of the positive instances, while a low recall value indicates that the model is missing many positive instances.

ROUGE (Recall-Oriented Understudy for Gisting Evaluation) A set of metrics used to evaluate the quality of summaries generated by automatic text summarization systems and machine translations by comparing them to reference summaries or translations (typically human-produced).

Regulatory adherence scores A set of metrics used to evaluate how well AI systems comply with relevant legal and regulatory standards.

Reinforcement learning A distinctive branch of machine learning known for its ability to autonomously learn from its own actions and subsequent rewards.

Reinforcement learning from AI feedback (RLAIF) A methodology that integrates reinforcement learning algorithms with feedback from other AI models to enable hybrid learning. By leveraging AI-generated feedback, the system enhances the decision-making capabilities of the learning agent. Transitioning from RLHF to RLAIF resolves the issue of limited human feedback in RLHF, leading to a more efficient and scalable learning process.

Reinforcement learning from human feedback (RLHF) A methodology where a reinforcement learning agent improves its decision-making capabilities by learning from feedback provided directly by humans. This approach allows the learning agent to refine its actions based on human preferences or decisions, thus aligning the behavior more closely with human values and expectations.

Relevance The extent to which a feature or input variable helps accurately predict the target variable or outcome of interest. This concept is crucial in model building and data analysis, where determining the most impactful variables can enhance the precision and effectiveness of the predictions.

Resource allocation efficiency The effectiveness with which available resources, such as time, money, and personnel, are allocated and utilized to achieve desired objectives or outcomes.

Resource utilization efficiency Describes how effectively available resources, such as CPU, memory, disk space, network bandwidth, and human resources, are used to perform tasks or deliver services within a system or organization. It measures the degree to which resources are allocated, managed, and utilized to achieve desired outcomes or objectives while minimizing waste, idle time, and underutilization.

Responsible AI (RAI) Designing, developing, and deploying artificial intelligence systems in an ethically sound, transparent, and accountable manner. The concept encompasses a broad range of principles, including fairness, transparency, accountability, privacy, security and inclusivity, ensuring that AI technologies do not perpetuate biases, invade privacy, or cause harm.

Retention Strategies and practices aimed at keeping customers or clients engaged and satisfied with a company's products or services over time. The goal is to reduce customer churn and enhance loyalty by providing continuous, value-added support and services.

Retraining The process of updating or refining a trained model by integrating new data. This involves inputting additional data into the existing model and adjusting its parameters or structure to improve its performance and adapt to changes in the underlying data distribution.

Retrieval augmentation Enhancing information or data retrieval by augmenting the original query with additional relevant information or context. This technique improves the accuracy and relevance of search results and recommendations.

Return on investment (ROI) A performance metric used to evaluate the efficiency or profitability of an investment by comparing benefit (or return) to the costs involved in creating, deploying, and maintaining a particular solution. It is calculated by dividing the net profit by the investment cost and expressed as a percentage or ratio.

Robustness The ability of a model to maintain high performance and reliability under expected or unexpected variations in conditions and datasets. Robust model design involves creating models that are minimally susceptible to errors or disruptions, ensuring consistent accuracy across diverse scenarios.

S

Scalability metrics Measures used to assess the ability of a system, application, or infrastructure to handle increasing workloads or demand without compromising performance, reliability, and efficiency. These metrics typically quantify aspects such as throughput, response time, resource utilization, and system capacity, providing insights into how well a system can expand to accommodate a growing user base, data volume, or computational requirements.

Security compliance metrics These metrics assess the robustness of AI systems against cyber threats and vulnerabilities.

Self-consistency The ability of a model or algorithm to generate predictions or outputs that are internally coherent and consistent with its learned patterns or principles, ensuring the reliability and robustness of the model's performance.

Semi-supervised learning A machine learning approach that combines a small amount of labeled data with a large amount of unlabeled data during training. This method leverages the labeled data to guide the learning process while utilizing the unlabeled data to improve the model's performance and generalization. It is useful when obtaining labeled data is expensive or time-consuming.

Sentiment analysis A natural language processing technique used to analyze and categorize text based on the sentiment it expresses, identifying it as positive, negative, or neutral, to understand the subjective opinions or attitudes conveyed within the text.

Service Level Agreement (SLA) A formal contract between a service provider and a customer that defines the expected standard of service. It specifies the metrics by which the service is measured and the remedies or penalties should agreed-upon service levels not be achieved.

Simple rating A straightforward method used to assign scores or ratings to items or entities based on a limited set of criteria, often used in evaluations, reviews, or assessments.

Skip-Gram One of the unsupervised learning techniques used to find the most related words for a given word. It's the reverse of a continuous bag of words (COBW). Given a specific word, skip-gram tries to predict the surrounding words, helping the AI grasp the context and relationships between words in a sentence.

Smoothing Smoothing in the context of language modeling and statistics refers to adding small values to the counts of n-grams to avoid assigning zero probabilities to unseen events or sequences. This adjustment helps models deal more effectively with the issue of data sparsity and ensures that all possible sequences have a non-zero chance of occurring, which is crucial for making reliable predictions, especially in tasks involving natural language processing.

Statistical language model A computational model that quantifies the probabilities of word sequences within a given language. It utilizes statistical methods to analyze the structure and patterns of natural language, allowing it to predict the likelihood of specific word sequences based on their context.

Statistical or demographic parity A scenario where various groups, such as different races or genders, have an equal likelihood of experiencing a particular outcome, such as being hired for a job or accepted into a program. This concept ensures fairness across demographics by aiming for equal representation and opportunities for all groups. In the context of AI, the fairness of a model relies on the parity of the data it learns from during training, emphasizing the importance of unbiased and representative datasets.

Stratified sampling A sampling technique where the population is divided into distinct subgroups, or strata, based on specific characteristics. Random samples are then taken from each stratum to ensure that all subgroups are represented proportionally in the final sample.

Stress testing A method used to evaluate a system's robustness, reliability, and performance by subjecting it to extreme or challenging conditions, often beyond normal operating parameters. This evaluation helps identify potential weaknesses or failure points in the system and ensures its ability to withstand adverse circumstances.

Subject matter expert (SME) A person who is an expert in a particular topic or subject.

Supervised learning A type of machine learning where an algorithm is trained on labeled data. This means the input data is paired with the correct output, allowing the model to learn the relationship between them. The goal is to enable the model to predict the output for new, unseen data accurately.

Support engineer A professional who provides technical assistance and support to customers, typically related to software, hardware, or other technological products. Their primary role involves troubleshooting, resolving, and offering solutions to ensure optimal functionality and customer satisfaction.

Synthetic transactions   Artificially generated interactions within AI systems or models. These interactions are scripted to mimic real-world scenarios or user behaviors. Synthetic transactions in AI are often used for testing and validation before real-world deployment.

T

Task-switching overhead   Denotes the additional time and resources required to switch or transition from one task or process to another, resulting in reduced efficiency and increased computational load.

Telemetry   Collecting and transmitting data from remote or inaccessible sources to a central location for monitoring, analysis, and decision-making purposes.

Tensor processing unit (TPU)   A custom-built application-specific integrated circuit (ASIC) developed by Google to accelerate machine learning workloads. TPUs are designed to efficiently perform matrix operations on tensors, which are the primary data structures used in machine learning algorithms, such as neural networks. These chips are optimized for high-speed, low-power processing, making them very effective for training and executing large-scale deep-learning models.

The Diffusion of Innovations Theory
A social science theory that explains how new ideas, products, or technologies spread and are adopted within a population over time, considering factors such as communication channels, social networks, and the characteristics of the innovation itself. The theory was popularized by Everett Rogers in 1962.

Thermal throttling   A protective mechanism employed by hardware components like CPUs or GPUs to mitigate the risk of overheating and potential damage. When temperatures rise to levels that could jeopardize the integrity of

the component, thermal throttling kicks in, reducing the performance of the hardware to lower its temperature.

Throughput   The capacity of a system, process, or component to handle and process a specific amount of work or data within a defined period. It is typically quantified by the rate at which units of work or data are processed per unit of time, such as transactions per second, requests per minute, or bytes per second.

Time to close (TTC)   Time to close, also known as days to close (DTC), is a metric used to measure the time, usually in days, required to complete the support cycle closing the customer incident or ticket.

Time to resolution (TTR)   A customer service metric measuring the time between when a customer issue is reported and when it is fully resolved.

Tokenization   A common form of chunking where text is broken down to the smallest meaningful unit in a language, known as tokens. These tokens are typically words but can also be subwords or characters, depending on the specific tokenization strategy used.

Token   The smallest meaningful unit of data that an AI model processes. Here are some helpful rules of thumb for understanding tokens in terms of lengths according to OpenAI:

1 token $\sim=$ 4 chars in English, 1 token $\sim=$ ¾ words, 100 tokens $\sim=$ 75 words

Or

1-2 sentence $\sim=$ 30 tokens, 1 paragraph $\sim=$ 100 tokens, 1,500 words $\sim=$ 2048 tokens

Training data   The set of data and examples used to teach a machine learning model how to make predictions or classifications. It consists of input-output pairs, where the inputs represent the features or attributes of the data, and the outputs are the corresponding labels or target values that the model seeks to predict or classify.

Transfer learning (TL)   A technique in machine learning in which knowledge gained for one task or dataset is repurposed as the starting point for a related or different task instead of starting the learning process from scratch.

Transformer   A deep learning architecture introduced by Google in 2017 that processes data simultaneously rather than sequentially, using a self-attention mechanism to dynamically focus on different parts of the input. These models can translate text and speech in near-real-time. This architecture efficiently handles long-range dependencies within the input data, making it powerful for tasks like translation, text generation, and more.

Transparency and explainability indexes   Qualitative assessments that evaluate the clarity and understandability of an AI model's decision-making processes. These indexes aim to measure how easily humans can understand and interpret the reasoning behind the model's predictions or actions.

Tree of Thoughts (ToT)   A prompting technique based on a metaphorical concept that describes the hierarchical organization of ideas or concepts in the human mind. Like the branches of a tree, thoughts branch out from central themes or concepts, creating interconnected networks of cognitive structures.

Two-stage combination test   A statistical methodology designed to mitigate the risk of false positives by conducting tests in two sequential stages. In the first stage, initial tests are performed to identify potentially significant results or signals. Then, in the second stage, further testing is conducted to confirm or scrutinize the findings from the initial stage. This approach helps reduce the likelihood of false positives and enhances the reliability of statistical inference.

U

Underfitting   Underfitting in machine learning occurs when a model is too simplistic to adequately capture the underlying patterns or structure of the data, resulting in poor performance on both the training data and new, unseen data. Underfitting can be addressed by using more complex models, increasing the model's capacity, or providing more relevant features or data to train on.

Ungrounded content   Information or data lacking sufficient evidence, validation, or factual basis, often leading to uncertainty or skepticism regarding its accuracy or reliability.

Universal Basic Income (UBI)   A social welfare concept that proposes providing all citizens or residents of a country with a regular, unconditional cash payment. Unlike traditional social assistance programs, UBI does not require recipients to meet specific criteria, such as employment status or income level, to qualify for this basic income level to meet their essential needs.

Unsupervised learning   A type of machine learning where the algorithm is trained on data without labeled responses. The system tries to learn the underlying patterns and structures from the data on its own, often used for clustering and association. The aim is to identify hidden patterns or groupings in the data.

User engagement metrics   How users interact with an AI system, including frequency, duration, and depth of interaction.

User experience optimization (UXO)   A systemic process for enhancing the overall experience of users when they interact with a product, service, or system. It involves analyzing user behavior, preferences, and feedback to identify areas for improvement and implementing design changes to optimize usability, accessibility, and satisfaction.

User retention rate   A metric used to measure the proportion of users who continue to use an AI system over a specified period of time. It provides insights into the system's ability to retain users and sustain their interest and engagement over the long term.

V

Virtual reality (VR)   An immersive technology that simulates realistic three-dimensional environments, allowing users to interact with and experience artificial worlds as if they were physically present. Users can explore and manipulate virtual environments in real time through specialized hardware, such as VR headsets and controllers, often with a high degree of interactivity and immersion.

W

Word2vec   A natural language processing technique developed by Google researchers that converts words into numerical vectors based on their contextual usage and surrounding words. These vectors capture information about the word's meaning based on its context, improving machine learning effectiveness, particularly in tasks involving natural language understanding.

Z

Zero-shot prompting   Providing instruction to an AI model without any examples or training data on how to respond. It's a task given to the model for which it hasn't been explicitly trained. Despite lacking specific examples, zero-shot prompts rely on the model's ability to generalize and understand the task based on its pre-existing knowledge and training.

Index